VIRTUES AND

VIRTUES AND REASONS

PHILIPPA FOOT AND MORAL THEORY

Essays in Honour of Philippa Foot

Edited by
ROSALIND HURSTHOUSE
GAVIN LAWRENCE
WARREN QUINN

CLARENDON PRESS · OXFORD

Oxford University Press, Great Clarendon Street, Oxford OX2 6DP

Oxford New York

Athens Auckland Bangkok Bogota Bombay Buenos Aires
Calcutta Cape Town Dar es Salaam Delhi Florence Hong Kong Istanbul
Karachi Kuala Lumpur Madras Madrid Melbourne Mexico City
Nairobi Paris Singapore Taipei Tokyo Toronto Warsaw
and associated companies in
Berlin Ibadan

Oxford is a registered trade mark of Oxford University Press

Published in the United States
by Oxford University Press Inc., New York

First published 1995
First issued in paperback 1998

British Library Cataloguing in Publication Data
Data available

Library of Congress Cataloging in Publication Data
ISBN 0-19-824046-5
ISBN 0-19-823793-6 (Pbk.)

Printed in Great Britain
on acid-free paper by
Bookcraft (Bath) Ltd
Midsomer Nortan, Somerset

Preface

Philippa Foot was born in 1920 and educated mainly at home in the country before going up to Somerville College, Oxford, on a scholarship in 1939 to read Philosophy, Politics, and Economics. She has been associated with Somerville ever since. She received her BA with First Class Honours in 1942, her MA in 1947, became Somerville's first philosophy Tutorial Fellow in 1949, and Vice-Principal in 1967.

In 1969 she resigned her tutorial fellowship, becoming a Senior Research Fellow instead, and began to freelance in the USA. She had already held visiting professorships at Cornell and the Massachusetts Institute of Technology. Between 1969 and 1976 she was a Visiting Professor at the University of California at Los Angeles, the University of Washington, the University of California at Berkeley, and the Graduate Center at the City University of New York; the First Senior Visiting Professor in the Society for the Humanities at Cornell; Old Dominion Fellow at Princeton; Fellow at the Center for Advanced Studies in the Behavioral Sciences at Stanford; and Professor in Residence at UCLA, where she finally settled, as a full Professor, in 1976. In 1988 UCLA appointed her as the first holder of the Gloria and Paul Griffin Chair in Philosophy, a position she held until her retirement in 1991.

In a letter to Oxford University Press in 1991 to explain 'why Philippa Foot is worthy of a *Festschrift*', Warren Quinn wrote:

no one has stayed at centre-stage in moral theory for such a long period of time. Indeed, far from resting on her impressive past laurels, she is now embarked on her most important and promising work: a book giving a new account of practical reason and its relation to moral action, desire, and happiness. And while she has as yet refused to publish anything of this new account, interest in it is keen in America (where she presented part of it in a series of lectures at Princeton and in the Whitehead Lecture at Harvard), France (where a recent lecture on happiness given in Paris is to be brought out by the Presses Universitaires de

France), Israel (where she lectured this summer at Haifa, Tel Aviv, and Beersheba), and, soon I'm sure, Oxford . . .

She has been honoured and continues to be honoured around the world. She is one of the few academics who are regular Fellows of both the British Academy and the American Academy of Arts and Sciences. She has given the Whitehead Lecture at Harvard, the Lindley Lecture at Kansas, the Berkeley Lecture at Trinity College Dublin, etc. Her publications in learned journals, her collections (*Theories of Ethics* must be one of your all-time best-sellers), as well as her more popular reviews—in the *New York Review of Books* (where she recently published a brilliant piece on Nietzsche), in the *London Review of Books*, and in *The Times Literary Supplement*—are widely read, admired, and in many cases widely reprinted.

She has also lectured in Moscow and Prague, given the Romanell Lecture at the American Philosophical Association, the Clark Library Lecture at UCLA, the Oxfam Gilbert Murray Memorial Lecture, and the Hart Lecture on Jurisprudence and Moral Philosophy in Oxford. Her new work will be appearing in a book, *The Grammar of Goodness*, to be published by Oxford University Press.

In her own Introduction to *Virtues and Vices* Philippa identifies her two main themes as 'opposition to emotivism and prescriptivism, and the thought that a sound moral philosophy should start from a theory of the virtues and vices', and says that it was her early reading of Aquinas (not Aristotle) on the virtues that first made her suspicious of the 'fact–value' distinction. This description might lead a reader unacquainted with her work to expect much of what he would, indeed, find—the emphasis on the virtues and vices, the naturalism, the attacks on non-cognitivism, Kantianism, and utilitarianism; he might even be unsurprised to find her discussing Thomistic distinctions between doing and allowing, and what is intended and merely foreseen. But it would not, perhaps, quite prepare him for the extent to which a third theme is interwoven with these two, namely the problem of the rationality of acting morally. This is a problem she has returned to again and again, her (changing) thoughts about it having inspired many of the papers in this volume, and is the problem that informs the new work which Warren Quinn described.

In recognition of more than forty-five years of scholarly achievement, inspired philosophical thought, and leadership in teaching, we offer these essays in her honour.

Rosalind Hursthouse
Gavin Lawrence

The editors much regret the death of their fellow editor, Warren Quinn, during the preparation of this volume, for which he was a driving force.

Contents

List of Contributors

G. E. M. ANSCOMBE is Emeritus Professor of Philosophy of the University of Cambridge and Honorary Fellow of Somerville College, Oxford. Her publications include *Intention, An Introduction to Wittgenstein's Tractatus*, and *Collected Papers*.

SIMON BLACKBURN is the Edna J. Koury Distinguished Professor of Philosophy at the University of North Carolina at Chapel Hill. He is the author of *Spreading the Word* and the collection *Essays in Quasi-Realism*. His *Oxford Dictionary of Philosophy* appeared in 1994.

ROSALIND HURSTHOUSE is Head of the Philosophy Department at the Open University. She is the author of *Beginning Lives* and articles on moral philosophy.

ANTHONY KENNY is Warden of Rhodes House in Oxford. His more recent publications include *The Metaphysics of Mind, Aristotle on the Perfect Life*, and *Aquinas on Mind*.

GAVIN LAWRENCE is Assistant Professor at the University of California at Los Angeles.

JOHN MCDOWELL is University Professor of Philosophy at the University of Pittsburgh and Emeritus Fellow of University College, Oxford. He is the author of numerous papers on moral philosophy, philosophy of mind, and philosophy of language.

WARREN QUINN was Professor of Philosophy at the University of California at Los Angeles until his tragic death in 1991. His collected papers, *Morality and Action*, edited by Philippa Foot, appeared in 1994.

DAVID SACHS, who died in 1992, was Professor Emeritus at Johns Hopkins University. His publications included articles on moral philosophy, both ancient and modern, Wittgenstein, and Freud.

T. M. SCANLON is Professor of Philosophy at Harvard University. He is the author of 'Contractualism and Utilitarianism' and many other essays in moral and political philosophy.

MICHAEL THOMPSON is Assistant Professor at the University of Pittsburgh.

DAVID WIGGINS was at the time of writing Professor of Philosophy at Birkbeck College, London. He is now Wykeham Professor of Logic at the University of Oxford. His publications include *Sameness and Substance* and *Needs, Values and Truth*.

BERNARD WILLIAMS is White's Professor of Moral Philosophy at the University of Oxford and Deutsch Professor of Philosophy at the University of California at Berkeley. His books include *Ethics and the Limits of Philosophy* and *Shame and Necessity*.

1

Practical Inference

G. E. M. ANSCOMBE

Logic is interested in the UNASSERTED propositions.

(Wittgenstein)

I will write in appreciation of, but some dissent from, this paragraph of von Wright's:

Now we can see more clearly, I think, wherein the claim to logical validity of the practical inference consists. Given the premises

X now intends to make it true that E
He thinks that, unless he does A now, he will not achieve this

and excluding, hypothetically or on the basis of investigations, that he is prevented, then his actual conduct, whatever it may "look like", either is an act of doing A or aims, though unsuccessfully, at being this. Any description of behaviour which is logically inconsistent with this is also logically inconsistent with the premises. Accepting the premises thus forces on us this understanding of his conduct,—unless for some reason we think that a preventive interference occurred right at the beginning of his action.[1]

1

If there is practical inference, there must be such a thing as its validity. Validity is associated with necessity. I take it that this is what leads von Wright always to consider only the "unless" forms, giving

Under the title 'Von Wright on Practical Inference', this article, written in 1974, originally appeared in P. A. Schilpp (ed.), *The Philosophy of Georg Henrik von Wright* (La Salle, Ill.: Open Court, 1989), in the Library of Living Philosophers series. In response to Philippa Foot's especial request, it is reprinted here, with the kind permission of Professors Anscombe and von Wright and Open Court Publishing Co.

[1] G. H. von Wright, 'On So-Called Practical Inference', *Acta Sociologica*, 15/1 (1972), 49.

I want to achieve E;
Unless I do A, I shall not achieve E

as a scheme in the first person. Suppose, having that end and that opinion, I do A. 'What sort of connexion would this signify between want and thought on the one hand, and action on the other? Can I say that wanting and opining *make* me act? If so, would this be a form of causal efficacy? Or would it be more like a logical compulsion?'[2]

Donald Davidson opts for "causal efficacy" here, on the ground that there is a difference between my having a reason and its actually being my reason. I act because . . . We need an account of this "because". The psychological "because", he supposes, is an ordinary *because* where the *because* clause gives a psychological state. The solution lacks acumen. True, not only must I have a reason, it must also "operate as my reason": that is, what I do must be done *in pursuit* of the end and *on grounds* of the belief. But not just *any* act of mine which is caused by my having a certain desire is done in pursuit of the object of desire; not just *any* act caused by my having a belief is done on grounds of the belief. Davidson indeed realizes that even identity of description of *act done* with *act specified in the belief*, together with causality by the belief and desire, isn't enough to guarantee the act's being done *in pursuit of the end* and *on grounds of the belief*. He speaks of the possibility of "wrong" or "freak" causal connexions. I say that any recognizable causal connexions would be "wrong", and that he can do no more than postulate a "right" causal connexion in the happy security that none such can be found. If a causal connexion were found we could always still ask: "But was the act done for the sake of the end and in view of the thing believed?"

I conjecture that a cause of this failure of percipience is the standard approach by which we first distinguish between "action" and what merely happens, and then specify that we are talking about "actions". So what we are considering is already given as—in a special sense—an action, and not just any old thing which we do, such as making an involuntary gesture. Such a gesture might be caused, for example, by realizing something (the

---

[2] G. H. von Wright, 'On So-Called Practical Inference', *Acta Sociologica*, 15/1 (1972), 40.

"onset of a belief") when we are in a certain state of desire. Something I do is not made into an intentional action by being caused by a belief and desire, even if the descriptions fit.

Von Wright has no taste for this explanation by causal efficacy, but is drawn to the alternative which he gives—logical compulsion. He has difficulties with this which lead him to substitute "intend" for "want" and the third person for the first, prefixing "he believes" to the second premise. Even so, there is still a time gap; so he closes the gap with a "now" which is to be quite narrowly understood. He must also exclude instant prevention. But he now has a rather obscure difficulty about the "instantaneous" application of the argument. 'Is there explanation of action only on the basis of what is *now* the case—and is there intentional action which is *simultaneous* with the construction of a justification of it?' He thinks not; but he does not explain why not.

He *seems* to conceive the application like this: one *makes use* of an argument. Now one can hardly be said to make use of an argument that one does not produce, inwardly or outwardly. But the production takes time. If I do *A* "on the instant", there isn't time. Given time, the argument or calculation will look to a future action. Or, if I have done the action, I may be justifying it. I cannot *be reaching* the action as a conclusion. (This is interpretation on my part; I hope not unjust.)

This raises the interesting question: is inference a process? Is "infer" a psychological verb? Is 'reasoning' a psychological concept? If so, it is perhaps curious that people don't usually put inference and reasoning into lists of mental phenomena. Bernard Williams once wrote that an inference must be something that a person could conduct. What has one in mind, if one speaks of someone as "conducting an inference"? Presumably not reproducing an argument, but rather: thinking first of one proposition, say, and then another, which is seen to follow from the first. Is there something else which one could call not just *seeing* that the second follows from the first, but actually *inferring* it? I take it, no. That is, it is of no importance that I "wouldn't have produced the one except because I had produced the other". One may feel inclined to say such a thing in a particular case, but one wouldn't say "You didn't infer, if the second proposition merely flashed into your mind; you saw it followed from the first and added 'then' to it!" Nor need one even have added "then". If inferring is a particular mental act, one might suppose that it was "conceiving the second proposition under the aspect *then* in relation to the first". But now, how is it that when one considers or examines inferences, one has no interest in whether anything like that has gone on in someone's mind, i.e. whether he has experienced something which he would like to express in that way? It is because we have no such interest that it does not come natural to classify inference as a mental content, "infer" as a psychological verb.

Von Wright's observation about the simultaneous construction of a justification comes in a passage where he is asking 'what uses has the type of argument which I here call practical inference?' and it therefore seems entirely fair. Construction, production, going through, all these take some time; therefore no "instantaneous" use. And yet it appears as if something deeper had been said. Has he perhaps not exhausted the "uses" of this type of argument?

Practical inference was delineated, as anything called "inference" must be, as having validity. The validity of an inference is supposed to be a certain formal character. The appreciation of validity is connected with the evaluation of grounds *qua* grounds. Therefore, one use (which von Wright has not mentioned) of his type of argument will be not to get at a conclusion or explain or justify an action, but to form an estimate of an action in its relation to its grounds. Now can a person act on grounds upon the instant? For example, he steps behind a pillar to avoid being seen, as soon as he sees someone enter the building. If so, the setting forth of the grounds, displaying the formal connexion between description of the action and propositions giving grounds, will indeed take time but will relate to something instantaneous.

Von Wright's investigation has led him to the curious position that there is such a thing as the validity of a practical inference, but that when it *is* valid, it has no use as an argument—that is to say, as an inference. Its use is connected, rather, with understanding action. Where it is of use as an argument it lacks validity because of the time gap: 'with this gap there is also a rift in the logical connexion between the intention and epistemic attitude on the one hand and the action on the other'. Thus when we obliterate the time gap we 'obliterate the character of an argument or an inference': we obliterate it from the propositional connexions which we were investigating.[3]

.2

If there is such a thing as practical inference, it is surely exhibited not only by the "unless" form:

I want to attain *E*;
Unless I do *A* I shall not attain *E*;

after considering which I do *A*.
It is also exhibited by the "if" form:

I want to attain *E*;
If I do *A* I shall attain *E*.

I have conjectured that von Wright does not consider this latter form because with it there is no shadow of a sense in which doing the action *A* is necessitated by the premises. With the "unless" form, the action is required if my desire is not to be frustrated. However, we have seen the difficulty in making out a necessity about *its being true that the action happened*, which I take to be his picture of making out the *validity* of inference here. He looked for the relation to be 'one of logical compulsion'.

He notices my remark that the conclusion of a practical syllogism is not necessitated; perhaps he thought I said this because of these difficulties. But in fact my view was completely different: I thought that the relation between the premises and the action which was the conclusion was this: the premises shew what good, what use, the action is.

If someone acts on the premises, that shews that he is after—or perhaps that he wants to avoid—something mentioned in the first premise. In 'On So-called Practical Inference', von Wright says: 'According to Anscombe the first premise . . . mentions something wanted', and he claims that this doesn't fit Aristotle's version of practical inference, which 'subsumes a particular thing or action under some general principle or rule about what is good

---

[3] G. H. von Wright, 'On So-Called Practical Inference', *Acta Sociologica*, 15/1 (1972), 50.

for us or is our duty'.[4] He contrasts with this the inference in which the first premise mentions an end of action, and the second some means to this end.

He seems to think that "mentioning an end of action" or "mentioning something wanted" is saying that a certain end is wanted. Otherwise, he would not contrast the well-known Aristotelian forms with the form "in which some end of action is wanted".

> Pure water is wholesome;
> This water is pure,

followed by drinking the water, would be an example on the most frequent Aristotelian pattern. It mentions the wholesome, and this is shewn to be what the person wants by his acting on these propositions as grounds for drinking the water. It seems to me incorrect to call such a premise "A general rule about what is good for us". It is a general statement about what is good for us, not a rule.

It is true that Aristotle's first premises in these forms are always some sort of "general principle". But "principle" here only means "starting-point". This generality is indeed important, and I will return to it. However, an end calculated for certainly might be very particular and no general considerations about the kind of end be stated. Let us concentrate for the moment on the question whether the wanting or intention of the end *ought to figure in the premises*.

As I formerly represented the matter, "I want" does not go into the premises at all unless indeed it occurs as in the following example. (I owe the point and example to A. Müller.)

> Anyone who wants to kill his parents will be helped to get rid of this trouble by consulting a psychiatrist.[5]
>
> I want to kill my parents;
> If I consult a psychiatrist I shall be helped to get rid of this trouble.

[4] G. H. von Wright, 'On So-Called Practical Inference', *Acta Sociologica*, 15/1 (1972), 39–40.

[5] This is the Aristotelian general premise which does not appear in von Wright's examples. It is easily supplied; e.g. "Unheated huts in cold climates are uninhabitable by humans" or "Unheated huts are not rendered inhabitable unless they are heated". But the hypothetical statement seems to make the general one redundant and vice versa. See Section 4.

NN is a psychiatrist;
So I'll consult *NN*.

Here my wanting to kill my parents is among the facts of the case; it is not that wanting which we picture as, so to speak, constituting the motor force for acting on the premises. *That* is evidently the desire to get rid of the trouble. The decision, if I reach it on these grounds, *shews* that I *want* to get rid of the trouble. It is clear that the roles of these two statements of wanting are different.

If a set of premises is set out without saying what the person is after who is making them his grounds, then the conclusion might be unexpected. It might be opposite to what one would at first expect. For example, in the given case: "So I'll avoid consulting *NN*". This seems perverse and pointless; why then get as far as specifying consulting *NN*, at least if it is a thing one would be in little danger of doing inadvertently? On the other hand identical considerations:

Strong alkaloids are deadly poison to humans;
Nicotine is a strong alkaloid;
What's in this bottle is nicotine

might terminate either in careful avoidance of a lethal dose, or in suicide by drinking the bottle.

That being so, there is a good deal of point in having the end somehow specified if we want to study the form. This at least is true: if you know the end, you know what the conclusion should be, given these premises. Whereas if you do not know the end, (1) the conclusion may be either positive *or* negative. Aristotle, we may say assumes a preference for health and the wholesome, for life, for doing what one should do or needs to do as a certain kind of being. Very arbitrary of him. But also (2) how do we know where the reasoning should stop and a decision be made? For example, note that in the case above we left out a premise, "I am human". As Aristotle remarks somewhere, this premise is one that would seldom be formulated, even by someone who was actually going through the considerations of a practical inference, and though "strictly" that premise belonged among them. Replacing it by "*NN* is a human" can suggest a different tendency altogether for the reasoning! However, in saying that, we are betraying our actual guess what the reasoning is for. Our idea of where the reasoning should terminate depends on this guess.

Thus the end ought to be specified, but the specification of the end is not in the same position as a premise.

A rather pure example of practical reasoning, as we are at present conceiving it, is afforded by the search for a construction in geometry. In Euclid all we are given is the problem, the construction, and then the proof that it does what is required. That saves space, but it does not represent the discovery of the construction.

We have the requirement stated, e.g. *To find the centre of a given circle.* We may then reason as follows, reaching Euclid's construction:

> If we construct the perpendicular bisector of a diameter, that will give us the centre.
> If we construct the perpendicular bisector of a chord, and produce it to the circumference, that will give us a diameter.

We can draw a chord, and we can construct the bisector of any given line. So we conclude by drawing a chord, bisecting it, and bisecting the resultant diameter.

This is different from most of Aristotle's examples. It is of the form:

> Objective: to have it that p.
> If q, then p.
> If r, then q.

Whereupon, r being something we can do, or rather immediately make true, we act. But this form is something like one once sketched by Aristotle:

The healthy state comes about by reasoning as follows: since health is such-and-such, it is necessary, if health is to be, that such-and-such should hold, e.g. homogeneity, and if that, then heat. And so one goes on considering until he comes to some last thing, which he himself can do.[6]

This last thing, Aristotle indicates, may be rubbing: "In treatment, perhaps the starting-point is heating, and he produces this by

---

[6] Aristotle, *Metaphysics* Z. 1032b7–10.

rubbing". Here "starting-point" evidently means the thing the doctor starts by considering how to procure.[7]

In the geometrical example, the construction of a diameter is not the only possible construction for finding the centre of a circle, but in Aristotle's example, the "homogeneity" is said to be *necessary* for restoration of health, and heating for homogeneity. Friction, however, is merely a way of producing heat. What is important is surely that the end will be attained by the means arrived at, not whether it is the only means.

The relation between the premises given for the more usual type of Aristotelian reasoning, and these "if, then" premises, is an obvious one. "The healthy is such-and-such" is rather of the standard type. Somewhat tediously, we could put the two side by side. For "such-and-such" I put "X":

Being healthy is being X.	Only if this patient is X will he be healthy.
Only the homogeneous is X.	Only if he is homogeneous will he be X.
Only by heating does the unhomogeneous become homogeneous.	Only if he is heated will he be homogeneous.
This patient is in an unhomogeneous state.	
Rubbing is heating.	If he is rubbed, he will be heated.

Similarly, we could equip our "if, then" propositions in the geometrical search with accompanying justifications. "The centre of a circle is the mid-point of a diameter." "The perpendicular bisector of a chord, produced to the circumference, is a diameter." These might have stood by themselves as premises on which the enquirer acts by constructing a chord, etc. Aristotle's "light meats" syllogism again can be cast in the "if, then" form:

Light meats suit so-and-sos.	
I am a so-and-so.	If I eat light meat, I'll be eating what suits me.

---

[7] Ibid. 25–6.

| Such-and-such a kind of meat is light. | If I eat such-and-such, I'll be eating light meat. |
| This is such-and-such a kind of meat. | If I eat this, I'll be eating such-and-such. |

There is an interesting difference between the forms. I said that the first premise mentions, not *that* one wants something, but something that one wants. Applying this to the left, it claims that what is wanted (by someone acting on these grounds) is something that suits beings of a certain kind—to which, indeed, he belongs. Applying it to the right, it claims that what is wanted is to eat something that suits oneself.

Suppose we refashioned the right-hand column in an attempt to avoid this apparent difference:

If a so-and-so eats light meat, he eats what suits him.
If a so-and-so eats such-and-such, he eats light meat.
If I eat this, a so-and-so eats such-and-such.

This would make it look as if the objective were the somewhat abstract or impersonal one, that a being of a certain kind should eat suitable food. This is, after all, not what is suggested by the left-hand column together with the comment that if these are premises of practical reasoning, what is wanted is something that suits beings of a certain kind. I shall return to this matter when I take up the topic of the nature of the *generality* of Aristotle's first premises.

For the moment, it is only necessary to say first that the considerations on the left justify (prove) those on the right, a point that we saw also for the geometrical example; and also that the "abstract" aim would seem to be an absurdity. I do not mean, however, that all aims must concern one's own doing or having something. That there should be adequate food in prisons, or a Bible in every hotel room, or fireworks on every New Year's Day are possible aims in which the reasoner's doing or having something are not mentioned. I mean only that *in this case* the abstract aim is absurd. In other cases, indeed, one might do something so that *someone* of a class to which one belongs shall have done a thing of a certain kind. But that is evidently not what is in question in Aristotle's "light meats" syllogism.

3

The previous section has shewn not what practical reasonings are, but at any rate what are practical reasonings, and how great is the contrast with reasonings for the truth of a conclusion. Practical grounds may "require" an action, when they shew that *only* by its means can the end be obtained, but they are just as much grounds when they merely shew that the end *will* be obtained by a certain means. Thus, in the only sense in which practical grounds *can* necessitate a conclusion (an action), they need not, and are none the less grounds for that.

The difficulty felt is to grasp why this should be called "inference". Inference is a logical matter; if there is inference, there must be validity; if there is inference, the conclusion must in some way *follow* from the premises. How can an action logically follow from premises? *Can* it be at all that, given certain thoughts, there is something it logically *must happen* that one does? It seemed no sense could be made of that. Von Wright indeed came as near as he knew how to making sense of it, but he did not succeed. He was indeed assured of failure by the move which ensured that he was speaking clearly in speaking of logical necessity—namely by going over into the third person. What—hedged about by various saving clauses—became the logically necessary conclusion was not the doing, but merely the *truth* of the proposition that the agent would do something. But in this way the practical inference degenerated into a theoretical inference with the odd character of being invalid so long as it was truly inferential!

I have given a very different account, but the question remains outstanding: in what sense is this *inference*? One speaks of *grounds* of action indeed, as of belief; one says "and so I'll . . ." or "Therefore I'll . . .", and we understand such expressions. But are they more than mere verbal echoes? The frequent non-necessity of the "conclusion" is a striking feature. In order to eat *some* suitable food, one eats *this*. Or again: either *A* or *B* will do, and so one does *A*.

Some philosophers have tried to develop an account of "imperative inference"—inference from command to command, or from command to what to do in execution of a command, conceived as self-administration of a "derived" command by one

who seeks to obey the first command. This has some bearing on
our topic. If someone has the objective of obeying an order which
does not tell him to do what he can simply do straight off, his
problem is a problem of practical inference: he has to determine
on doing something, in doing which he will be carrying out the
order. The picture of this as reasoning from a more general to a
more specific command, or from a command to achieve something to a command to do such-and-such with a view to this, is of
some interest to us.

R. M. Hare maintained that imperative inference repeated ordinary inference; if one proposition followed from another, the
corresponding imperatives were similarly related. And also, from
an imperative $p!$ and a proposition *if p then q*, there would follow
an imperative $q!$

Anthony Kenny was struck by the "non-necessary" character of
many Aristotelian inferences. He suggested that there was a
"logic of satisfactoriness" by reasoning within which one could
move from "kill someone" to killing a particular individual, from
a disjunctive command to obeying one of the disjuncts, and from
a requirement that q, with the information that if p then q, to the
decision to effect p. All these reasonings would be fallacious in
the logic of propositions. Accordingly, Kenny suggested that this
logic was the mirror image of ordinary logic; what would be
conclusions in ordinary logic figure as premises in this logic—
premises of the form Fiat $p!$—and the reasoning proceeds to conclusions, also Fiats,[8] which are what in the indicative mood would
be premises in ordinary logic. To see whether an inference in the
"logic of satisfactoriness" is valid, you check whether the reverse
inference is valid when instead of Fiats you have the corresponding propositions.

Hare's "imperative inference" of course does not allow of such
inferences as these. Also, as had earlier been pointed out by Alf
Ross, such a "logic" admits the inference of $(p$ or $q)!$ from $p!$
Kenny's system allows many natural moves, but does not allow
the inference from "Kill everyone" to "Kill Jones!" It has been
blamed for having an inference from "Kill Jones!" to "Kill everyone!" but this is not so absurd as it may seem. It may be decided

[8] In a special sense: not that the "conclusion" has to be fulfilled or implemented.
But the proposition is given the "Fiat" form to shew that it is not being asserted or
supposed, but proposed as something to make true.

to kill everyone in a certain place in order to get the particular people that one wants. The British, for example, wanted to destroy some German soldiers on a Dutch island in the second world war, and chose to accomplish this by bombing the dykes and drowning everybody.[9] (The Dutch were their allies.)

This "logic", however, curiously and comically excludes just those forms that von Wright has concentrated on. Expressing the end as a "Fiat", and given that unless one does such-and-such the end will not be achieved, it seems obvious that if there is such a thing as inference by which a command or decision can be derived, there must here be an inference to "do such-and-such". It also seems absurd that $(p \& q)!$ for *arbitrary* q, follows from $p!$ Effecting two things may indeed often be *a way of* effecting one of them; but the admission of arbitrary conjuncts is one of those forced and empty requirements of a view which shew that there is something wrong with it. It is in this respect like the derivation of $(p \lor q)!$ from $p!$ in Hare's system.

Kenny's suggestion has this value: it suggests that we consider a passage *from* what would be a conclusion of inference from facts *to* what would be premises of such a conclusion, when the conclusion is something to aim at bringing about, and the premises are possibly effectable truth-conditions of this, or means of effecting them. A truth-condition is a circumstance or conjunction of circumstances given which the proposition is true. Execution-conditions for commands are truth-conditions for the corresponding propositions. A proposition implies that a (some or other) truth-condition of it holds, but the truth of a given truth-condition of it does not usually follow from its truth. If we find a conjunctive truth-condition, it may be that the truth of one of the conjuncts follows from the truth of the proposition, but this need not generally be so.

In reckoning how to execute an order, one may be looking for straightaway practicable execution-conditions. Also, perhaps, for practicable conditions whose falsehood implies that the order is not carried out. If there is something of this sort, the proposition stating that it is true *will* follow from the proposition corresponding to the original order. But there may be no particular condition

---

[9] Alf Ross shews some innocence when he dismisses Kenny's idea: "From plan *B* (to prevent overpopulation) we may infer plan *A* (to kill half the population) but the inference is hardly of any practical interest." We *hope* it may not be.

of that sort. Thus, one may not be looking for anything, and
certainly will not be looking for everything, which will necessarily have been made true if the original order is carried out.

Let us illustrate. An administrator for a conquering power
gives the order "Bring all the members of one of these committees
before me". There are a dozen or more committees in question. So
if all the members of any one of them are brought before him, the
order is obeyed. But there is no committee that must be brought
before him. If, however, there is someone who is a member
of all the committees, then if *he* is not fetched the order has not
been obeyed. Let there be such a man. The executor of the order
picks up this man and one by one a number of others,
until he knows he has a set among them that comprises a committee. He may not aim at any particular committee but let
chance decide which one he makes up as he gets hold of now this
man, now this pair of alternatives, now that man. All the
time he is calculating the consequences of his possible moves
as contributions to the achievement of his goal, and acting
accordingly.

This brings out the relation we have mentioned between the
idea of practical inference and imperative inference. The one seeking to obey this order has a goal, expressed by what the order
requires should become the case.

But now, it appears that all the reasoning is ordinary "theoretical" reasoning. It is, for example, from potential elements of truth-
conditions for the attainment of his goal. "If he does this, he will
have that situation, which has such-and-such relevance to the
attainment of the goal." Such conditionals and such relevance will
themselves be established by "ordinary" inference from various
facts. What he is trying to do is to find a truth-condition which he
can effect, make true, (practicable ways of making not straightaway practicable truth-conditions true). As he does so, or as he
finds potential conjuncts of a truth-condition which he can effect,
he acts. Where in all this is there any other than "ordinary"
reasoning—i.e. reasoning from premises to the truth of a
conclusion?

Let us suppose that the order is placed at the beginning of a set
of considerations, but is cast in the form of a "Fiat" ("May it come
about that") adopted by the executive.

Fiat: some committee is brought before X.

He now reasons:

If I get all the members of some committee rounded up, I can bring them before X

and adopts a secondary Fiat:

∴ Fiat: I get all the members of some committee rounded up.

He reasons further:

Only if A is rounded up will all the members of any committee be rounded up.

And he can pick up A, so he does. Let us verbalize his action:

∴ Let me pick up A. (Or: So I pick up A.)

He reasons further:

If the occupants of this bar are rounded up, several members of committees will be rounded up.

If several members of committees are rounded up, we may be able to pick a whole committee from among them, together with A.

And he can round up all the occupants of the bar, so he does. Verbalized:

∴ Let me round up all the occupants of this bar. (Or: So I round up all the occupants of this bar.)

He now finds he hasn't yet got all the members of any one committee, but he reasons:

If I pick up B and C, or D, or E and F, or G or H, then, with what I have already I shall have a whole committee.

He now gets an opportunity to pick up B, C, and G. Verbalizing his action as before, we have:

∴ Let me pick up B, C, and G. (Or: So I pick up B, C, and G.)

or: ∴ Let me pick up B and C. (Or: So I pick up B and C.)

or: ∴ Let me pick up G. (Or: So I pick up G.)

Now, what is the relation between the original Fiat and the secondary Fiat, and between the secondary Fiat and the actions (or, if you like, their verbalizations)? The relations, if the man is right, are severally given in the reasoning; that is, in the conditionals that I prefaced with the words "he reasons".

What, then, does the *therefore* signify? "Therefore" is supposed to be a sign of reasoning! But what we have been calling the *reasoning* was the considerations. These will just be truths (or, if he is wrong, falsehoods). If they in turn were conclusions, the reasoning leading to them wasn't given. If we say "He reasons . . .", should it not run "He reasons . . . (∴) . . ."? We gave a "therefore" indeed, but it is just what we are failing to understand. The therefores that we'd understand are these:

(a) I pick up B and C.
∴ I have a complete committee rounded up.
(b) I get all members of some committee rounded up.
∴ I can bring some committee before X.
(c) A will not be picked up.
∴ No complete committee will be rounded up.
(d) A will not be picked up.
∴ It will not be possible to bring a complete committee before X.

whereas the corresponding ones that we actually gave were:

(a^1) Let me get a complete committee rounded up.
∴ Let me pick up B and C.
(b^1) Let me bring some committee before X.
∴ Let me get all the members of some committee rounded up.
(c^1) Let me get a complete committee rounded up.
∴ Let me pick up A.
(d^1) Let me bring a complete committee before X.
∴ Let me pick up A.

Now first note this: what I implicitly called the "reasoning"—by putting "he reasons" in front of the examples—were considerations which would be the same in corresponding cases; I mean that the same conditional propositions mediate between "premise" and "conclusion" for a and a^1, for b and b^1, for c and c^1, for d and d^1.

For a and a^1 it is:

> If I pick up B and C, with what I already have I shall have a whole committee.

For b and b^1:

> If I get all the members of some committee rounded up, I can bring some whole committee before X.

And so on. Criticism of the transition as incorrect, whether in the "Fiat" or the "ordinary" form, will be exactly the same, e.g. "What makes you think that if you round such people up, you will be able to bring them before X?"

Let us also note that the "reasoning" that we seemed to understand, where there was "ordinary" inference, was purely suppositious. The premises were not asserted; they concerned future possible happenings, and were merely supposed.

With these observations we have already indicated the relation between the different "Fiats" and between them and the decisions. Where this relation exists, *there* we have the practical "therefore".

We should note, however, that to the transition

> Fiat q!
> ∴ Fiat p!
> or: ∴ I'll make p true

there corresponds not one but four different patterns of suppositious inference:

p will be.	$\sim(p$ will be).	p will be.	$\sim(p$ will be).
∴ q will be.	∴ q will not be.	∴ q will be possible.	∴ q will not be possible.

The hypotheticals "If p will be, q will be" etc. prove the correctness of the inferences "p will be, ∴ q will be" etc. Such a hypothetical may be true, either because p is or is part of a truth-condition of q, or because the coming about of p will bring about the truth of q, or of at least part of some truth-condition of q. The difference between these is not reflected in the schemata. That is quite as it should be. In his reasonings our executive considered execution-conditions and ways of bringing about the truth of execution-conditions all in the same way. Nor in "ordinary" inference, when, for example, we use "if p, then q" in *modus ponens*, do we have to ask ourselves whether p is a truth-condition of q, or q is some other sort of consequence of p.

And now we can say in what sense there is, and in what sense there is not, a special "form" of practical inference. We can represent any inference by setting forth a set of hypothetical considerations:

If p, q.
If q, r.

The question is: what are these considerations *for*, if they are not idle? There may be at any rate these uses for them: We may be able to assert p, and go on to assert r. Or we may want to achieve r, and decide to make p true—this being something we can do straight away. In either case we may appeal to considerations. Looked at in this way, we find no special form of practical inference; we have a set of propositions connected with one another the same way in the two cases. The difference lies in the different service to which they are put.

Not that these two are the only uses. These hypotheticals might of course be used to make a threat or offer a warning. But we are interested in cases where the first and last propositions get extracted from the hypothetical contexts, and the hypotheticals get used to mediate between them. In the cases we have considered, the extracted propositions are either asserted or made the topic of a Fiat.

But again, those are not the only cases. There is also a use in seeking an explanation; we have it given that r, and the hypotheticals suggest p, which we will suppose is something we can check for truth. If p turns out true, it may perhaps explain r.

The hypotheticals can be put to *practical* service only when they concern "what can be otherwise", that is: what may happen one way or the other, that is: future matters, results which our actions can affect. Then the hypothetical mediates between will for an objective and decision on an action.

A passage in von Wright's 'On So-called Practical Inference' is relevant here:

The conclusion of the first person inference, we said, is a declaration of intention. This intention may not have been formed until we realised practical necessities involved in our aiming at a certain end. So its formation may come later, after the first intention was already formed. We can speak of a *primary* and a *secondary* intention here. The connexion between the two intentions is, moreover, a kind of logically necessary connexion. The second (epistemic) premise can be said to "mediate" between the primary intention of the first premise and the secondary intention of the conclusion. One can also speak of a transfer or *transmission of intention*. The "will" to attain an end is being transmitted to (one of) the means deemed necessary for its attainment.[10]

I have taken cases where the means chosen aren't supposed to be necessary. Yet here too there can be a "transmission of intention". Von Wright finds 'a kind of logically necessary connexion' between the primary and secondary intentions. Now can we not say that there is a logical connexion—but beware! this does not mean "a relation of logical necessitation"—between the truth-connexion of p, $p \supset q$, and q on the one hand, and the transmission (1) of belief from p to q and (2) of intention from Fiat q! to Fiat p!? But the logical necessity involved is only the truth-connexion of p, $p \supset q$, and q; this truth-connexion is common to both kinds of inference.

"But the logical necessity is *the justification* of assertive inference from p to q, and its apprehension *compels* belief!" That is a confusion. The justification is simply the truth of p and $p \supset q$: Where there is such a justification, we *call* the connexion one of "logical necessity". And how can belief be "compelled"? By force of personality, perhaps, or bullying. But that is not what is in question. One may also *feel* compelled, but again, that is not what is in question. What is claimed is that the belief is "logically" compelled. But what can that mean except that there is that "logical necessity", the truth-connexion? But it was supposed to be not *that* necessity, but a compulsion produced by perceiving that necessity. Once again: if it is a feeling, a felt difficulty so strong as to create incapacity to refrain from belief, that is still not "logical". And the same would hold for any other "state of the subject". As soon as we speak of "logical" compulsion, we find that we can mean nothing but the "necessity" of the truth-connexion.

(Von Wright would here slide into the third person: "X consciously believes p and consciously and simultaneously believes $p \supset q$ and the question whether q is before X's mind" *entails* "X

---

[10] von Wright, 'On So-called Practical Inference', 45.

believes *q*". But how do we know this? Only as we know "Treason doth never prosper": if *X* doesn't then believe *q*, we won't *allow it to be said* that those other three things are true of him.)

I conclude that transmission of intention and transmission of belief should be put side by side; that there is no such thing as the transmission's being "logical" in the sense that the "necessity" of the truth-connexion has an analogue in a "logical compulsion" to be in one psychological state once one has got into another. And therefore that there never was a problem of how the action or decision could be "logically compelled". This is obscured for us if we make the assumption that there is such a thing in the case of belief, and that *it* at least is unproblematic. I believe this is a common scarcely criticized assumption.

Nevertheless, we cannot *simply* say: practical inference is an inference, a transition, that goes in the direction from *q* (Fiat *q!*) to *p* (Fiat *p!*) when, for example, we have the truth-connexion of *p*, *p* ⊃ *q*, and *q*. For that is not the whole story. We have observed that when the propositions are turned into Fiats they are restricted in their subject-matter to future matters which our action can affect. But we have also noticed that not just any effectable truth-conditions are of practical relevance. That is, that *p* & *q* may be a condition of *r merely* because *p* is so, merely a truth-condition. If there is a way of effecting *p* & *q* jointly, that may be a practical conclusion, however outrageous, for one who wants to effect *r* (like burning the house down to roast the pig). But what if the only way of effecting *p* & *q* is to effect them separately?

In such a case "If *p* & *q*, then *r*" may still have practical relevance; namely, that effecting *q* as well as *p* does not impede *r*. "If *p* then *r*, and if *p* and *q* then still *r*", the agent may say. The consideration is of service to him if, for example, he independently wants to effect *q*. (Or someone else does.) But there is here no "transmission of intention" via (*p* & *q*) ⊃ *r*, from the primary intention that *r* to a secondary intention that *p* and that *q*. That is, the truth-connexion of (*p* & *q*) and (*p* & *q*) ⊃ *r* does not "mediate" such a transmission.

We cannot state *logical* conditions for this restriction on the relevance of effectable truth-conditions. We cannot do it by saying, for example, that *p* & *q* won't be a relevant effectable truth-condition of *r* if *p* & ~*q* too is an effectable truth-condition of *r*. For that may be the case, and effecting (*p* & *q*) *still* be *a* way of effecting *r*. For example, I invite a married couple to dinner; I really want to just see the wife and I could invite her alone, but (for some reason or none) the way of getting to see her that I choose is to issue a joint invitation.

What is in question here is something outside the logic that we are considering, namely whether there is "one action" which is a way of effecting (*p* & *q*) and therefore a way of effecting *p*. But what counts as "one action" may be very various in various contexts and according to various ways of looking at the matter.

We have now given the sense in which there is *not* a special "form" of practical inference. The considerations and their logical relations are just the same whether the inference is practical or theoretical. What I mean by the "considerations" are all those hypotheticals which we have been examining, and also any propositions which show them to be true. The difference between practical and theoretical is mainly a difference in the service to which these considerations are put. Thus, if we should want to give conditionals which are logical truths, which we might think of as giving us the logically necessary connexions which "stand behind" the inferences, *they will be exactly the same conditionals* for the practical and for the corresponding "theoretical" inferences.

I must therefore make amends to Aristotle, whom I formerly blamed for speaking of practical inference as "just the same" as theoretical. I wanted to say it was a *completely different form*. I believe Aristotle might have had a difficulty in understanding the debate that has gone on about "whether there is such a thing as practical (or imperative) inference". For what I believe has lurked in some of our minds has been something which his mind was quite clear of.

That is the picture of a logical step: an act of mind which is making the step from premise to conclusion. Making the step *in logic*, making a *movement* in a different, *pure*, medium of logic itself. So the dispute seemed one between people who all agreed there was such a thing as this "stepping" for assertions or suppositions; but some thought they could see such a "step" also in the case of practical inference, while others just couldn't descry it at all. But there is no such thing in any case!

There is, however, a distinct "form" of practical inference, if all we mean by the "form" is (1) the casting of certain propositions in a quasi-imperative form, and (2) how the matters are arranged. What is the starting-point and what the terminus? The starting-point for practical inference is the thing wanted; so in representing it we put that at the beginning. Then there are the considerations (to which I formerly restricted the term "premises") and then there is the decision, which we have agreed to verbalize. So:

Wanted: that p. (Or: Let it be that p.)

If q, then p.

If r, then q.

Decision: r!

While for theoretical inference the starting-point is something asserted or supposed:

r. (Or: Suppose r.)

If r then q.

If q then p.

p.

The change of mood and different order of the same elements give what may be called a different form. But that is all. We would have as much right to call "a different form" that search for an explanation which we noticed. In arrangement it is just like practical inference. The mood is not changed, and the reasoning is towards a hypothesis proposed for investigation.

Given: p.

If q, then p.

If r, then q.

To investigate: r. (Is "r" true?)

For example, we may either seek to attain something, or to explain it when given it as a phenomenon:

To attain: Spectacular plant growth.	To explain: Spectacular plant growth.

If plants are fed with certain substances,
there will be spectacular plant growth.
If these substances are in the soil,
the plants will be fed with them.

| Conclusion: To put those substances in the soil. | Conclusion: To examine the soil so as to check whether those substances are present. |

Both of these uses are different from the "theoretical" use to reach the truth of a conclusion:

Premise: There are certain substances in the soil.

If those substances are in the soil, the plant will be fed with them.

If the plants are fed with those substances, there will be spectacular plant growth.

Conclusion: There will be spectacular plant growth.

If the common characteristics of these three patterns are recognized, and it is also clear wherein they differ, then it seems a matter of indifference whether we speak of different kinds of inference or not.

Those, however, who have objected to the idea of "practical inference" have this speaking for them: though there is a "validity" of practical inference, it is not of a purely formal character. By that, I mean one that can be displayed by the use of schematic letters, such that any substitution instance of the forms so given will be valid. The restriction of subject-matter to future contingents may be formally characterizable. The restriction, which we have mentioned, on inferences to *bringing it about that p and q,* apparently cannot be.

The transmission of belief can be called "logical" in a derivative sense: if *r* follows from *p and q* and one *believes r "because p and q".* Given the truth-connexions of the propositions, *any* such belief will be "logically transmitted" in our derivative sense. A parallel sense of "logical transmission" for practical inference would be empty and vain, failing to catch the idea of "transmission of intention". For there *is* such a thing, but it is excluded in the case where *p* will be relevant to the end and we add just any arbitrary conjunct *q,* whose truth would have to be effected "separately".

In his earlier 1963 article on practical inference, in the *Philosophical Review* von Wright mentions a form in which the second premise says that the end won't be attained unless someone *else,*

B, does something. With his assumptions, he cannot give an account of a reasoning whose conclusion is *B*'s action; 'the agent who is in pursuit of the end and the agent upon whom the practical necessity is incumbent must be the same'.

Nevertheless, there are such forms. They will be practical (rather than idle) if the considerations on the part of *X*, whose objective is mentioned in the first premise, lead to the other's doing the required thing. But this might be because *X forces B* to do it! If so, then the terminus is that action on *X*'s part which compels *B* to do *A*. But it might also exemplify some relation of affection or authority or co-operation. Then we could treat the action on *B*'s part (without verbalization) as the conclusion. At any rate, we can do so just as much as where the person who acts is the same as the person whose objective is promoted.

If the reasoning terminates in the utterance of an order, then of course *B* does not have to derive that conclusion; he is already given it. That will not be a case that interests us; the cases we are after are ones where *B* makes the inference. Now in discussion of "imperative inference", people have usually had in mind the derivations to be made by someone obeying other people's orders. I described this as a problem of practical inference: such a person, I supposed, has the objective of executing an order. But what have people in mind who discuss whether "*Do r!*" follows from "*Do r or q*", or conversely? I think that either the initial order is supposed to be accepted, in the sense that the one who accepts it as it were administers it to himself, after which he "infers" derivable orders, or he is conceived of as ascribing the derivable orders to the person giving the initial order. In either way of looking at it there is a supposed or putative inference on the part of someone who seriously means the first order, to the derived order.

Reverting to von Wright's first-person form, suppose I say to you:

> I want to get this message to *N* by four o'clock. Unless you take it to him, I shan't get it to him by four o'clock.

and suppose I then hand you the message with nothing more said, whereupon you carry it to *N*. (Such is our relationship.) So *you* act on *my* grounds. I state the premises (as premises are conceived by von Wright); you draw the conclusion.

Now if it were "theoretical" reasoning, i.e. reasoning to the truth of a conclusion, you might "draw the conclusion" without believing it. I make assertions, you produce a statement that is implied by them. If you did believe what I said, and are clear about the implication, very likely you will believe the conclusion. But you may not have believed me. None the less, you can still produce the conclusion precisely as a conclusion from the premises without asserting it and without believing it.

How is it with action? The way we are looking at the matter, drawing the conclusion in a practical sense is acting. Then you act in *execution* of my will. But what are you after yourself?

You may be after promoting my objectives. If so, we might represent the matter by setting forth *your* "practical grounds":

I want what she wants to be attained.

Unless I do *A*, what she wants won't be attained,

so . . . But may it not be that you have no objective of your own here? That you are functioning as an instrument? Asked for the grounds of your action, you point to *my* grounds, as a man may point to his orders.

You are then speaking as one who had a certain role, but whose own objectives do not yet come into the picture.

Do you, for example, have to believe the "second premise"? No! Then you act, but perhaps woodenly or even as it were ironically. Surely slaves and other subordinates must often act so.

Not aiming at what the directing will aims at, not believing his premises, but still drawing the conclusion in action: *that* will be what corresponds to not believing the assertions and not believing the conclusion but still drawing the conclusion in the theoretical case.

These considerations make a distinction between what a man is up to and what he is after. In the case imagined, what he is up to is: being the executive, the instrument, a kind of rational tool, and *so* acting as a subordinate. But this does not show what, if anything, he is after: it does not show *for the sake of what* he acts. It might be objected that he *has* the objective of "acting as a subordinate"; this no doubt is an intermediate end, for him, pursued perhaps for the sake of getting by, of not getting into trouble. This may be so sometimes. Then the man does not merely act as a subordinate, *he thinks* he had better do so in order to keep out of trouble. But it would be a mistake to think this must always be the situation. We can go directly from taking the message in these circumstances to the end of not getting into trouble. The means, acting as a subordinate, are not required as an intermediate term. That he acts as a subordinate in the way I have described is a true characterization or summary description of his thus acting under the will of his master or superior. But perhaps his "consciousness has not been raised" sufficiently for the idea to enter into his calculation.

Now I can at last bring out the objection to von Wright's putting wanting and believing—the psychological facts of wanting and believing—into the premises. It is as incorrect as it would be to represent theoretical inference in terms of belief. No doubt we could argue that "*A* believes that *p* and that if *p* then *q*" entails "*A* believes that *q*". I have already remarked on a certain emptiness in this contention when it is decked out with such saving clauses as are needed to make it true. One will then take the failure to believe *q* as a criterion for the falsehood of the statement of conjunctive belief: we won't *call* it "really" believing that *p* and if *p* then *q*. Similarly for "*X* intends to attain *E* and believes that unless he does *A* he will not"—if he does not now do *A*. Yet the objection may not impress. For if *p* entails *q*, then of course *not-q* will entail *not-p*, and one may not be sure of the weight of the notion of a "criterion" here.

But there is a clearer objection. We would never think that the validity of "*p*, if *p* then *q*, therefore *q*" was to be expounded as the entailment of "*X* believes *q*" by "*X* believes that *p* and that if *p* then *q*". It is, we feel, the other way around.

Belief is the most difficult topic because it is so hard to hold in view and correctly combine the psychological and the logical aspects. Beliefs are psychological dispositions belonging in the histories of minds. But also, a belief, a believing, is internally characterized by the proposition saying what is believed. This is (mostly) not about anything psychological; its meaning and truth are not matters of which we should give a psychological account. Propositions, we say, are what we operate the calculi of inference with, for example the calculus of truth-functions; and here is the calculus. We then display it. Certainly what it is *for* is, for example, to pass from beliefs to beliefs. But we should throw everything into confusion if we introduced belief into our description of the validity of inferences. In setting forth the forms of inference we put as elements the propositions or we use propositional variables to represent them.

Just the same holds for the patterns of practical inference. I have argued that the *logical facts* are merely the same as for theoretical: e.g. the truth-connexions of p, if p then q, and q; and of *not-p*, only if p then q, and *not-q*. But the patterns are different; the elements are put in a different order; and the propositions are not asserted but propounded as possibilities that can be made true.

There would be no point in the proof patterns, if they were never to be plugged into believing minds, if nothing were ever asserted; and equally no point in patterns of practical inference if nothing were aimed at. But *still* one should not put the wanting or intending or believing into the description of the inferences.

Now this point about the inference itself appears to me capable of demonstration from the cases we have just been considering. Just as, without believing it, I can draw a conclusion from your assertions, so our ironical slave can draw a conclusion in action from the specified objective and the assertion made by his master. In both cases the inference is something separable from the attitude of the one who is making it. The elements of the inference must all be in one head, it is true; that is, they must be known to whoever makes the inference; but the cognate believing and willing do not have to exist in that soul. So the inference patterns should not be given as ones in which these psychological facts are given a place.

Theoretical inferences do essentially concern objects of belief, and practical ones do concern objects of will and belief. This can put us on the wrong scent if we think that belief and will are themselves experienced soul or mind states, happenings, actions or activities, as are pains, feelings of all sorts, images, reflections, and sometimes, decisions. It is easy to think this. Then "I believe p" would mean, say, "I get assent-feelings about the idea that p". But if one does adopt such a view, one will find the greatest difficulty in maintaining that there is anything at all in the entailment: "X believes that p and that if p then q, therefore X believes q"; Or by the same token, anything at all in the argument "X

intends to attain end E; X believes that unless he does action A now he will not attain E; so X is just about to do action A''.

4

One of von Wright's moves, which helped to obtain necessity in the conclusions of practical inferences, was to change "want" to "intend": X intends to make the hut inhabitable. This has the effect of restricting his first premise to definitely accomplishable objectives. A man may hubristically say that he intends to be rich, healthy, happy, glorious, to attain the knowledge of things worth knowing, or to enjoy life. Whether he will do so is very much on the knees of the gods. If we speak, as I am willing to speak, of an *intention of the end* even for such ends, intention here means nothing but "aiming at", and the verb "intend" remains inept.

We have seen that the pursuit of necessary connexion or logical compulsion is pursuit of a Will-o'-the-wisp. So we need not limit ourselves to such restricted ends. Von Wright himself did not stress the purpose of securing some kind of necessity of a conclusion; nevertheless, that purpose was served by the restriction in the following way: when ends are of such a diffuse character as the ones I have just mentioned, it is rare for some highly specific action here and now to be quite necessary in pursuing them. Not that it is out of the question. I might, for example, have the end of leading an honourable, unblemished life, and then there will sometimes be situations in which, as we say, some "quite particular" act is necessary for me. All the same, the case is exceptional. But it is a quite frequent one for the attainment of such very specific objectives as I can properly be said to *intend to bring about*.

Von Wright gives a different reason for the restriction: a man may want incompatible things. But his purpose of ruling out incompatible ends is not guaranteed success by changing "want" to "intend". Although no doubt a man can intend only what he at least thinks he can achieve, still the objective is always at a remove from the action; it is thus quite possible for him in his actions seriously to intend to achieve things which are severally possible, but not possible together; nor does he have to *think* that they are compossible; he may never have brought them together in his mind—if he had, he would perhaps have realized at once that they were not possible together. Thus he may do one thing to help bring it about that two people meet, and another to help bring it about that one of them travels overseas, though this will prevent their meeting.

We may therefore confidently abandon this impoverishing restriction. This allows us to consider an important fact of human nature, namely, that men have such "diffuse" ends. They are not merely concerned to bring about such circumstances as that object *A* be moved to point *B*. They want, for example, happiness, glory, riches, power.

We might call these ends "generic". But here we must avoid a confusion: "generic" does not mean the same as "general". The generic is contrasted with the more specific: what *form* of wealth, for example, is a man who wants to be wealthy aiming at in his calculations, when he has worked out something to do in order to be wealthy? The possession of lands, or of a regular income, or of a large sum of money? His heart may just be set on being wealthy, but if he is to achieve this it must take a more specific form, perhaps determined for him by his opportunities.

An end may be called "particular" either by contrast with being generic or by contrast with being general. It will be convenient to avoid this ambiguity. When I call an end *particular*, I will henceforth mean that the end is that something shall hold about a given individual. *This hut* is to be inhabitable, *I* am to be rich or happy. Thus all these generic ends of health, wealth, knowledge, etc. are in this sense particular. That *this hut* is to be inhabitable is particular but not very specific. More specific is that it is to be warm, or furnished. Still more specific: that it is to be warmed with a coke stove. We descend from the merely specific to the particular on the side of *what is to be done* to the hut if I make it my objective that it be warmed with the stove I found in a certain shop; at least, if I mean the very example of the stove, and not the type.

Ends can be general. I may not be aiming at *NN*'s doing or being something, but have, for example, the aim that some men know classical Greek, or again that men be free. This last is not merely general but generic. But if my aim is: that there be a copy of the Bible in every hotel room, that is a general but specific end.

It is human to have generic ends. These are particular when they are ends that one shall oneself be or do something. I don't know if it is humanly possible to have no *general* ends. I suppose that a good man will be likely to have some. (Though I don't mean that it *takes* a good man to have any.)

Having thus far cleared the ground, we can make some observations on the role of "general principles" in practical inference.

If, as in Aristotle, "principle" means "starting-point", we might first think that a starting-point is wherever you happen to start. But this would not be quite satisfactory, since you might happen to *start* with some quite particular fact, as, that N is married to M. It is not a historical order of actual consideration that is meant; a man's considerations leading to an action can be arranged in an order that displays a progress from something mentioning an end to the particular action adopted. This is so whether the first thing merely mentions an end as "pure water is wholesome for humans to drink" mentions the wholesome to drink, or specifies it *as* an objective, as "Health is to be restored" does. In either case we can call the thing aimed at the starting-point. If the objective is not specified *as* an objective, then the statement mentioning it which we put first in an orderly arrangement *may or may not be a general statement*. Thus, "Only if this hut is heated will it be habitable" is not a general statement; yet it might be the first in a set of considerations which we give as the grounds of an action.

However, its truth will be connected with general facts as well as a particular one. For example, "Humans need a certain degree of warmth in their habitations" as well as "This hut lacks such a degree of warmth as it is".

Aristotle's "general" or "universal" premises are of that kind. It is a reasonable view that such premises are always, in some sense, in the offing. But maybe only in the sense that they ought to be reachable. "*This* hut needs heating if *you* are to live in it" might be the judgement of a sensible person who had not formulated a general statement—for perhaps another person rather hardier could manage well without heat in this hut. "General propositions derive from particular ones,"[11] Aristotle remarks, and an experienced person may just have good particular judgement. He has just spoken of "intelligence" (*nous*), which in practical considerations—and here I will translate with the uncouthness of a close rendering of the Greek—"is of the particular, of the possible and of the second premise; for these are starting-points of that for the sake of which". Here "starting-points" does not mean

---

[11] *Nicomachean Ethics* 1143ᵇ4 ff.

considerations or things put in some arrangement of propositions; it means rather *causes*. That for the sake of which something is done has its source, if it does get achieved, in perfectly particular contexts, where there is possibility of things turning out one way *or* another, and in the particular premise, which is the immediate ground of action. Thus the general premises may be dispensable. But if we could not simply and directly judge the particular "*You* need *this* hut to be heated" we might reach it from generalization, as also if we heard it and looked for a justification of it. Somewhat vague generalizations like "Humans need a certain degree of warmth in their dwellings" are of course readily available.

So much for the relation of general and particular premises. I now turn to what is much more important, the matter of generic ends.

Aristotle has a teaching which is useful to mention because of the contrast that it offers with von Wright's. I stick to my principles of close translation:

> Of theoretical thinking which is neither practical nor productive, the *well* and *badly* is the true and false, for this is the business of any thinking; but of what is practical and intellectual, [it is] truth in agreement with right desire.[12]

By contrast, we may say: in von Wright's picture the business of practical thinking is simply *truth in agreement with desire*,[13] i.e. getting things the way you want them to be without the qualification that Aristotle puts in "getting things a way it's all right to want them to be".

This may be a little unfair to von Wright, who after all has not addressed himself to the question. But we can ask: is not the truth about it a necessary component of the essential characterization of practical inference?

I claimed that in practical inference the relation between the premises and the conclusion (the action) is that the premises show what good, what use, the action is. Now if, following von Wright, we put "I want" into the first premise, this aspect assumes insignificance. It could be admitted, but it would be of no consequence.

---

[12] Ibid. 1139ª27–30.
[13] I mean truth which you make true by acting. For some reason, people find this idea very difficult. In lecturing I have sometimes tried to get it across by saying: "I am about to make it true that I am on this table." I then climb on the table. Whether I have made it true that my hearers understand, I do not know.

Of course the premises show what use the action is—it is that of bringing about something one wants, which has to be achieved, if it is achieved, by some means.

But in Section 2 I shewed that the wanting, the drive towards the end, does not properly go into the reasoning at all. This "I want" is not a reason; a reason must shew or be connected with further reasons that show what good it is to do the thing. Now does this mean merely; what it will effect or help to effect—which, as it happens, one wants?

Admittedly, that is how I have been presenting it so far. There are strong reasons for doing so. If an end, an objective, is specified, then how is correctness of calculation to be judged? By whether it indicates an action that is necessary for, or will secure, that objective. Not *only* by this, indeed, since an effective means may be cumbersome or clumsy or difficult, and a better means may be available. But a criticism of the means on any other ground, for example on grounds of outrageousness, makes an appeal to other ends which ought not to be violated in pursuing this one. If you don't mind burning the house down to roast the pig, and it is easy and effective, the pig getting well roasted that way, then why not do it?

Criticism of means which are good purely in relation to the given end, must be in the light of other ends which it is assumed that you have or ought to have. If you have them, we can put them in and criticize the calculation for failure in relation to its ends. If not, then this criticism of means is a criticism of ends and can be considered together with a possible criticism of the given end, either as such or in those circumstances. Now the question becomes: what has a criticism of ends got to do with an evaluation of practical reasoning as such?

Aristotle discusses an intellectual virtue, *euboulia*, which is translated "good counsel". This does not imply that one is a giver or receiver of advice, only that the actions of one who has it are, as we might say, "well-advised", of one who lacks it "ill-advised". He observes that it is a certain kind of correctness of calculation; not every kind, because "the self-indulgent or bad man will get what he purposes by calculation if he is clever, and so he will have calculated correctly, but will obtain for himself a great evil"— whereas good counsel will not produce such a result. We can now say: hitherto we have been considering that "correctness of calculation" which can be common to the well-advised and the ill-advised. That correctness of calculation which produces "truth in agreement with desire", i.e. things as one wants them to be.

It is easy to say at this point: "Ah, what is in question here is *moral* criticism, and that is something else. It is not a criticism of practical inference as such". But I cannot accept this observation: I have long complained that I don't know what "moral" means in this sort of use. "Perfectly sound practical reasoning may lead to bad actions." Yes, that is true, in just the same sense as it is true that "Perfectly sound theoretical reasoning may lead to false conclusions". If we limit what we mean by "soundness" to what is called "validity", both observations are correct. And in our philosophical training we learn carefully to use this idea of soundness of reasoning and to make the distinction between truth and validity and we are right to do so. Equally right, therefore, to distinguish between goodness and validity; for in the sphere of practical reasoning, goodness of the end has the same role as truth of the premises has in theoretical reasoning.

This is the great Aristotelian parallel: if it is right, then the goodness of the end and of the action is as much of an extra, as external to the validity of the reasoning, as truth of the premises and of the conclusion is an extra, is external to the validity of theoretical reasoning. *As* external, but not *more* external.

We know that the externality is not total. For truth is the object of belief, and truth-preservingness an essential associate of validity in theoretical reasoning. The parallel will hold for practical reasoning.

In the philosophy of action we often hear it debated to and fro whether something, p, "is a reason" for action. We sometimes hear it said that "moral considerations" *just are* "reasons". But what does all this mean? It seems to be discussed independently of anybody making the thing *his* reason. With our present insight, we can clarify. "p is a reason", in theoretical contexts, assumes that some proposition q is in question. It may mean that *if p* is true to believe, then q is true to believe or is probable. And that someone believing p would intelligibly believe q "because p". Or it may mean that p *is* true, and that anyone would be right to believe q, absolutely or with more or less confidence, "because p". Similarly in practical contexts "p is a reason" assumes that some act A is in question, and then it may mean one of two things. Either that p

mentions an end E or states something helping to shew that A will promote an end E, such that *if p* is true *and* E is good to pursue, A is good to do. And that someone who had the end E would intelligibly do A "because *p*". *Or*, that E *is* good to pursue, that *p* is true, and someone would be right to do A "because *p*".

What sort of proposition is "that E is good to pursue"? There are two types of case: one, where one can ask "good for what?" As, for example, if I am proposing to do various things to build a bonfire. Building a bonfire is my aim—what's the good of that? In the second type of case E is already specified as some good, for example as health is the good state of the body, knowledge of what is worth knowing the good of the intellect. Pleasure is a specially problematic concept, pleasantness therefore as a terminal characterization especially problematic and I won't concern myself with that question here.

But may not someone be criticizable for pursuing a certain end, thus characterizable as a sort of good of his, where and when it is quite inappropriate for him to do so, or by means inimical to other ends which he ought to have?

This can be made out only if man has a last end which governs all. Only on this condition can that illusory "moral ought" be exorcised, while leaving open the possibility of criticizing a piece of practical reasoning, valid in the strict and narrow sense in which in theoretical contexts validity contrasts with truth. The criticism will be of the practical reasoning as not leading to the doing of good action. An action of course is good if it is not bad, but being inimical to the last architectonic end would prove that it was not good.

Now, that practical reasoning so understood should be of use in understanding action, including the action of a society, I can accept.

2

The Flight to Reality

SIMON BLACKBURN

But where is the reward of virtue? And what recompence has nature provided for such important sacrifices, as those of life and fortune, which we must often make to it? Oh, sons of earth! Are ye ignorant of the value of this celestial mistress? And do ye meanly enquire for her portion, when ye observe her genuine charms? But know, that nature has been indulgent to human weakness, and has not left this favourite child, naked and unendowed. She has provided virtue with the richest dowry; but being careful, lest the allurements of interest should engage such suitors, as were insensible of the native worth of so divine a beauty, she has wisely provided, that this dowry can have no charms but in the eyes of those who are already transported with the love of virtue. GLORY is the portion of virtue, the sweet reward of honourable toils, the triumphant crown, which covers the thoughtful head of the disinterested patriot, or the dusty brow of the victorious warrior. Elevated by so sublime a prize, the man of virtue looks down with contempt on all the allurements of pleasure, and all the menaces of danger. Death itself loses its terrors, when he considers, that its dominion extends only over a part of him, and that, in spite of death and time, the rage of the elements, and the endless vicissitude of human affairs, he is assured of an immortal fame among all the sons of men.

(David Hume, *Essays, Moral and Political*, pt. 1: 'The Stoic')

1. Professor Foot's Journey: Against Existentialism

In her introduction to *Virtues and Vices* Philippa Foot describes her essays as ones in which 'I was making a painfully slow

This chapter was originally received by the editors in 1989, prior to the publication of Allan Gibbard's *Wise Choices, Apt Feelings* (Cambridge, Mass.: Harvard University Press, 1990), to which the author would have made many references if he were writing it now.

journey, upward or downward according to your opinion, away from theories that located the special character of evaluations in each speaker's attitudes, feelings, or recognition of reason for acting.'[1] Given the evident quality of the essays, they must be recognized as posing a major challenge to those of us who feel, in however qualified a way, that attitudes, or feelings, or the recognition of reason for action contain some kind of key to the nature of ethics. That is, they challenge those of us who think that attitudes, feelings, or recognition of reason for action should form the centre-piece of some successor of 'Humean' theories of ethics. I shall call such successors projective theories, and I shall call the attitudes, feelings, or recognition of reason they seem to need conative states. Neither term is entirely happy, and some of the unhappiness will be on view later in this essay, but at present they only point in the direction of an issue. The issue, then is Foot's challenge to the view that these states and their expression might offer the best clue to the slippery subject of ethics.

We might start by recognizing a battle that Professor Foot fought, and in my view won. It was fought on a field that certainly needed winning at the time she was writing, but that might, I believe, be conceded without loss. It was a mistake of allies of the projectivist to occupy the ground. Indeed, its occupation seems to me to have been part of an existentialist current in the spirit of the age, surfacing in the unlikely pages of Oxford moral philosophy. Thus when Professor Hare's lone cactus importer contemplates his object, he can undertake to dub it good of its kind, just like that.[2] And he can *choose* the standards that are to apply to good cacti, again, just like that. Generalized to more serious ethics, the image must be that of the hero choosing his aims and standards from a romantic vantage-point of pure untrammelled freedom; his standards then gain what authority they have from his free act of selection of them, somehow translated into a position of submission to them. Surely we have to be grateful to Professor Foot for opposing this fantasy, and we should applaud two different elements in her opposition. First, even choice (the paradigm existentialist act) is not bare *pointing*: choosing is choosing for a role or purpose, and it is essential to it that grounds may be offered and

[1] Philippa Foot, *Virtues and Vices* (Berkeley, Calif.: University of California Press, 1978), p. xiv. Subsequent references to Foot's writing refer to this work.
[2] Ibid. 142–3. R. M. Hare, *The Language of Morals* (Oxford: Clarendon Press, 1952), 96–7.

discussed; these grounds will (at least typically) make use of some sense of what is the best thing to choose in the context. Making pure choice antecedent to values flies in the face of this involvement of values in our very concept of choice. Foot acknowledges the appearance of a counter-example, in the picking of a card, in response to a conjuror's request, which is as pure a case of an untrammelled, existentialist choice as we could meet. But it is noteworthy in part because it serves as no basis for the view that the subject took what he thought was the best card. That only arises if a question of reason or justification can be answered, and in its absence there is no route from choice to value.[3] So this sort of existentially pure choice is not only highly atypical, but also useless for the purpose of finding a behavioural basis for values.

I shall return to this after introducing the second point, which is that standards may in some circumstances be chosen and set, but only by people in some acknowledged position of authority. Out of context I cannot successfully announce that I hereby set such-and-such standards for some kind of object: I would be essaying an essentially social act, needing a rooted social context for success. On both questions, then , the existentialist fantasy forgets the sheer scene-setting necessary for acts of choice and standard-setting (or using) to take place.

Foot extends the second point in her later essay 'Approval and Disapproval', arguing that 'it is no more possible for a single individual, without a special social setting, to approve or disapprove than it is for him to vote'. She points out that while parents or guardians may approve or disapprove of someone's marriage or move of house, it is not open to bystanders to do so in the same way. Bystanders may want or dislike some action, but they are not in a position to approve or disapprove of it. The difference is that there is no tacit agreement that bystanders are to be listened to on such matters: 'the attitudes of approval and disapproval would not be what they are without the existence of tacit agreement on the question of who listens to whom and about what'.[4] Carefully separating and comparing what might seem to be the relatively brute 'being for or against something', she finds that here too a social setting of some kind is presupposed: 'the position of being against something is one that only society can create'.

---

[3] Foot, *Virtues and Vices*, 142–3.   [4] Ibid. 198.

Turning to morality, Foot finds the situation significantly similar. Normal moral practices do not involve special relationships to events, for anyone may disapprove of an action on moral grounds. But this democracy is also the upshot of a social practice, albeit one that is so familiar that it is hard for us even to notice it. The social practice is one of allowing (virtually) everyone a voice in some matters. This is essential to creating the context in which it is possible to approve or disapprove morally, and it arguably helps to put limits on the extent to which a moral reformer can speak with authority while departing from common ground, although the picture here is subtle.[5]

The first point then involves values in the very activity of choosing; the second involves society in the creation of positions from which approval and disapproval are even possible. Of course, Foot's journey away from the theories she describes contains other elements, which I come to in due course. But if we grant, as I think we should, that on these two points she is correct, what modifications in such theories might it suggest? The first shows that we cannot first locate a simple or fundamental behavioural reaction, dubbed 'choice', and out of choice construct values as theoretical constructs further down a one-way system. Granting this point indeed means abandoning this simple behaviourist model. But a simple behavioural manifestation of moral attitudes would not now seem a good thing to expect in any case. We have become familiar with the idea that mental states manifest themselves in behaviour in holistic and indirect ways, indefinitely subject to modification in the light of other elements of the web. I do not say that it is easy to absorb all the lessons of that new orthodoxy. I merely suggest that if it is true of beliefs, there is no reason why it should not also be true of attitudes, or feelings, or the acknowledgement of reasons for action. Just as belief can manifest itself variably in action, depending at least on what else is believed and what is desired, so attitude can manifest itself in various ways in action, depending at least on those same variables. So far as this complexity goes, the question whether to put attitudes rather than beliefs at the centre of our understanding of ethics remains moot. We return to it later.

The same structure seems to apply to the second point that I

[5] Foot, *Virtues and Vices*, 204.

conceded to Foot. Her point is presumably not a purely nominal one, that whatever state a person is in, it would be wrong to *call* it approval unless various social conditions were met. As far as that goes, a person missing the social scene-setting could actually have the same attitude as those who approve, although it should not be called that, just as a Martian might possess an object identical with an American baseball, but it not be a baseball if the scene-setting or the history is lacking. The point is to be a more substantial one, making the setting constitutive of the attitude: talking, as it were, of its real rather than nominal essence. Again, this is a point that is frequently conceded for beliefs. Whatever words go through my head, and whatever description at a choreographic level my behaviour admits of, I cannot believe that Fischer checkmated Spassky unless I am set in a scene that includes those two persons, the institution of chess, and a great many links between me and all three. Of course, there is great difficulty in knowing what about my belief could be thought of as constant if some of the scene were different, and controversy about this is the upshot of all the thought experiments where some part is kept constant, and other parts, such as the identity of external objects or kinds, is varied. Again, however, if we are disposed to find the external scene-setting essential to the belief, we might expect the same arguments and the same outcome to apply to attitudes. Indeed, if Foot is right, as I am conceding she is, it may be slightly easier to see how the scene-setting is constitutive of the attitude. If I am only able to approve of something because I am set in a scene in which other people recognize me as having the right to be heard on the subject, then the social essence of the state is very evident. Any post-Humean must be willing to see in ethics, and therefore in the states of mind it expresses, an intricate social construction designed to meet the needs of people in social settings; it should not surprise us if such a social construction has constitutive rules of this kind.

Foot's claim stands in the way, of course, of any reductionist account, such as that recently proposed by David Lewis, of approval to a complex of desire (e.g. desiring to desire, desiring that others desire, etc.).[6] At least, it stands in the way unless either

---

[6] David Lewis, 'Dispositional Theories of Value', *Proceedings of the Aristotelian Society*, supp. vol. 63 (1989), 113–37. Lewis proposes his reduction not for approval, but for something being a value, or taken to be a value.

desire is itself given a socially identified essence, or unless the necessary social setting can somehow be grafted into the analysis. So she marks a reef on which varieties of approach can certainly founder, through having too simple a notion of the kinds of conative state available to anchor the theory.

But for all that, the state may be better thought of as conative rather than cognitive, or an attitude rather than a belief. For neither of these two points seems to undermine the distinction here, although they undermine on the one hand crudely behaviourist ways, and on the other hand methodologically solipsistic ways, of drawing it.

There is one way of reading the first point that would sharpen its teeth. I have treated it as showing that choosing and valuing come in a package, and that neither can be given a simple priority, in any philosophically important ordering. Foot may have had in mind the stronger claim that there is a significant ordering in exactly the reverse direction. This would mean that we could not understand some actions as genuine cases of choosing, unless we antecedently see the subject as capable of believing things good, so that the priority runs directly opposite to that of the behaviourist. But I do not think she proves this, and it would indeed be extremely hard to prove. Consider a simpler system, such as a cat. We say that the cat always chooses the cat flap rather than the upstairs window just because that is the way it comes in. We might listen to the inextricability of choice and value enough to wonder whether we are being too anthropocentric, given that we have no sense of the cat having values. But I do not think we would regard this as a knock-down proof that we should not, strictly and literally, talk as we do. Yet if there was complete one-way traffic in the opposite direction, this is how we should react. More substantially, we should remember the inextricability of choice and values in teaching. To teach the child that eating dirt is not on, we encourage expressions of distaste, avoidance, and the view that eating dirt is BAD for you in a seamless activity.[7] The child has only absorbed the value when she has absorbed the attitude, and internalized the avoidance of the activity. This is, of course, a point that should be thoroughly congenial to Foot, but it stands in the way of the straight reversal suggested.

---

[7] I am indebted to Rosalind Hursthouse here.

There is, as well, a way of taking the second point that would sharpen its teeth, although it might then be poised to bite its owner. There is a latent danger of regress in Foot's description of the necessity of social setting for approval to be possible. The feature that she finds in the social setting is a shared presumption or agreement about 'who listens to whom about what'. And she makes it clear that this is not agreement about who in fact has power or influence over decisions (for a start, that needs no agreement). It is an agreement about who has something like a *right* to be listened to, or who may *properly* exert influence. But then something like approval is in the offing when we think of this kind of social set-up. In fact, it is in two offings. Firstly, a society with no mechanisms of approval is incapable of entering into tacit agreements: an agreement is distinctive because of its normative consequences, and if approval does not yet exist a tacit agreement cannot be made to generate it. The point is parallel to the familiar one that we cannot create the institution of obligation to promises by sitting around and undertaking an agreement to honour promises. But secondly the content of the agreement is represented as itself normative: we agree about who is to listen to whom, and this is an agreement not about a fact of actual influence or power, but about an arrangement of something like rights of access. Again, a society without a going concept of approval cannot generate it by building on an antecedent notion like 'who is to be listened to'; the gerundive implies that they are already capable of the distinction between proper and improper occupation of roles, proper and improper influence.

It might be tempting to use this point to attack the projectivist, as if he alone needs to give a non-circular and non-regressive account of what the normative attitudes are. But this would be unduly sectarian. *Anyone* with an interest in placing ethics in the natural world will be worried by the hint of regress or circularity. If our best account of how a social position is available has to finish with it being so because other social positions of essentially the same kind are already available, our understanding is baffled. We need not have been aiming for a reductive analysis of what it is to approve of something, but we must have been aiming at some understanding of how the whole show got off the ground, and by those standards a reminder that one part could get off the ground only because other parts were already airborne is not good enough. So the right reaction is not to sharpen the teeth of this point, but to recognize that it leaves a further task that needs to be addressed by anyone who wants to understand the place of ethics in human psychology.

2. Professor Foot's Journey: More Landmarks

Before sketching more positive suggestions, we can attend to three further related landmarks on Foot's road from projective theories. The first two emerge from the comparison with etiquette which Foot uses to such effect in several of her papers. We can recognize considerations of etiquette for what they are without caring about them at all, and similarly with ethics. We can also care about considerations of etiquette without making its norms overriding, and similarly with ethics. In each case, then, we have latitude in whether we care, and how much we care. Of course, in each case we can use this latitude so as to invite criticism: in the one case we are rude and boorish, or at best not polite enough, and in the other case we are unprincipled, or at best not principled enough. But such psychologies exist, and must not be ruled out by bad philosophical theories. A theorist might, for example, drive herself to the position that an ethical consideration cannot be recognized for what it is without influencing the will to some degree, or to the stronger position that we cannot care about an ethical consideration at all without hearing its demands as overriding all non-ethical considerations. Foot is rightly and realistically opposed to these excesses.[8] She recognizes that it is contingent whether we are confronted with people who simply do not care, or do not care enough, about what they know to be ethical considerations. In this confrontation we meet the third landmark that I detect on her road, which is the need to invoke contingent human concern for the considerations of ethics: her opposition to the mesmeric command that can seem to lie at the bottom of things, notably in the form of the Kantian 'ought' that conjures up an outside writ coercing all who would be rational into the ranks of the ethical. It is undeniable that these landmarks have seemed to many to signpost a road away from any kind of

[8] See esp. Philippa Foot, 'Are Moral Considerations Overriding?', in *Virtues and Vices*.

projective theory, and I have met people who cite them as their own reasons for avoiding such theories. I do not know quite how Foot herself would draw the ground, but we can agree that the initial appearance is of a progressive distance from such a theory. For 'ethical considerations' now seem to occupy the place of one set of considerations, potentially amongst others, with no proprietary writ over the will. Whether they move us or not is contingent, and the hope that they do remains a hope, underpinned by nothing but education, good breeding, and whatever else enables social life to survive without catastrophe. If we substitute for Hume's is–ought gap a recognize–act gap, then ethics seems to be placed on the 'recognize' side, and the gap to action is filled, when it is, only by the correct sentiments of good people. If we ask what it is that is recognized, Foot can draw upon the common consensus: we know what ethical considerations are, and the range from which they come, whatever difficulties we have in drawing boundaries and assessing rankings. We can recognize courage, prudence, charity, and justice well enough, and then sometimes we love them enough to don them as best we may. Thus the three landmarks: the possibility of not caring at all about ethical considerations, of caring very little, and.the need for a proper sentiment to cross from any recognition of them to a joyful conformity of the will. They all seem to signal a road taking us away from a recognizable projectivism.

And yet. Our suspicions might be roused if we ask which of these landmarks signals a road that Hume could not comfortably travel. To take the last point first: the culminating opposition to Kant and to the mesmeric ought that pretends to provide a foundation, outside of our contingent sentiments, for the influence of the right considerations on the will can hardly be uncongenial to the author of book III, part i, section 1 of the *Treatise*. And on the other two issues, surely there is abundant recognition in Hume of the fragile connection between recognizing an ethical consideration for what it is and its having any influence on the will. This consorts, of course, with stress on the overwhelming consensus of mankind in recognizing the virtues, sometimes in the same paragraph:

In this kingdom, such continued ostentation, of late years, has prevailed among men in active life with regard to public spirit, and among those in speculative with regard to benevolence; and so many false pretensions to each have been, no doubt, detected, that men of the world are apt, without any bad intention, to discover a sullen incredulity on the head of those moral endowments, and even sometimes absolutely to deny their existence and reality. In like manner, I find, that, of old, the perpetual cant of the Stoics and Cynics concerning virtue, their magnificent professions and slender performances, bred a disgust in mankind; and LUCIAN, who, though licentious with regard to pleasure, is yet, in other respects, a very moral writer, cannot, sometimes, talk of virtue, so much boasted, without betraying symptoms of spleen and irony. But surely this peevish delicacy, whencesoever it arises, can never be carried so far as to make us deny the existence of every species of merit, and all distinction of manners and behaviour. Besides discretion, caution, enterprise, industry, assiduity, frugality, economy, good-sense, prudence, discernment; besides these endowments, I say, whose very names force an avowal of their merit, there are many others, to which the most determined scepticism cannot, for a moment, refuse the tribute of praise and approbation. Temperance, sobriety, patience, constancy, perseverance, forethought, considerateness, secrecy, order, insinuation, address, presence of mind, quickness of conception, facility of expression; these, and a thousand more of the same kind, no man will ever deny to be excellencies and perfections. As their merit consists in their tendency to serve the person, possessed of them, without any magnificent claim to public and social desert, we are the less jealous of their pretensions, and readily admit them into the catalogue of laudable qualities. We are not sensible, that, by this concession, we have paved the way for all the other moral excellencies, and cannot consistently hesitate any longer, with regard to disinterested benevolence, patriotism, and humanity.[9]

If peevish delicacy can lead us to sneer where we should not, other vices can make us indifferent where we should not be, and inconstant in our principles, where we should not be. Yet if Hume can say all this, and also be as steadfast in opposition to the external Kantian bludgeon as it is possible to be, how are we to see Foot's landmarks as posting a road away from him?

One solution, obviously, is to see Hume as inconsistent, or as betraying his (alleged) projectivism in such passages as these. But

---

[9] David Hume, *Enquiry Concerning the Principles of Morals*, VI. i, para. 199. Of course, I am not here concerned with the relationship Hume finds between personal and moral merit, attacked for example by Foot in *Virtues and Vices*, 75. But it should be noticed that he doesn't quite *equate* personal and moral merit, but thinks that the first is a Trojan horse with which to defeat a sceptic about the second.

such lack of charity needs to be forced on us, and it is far from clear that it is. Take, as central, the problem of the variable effect of recognition of something as good—the problem that this might leave us cold, or colder than we ought to be, or even, as in Hume's example, actively irritated by the recognition. Is this really inconsistent with the idea that recognizing something as good or as a virtue or duty is better classified as conative, as a 'passion', than as a cognition? If it is inconsistent it is a massive incoherence in Hume, for he constantly returns to the variable and fragile nature of our love of virtue, and in particular to the amazing fact that we can be swayed at all by the artificial virtues when they oppose personal interest and even genuine altruism.[10] Our capacity for this kind of motivation is one of the main problems to be solved before the Newtonian theory of the mind can begin to look successful. And along with our capacity for such motivation lie our frequent lapses, explicable because ' 'Tis seldom men love heartily what lies at a distance from them, and who no way redounds to their particular benefit' (p. 583). The theme is pervasive from first to last in Hume. Consider that it is a *task* that the easier kind of philosophers undertake when they:

make us feel the difference between vice and virtue; they excite and regulate our sentiments; and so they can but bend our hearts to the love of probity and true honour.[11]

And the vicissitudes in front of us are as frankly confronted:

And though the heart takes not part entirely with those general notions, nor regulates all its love and hatred, by the universal, abstract differences of vice and virtue, without regard to self, or the persons with whom we are more intimately connected; yet have these moral differences a considerable influence, and being sufficient, at least, for discourse, serve all our purposes in company, in the pulpit, on the theatre, and in the schools.[12]

Hume is in fact half-way between the ludicrously optimistic, allegedly Greek idea that it is always conducive to the happiness of a person to be just, and the not so ludicrously pessimistic Chekhovian idea that the good man cannot possibly be happy,

[10] See particularly David Hume, *A Treatise of Human Nature*, 2nd edn. (Oxford, 1981), III. iii. 1, 575–83.

[11] David Hume, *Enquiry Concerning Human Understanding*, I. 1.

[12] *Enquiry Concerning the Principles of Morals*, v. ii. 27.

since happiness is only made possible by ignoring the plight of others.[13] My contention is that he is far from inconsistent, but betrays a greater awareness of the real contours of human motivation than his successors.

Consider this parallel: most people would think of 'being in love' as a passion rather than a cognition: a special way of being drawn, and drawn too away from facts and factors that determine one's normal actions. But is there any limit to the reactions that one might have, either towards the object of the feeling, or towards recognition that it is *that* feeling? Does it always conquer everything? You might as well say that every wave in the ocean makes straight for shore, regardless of the swirls and vortices capable of engulfing it, or annihilating it, or tossing it back upon itself. Is there a limit to the actions ('choices') that may result? Peevish delicacy is about the least of the eddies a passion may encounter. And if this is true for such a turbulent passion, how much more is it likely to be true for a calm passion, and a passion that, because of its social setting and its potential for opposing self-interest, is especially apt to generate a sense of resentment: for example, in circumstances in which the person who behaves well can easily feel herself to be a victim.

We are, inevitably, subtle. Not everything goes: lip-service, self-deception, imitations, and inverted commas plague our interpretations of ourselves and of others equally. But not everything does not go, either—everything, that is, short of a one-dimensional, single-minded elevation of the object of the passion.

It might be countered that the situation is not the same with ethical approval. Even if a passion can occur in such divergent

---

[13] 'I saw a happy man, one whose cherished dream had so obviously come true, who had attained his goal in life, who had got what he wanted, who was satisfied with his lot and with himself. . . . I was assailed by an oppressive feeling bordering on despair. . . . I said to myself: "How many contented, happy people there really are! What an overwhelming force they are! Look at life: the insolence and idleness of the strong, the ignorance and brutishness of the weak, horrible poverty everywhere, overcrowding, degeneration, drunkenness, hypocrisy, lying—Yet in all the houses and on all the streets there is peace and quiet; of the fifty thousand people who live in our town there is not one who would cry out, who would vent his indignation aloud . . . we do not see or hear those who suffer, and what is terrible in life goes on somewhere behind the scenes—And such a state of things is evidently necessary; obviously the happy man is at ease only because the unhappy ones bear their burdens in silence, and if there were not this silence, happiness would be impossible."' 'Gooseberries', in *A Doctor's Visit: Short Stories by Anton Chekhov*, tr. Avrahm Yarmolinsky (New York: Bantam, 1988).

psychologies that there is no telling how it might manifest itself, still it is essentially *active*. The person in love is *disturbed*, and the disturbance will come out somewhere: even if the wave does not crash on the shore, it creates havoc on the neighbouring surface. Whereas recognition of a moral consideration for what it is may be as calm as we like, and in those whose peevish delicacy or other alienation from the ethical balances any ordinary sentiment of being drawn to virtue, it may sit there as inert as any belief. The suggestion will be that since it may be so inert, it is better theorized about as itself simply a belief, which, like other beliefs, takes some kind of desire or other motivating force to prompt action. It is as if Foot would turn the difficult question for prescriptivism 'How is weakness of will possible?' on its head, substituting 'How is strength of will possible?' It takes a contingent, and in its way remarkable, sentiment to carry us from knowledge of the good to an inclination to do anything with the knowledge. In Foot, the connection is our fortunate capacity to be moved by the common good, coupled with an appreciation that the virtues further that good.[14]

But before substituting this polar opposite to a Humean view, we must be careful of a trap that Foot herself warns us against, which is that of generalizing from the one case. Just as 'a word which applies only to such activities [just picking a card from a pack] would not properly be translated by our word "choice", so a word which applies only to an inert state of approval might not properly be translated as approval'.[15] In other words, it may take special scene-setting for approval to be utterly passive, and the scene-setting in effect requires balancing states of mind: peevish delicacy, resentment of the chains of ethics, despair that nothing matters, and so on. Approval, and other ethical states such as recognition of a trait as a virtue, seem to require *neutralizing* if they are to be ineffective in directing action. We cannot generalize from cases in which they have been neutralized and suppose that they have nothing essentially active about them, any more than we can generalize from the listless lover, and suppose that love

---

[14] Philippa Foot, 'Hume on Moral Judgement', in D. F. Pears (ed.), *David Hume: A Symposium* (London: Macmillan, 1963), 80. Foot moved away, in my view entirely fortunately, from the idea that justice could on each occasion be motivated by self-interest. On this, see the quotation from Chekhov above.

[15] Philippa Foot, 'Goodness and Choice', in *Virtues and Vices*, 143.

has nothing essentially to do with being drawn towards the object of the passion.

An analogy would be the association of beauty and pleasure. Seeing something as beautiful is well thought of in terms of taking pleasure in its visible features. If we never did this, we would not have our concept of visual beauty.[16] And this is true even although a person may take no pleasure in what they know to be another's beauty, and may be too dispirited to be moved, or even be disgusted by it or hate it.

It is, then, too swift to move from the occasional passivity of recognition of the good to imagining that it might always be like that, and indeed always is like that if concern with the common good is absent. Foot, I think, never confronts squarely the question whether we could have ethics even if we were constitutionally indifferent to all its judgements. But it is difficult to imagine, to use her own criterion, that we could rightly translate a society as making ethical (or aesthetic) judgements, if there were no inclination to take them into account in the business of practical reasoning. Even if they cast some kind of extensionally adequate lasso around the traits that we denominate virtues, we would be wrong to interpret them as seeing these traits under the heading of virtues. With this point in place the possibility arises that Foot's marvellously subtle journey is not, in fact, taking her as far from the territory of a projective, post-Humean theory of ethics as she supposes. How is the matter to be decided?

3. A Place for Unbelief

If we return to the quotation from Foot with which I began, we may take note of its individualistic cast. Her journey takes her away from theories that 'locate the special character of evaluations in *each speaker's* attitudes, feelings, or recognition of reason for acting'. Now it is certainly not clear that the speaker's own attitudes and other states deserve centre-stage. We will incorporate a speaker who so expresses herself into the conversation of

[16] The association is well defended in Mary Mothersill, *Beauty Restored* (Oxford: Oxford University Press, 1984). I am not, however, endorsing Mothersill's dispositional analysis of the concept; I think the association between the perception of beauty and pleasure is better made quasi-realistically.

ethics, even when her own contours of concern and choice are pretty peculiar.[17] But it is not clear either that a projective theory needs to claim that they do. It can be urged as an objection to 'projectivism' that the image it conjures up is one of a particular internal sentiment, perhaps *sui generis*, perhaps reducible to a complex of others, that is voiced when we approve or evaluate sincerely.[18] Perhaps the term should be abandoned, but how much of the position remains?

A highly individualistic model of meaning would be the Lockean one, in which on each occasion a word or sentence serves to express the Ideas of its user. These Ideas are thought of as mental existences, complete in themselves in the mind of the user at the time, although also (fortunately) capable of being shared and transmitted, in the sense that others can have Ideas of the same kind. A Lockean projectivist model would substitute for the Idea an Attitude: the speaker would possess his own particular Attitude or profile of Attitudes, and it would be this conative state that he is concerned to express, and usually to transmit to others.

I suppose that nobody believes the Lockean model in the philosophy of language any more. The central mistake is to over-look the role of public usage as the primary determinant of what is being said. A speaker's Ideas, thought of in the individualistic way I tried to indicate, may be as idiosyncratic as we like, but while the speaker is a member of a speech community words used are subject to public norms, and these norms mean that people are liable to be *told* what they said. Subjective states are not the authority: we are entered into a conventional system, and can no more escape its norms than we can make the coins we tender worth what we think they are worth. So far so good, but it is important that the same moral applies when public expression of attitude is in question. Just as we do not look to the speaker's private idiosyncrasies in determining what he said, so we should not look to the particular profile of his conative states to deter-mine what he is doing, when what he is like is expressed by a shared language. What he is doing is determined by something social and public, not by the extent to which he conforms to

---

[17] See e.g. my 'Just Causes', in *Essays in Quasi-Realism* (New York: Oxford University Press, 1993), esp. pp. 199–201.

[18] See further my 'Reply to Sturgeon', *Philosophical Studies*, 61 (1991), 39–42, which pursues this problem as it was urged against me by Nicholas Sturgeon.

central patterns of attitude. This may mark a point at which the title 'projectivism' is not perfectly happy, for that suggests too strongly an individualistic cast, in which a particular kind of mental state is the determinant of meaning. But once the point is noticed, I do not think it does any harm. The essential task remains the same. It is that of describing the socially embedded attitudes (or beliefs) that make up ethics, and of seeing how, if the notion of an attitude is central, our propositional forms of discourse are to be understood.

This being so, it follows that we should not concentrate on the individual speaker's particular configuration of pressures and policies, passions and attitudes, to decide what ethics, as a socially going concern, actually consists in. To decide what it consists in we need to find an idiom to theorize about it as such a concern; we cannot expect concentration on individual desires and choices to do the work for us. This is, of course, a lesson fully concordant with the first two points we allowed Foot in the previous section. And it is a point that is to be respected by all parties in the field. The question becomes whether, when we do theorize about ethics in an idiom respecting its social essence, it is the notion of an attitude or that of a belief that gains the central role. When we try to think intelligently about ethics as an aspect of life, do we need to think firstly in terms of belief in virtue, duty, and so on (call this representationalism), or do we need to think firstly in terms of certain kinds of pressure on action (projectivism)? Or is the amalgam so close, the intertwining of attitude and belief so seamless, that nothing useful can be said by taking either as primary?

When the question is put as starkly as this, the answer to representationalism seems to me to be evident. We could expect no satisfactory natural placing of ethics in the human scene if we gave priority to belief with ethical content at this point. Ethical features are not simply or barely present, as colours are, but are recognized in virtue of other features of characters and actions—in the jargon, they supervene upon other features of things. So making belief with moral content primary gives four factors. We need (1) underlying features that (2) give rise to the ethical features of things, (3) a capacity to recognize what they give rise to, and (4) a contingent sentiment of concern, in the well-bred and principled, meaning that those features, when recognized, tend to act on the will. And the reason that this seems to be a bad package to offer as *fundamental* is that it invites a short-circuit: we could have reached the same end-point by thinking of underlying features of things generating sentiments and pressures on action, and missing out the second and third stages.

The point can be made evolutionarily: if evolution selects for societies whose members have achieved some kind of co-ordination in their actions and feelings, the first route is relatively cumbersome; the second gets to the same place more economically. On the first route we must start by getting into shape to cognize values, and then we have to get into shape to make something of what we have cognized. How much simpler if there were instead just the underlying properties, and a properly conative sensitivity to them: a propensity to form attitudes and choices and policies in the light of them. And this, in effect, is what the projectivist says that we have done. Of course, we have also evolved ethical discourse as part of the package. It too comes with a social function, enabling conflict to be discussed, and enabling co-ordinating or competing ethics to be recognized and negotiated.

But now consider the following parallel.[19] Financial relations between people supervene on other relations; financial relations also have normative aspects (that I owe you money is at least largely a question of my obligation to you). But nobody would think that recognition of the financial aspects of life could be 'short-circuited', in favour of a fundamental story in which persons have purely conative, or motivational, states in response to bits of paper, signatures, and so on. Why not with ethics as with finance? Again to use an analogy that Foot enjoys, why think that the requirements of etiquette can be short-circuited, in favour of a reaction to behaviour described outside that vocabulary? And especially why think it when people so visibly vary in their reactions to questions of etiquette? The parallel suggests that the seamless approach, just as much as projectivism or even more, stands to profit from the last two paragraphs.

One difference is this. We should beware of overdoing the parallel between ethics and an institution. Although aspects of ethics are no doubt institutional, ethics allows the open-question

---

[19] The importance of this in the thought of both Mrs Foot and Miss Anscombe was again urged upon me by Rosalind Hursthouse.

standpoint, where we ask what is the point and purpose, the *good* of things, including institutions (you cannot in the same way ask what is the financial point of financial institutions. You can only ask what they are good for). It is here that the conative puts its nose in front: it is revealed as *driving* the design of richer or thicker ethical institutions.[20] You can ask what they are good for, with an eye to comparing them, which is asking the question which is better. But to compare ways of embedding ethics in social arrangements is to take up an attitude to different arrangements: to change an ethic requires *conversion*, not just an apprehension of new facts.[21]

Now suppose we stick with the analogy with institutions, and the plethora of 'oughts' they engender: those of law, finance, etiquette, and so forth.[22] We can hear the unconverted, those outside the institution who acknowledge no allegiance to its verdicts, describing people as 'bound' to pay money, curtsy, and so on. But their usage is clearly parasitic upon the existence of *insiders*, who do acknowledge allegiance, or in other words who are governed by the norms of the institution. If it were not for the insiders, past or present, there would be nothing for the indifference of the outsiders to have as an object. Now if we ask what distinguishes the insiders, the answer is clearly from the conative, sentimental side of things. These are people who function differently in practice; they feel pressures and pulls to which, for better or worse, the outsiders are immune. They cannot at this point simply be described as those who are aware of what the law and etiquette and finance require, since the outsiders are aware of that, and indifferent to it. The difference has to be seen in other terms. So it seems misdirected to cite the possibility of outsiders as a point against a suitably social version of projectivism, for as long as the central, fundamental functional difference on which all other complexity depends is correctly described in the non-descriptive, non-representative way, the flight from Hume is still

[20] The debate on Searle's notorious derivation of 'ought' from 'is' would be relevant to a full discussion of this comparison.

[21] As Wittgenstein said about the parallel contrast between treating mathematics as a description, and as a system of rules, 'But that is not to say that this contrast does not shade off in all directions. And *that* in turn is not to say that the contrast is not of the greatest importance' (*Remarks on the Foundations of Mathematics* (Oxford: Blackwell, 1956), pt. v, p. 163.

[22] I am indebted to Michael Smith for the line of thought of this para.

not off the runway. And so far as this part of the argument goes, that is how it appears.[23]

Nevertheless, we can see how the seamless approach might continue. Its shield would be the distinction deployed in a parallel context by Professor Strawson, between a 'genetic-psychological' and an 'analytic-philosophical' theory.[24] A genetic-psychological theory might try to describe the development of ethical thought either in societies through long times, or in infants in shorter times. But an analytic-philosophical theory will be a different thing. Its subject is mature, adult experience and 'it will be important to run no risk of characterizing mature sensible experience in terms adequate at best only for the characterization of some stage of infantile experience'. Strawson is discussing sensory experience and its involvement, in mature adults, with content given by the conceptual scheme of the external world. But it is natural to generalize the point. Even if in genetic theorizing about the emergence of norms it is satisfactory and economical to deal only with non-ethical features and socially reinforced pressures on us to respond to them, it does not follow that 'mature' ethical experience admits of this description. To put it bluntly, we have created something that involves us essentially in the cognitive: in judgement, reason, truth, fact. A pointed way of bringing this out is that the *object* of the mature ethical experience may be the virtue or the iniquity of an action, just as the object of a hope or fear may be the financial outcome: what has come to exist plays its own role in intentional psychology, and that role is not reducible to a concentration upon the subvening relations.

Strawson's principal target was the view that the interpretation of experience in terms of perception of distant, solid, extended independent objects has the status of a 'theory'. On the contrary, such an interpretation is not an inference we make or an explanation we arrive at, but a content carried by the experiences themselves. Distance, for example, is not something we infer from the nature of a two-dimensional presentation, but something given in visual experience itself, which would not be as it is did it not carry

[23] Would it affect the argument if it were shown that the outsiders could not understand the form of life of the insiders? Perhaps, but since this cannot be shown the point stands.

[24] P. F. Strawson, 'Perception and its Objects', in G. McDonald (ed.), *Perception and Identity: Essays Presented to A. J. Ayer* (London: Macmillan, 1979), 42.

this content within it.[25] How it came to do so is the subject of the genetic-psychological story; that it does so is a datum for any philosophical reflection on appearance and reality.

Strawson is clearly right about this, but the transfer of his distinction is not straightforward. For there is no parallel at all between the position of the projectivist and that of someone advocating a 'theory-theory' about belief in the external world. The projectivist in this social guise does not have us, the vulgar, doing a piece of theory which is in fact a figment of his own imagination. He is, or should be, perfectly happy with what I call the 'propositional surface' of ethics; he does not suppose that in ordinary thought there is a constant theoretical commentary busy explaining and justifying the use of propositional forms. There is no level of psychology in which he represents the mature adult thinking: 'here is a passion of mine, against bullfighting; let me see, if I play my cards right it may be legitimate for me to voice this by saying "bullfighting is wrong"; yes, I can step to doing that!' On the contrary, the upshot of our experience in ethics, just as much as the upshot of our experience with the external world, is the immediate judgement. Anything else falsifies the phenomenology.

But what if the immediate judgement has the virtue or iniquity of an action as its object? What is the projectivist reconstruction of the phenomenon, and how can it be more plausible than a 'reconstruction' that interpreted fear of financial failure as having any other than its apparent object? In fact the parallel is suggestive: to fear financial failure is not separable from fearing the typical concomitances of the failure, and to fear the attitudes to which one will then be subject and perhaps the lack of defence one will be able to give. To love virtue is not readily separable from loving the traits that are virtuous, and that which makes them so, and as the discussion earlier showed, that is a psychological state that can wax and wane. The phenomenology here is not simple, and the interplay between paying attention to the subvening features, on the one hand, and thinking as if there is a supervening property, on the other, should not be overlooked. Would it be an objection to projectivism about the niceness of tastes if we found

[25] The theme is emphasized in much phenomenology. Cf. Merleau-Ponty, *Phenomenology of Perception*, tr. Colin Smith (London: Routledge & Kegan Paul, 1962), 36–7.

ourselves having that itself as an intentional object, abstracted from both particular tastes and reflection on the human pleasures that underlie the predicate?

The threat from the 'seamless approach' is that projectivism retreats to consort with fairly shabby armchair genetics. But surely these options do not exhaust the field. A theory may not be a phenomenological theory, but may be an 'analytic-philosophical' theory for all that. A theory—and the point goes beyond its immediate application in ethics—may be silent about common phenomenology, and irrefutable by evidence that it has this or that nature, but be philosophical for all that. It will be so if it explains how that phenomenology comes to be as it is not merely historically or genetically, but rather metaphysically—in other words, if it explains how our thoughts come to be what they are in a world of one kind rather than another.

Let me give a simple example, albeit one where the eventual rights and wrongs are even more controversial than in the present case. In Hume's account of causation a world of independent, atomistic events, a mosaic of just 'one thing after another', so works on the mind that it falls into the firmest habits of expectation, and these habits gain expression in the commitments to causal connection to which we so fervently adhere. Now it may *add* to this theory, but it surely does not *refute* it, if we remind ourselves how experience is permeated with causal interpretation: the objects of experience come to us not only in space and extended, but surrounded, as it were, with a halo of powers.[26] It is good that this is the phenomenology, for it makes life possible, and nature might be thanked for doing that for us too, in the world that Hume describes: the fact that it does not 'feel like that' no more refutes the view that it is like that, than the fact that a suitable sequence sounds like a melody rather than a sequence of notes refutes the view that the melody is a sequence of notes.[27]

Yet Hume's theory is not merely 'genetic-psychological', for it marks about as profound an ontological assertion as a theory well

[26] Not that I think extension is any different from possession of such a halo, but that is another story.

[27] Would it refute the view if we thought that a note, as it occurs within a melody, is literally a different thing from a note occurring without? For a discussion see my 'Has Kant Refuted Parfit?', in Jonathan Dancy (ed.), *Reading Parfit* (forthcoming).

could. Or, if it is insisted that this is where it is (and one can indeed associate it with developmental psychological testing on the emergence of the perception of causality) this is no mere assertion, but a deliberate, almost political, statement of the powers and limits of philosophy itself.

The example of causality is deliberately provocative. It raises a host of questions. Clearly we may query the authority of the metaphysical vision. What is the compulsion to go beyond the common-sense world as we do this kind of 'metaphysics'? What is the authority of the starting-point? And we may voice despair at the determinacy of any investigation conducted once we have allowed the starting-point: if we engage this metaphysics as a serious possibility, where is the methodology and the range of considerations that legitimately bear on it? Once phenomenology, and the surface reactions of the vulgar, and the proprieties of propositional modes of discourse have all been neutralized, how can any debate find a foothold? And then it requires only a smattering of verificationism to fear that things have got out of hand, and we are being presented with dreams and images rather than positions and theories.

We have to tread softly, even when we tread on dreams. But however it is with causality, where so many of us are content to sit with Dr Johnson and kick the stone and thump the table, it is surely clear that in the case of ethics we are not in a domain of dreams and images, but if not exactly in one of scientific theory either, at least in one where art and judgement are possible. It is not an existentialist decision to see matters as the projectivist does. Hume so saw it, and we can do so too, because of a serious desire to remove the mystery from the subject, and to place ethics in the natural world of fallen, mainly selfish, grudgingly co-operative animals beset by a niggardly and stepmotherly nature. What these creatures need are co-operation and sentiments and policies and susceptibilities to pressure that enable them to cope. In time, they, and we, can describe them as recognizing what things had to be done and were good to do, but that is after the event, when we work within a framework of thought that has first to be understood in other terms.

Applying Virtue Ethics

ROSALIND HURSTHOUSE

A standard criticism made of virtue ethics is that it does not tell us what we ought and ought not to do, that it cannot be applied to real moral issues such as abortion or euthanasia; in contrast to monistic (e.g. utilitarianism) or pluralistic rule-based ethical systems, which do. In this paper I want to explore this criticism, to see how virtue ethics fares in comparison with an "ethics of rules" and to try to uncover what basic disagreements there are—if any—between virtue ethicists and deontic ethicists as such.

It is true that there is not much around in the way of books and articles discussing "real" moral issues, or "applied" ethics, in the terms of virtue ethics. There is a growing number of articles on particular virtues—but their concern, it is said, is the delicate exploration of moral psychology. They precisely fail to shed light on the area which ethical theory is supposed to deal with, namely what we ought and ought not to do—on action. And the philosophers usually cited as "virtue theorists"—Foot, McDowell, MacIntyre, Anscombe in 'Modern Moral Philosophy'—have been particularly concerned with theory, not with applying it to yield conclusions about action.

But this fact on its own could hardly justify a criticism of the theory, as opposed to its proponents. Even if its proponents do not tell us about the rights and wrongs of abortion and eutha-

This *Festschrift* has taken a long time to get together. Rather than exploiting my position as an editor and putting in my very latest thoughts, I have stuck with the paper I originally put in in 1989, which benefited greatly from discussions with Ron Condon and Andrew Hsu. This has had the advantage of enabling me to take a high moral tone with tardier contributors, and to fend off more conscientious ones who sought (potentially unlimited) licence to change papers they had sent in. The attendant disadvantage is that it has been superseded by several other papers I have published, which repeat some things said here, and deny others. I'm not particularly worried about the repetitions, but on the denials see n. 5 below, and 'Moral Dilemmas', in *Argumentation* (1995), which is much less combative than the paper printed here.

nasia—and what about Foot's famous article on the latter?—this hardly shows that their theory does not.

Moreover, the critics of the theory do not point merely to the fact that its proponents have not as yet managed to come up with any specific answers to the questions 'What ought we to do and what ought we not do?' They imply that this is no accident; that virtue theorists not only have not but *cannot* come up with answers.

So, for example, a reviewer of fairly recent work on virtues[1] claims that the promise that a theory of the virtues could replace deontological or utilitarian theories has not been made good and strongly implies that it cannot be. A typical critic claims that virtue ethics *cannot* answer the question 'What ought I to do?' or tell us which acts are right and which wrong; and concludes that, at best, virtue ethics has a supplementary role to play, the major role to be played by an "ethics of rules".[2] It may be admitted that utilitarians and deontologists who focus on principles, rules, and duties should not overlook character and virtues, if it is admitted that these are a significant part of the moral life and cannot be ignored in ethical theory. But some critics are struck by the fact that 'persons of good moral character ... are often the first to recognise that they do not know what ought to be done' and conclude '*Hence*, a discussion of the morality of acts remains important, indispensable *and primary* in establishing what morally good people ought to do.'[3]

Now why is it asserted so confidently by the critics of virtue ethics that it cannot come up with any answers? This claim is too often made, and Foot's paper on euthanasia too well known, for us to suppose that all those who make the claim are ignorant of it. So it must be true of at least some of the critics that they regard Foot's paper as the exception that proves the rule. Exceptionally for a paper by a virtue ethicist, it *tries* to say some-

[1] Gregory E. Pence, 'Recent Work on Virtues', *American Philosophical Quarterly*, 21 (1984), 281–97. However, Gregory Trianowsky, 'What is Virtue Ethics all About? Recent Work on the Virtues', *American Philosophical Quarterly*, 27 (1990), 335–44, is a little more optimistic.

[2] Robert B. Louden, 'On Some Vices of Virtue Ethics', *American Philosophical Quarterly*, 21 (1984), 227–36.

[3] Tom L. Beauchamp and James F. Childress (eds.), *Principles of Biomedical Ethics*, 2nd edn. (New York: Oxford University Press, 1983), 264 (my italics). It is noteworthy that, by the 3rd edn. (1989), they have considerably modified their position.

thing about what we ought and ought not to do; but the rule that
virtue ethics cannot yield any answers survives this test; in some
sense the paper totally fails to give any answers. But in what
sense?

The previously mentioned critic says that all attempts of virtue
ethicists to answer moral questions have been 'useless'. On what
grounds might someone say that about the attempts to give answers in Foot's paper?

Someone might think that every conclusion she comes to about
what we ought and ought not to do with respect to euthanasia is
false. That seems a little unlikely, since many of her conclusions
are fairly orthodox and have been reached by other means by
various deontologists.

Is it perhaps something about the very orthodoxy and the form
it takes that troubles people? The critic complains of her discussion of practical wisdom (in the 'Virtues and Vices' paper) that
it does little more than 'repeat conventional wisdom on the topic';
and I can imagine that someone might make the same complaint
about the euthanasia paper. For such conclusions as are reached
in it are not *codifiable*; not capturable in the sorts of rules that
legislators and rule-followers want us to come up with. Foot's
article does not give one any simple rule or even rules about the
permissibility or otherwise of euthanasia *tout court*; it leaves the
problem, one might say, in exactly the same difficult and perplex-
ing state as those of us who worry about it found it to be in in the
first place. We began with a set of intuitions about the seriousness
of taking human life, and the value of 'death with dignity', about
the significance of the fact that euthanasia is done for the sake of
the one who dies, about the relevance of whether or not the
person wants to die, and the distinction between active and passive, and the special duties of doctors, and so on; all of this counting as 'conventional wisdom'. Then we turned to ethical theory in
the expectation that it would sort these out for us and tell us when
and how to take them into account in such a way as to reach the
rational answer to the question 'What ought I to do in such-and-
such a case of euthanasia?' And, it might be said, Foot's paper
does not even profess to do this; in effect all it does is to say 'Yes,
all these things are relevant, and make the problem intractably
difficult, except in these few cases that we are (nearly) all agreed
on anyhow.'

People like Michael Tooley and James Rachels, it might be said, even if they do not come up with the right answers, at least come up with the right *sort*. Tooley tells us that if the patients are not persons any more we can kill them off and do not have to worry about all those other considerations; and Rachels that there is no distinction between active and passive, so we can at least forget about that consideration. They impose some theoretical order on the chaos of our intuitions, and thereby come up with solid, concrete guidance about the matters that we find difficult, and *that* is what ethical theory is supposed to do. A so-called ethical theory that cannot do that is useless.

Now it is the mark of all the other theories around—rights-based, duties-based, or consequentialist—that they not only aim to answer 'What ought I to do?' but also that they may be used—they have the right formal shape—to give us clear guidance, in agonizing cases, about what's right and what's wrong, in the form of rules or principles—to *codify* morality, or, in the words of Onora O'Neill, to provide an algorithm not just for some situations but for life.

And, when we look at the criticisms that are made of virtue ethics, it seems that at bottom they may come to this objection—that virtue ethics does *not* aim to produce such an algorithm. Those of its proponents who follow Aristotle closely always quote him with approval on ethics not being definable by rules, but resting in some cases on a decision based on perception.

Hence, characteristically, Louden says:

Due to the very nature of the moral virtues, there is a very limited amount of advice on moral quandaries that one can expect from the virtue-oriented approach. We ought, of course, to do what the virtuous person would do, but it is not always easy to fathom what the hypothetical moral examplar would do were he in our shoes . . . Furthermore if one asks him why he did what he did . . . the answer might not be very enlightening. One would not necessarily expect him to appeal to any rules or principles which might be of use to others.[4]

Now who is right and who is wrong here? Should we expect a decent moral theory to provide such an algorithm or not? Is this, in particular, what we should expect a *secular* moral theory to do? If so, why?

---

[4] Louden, 'On Some Vices of Virtue Ethics', 229.

I emphasize 'secular' here, for the following reason. If we thought that we were living in a world created by a good God, a God who wanted us to live well and who had organized the world and us in such a way that our reason could discover how to live well, then we might indeed expect our moral theory to consist of codifiable rules and principles. But a genuinely secular morality must be more than a morality that does not happen to mention God explicitly; and more than a morality espoused by people who make a point of claiming proudly that they have thrown off the shackles of Judaeo-Christian tradition. It must be one which does not, even implicitly, presuppose the existence of a God. But then it is quite unclear what could entitle it to presuppose that every aspect of the world will fall within the realm of rational understanding; and, in particular that our categories of right–wrong, good–bad, permitted–required, etc. are guaranteed to fit on to the world neatly.

Having emphasized that point, let me ask again: should we expect a secular morality to consist of a complete code of rules and principles which settles all our dilemmas? And if so, *why* do we expect that such rules and principles can be found?

And let me ask further; how do we think a secular theory could do this? What is it going to be based on? No secular theory can ultimately be based on anything but some favoured set of our moral intuitions. If all our judgements within some area are perfectly clear and consistent, then we can, if we like, sum them up in a rule—but then we do not need the guidance of a theory. If, on the other hand, we are not clear, as, for instance, in areas such as euthanasia and abortion, and find it all very difficult, why do we think a *theory* is going to help us and resolve our dilemmas? Why should it be a condition of adequacy on a moral theory that it should provide an algorithm for life?

Rather than criticizing a secular theory for failing to come up with rules that settle difficult cases, we might say that it is entirely to its credit that it does not do so. It is not an accident, we might insist, that (within secular morality at least) so many people should find particular decisions about abortion or euthanasia so agonizingly difficult, and decisions about foetal experimentation, or vegetarianism, if not personally agonizing, at least still very difficult. For what we should accept is that they really *are* difficult, and we should make it a condition of adequacy on a theory that it can leave some cases *un*resolved.[5]

If we do so, then virtue ethics emerges in a new guise. Far from its being a failure on the part of agent-centred virtue ethics that it cannot resolve various dilemmas, a failure which shows that it needs to be supplemented by a theory of right and wrong acts, it turns out that on the contrary virtue ethics, to its credit, is well positioned (or propositioned!), perhaps uniquely so, to admit not merely the possibility but the likelihood of there being, as Wiggins puts it, 'some absolutely undecidable questions—e.g. cases where the situation is so appalling or the choices are so gruesome that nothing could count as the reasonable practical answer'.[6] Why is virtue ethics well positioned, and perhaps uniquely so, to admit undecidability (in Wiggins's sense)? Because virtue ethics, putting the virtuous agent at the centre of its theory, can appeal to the very fact mentioned above, namely that 'persons of good moral character are often the first to recognise that they do not know what ought to be done'.

In the mouths of the critics of virtue ethics, this is taken to mean that the morally wise are the first to recognize the need for a moral theory which settles every issue—as if they were thinking of the virtuous as saying 'Well, I know there must *be* a perfectly clear answer to the question of what we ought to do about abortion, or about using the material the Nazi doctors put together in the concentration camps, or to what I ought to do about my mother's staying on the life support system, but I can't see what it is'. Whereas I think of the virtuous as, rather characteristically, saying 'This *is* a complex, difficult issue, isn't it; well, let's consider some particular cases . . .'; or as saying, after their decision in a particular case, 'No, of course I didn't think it was the *right* decision; how could either have counted as the right decision in such a terrible set-up?'

The set-up, it should be said, does not have to be terrible; as

---

[5] I have subsequently come to realize that this is too strong a claim. I now believe that an adequate ethics should be sufficiently flexible to allow for a comprehensible disagreement on the question whether there are unresolvable dilemmas. See my 'Normative Virtue Ethics', in Roger Crisp, *How Should one Live?* (Oxford: Clarendon Press, forthcoming).

[6] David Wiggins, 'Truth, Invention and the Meaning of Life', *Proceedings of the British Academy*, 62 (1976), 371.

Foot has noted,[7] formal undecidability can arise in delightful as well as appalling situations, where the choices are enticing rather than gruesome. Quite generally, virtuous people may make moral decisions without believing that what they are doing is *the* right, one and only thing to do in the situation. But it is the "tragic dilemmas" which command our concern.

It must be, I think, a thesis in virtue ethics that two virtuous people cannot, in the same circumstances, act differently, each thinking that what she does is right and what the other does is *wrong*. But to insist on that is a far cry from insisting that the two must always act as one. If they agree on what is good and evil in each choice, and believe that each is a choice of the good, though not of the best, it seems that they can, consistently with their virtue, act differently.

This looks like a point that gives real substance to the rather vague claim that virtue ethics is 'agent-centred rather than act-centred'. For at the theoretical level the point is this. If we have two virtuous people, both of whom have practical wisdom, who agree to disagree about what they are going to do, despite being in the same circumstances, then that *settles* the fact that there is no answer to the question 'What is *the* right thing to do in these circumstances?' For the central question is 'What would a virtuous agent do?' not 'Which is the right act?'; and if the virtuous agents act differently, that is how the first question is answered, by, for example, 'Well, this one had an abortion, and this one didn't, but went ahead with the pregnancy' or 'This one asked the doctor to switch off the life support machine her mother was on, and this one asked the doctor to continue the treatment'.

Now is virtue ethics, by its appeal to virtuous agents, uniquely positioned to build in this sort of undecidability, or can deontic ethics too? It cannot, of course, in the hands of proponents demanding an algorithm for life; but sophisticated deontologists, such as Onora O'Neill, may well be anxious to reject such an essentially adolescent view. As she points out, deontologists may recognize that principles underdetermine decisions, and may indeed maintain, with the Aristotelians, that what enables a person to apply them correctly is a virtuous disposition engendered by habituation. But it is not clear to me that underdetermination is,

[7] Philippa Foot, 'Moral Realism and Moral Dilemma', *Journal of Philosophy*, 80 (1983), 379–98.

or entails, undecidability. Can even sophisticated deontology ac-
commodate the idea of there being absolutely undecidable questions? One might say, 'Of course it can; most obviously when two
equally important rules give conflicting injunctions in a particular
situation'. But how can deontologists, within the terms of their
theory, justify *accepting* the conflict, rather than looking for some
adaptation or refinement of the rules which will yield a clear
direction? As I heard a deontologist say in discussion once, 'Of
course universalizability is consistent with "circumstances alter
cases" because a principle can always be found to distinguish the
cases.' However complicated finding such a principle might be,
according to deontology, it must be there.

Well, maybe that is not true; perhaps it depends on where
deontologists think the rules come from or what they are like. I
will leave that as a moot point. But at least we can stake out a bit
more territory for virtue ethics. Its use is not limited to moral
psychology, nor even, as is sometimes conceded, to providing an
account of supererogatory action. It provides a nice account of
action in undecidable cases too, enabling one to say 'In doing *A*
she did *well* (though not 'the right thing') in so far as she did what
was, for example, honest'.

This may suggest a further problem. 'Surely,' it may be said,
'there are situations from which it is impossible to emerge with
"clean hands". And what does your hypothetical virtuous agent
do then?'

Let us suppose that there are some things a virtuous agent must
die rather than do; this is recognized in common morality, which
condemns at least some cases of saving one's own life by betraying or killing others. In such cases it is indeed impossible to
'emerge' with clean hands, but we know what virtuous agents
would do, and actually have done, all right—they allow themselves to die or be killed; perhaps even commit suicide.

'But' it will be said 'what about the cases in which one's own
death is not an option, being either impossible to achieve, or itself
an immoral abnegation of responsibility? What does the virtuous
agent do then?'

What problem for virtue ethics might be thought to lie in the
existence of such cases? I take it that the thought is 'Aha. We trap
the proponent of virtue ethics in an inconsistency; her so-called
virtuous agent may be forced, in such a a case, to act like a rogue,

emerging, perforce, with dirty hands.' But 'the virtuous agent' is not so-called by *me*, proponent of virtue ethics though I am, but by all of us; a virtuous agent, real or hypothetical, is one who has the character traits of, for example, justice, compassion, honesty, charity . . . The claim that there are cases in which an agent, perforce, emerges with dirty hands is thus tantamount to the claim that there are, or could be, cases in which the just, compassionate, honest . . . agent is forced to act unjustly, callously, dishonestly . . .

But there could not be any such cases; the claim embodies a conceptual confusion created by a misinterpretation of the adverbial qualifications 'unjustly, callously' etc. The just or compassionate agent does not act unjustly or callously, that is, '*as* the unjust or callous one does'. She acts with immense regret and pain instead of indifferently, or gladly, *as* the unjust or callous agent acts.

This does not mean that I deny the possibility of cases from which a virtuous agent could not emerge with 'clean hands', though I suspect these are not as common as is usually supposed. It seems to me that, by and large, we have tailored our virtue concepts in such a way that the virtuous agent *is* allowed to emerge from extremely difficult situations with 'clean hands'; *if*, for instance, we think that the only way out of a situation was to lie, and the putatively honest agent lied, we do not say that this is any reflection on her honesty, though we do not say it was an exercise of it either. We say, in explanation, 'Well, she couldn't act honestly here you see, because . . .' But there is no reason to suppose that we have tailored all, or any, of them so carefully. So, as I say, I do not deny the possibility of enforced 'dirty hands'. What I deny is that they present a particular problem for virtue ethics.

Acknowledging their existence, as I have just argued, does not trap the virtue ethicist in the position of maintaining, inconsistently, that the just may act unjustly, the compassionate callously, etc. All it amounts to is the claim that there may be situations from which no one, even the most virtuous, can emerge with their life unmarred. And if indeed there are, they can be described in terms of the virtuous agent. Some people, for instance, think that what has to be said about situations such as Williams's Jim and Pedro case is that one kills the two, or refuses to, and then kills oneself when the opportunity is available, i.e. *that* is what the virtuous agent would do. Others say, no, that would be cowardly, so (*ex hypothesi*) the virtuous agent cannot do that. So she must live out the rest of her natural life haunted by remorse.

We should note that the 'must' here is not action-guiding but conceptual—'one who is truly just and compassionate cannot ever rest content with the knowledge that she has killed the two (or not saved the eighteen); one who is truly brave cannot kill herself to escape the knowledge; it follows that a virtuous agent who has done what she has done will never rest content again; her life will be forever marred'.

I am not necessarily endorsing any of this, only pointing out what can be said about situations of which it is supposed that no one can emerge from them with clean hands, in terms of the virtuous agent. Given that these situations are those in which, *ex hypothesi*, there is no virtuous *choice* to be made, no action which is partially constitutive of living well, virtue ethics is logically debarred from saying 'In such situations, the virtuous agent *chooses* to do such and such'. But it is not debarred from describing what the virtuous agent "does" without choosing to do so; perhaps she suffers for the rest of her life.

So much for what virtue ethics can say about tragic dilemmas, or situations from which it is impossible to emerge with 'clean hands'. It can give at least a plausible and, I would say, the right account of each. But this is quite a modest claim; we are really interested in the question of whether it can do much more. So now let me turn to another issue, one which rapidly unfolds into a nest of others.

In the discussion so far I have left unquestioned the standard claim that virtue ethics does not aim to come up with any rules or principles. But in one way this is trivially false. Virtue ethics does aim to sort out amongst character traits which ones are virtues and which vices; and settling on some particular one, e.g. honesty, as a virtue, and another, e.g. cruelty, as a vice certainly seems to entail settling on 'Act honestly' and 'Don't act cruelly' as rules or principles. Of course, it entails more than that, for we are supposed to *be* honest too, which covers at least our unintentional reactions as well as our intentional actions; nevertheless, it shows that the favoured catch-phrase that is used to sum up virtue ethics—that it is concerned with being rather than doing—is seriously misleading.

So when philosophers say that virtue ethics needs to be supplemented with a theory of rules—as though it did not offer any—do they overlook our offering all these obvious ones? Or is their complaint something like 'Oh I don't mean *those* sorts of rules, because they're *no use*'. The first is not an interesting possibility, so let us explore the second.

Why might one say that the virtue ethicists' "rules" were no use? One very 'act-centred' thought would be: 'Such rules do not give me any guidance about the rights and wrongs of *types of act*— such as abortion or euthanasia or foetal or animal experimentation or eating meat or not telling the truth. And that is what is called for.'

It is hardly true to say that the virtue ethicists' rules do not give me any guidance about the rights and wrongs of types of act in *some* sense of 'types of act'. For I cannot act honestly by performing dishonest acts, generously by performing mean ones; I cannot eschew acting cruelly by performing cruel ones; and so on; so the virtue ethicists' rules give me some guidance about the rights and wrongs of those types. Does this not show that the rules are of some use?

A reply to this might be as follows: 'The level of act description which virtue ethics employs in its "rules"', it might be said, 'is already morally laden, being in terms of the virtues and vices'. And then there are at least two different lines of thought that may be developed.

One is that whether a particular character trait is a virtue or a vice or neither is culturally or socially determined; hence the virtue ethicists' "rules" determine only what is right or wrong in their culture or society. So unless we are prepared to accept rampant cultural relativism, they are of no use for determining what is *really* right and wrong, independently of one's culture.

My response to this line of thought, briefly, is simply to deny that whether a particular character trait is a virtue, a vice, or neither is culturally determined. Of course, this is hard to argue; but only, I would say, in so far as it is, in general, hard to argue against cultural relativism, a problem that deontic and virtue ethicists share. Formally speaking, the concept of a virtue is specified in terms that make no reference to culture. The specification is something like: a virtue is a character trait that human beings, given their physical and psychological nature, need to flourish (or to do and fare well)—flourish *in this world in which we inevitably find ourselves*, not *in the particular culture or society we happen to find ourselves in*. Indeed, a fundamental criticism that can be made of a society or culture, from the standpoint of virtue ethics, is that it disallows, or makes impossible, or fails to encourage, a particular virtue in all *or* some of the human beings within it. So I put this objection to one side.

A second line of development goes something like this. 'Of course we all know', it might be said, 'that we shouldn't act dishonestly and perform dishonest acts. But that's no help or guidance when I'm trying to decide, for instance, whether or not to tell a patient the truth about the fact that he has cancer. My quandary about whether or not I ought to tell him just is the quandary about whether not telling him is dishonest or not. Some people will maintain it is, and that I ought to tell him; and some will say it isn't, and that I needn't, and then I'm just stuck. And that shows the uselessness of starting with rules that are already morally laden, as the virtue ethicists' rules inevitable are. We need a different *sort* of rule.'

What assumption or assumptions lie behind this line of thought? One seems to be another version of the 'we need an algorithm for life' point again; not with particular reference to undecidability, but more generally with reference to easiness. The trouble with the virtue ethicists' "rules", it seems, is that they are too *difficult* to apply. 'Virtue theorists tell us that the fully virtuous agents know when an act is dishonest and when it is not, but of what use is that to the rest of us, who lack their (hypothetical) special insight?'

The virtue ethicists' response to this is 'Well of course it is difficult. Are you seriously suggesting that a condition of adequacy on a moral theory is that it should make life easy, that it should represent moral wisdom as something that any clever adolescent could acquire just by being taught the right rules? Surely a constraint on any adequate moral theory is that it should have built into it an explanation of a truth expressed by Aristotle, that moral knowledge—unlike mathematical knowledge—cannot be acquired merely by attending lectures, and is not characteristically to be found in people too young to have much experience of life. There are youthful mathematical geniuses, but rarely, if ever, youthful moral geniuses, and this shows us something significant about the sort of knowledge that moral knowledge is. Virtue ethics builds this in straight off precisely by couching its rules in terms whose application may indeed call for the most delicate and sensitive observation and judgement.'

In fact, I find it hard to believe that many deontic theorists believe that an adequate theory has to come up with rules that are easy to apply. Most deontologists want some sort of rule about not harming others; and the concept *harm* is no easier to apply than the concept *dishonest*.

Still, perhaps the thought is that there is some especial difficulty, amounting indeed to an impossibility, in applying the virtue ethicists' "rules", which shows that in some sense they are useless and need to be supplemented with real rules. Suppose the objection goes like this. 'The act descriptions which figure in the virtue ethicists' "rules"—the way in which they classify types of act—are parasitic on classifications of people by character traits. Cruel people characteristically go in for inflicting pain on other people, and thereby we have the concept of cruel acts. Honest people characteristically go in for eschewing lying and cheating, and thereby we have the concept of honest acts. Now it is true that whether an act is of the type *cruel* or *honest* is morally important; we need rules about such types of act and, yes, virtue ethics provides them, and is thus far of some use. *But*, there are other types of act—types such as abortion, or euthanasia, or animal experimentation—where an act's being of that type is morally significant. So we need rules about them too. And virtue ethics obviously is useless in these cases, because these act descriptions are entirely independent of classifications of people. There isn't a particular sort of character who typically goes in for, or even approves of, abortion or euthanasia or animal experimentation. So it is impossible to apply the virtue ethicists' rules to these sorts of case. Hence, to go back to the original complaint with a new emphasis, virtue ethics, as was originally said, does not, and cannot, give us guidance about the rights and wrongs of types of act *such as* abortion, euthanasia, animal experimentation, etc. We must have rules couched explicitly in terms of *those* sorts of act description. *That* is what is called for.' (There is something not quite right about this, because a particular supporter of deontic ethics might want to say that the very idea that *abortion* and *euthanasia* are morally significant categories already contains the improper notion that the two do not fall straightforwardly under the rule prohibiting murder or the taking of human life. But I shall ignore this complication.)

So the claim is that, for example, *abortion* or *euthanasia* is a morally significant category and the move is from that premise to the conclusion that there must be a rule or principle which governs it. But why should one think that inference is valid?

I take it that the reason cannot be the algorithm-for-life point again, that is that since *abortion* and *euthanasia* are morally significant act categories, i.e. pick out types of act that we are deeply troubled about, they must each be governed by a simple rule which solves all our problems; which tells us, for instance, that all abortion is impermissible and all euthanasia permissible or vice versa. Deontic theorists do not as such expect *the* rule governing abortion to make it a black or white issue (though it is true that much of the ink that has been squandered in pursuit of the question 'What is the status of the foetus?' can be understood only on the assumption that it represents the attempt to get abortion firmly under one rule, either (something like) 'Taking human life is wrong' or (something like) 'Killing things that do not have the right to life is permissible'). So I take it that that cannot in general be the thought which tempts people to the inference. What other thought could it be?

It seems that it must be some form of our old friend (or enemy) universalizability. The thought is this: 'Granted the basic premise that abortion is at least sometimes permissible and sometimes wrong, one must be able to say in any particular case *why* it is permissible or wrong. And giving the reason why commits one to some sort of universalization to the effect that any case of abortion similar in the relevant respects would be permissible or wrong. And that would be the statement of a rule or principle.'

If this is right, how does virtue ethics fare? Suppose the virtue ethicist and deontic theorist agree in their normative judgement on some particular example; say, to take Thomson's famous case, that a woman who is seven months pregnant ought not to have an abortion in order to go on holiday; that this would be wrong. And let them agree further that each of them must be able to say something about why she ought not to, why it would be wrong. I leave it to interested parties to fill in what the deontic theorist could say about this. My question is: 'What could the virtue ethicist say?'

The implication of the claim that 'virtue ethics can't come up with rules couched in terms of act descriptions such as, for example, "abortion"' was clearly supposed to be that the answer to that question must be 'damn all'; that at best the "answer" would be 'The virtuous agent wouldn't do that'—which adds nothing to the agreed ground, namely that it would be wrong. Recall the complaint that when we ask our hypothetical moral exemplar what she would do (or would not do in this case) we shall not get anything enlightening *because* we shall not get an appeal to a rule or principle.

But the virtue ethicist has not lost the resources of her character-trait vocabulary simply because we are now talking about, for example, abortion rather than, for example, dishonest acts, so we have no reason to believe that she is struck dumb. There is lots she could say about why it would be wrong of the woman in Thomson's case to have the abortion. For instance, she could say that it would be wrong because it would be callous, wrong because it would be stunningly light-minded, very likely (pending further details) to be wrong because it was very selfish, or self-centred, or cruel. She could also say it was wrong because it was folly. And all such claims universalize in the required way; any abortion which is similarly callous, or light-minded, or cruel, etc. is wrong. So, in a way, virtue ethics can produce "rules governing abortion"—not of course the sort which the deontic theorist expected, but nevertheless rules which rebut the claim 'virtue ethics can't say anything about the rights and wrongs of acts *such as* abortion, and hence needs to be supplemented by rules governing them'.

Even supposing this much is conceded, a deep dissatisfaction and a suspicion that the virtue ethicist is cheating may still be felt. The next natural question would be: 'But what does the virtue ethicist say about *why* the abortion in Thomson's case is, say, callous or light-minded? Surely, in making this out, she is going to have to have to say something like "It is callous to regard what is in effect a premature baby as something whose life can be disposed of for the sake of a holiday", and this is just tantamount to the claim that killing babies is wrong, i.e. tantamount to one of our rules.'

Now the virtue ethicist can reject this, and say she is claiming no more than that killing babies, or indeed taking human life at any stage, is a serious matter, never anything to be undertaken lightly. But here too the objection may be: 'But you are just helping yourself to non-virtue-based concepts. What account can *you* give of the taking of human life's being a serious matter beyond claiming that it is a consideration which the virtuous happen to take seriously?'

With this objection we reach a common misunderstanding of what virtue ethics involves. It is often thought that virtue ethics, in being agent-centred rather than act-centred, in starting with the virtues and vices rather than right or wrong acts, is committed to a sort of reductionism. It is thought that virtue ethics maintains that the concept of the virtuous agent is the only piece of conceptual apparatus relevant to moral philosophy and that the theory promises to be able to give a reductive analysis of all our moral concepts in terms of the virtuous or vicious agent.

Hence, I suspect, to go back to the example with which I started this paper, another source of the view that Foot's paper on euthanasia fails to show that answers to real questions can be yielded by virtue ethics. For even those who admit the paper does more than repeat conventional wisdom may say that it succeeds in doing so only in so far as Foot has illegitimately helped herself to a number of moral concepts which are not derived from virtue ethics—particularly those of a *right*, and of a *good* or a *benefit*.

It is certainly true that these, along with the concepts of the two virtues of justice and charity, figure essentially in her article. 'Charity' she says 'is the virtue that gives attachment to the good of others, and because life is normally a good, charity normally demands that it should be saved or prolonged.'[8] Now, unless she can employ the concept of the *good* of others, she cannot characterize charity; and unless she can maintain that life is normally a good or a benefit to a human being, she cannot connect the virtue of charity to questions about saving, prolonging, or ending human lives. And unless she can say something about 'the sense in which life is normally a good, and (of) the reasons why it may

---

[8] Philippa Foot, *Virtues and Vices* (Oxford: Blackwell, 1978), 54.

not be so in some particular case',[9] she cannot connect charity to questions explicitly about euthanasia. But why should her employment of this concept be claimed to be illegitimate? Why should a virtue ethicist not employ moral concepts other than those of the virtues and vices?

People tend to sum up different ethical theories in catch-phrases such as 'Utilitarians define (the concept of) the Right in terms of (the concept of the) the Good, whereas Deontologists define the concept of the Good in terms of the concept of the Right'. Within this procrustean framework, virtue ethics is then defined as a theory committed to the daunting task of reductively defining the Right and the Good in terms of the virtuous agent. I myself do not believe that any serious utilitarian or deontologist has ever attempted any such wholesale reductive definition as these catch-phrases suggest; but regardless of whether or not they have, virtue ethicists do not. The question whether neo-Aristotelian virtue ethics already involves the concept of the Right, or Duty, might be regarded as the topic of this paper, but it is beyond question that it relies, non-reductively, on the concept of the Good, as the most cursory glance at, for instance, Anscombe's 'Modern Moral Philosophy', or indeed at Aristotle himself, should reveal. For built into the theory is the claim that part of the virtuous person's practical wisdom is her knowledge, her correct appreciation, of what is truly good, and, indeed, of what is truly pleasant, truly advantageous, truly worth while, truly important, truly serious (and, correspondingly, of what is truly bad, unpleasant, or painful, disadvantageous, worthless, unimportant, and trivial).

So the virtue ethicist does not say, 'Taking life is a serious matter because it is a consideration which the virtuous happen to take seriously'. She says, 'The virtuous do not just happen to, but *qua* virtuous, have to, regard the fact that a proposed act is one of taking life as a serious consideration because taking life *is* a serious matter'.

Now does *this* show that virtue ethics is useless?

I began this paper with the standard complaint against virtue ethics; that in some sense it cannot answer questions about real moral issues such as abortion or euthanasia. I have granted that in

[9] Ibid. 43.

at least two senses that is true—it cannot resolve every dilemma
into the right and the wrong, and it cannot render difficult matters
of delicate judgement easy and obvious to the adolescent—but
claimed in both cases that this is to its credit. If the complaint has
now been tracked down to the point that virtue ethics can answer
questions about real moral issues *only* by appealing to premises
about what is truly good, worth while, serious, and so on, what
can I say about this?

Here too I claim that this is all to virtue ethics' credit. As before,
I ask, 'What can be envisaged as an alternative?' If truths about
what is truly good, worth while, serious, and so on do *not* have to
be appealed to in order to answer questions about real moral
issues, then I might sensibly seek guidance about what I ought to
do from someone who had declared in advance that she knew
nothing about such matters, or from someone who said that,
although of course she had opinions about them, these were quite
likely to be wrong but that this did not matter, because they
would play no determining role in the advice she gave me. And if
this is absurd, then, once again, a condition of adequacy on any
moral theory—which virtue ethics meets—is that it reflects why
this is so.

Perhaps what philosophers, as a body of professionals, tend to
find uncomfortable about virtue ethics is that it makes all too
explicit a fact we would like to think was not so; that we are not,
qua philosophers, thereby fitted to say anything true or even
enlightening on real moral issues. It requires that we give up the
pretence that all we bring to bear on them is the expertise of our
trade—our oft-claimed clarity and rigour of argument, our detachment, our skill in working out inconsistencies and dreaming
up counter-examples. It reveals that, if we are to say anything true
about them, we must also bring our knowledge of the correct
application of the virtue–vice terms—about which actions are,
say, charitable or dishonest—and, moreover, our knowledge of
what is truly good and bad, of what is worth while, of what
counts as a good, mature, developed human life and what as a
wasted, perverted, or childish one.

Given that this is essential, we are fortunate indeed in having
had, and having, Philippa Foot as virtue ethics' most distinguished modern exponent. It is, I suppose, just conceivable that
the subject should have appeared on the current philosophical

stage without her. But without all those articles in which the requisite knowledge is so richly displayed, what picture would we have had of that knowledge, and thereby of the subject? Only something that justified the critics' rejection of virtue ethics' normative claims as useless.

4

Philippa Foot on Double Effect

ANTHONY KENNY

St Thomas Aquinas, in discussing killing in self-defence, remarks that one and the same action may have two effects, one of them intended, and the other beside the intention. Later Catholic theologians developed from this a doctrine of double effect, stated as follows by John of St Thomas. If an act, not evil in itself, has both good and bad effects, then it may be permissible if (1) the evil effect is not intended; (2) the good effect is not produced by means of the bad; (3) on balance, the good done outweighs the harm.

The doctrine of double effect has been much criticized by utilitarians. At first sight, this is perhaps surprising. The principle's reference to an 'act not evil in itself' makes it appear totally to bypass the concerns of utilitarians. For a Catholic who believes in a natural law, there are various classes of acts evil in themselves; but for a thoroughgoing utilitarian, there is no such thing as an act evil in itself without regard to its consequences. Provided the overall outcome is positive, no act, however heinous on the face of it, is absolutely prohibited.

What has excited the ridicule of utilitarians is the consequence to be drawn from the principle of double effect that the intention with which one acts can be a matter of supreme moral significance.

Where Aquinas made a distinction between what was intentional and what was beside the intention, Bentham made a distinction between direct and oblique intention. An act, he said, might be intentional without its consequences being so: 'thus, you may intend to touch a man without intending to hurt him: and yet, as the consequences turn out, you may chance to hurt him'. A consequence may be either directly intentional ('when the prospect of producing it constituted one of the links in the chain of causes by which the person was determined to act') or obliquely intentional (when the consequence was foreseen as likely, but the prospect of producing it formed no link in the determining chain).

Adopting Bentham's terminology we can say that according to the principle of double effect it may sometimes be permissible to intend a state of affairs obliquely which it would be wrong to intend directly. Thus, Catholic theologians have held that if the uterus of a pregnant woman is diseased then in order to preserve her life it may be permissible to remove it, thus causing the death of the foetus. The same theologians would insist that it would be wicked to remove the uterus in order to cause the death of the foetus. Distinctions of this kind, which are applications of the principle of double effect, are commonly held by utilitarians to be sophistical. For this and other reasons the principle of double effect has been poorly regarded by many influential philosophers in the analytic tradition.

Professor Foot has twice devoted careful attention to the topic of double effect. In 'The Problem of Abortion and the Doctrine of the Double Effect'[1] she starts her treatment from a series of moral judgements about particular cases. The driver of a runaway tram is right to steer down a track where one man will be killed rather than an alternative track where five men will be killed. On the other hand, a judge who frames and executes one innocent man in order to save five innocents does wrong. Doctors who withhold a scarce drug from a patient who will otherwise die, in order to save five other patients, are right to do so; but it would be totally wrong for a doctor to kill one person to provide spare parts for grafting on to five others who needed them. People who are faced with a choice between rescuing five victims from torture and rescuing one victim are right to choose to rescue the five; on the other hand, there is something wicked about a man who, in order to save five victims from torture, is ready to torture a sixth himself.

The moral difference between the members of these pairs, Foot said, has often been explained by the principle of double effect: that sometimes it is allowable to intend obliquely what one may not intend directly. But this principle leads also to the conclusion that one may not kill an unborn child to save the life of its mother

---

[1] *Oxford Review*, 5 (1967), 5–15; repr. in her *Virtues and Vices, and Other Essays in Moral Philosophy* (Oxford: Blackwell, 1978).

even when both will die in any case; and this, she argued, is intolerable. The difference, therefore, between the members of the pairs is to be explained in terms of the distinction between positive and negative duties rather than in terms of the distinction between direct and oblique intention. We have a much stronger duty to avoid injury than we have to bring aid. The tram-driver faces a conflict of negative duties, the doctors with the scarce drug and the rescuers of the torture victims face a conflict of positive duties. But in each of the cases regarded as immoral the duty to avoid injuring is being sacrificed to the duty to bring aid.

In all these cases, Foot observed, the same moral conclusions could be reached by the use of the positive duty–negative duty distinction as were reached by the use of the direct intention–oblique intention distinction. In other cases, she claimed, the conclusions will be different, and the advantage seems to be on the side of the positive versus negative principle.

Suppose, for instance, that there are five patients in a hospital whose lives could be saved by the manufacture of a certain gas, but that this inevitably releases lethal fumes into the room of another patient whom for some reason we are unable to move. His death, being of no use to us, is clearly a side effect, and not directly intended. Why then is the case different from that of the scarce drug, if the point about that is that we foresaw but did not strictly intend the death of the single patient? Yet surely it is different.[2]

I have no difficulty in accepting Foot's assessment of the various cases which she takes as the basis of her discussion. Where it is difficult to follow her argument is in its application to the Catholic doctrine that one may not kill an unborn child to save the life of its mother even when both will die in any case. Foot claims that this is an indefensible moral judgement; but it does not appear that the line adopted in her article is sufficient to distinguish her position from the Catholic one at this point.

As we have seen, Foot wished to replace the disctinction between direct and indirect intention with the distinction between avoiding an injury and bringing aid. But in the kind of case she has in mind, we are doing an injury to the child in order to bring aid to the mother. The mother will die if we don't kill the child; to bring aid to the mother we do injury to the child. Foot, in this

---

[2] Ibid. 29.

article, deliberately refused to endorse the principle that we may never, whatever the balance of good and evil, bring injury to one for the sake of aid to others, even when this injury amounts to death. But, to judge by the examples on which she based her argument up to this point, she thought that the ratio of the aid given to the harm done must be something more than five to one. It is hard to see, therefore, how she justified killing the child in the case in which mother and child would otherwise both die.

However, in a situation in which nothing that can be done will save the life of child and mother, but where the life of the mother can be saved by killing the child, there is, according to Foot, 'no serious conflict of interests'. I think it is really here that she was looking for the justification of killing in this case. She didn't think, of course, and her whole paper showed this, that a case of this kind is to be settled by working out the interests of the people involved and then choosing that action which will, on balance, serve the greatest interests of the greatest number. For that principle would justify the framing judge and the doctors who kill the patient to produce transplant organs. What, in this context, the reference to the interests of mother and child must mean is that the injury done to the child by killing it is really a negligible injury, since it would soon die anyway.

It is not easy to frame an acceptable principle which would enable Foot to get the conclusion she wanted. It seems too sweeping to say that it is all right to do a certain harm to someone if that harm is going to happen to them anyway. This would mean you could steal anything which was about to be stolen, and rape anyone you saw about to be raped. Of course, it would seem to be reasonable to take something you saw about to be stolen, with a view to returning it later, at a safer time, to its owner. But a principle that you can harm someone to prevent greater harm of the same kind to herself seems to be insufficient to justify the injury done to the child for the sake of the mother. It is difficult to think of a case where one can harm someone to bring aid to someone else, because she is about to suffer that harm anyway, where it would not be justifiable to harm her for this purpose whether or not she was going to suffer the harm anyway.

One case might be where a mountaineer falls and is likely to carry the rest of his rope to their death with him unless the rope is cut between him and the next climber. But the morality of cutting the rope is as hotly debated as the morality of therapeutic abortion. But perhaps this is only because the *certainty* that the others will be killed is unobtainable in the time available for making the decision. The plea 'If I don't, someone else will' is often used to justify very bad things—e.g. the peddling of dangerous drugs to minors, or the supplying of arms to nations proclaiming their intentions to massacre. At the very least, the principle needed by Foot would have to state, if it is to be tolerable, that the alternative harm which is pleaded as a justification must not be harm produced by human agents. Otherwise, in a sufficiently wicked world, one will be able to justify anything whatever.

In the three cases mentioned by Foot as giving initial plausibility to the principle of double effect, the factor of alternative harm was absent: we were left to assume that the man to be framed would otherwise live in peace, that the corpse to provide the spare parts was a healthy one. In order to know whether Foot had really provided an alternative to the principle of double effect in these cases, we would need to know whether she thought it was all right for the judge to frame a victim, and the doctors to carve up a patient, who was about to die of cancer anyway. Those of us who would shrink from saying this may well wish to defend the importance of the principle of double effect; and if we wish, like Foot, to dissent from the Catholic view on therapeutic abortion we must do so on other grounds.

By the time she wrote 'Morality, Action and Outcome'[3] Professor Foot had come to accept the principle which she had attacked in her earlier article. It is not competely clear what made her change her mind, but in a footnote she explains that a case considered in the 1967 article had left her uncomfortable. In that article she had pointed out that it is possible deliberately to allow something to happen: we might, for instance, think of giving food to a beggar, but then allow him to die so that his body will be available for medical research. Here, she admitted, it did seem morally relevant that in allowing him to die we were aiming at his death. How, without something like the principle of double effect, could she distinguish this from a case where the food was withheld to be given to others in need? Her solution was to suggest

[3] In T. Honderich (ed.), *Objectivity and Value: Essays in Memory of John Mackie* (London: Routledge & Kegan Paul, 1985).

that the withholding of food was a violation of negative rather than positive duty. But, as she later came to see, this went far to undermine the positive–negative distinction on which she relied.

In the second article Foot sets out to defend two commonly accepted non-utilitarian principles. The first is that there is a morally relevant distinction between what we do and what we allow to happen. The second is that there is a morally relevant distinction between what we aim at and what we foresee as the result of what we do.

The first of these two principles is akin to the one which, in her earlier article, she wanted to bear the entire weight of supporting the intuitive moral judgements about the particular cases which she considered. The second of the two principles is the principle of double effect which her first article aimed to reject.

To illustrate the first principle, she draws attention once again to the contrast between withholding a scarce medical resource from one patient to save others and killing a patient to bring aid to others. A parallel example is the difference between driving past an injured man in order to bring aid, as fast as possible, to a number of injured people, and driving over a prostrate person for the same purpose.

The difference between doing something and allowing something to happen, Foot says, is not the same as the distinction between act and omission. It is essentially the difference between starting a new train of events and refusing to intervene to stop one. (There is also the interesting intermediate case of diverting a harmful sequence from one victim to another, as when a pilot whose plane is going to crash steers it from a more to a less inhabited area.)

Thus far the argumentation of the second article follows the same lines as the first. But Foot now says that she was wrong, in the earlier article, to say that the distinction between direct and indirect intention was irrelevant to moral judgement. The main part of the second article makes use of the double effect distinction, along with the doing–allowing distinction, in launching an attack on utilitarianism and all forms of consequentialism.

If we are to maintain these two principles, she argues, there is no way in which consequentialism can be amended to make it compatible with them. It will not suffice to modify the utilitarian definition of 'welfare'. Nor is it possible to preserve the principles by adopting a non-utilitarian consequentialism which takes account of rights, and of the violation of rights, in the evaluation of good and bad outcomes.

Some have sought to reconcile the principles with consequentialism by introducing a notion of 'agent-relativity'. But in fact, unless there is some morally relevant difference between my situation and yours, an immoral act done by me is no worse than the same act done by you. 'I do not refuse to kill or torture to prevent others from killing or torturing because I think that killing or torturing is, in the ordinary sense, worse when I do it than when they do.'

To see what is really wrong with utilitarianism, Foot argues, we have to take issue with the whole concept of 'the best state of affairs', the outcome which the utilitarian seeks to bring about. The attraction of utilitarianism is that it can hardly seem rational to prefer a worse to a better state of affairs. But in everyday life a good or a bad state of affairs is one which suits someone's particular interests. The impersonal use of 'good state of affairs' is problematic. Benevolence may be the overarching aim of the utilitarian; but it gives us no reason to say that it would be 'a good state of affairs' or 'a good total outcome' if the sacrificing of a few experimental subjects allowed us to get cancer under control.

Foot's analysis of the motivation of utilitarianism is illuminating, and she is wholly successful in exhibiting the incompatibility between any form of consequentialism and the moral principles from which her article takes its start. But so many philosophers are attracted by one or other form of consequentialism that if told that their theories are incompatible with the principle of double effect their reaction will be not to give up their theories, but to say 'so much the worse for the principle of double effect'.

Given that in her earlier article Foot had herself rejected the principle, one might have expected that in the later one she would have felt obliged to give a full defence of it before using it as a weapon against consequentialism. But at the crucial point of the argument we meet with no more than the following brief passage:

The moral relevance [of the double effect distinction] must be allowed. To be sure it often makes no difference to the injustice of an action whether an injury which it causes is something the agent aims at or something he foresees but has not made the object of his will. A merchant who sold food he knew to be poisonous in order to make money would be morally no better than an unemployed grave digger who deliberately killed to get trade. Nevertheless there are circumstances in which it is morally permissible to bring something about without aiming at it although it would not be morally permissible to aim at it; even though the balance of benefit and harm in the consequences remained the same. That this is so is proved, I think, by some facts about the permissibility of allowing an evil to come on some for the sake of saving others. For sometimes this is a regrettable moral necessity, as in our previous examples having to do with scarce medical resources and with the person lying injured by the roadside. But it does not follow that it would be morally unobjectionable deliberately to leave someone unattended because his death could allow us to save others.

In effect, the only argument used by Foot to show the necessity of the double effect principle (in addition to the distinction between doing and allowing) is the case of the beggar deliberately left to starve, which was mentioned, though not satisfactorily dealt with, in the earlier article. I do not question Foot's judgement that the principle is applicable to this case: but readers of her article may have wondered whether this single case is sufficient to undermine a superstition as widespread as utilitarianism.

In fact, the everyday thinking of ordinary people constantly involves the notion that there can be an important moral difference between aiming at a particular outcome and bringing about the same outcome without aiming at it. It is easier to see this if we concentrate, initially, on issues which are much less than matters of life and death.

It is an unfriendly act for a hostess deliberately to seat one of her guests at table next to another guest whom she knows he dislikes. The act is not unfriendly if she assigns the place to the guest not deliberately, but because such is the unintended outcome of a placement which takes account of the conventions about alternating between the sexes, separating husbands from wives, and so on.

In appointing the best candidate to a job, the electors know that they will be causing pain and disappointment to the unsuccessful candidates. This does not make their action wrong. It would be a very different matter to elect a candidate—even if objectively the best candidate—*in order to* cause pain and disappointment to one of the others.

Fixing the date of a board meeting, I may, for good reason, choose one which has the consequence that one of my colleagues cannot attend. That is morally quite different from choosing the same day for the purpose of ensuring that he will be absent.

There are many occasions when, for one reason or another, we have to allow our companions to form a false impression about our intentions or our state of mind. This is quite different from lying, or keeping silent with the purpose of deceiving. My fellow trustees, perhaps, are resolving on an investment in a company which I know, because of confidential information, to be quite unsound. My silence may lead to a disastrous investment; but I am in a very different position from someone who maliciously keeps silent *in order that* his colleagues may invest imprudently.

If we return to the topic of taking life, the necessity for the principle of double effect is in fact brought out by some of the cases which Foot used in the article in which she rejected the principle. Perhaps the clearest is that of the pilot who is steering his stricken plane towards a particular suburb. In one case we may suppose that he is doing this because he wants to minimize the damage caused by his inevitable crash, and the suburb is less populous than any other place he can hope to reach before hitting the ground. In another case we may suppose that he takes the course he does because the suburb is where his wife's lover lives, and he is anxious, when he leaves this life, to take this obnoxious person with him.

There seems to be a big moral difference between these two cases. The difference cannot be explained on utilitarian grounds: the evil outcome is the same in each case. The difference cannot be explained in terms of doing versus allowing: in each case the pilot kills his victims by crashing his plane upon them; neither is a case of his just allowing them to die. The difference cannot be explained in terms of the distinction between positive and negative duties; in each case the pilot's action conflicts with a negative, not a positive, duty. The crucial difference seems to be that in the one case the death of his victims is merely foreseen as the outcome of his steering away from a more populous area; in the other case the death of at least one of the victims is an end he seeks.

Those who maintain the necessity for the principle of double effect are not committed to maintaining that there will *always* be a moral difference between bringing about an outcome with direct intention and bringing about the same outcome with oblique intention. As Foot says in her second article, a merchant selling food known to be poisonous is no less murderous because his motive is only to make money. But it follows that the case she presented in her first article—of the doctors who produce a healing gas whose manufacture has lethal side-effects on a neighbouring patient—is not by itself any refutation of the doctrine of double effect.

Foot's second article is well inspired, I believe, in turning the tables on the utilitarians with respect to the burden of proof. It is not that the onus is on the double effect principle to defend itself against the presumption that utilitarianism is the only rational moral system. On the contrary, utilitarianism has to defend its abolition of the prima facie plausible double effect principle. Anyone who is not an out-and-out act utilitarian will need a double effect principle if she attaches moral importance to the observation of rules or the maintenance of rights. For there will always be cases where the same outcome can be achieved with or without the contravention of a rule or the violation of a right. For the act utilitarian, only the outcome will matter; for others, it will make a difference whether a rule has been contravened or a right violated. And only the principle of double effect enables one to give a consistent articulation of this difference.

Foot sums up the drift of her second article in the following words: 'So far, the argument has tended to resist the encroachment of any form of consequentialism on the "mixed" aim-and-rule morality that we actually seem to have.' To illustrate what is meant by an 'aim-and-rule' morality she insists that the aim of benevolence will not justify the killing of the innocent, and that the moral requirement to fight injustice does not imply that one must, or may, fight it by any means whatsoever.

Foot's treatment of the doctrine of double effect does indeed bring out in a vivid manner the essential structure of morality. There are three elements which are essential to a moral system: a moral community; a set of moral values; and a moral code. All three are necessary. First, it is as impossible to have a purely private morality as it is to have a purely private language, and for very similar reasons. Second, the moral life of the community consists in the shared pursuit of non-material values, such as fairness, truth, comradeship, freedom: it is this which distinguishes between morality and economics. Third, this pursuit is carried out within a framework which excludes certain types of behaviour: it is this which marks the distinction between morality and aesthetics.

A common morality, therefore, consists of values and rules. Rules may be absolute, but values are not in the same sense absolute. No value is absolute in the sense that its pursuit justifies the violation of every rule. Some rules are absolute in the sense that their violation is never justified, no matter what the value pursued by their violation. This is simply to say that there are no ends which justify every means, and that there are some means which no end will justify.

Foot's later article discusses in magisterial fashion the relation between values and rules in moral systems. The article does not—apart from references to 'us' and 'the morality we have'—treat explicitly of the nature and extent of the moral community. Moreover, and it may seem surprisingly, the article contains no mention of the issue of abortion which was so central to the 1967 article.

These two omissions are related more than coincidentally. For those who wish to justify abortion do so most effectively when they deny that the unborn are members of the same moral community as adult mothers and surgeons. In this denial, I believe, they are mistaken. But that is a topic for a different essay; for it is the question of membership of the moral community, rather than the principle of double effect, which is the crucial issue when we seek to make a judgement about the morality of abortion.

5

The Rationality of Morality

GAVIN LAWRENCE

1. Introduction: Four Suggestions

A central preoccupation of Professor Foot, as of Plato, to whom she often refers, is with the rationality of morality. This she has pursued in a series of brilliant and searching papers across several decades. And, like Plato, she invites trisection. My contribution takes off from criticisms of some views in her early and middle periods, and leaves aside her recent, and as yet unpublished, work. I wish to stress right from the start that these are not her present views, and that she is, if anything, too severe a critic of her earlier work. For, though I shall take issue with a certain strand of thought in her early and middle papers, I think they are among the very best in moral philosophy, demanding and deserving the very hardest of study. Where they are wrong, they are importantly and illuminatingly wrong, and where they are right, I do not think their points have even yet been fully appreciated.

Early Foot, in defending morality against a broad spectrum of emotivist and prescriptivist positions, rejected the then, and unfortunately still, current orthodoxy that moral arguments, unlike factual ones, may always break down without rational error. But she left unquestioned a second orthodoxy. This is the claim that 'moral judgements necessarily give reasons for acting to each and every man' (p. xiii; 161),[1] or, alternatively, that no one 'could be indifferent to morality without error' (p. xiv). Moral judgements—by which I take it Foot means moral considerations or

This paper draws on many discussions with Philippa both in Oxford and at the University of California at Los Angeles. I am immeasurably indebted to her as philosophical mentor and friend. Thanks are due also to audiences at the University of Southern California, UCLA, and the Oriel College discussion group, and in particular to Bill Fitzpatrick, Andrew Hsu, Houston Smit, Michael Thompson, and most especially to Torin Alter.

[1] All page references to Foot are to *Virtues and Vices* (Oxford: Blackwell, 1978).

moral requirements—are such that they should engage everyone's will, and the amoralist, on whom they fail to gain purchase,
thus stands convicted of some error of reason.[2] In fact, Early Foot,
so far from questioning this orthodoxy, supposed she had to
defend it, at least when interpreted in a way compatible with her
rejection of the first orthodoxy. Its truth, she held, rested on two
premisses: first that there is some end or interest that is universally held, and second that morality non-accidentally serves that
interest.[3] As regards the first, self-interest is, she thought, a plausible, indeed the only plausible, candidate for an end that can be
universally appealed to (p. xiii; 125; 128–9). If so, the second
premiss requires there to be a 'necessary connection' specifically
between virtue and self-interest: anything, if a virtue, must serve
one's self-interest. And this she undertook to argue at least for the
cardinal virtues, including the difficult case of justice, in the
second half of 'Moral Beliefs' (123–30).

Middle Foot found this defence of the second premiss flawed,
for two reasons. First she came to believe that the particular virtue
of justice could not after all meet the constraint—for while its
general practice may indeed be to a man's advantage, yet it requires that he be ready to go against his self-interest *in the particular case*.[4] Second, she was no longer prepared, as she had been
earlier, to countenance the rejection of justice as a virtue if it failed
the constraint (125; 128; cf. p. xiii). So self-interest could not, it
seemed, function as the source for the alleged universal reason-
giving force of moral considerations.

A natural move at this point is to cast around for some other
candidate for the universal end required by the first premiss. One
obvious suggestion, along Humean lines, is that of a universal
feeling of sympathy, or humanity—some minimal benevolence
towards all on the part of all.[5] This differs markedly from the first

[2] I understand this orthodoxy to be the claim that necessarily moral judgements
give everyone *some* reason, though not necessarily an *overriding* (or silencing)
reason. At times, however, Foot apparently has in mind the stronger claim (123).

[3] Unless of otherwise indicated, 'serves', like 'means', covers constitutive as well
as instrumental means. (This distinction needs more elucidation than I can give
here.)

[4] p. xiii; 154; cf. 155 and 168 n. 6. This way of putting it, which is Middle Foot's
(p. xiii), is misleading. For Early Foot was already aware of the problem, but
thought she could solve it ('Moral Beliefs', 129–30). See Section 2.

[5] 'One man's ambition is not another's ambition, nor will the same event or
object satisfy both; but the humanity of one man is the humanity of every one, and

suggestion. For it posits as the universal interest served by moral considerations one that is itself a moral end. So some moral considerations will serve this interest constitutively rather than instrumentally. But not, however, all. For it incorporates a theory about the internal structure of moral considerations, elevating one kind of moral concern or virtue, namely benevolence, above others. This is, so to speak, the first principle, or foundation, under which all other virtues can be 'brought' (128), that is, motivated and justified. What we have then is an instrumentalist structure *within* morality, between the other virtues and the favoured foundational virtue, where before it was between morality as whole and a non-moral end.

This suggestion of a universally extended benevolence faces, as Hume so clearly saw, a difficulty over justice exactly parallel to that faced by self-interest (a 'singular benevolence'). We can plausibly motivate and justify the general practice of justice through an agent's attachment either to their own private interest or to the public interest, but a particular act of justice may run counter to either concern.[6] If justice is founded on their attachment to private interest, there is the problem of 'sensible knaves', or free-riders: those particular occasions where, without seriously jeopardizing the benefits from the practice of justice, more private good can be secured by infringing it. If it is founded on their attachment to society's interest, there is the problem of 'profligate creditors': those occasions where, without seriously jeopardizing the benefits of justice, more public good can be achieved, say, by reneging on a debt. (This supposed foundational role, or priority, of benevolence over justice is utilitarianism's fatal commitment— one much exposed in Foot's writings.) Thus whichever way justice is founded, it may appear, 'he conducts himself with most wisdom who observes the general rule, and takes advantage of all

the same object touches this passion in all human creatures', David Hume, *An Enquiry Concerning the Principles of Morals*, ed. L. A. Selby-Bigge (Oxford: Clarendon Press, 1902), IX, §222; cf. I, §137: 'depends on some internal sense or feeling, which nature has made *universal* in the whole species'. Hume takes the feeling to be both universal to all humans ('common') and universal in extending towards all humans as objects ('comprehensive').

[6] David Hume, *A Treatise of Human Nature*, ed. L. A. Selby-Bigge, rev. P. H. Nidditch (Oxford: Clarendon Press, 1978), III. ii. 2, 496–7; cf. III. ii. 1, esp. 480–3; and also *An Enquiry Concerning the Principles of Morals*, app. III, §257. Cf. *Enquiry*, IX, §232; app. I, §234.

the exceptions', whether these be to the advantage of the agent's private interest or the general good. But this isn't what it is to be just.

Early Foot considers and rejects this second suggestion indeed in part for precisely this Humean reason, that, in the particular case, 'the actions dictated by benevolence and justice are not always the same' (128; cf. 155). But she rejects it *also* because 'even if the general practice of justice could be brought under the motive of universal benevolence . . . many people certainly do not have any such desire' (128). That is, contrary to Hume, she does not believe that a benevolence universal in being extended towards all, even if it could play a foundational role, is plausibly universal as a concern had by all.[7]

In fact Foot supposes there is *no* other interest or desire plausibly as universal as self-interest (128; cf. 152), and so if that fails, we cannot locate the source of the universal reason-giving force of moral considerations in any connection with a desire or interest that every agent plausibly has. There may then seem only one place left to look, and that is in the moral considerations themselves—whether 'in their form or content' (152–4). Indeed support accrues to this third suggestion from the common opinion that everyone has reason to act morally 'whatever their interests and desires' (152; 153; 158; 160; 163; 173)—that everyone simply ought, or has a duty, to act morally. But this tack is, Middle Foot argues, unsuccessful (e.g. 152–4). It severs any but a merely accidental connection between morality and interest, between the virtues and happiness. And how could something be a reason for any- and everyone *whatever* their interests and desires—that is, in complete isolation from anything at all that they care about? Wouldn't this be to endow it with a magically automatic reason-giving force? And no one, she claims, has as yet 'offered any valid argument for the proposition that moral considerations have an automatic reason-giving force' (156; 152–4). If this is a blind alley, it seems we must perforce 'be prepared to think that moral considerations give reasons for acting morally only in ordinary ways'

---

[7] It may be objected that some feelings of benevolence, such as those between family members or friends, are by nature universal. Early Foot will counter that, even if so, such feelings do not extend towards enough people to give us reason to be *just*; and that as we move to feelings of more comprehensive, even of universal, benevolence, we do so in inverse proportion to the plausibility of supposing such feelings universally possessed (127–8).

(154)—that is, via the 'ordinary' connection with an agent's interests and desires.

But now we are back to the problems of how we can do this compatibly with the second orthodoxy. Given that the just must be ready to go against their own self-interest in the particular case, the interests to which moral considerations speak must, at least sometimes, be, or include, something other than self-interest. Yet making the interest served itself a moral one, in the shape of universal benevolence, ran into a parallel problem over justice. The obvious solution to *this* problem is simply to abandon the *foundational* role accorded benevolence and broaden the kinds of moral ends and interests people may have, by including, alongside those of benevolence or charity, those of liberty and justice. This is indeed what Middle Foot does: we are now to 'allow as ends the things that seem to be ends' (165).[8] But it still leaves the problem of the *universality* of these moral interests. It is on this that the truth of the second orthodoxy may appear now to turn. And just as Early Foot had held that universal benevolence is not universal as an interest, so Middle Foot holds this also of justice (e.g. 152; 166–7; cf. 170; 155). If so, there is no universally shared goal which moral considerations serve, instrumentally or constitutively; so they do not offer reasons to each and every agent, and the second orthodoxy must apparently be given up.

But is this so bad? Middle Foot boldly argues that it is not: rather that

it was possible for someone who did not share standard desires to have no reason to choose the good cars or the good knives, or to choose to be a good rider, a good patient and all the rest. Might it not be the same with good actions and good character traits? (p. xiii; cf. 130 with 'interests' in place of 'desires'; 151; 154)

Moral considerations are thus reasons for those who have 'standard' interests and desires in benevolence and justice, but not for those who do not. If so, moral considerations turn out hypothetical: their force as reasons depends on the agent having the relevant desires or interests. Admittedly those who have such interests 'talk about what things should be done presupposing

[8] 155; 166; 165; 170. The move, reminiscent of Sidgwick, introduces the new problem of adjudicating between benevolence and justice, now viewed as two independent and potentially conflicting interests. But this is a problem within morality, not for morality.

these common aims', and for them 'these things are necessary', but this is so 'only subjectively and conditionally necessary, as Kant would put it' (170). For those whose interests or desires are not furthered by moral considerations there is simply no reason to act morally, and while they cannot escape the charge of villainy[9]—and what should they care!—their faults need not be ones of inconsistency, nor yet of irrationality, where irrational actions 'are those in which a man in some way defeats his own purposes, doing what is calculated to be disadvantageous or to frustrate his ends' (161–2).

The thesis seems refreshingly scandalous, and inimical to morality (130–1; 167; 171; p. xiv). In giving up the universal 'mustness' of moral reasons, don't we lose all sense of security in our society and in ourselves? It now appears mere happenstance that anyone cares about moral matters at all, and nothing guarantees that those of us who at present do happen to care will, if rational, continue to do so (167; 170–1). We cannot view the immoral as necessarily irrational, as defective plants in the human garden, but only as further varieties—ones which, however much the moral may dislike them and seek to weed them out, have interests and desires that are non-standard, or abnormal, in nothing more than a *statistical* sense. It is in fact this very *contingency* in moral, as in all, ends, that Foot urges we must perforce accept (130–1; 167; 170; p. xiv). And it is, she suggests, in part our very fear of accepting it that animates the second orthodoxy and leads us to accord to certain locutions—the moral 'ought'—a universal

---

[9] See 161; 172; cf. 179, and B. Williams, 'Internal and External Reasons', repr. in *Moral Luck* (Cambridge: Cambridge University Press, 1981), 110. Middle Foot distinguishes two uses of 'ought', or 'should', one a reason-giving use, the other a rule-stating use, that states what a certain system, 'game', or point of view, requires. The latter 'ought' is subscripted, or qualified—'ought X-ly'. The former is unsubscripted, or unqualified. This is the 'ought' of practical reason. What one takes to be the conditions for its proper use depends on one's theory of the conditions of practical reasonhood. Foot, holding a Humean theory, takes the proper use of this 'ought' to be desire-dependent, offering a reason only on the 'hypothesis' that the recipient desires the relevant end; if they do not, the 'ought' statement is 'withdrawn' (159), presumably as false. On this view unsubscripted 'oughts' concern only means, and if used to advocate ultimate ends would be senseless (169). By contrast, statements with the systemic, or subscripted, 'ought' are 'non-hypothetical' in that they keep their truth-value quite independently of the agent's actual desires, and thus constitute reasons only for agents who happen to have the goals of the system (or appropriately related systems) as objects of their desire or interest.

reason-giving force that is completely bogus. And because this feeling of morality's special inescapability is so socially useful, society is only too ready to exploit such a usage to inculcate and sustain that feeling (153; cf. 162; 166). Yet individuals, if they reflect, may find they happen to have no interest or desire that is served by moral considerations, and that they are the victims of a fraud (167; 153; 126; 128; 131). Foot would have us avoid such dishonest nostrums for our insecurities. We must face our fears, have 'confidence' in our moral interests (171), and be glad that at least some of us volunteer for that moral army into which Kant would have duty conscript us all (167; 170).[10]

Foot's progress at first glance traces in brilliant miniature the seemingly eternal triangle of modern moral philosophy. Modern teleology (*sic*)—hereafter 'instrumentalism'—attempts to justify moral actions, or being moral, in terms of their instrumental role in securing some supposedly non-moral good, whether the individual's or the common good. Modern deontology standardly and plausibly objects both that instrumentalism has difficulty in making out its case, and that anyway, by providing ulterior motives, it provides the wrong kind of justification for morality.[11] Yet deontology in turn fails to provide anything satisfactory by way of such justification—portentously mouthing that it is one's duty, or obligation, to be moral, without explaining why anyone should *care* about duty in the first place; indeed by its own rubric it cannot do so, for any such explanation would consist precisely in

[10] As with the first orthodoxy, Foot puts Wittgensteinian ideas to work in her attack on this 'mustness' of morality. For a 'mustness' can indicate the grip of a false picture and the wish for a guarantee at once unobtainable and unnecessary. Such insecurity needs dissolution (therapy), not a pseudo-explanatory philosophical theory. But Middle Foot, if anything, underestimates the impact of her naturalism. For example, we think that some ways of bringing up children are correct, and others not so, because we think of the values we strive to instil as correct. And we think that the wicked have not merely rival views of how best to go on—a fact that might lead us to view them as merely in natural competition for *Lebensraum*— but incorrect views. Foot, by contrast, would regard these claims of correctness as either systemic (with a hidden 'morally' before 'correct') or bogus. It is not a matter of correctness, but simply of our—now apparently unjustifiable—'confidence' in our practices in the face of rivals (171), an idea taken up in a big way by Williams in ch. 9 of *Ethics and the Limits of Philosophy* (London: Fontana, 1985). The thesis is terrifying. I believe both Foot and Williams to have misplaced the Wittgensteinian bedrock.

[11] 164–5. This is the import of Kant's example of the honest trader. Cf. Hume's objections to the 'selfish theory', which would deduce morals from self-love (*Enquiry*, v, §§174–8).

providing a motive of the wrong ulterior sort.[12] Humean naturalism steps in to resolve this conflict. The instrumentalist is
right that moral actions are justified in an 'ordinary' way; the
deontologist is right that the justification is not instrumental.
Humans as it happens have basic moral desires and interests, and
this gives them reason to do those things, moral actions, constitutive of the satisfaction of these ends. The price of this resolution,
however, is that there is no ultimate justification for having these
moral ends themselves—no reason why anyone ought to care
about such things (167), and no rational error in not caring. That
is just how we, or some of us, happen to be. Optimists about
human nature will, like Hume, think such interests universal
among humans; the more cautious will, like Middle Foot, be
thankful they are shared by at least some of us.[13]

Such sense as this position of Humean naturalism can give the
second orthodoxy—if it does not reject it as bogus—would make
its truth an empirical or contingent matter of whether everyone
happens to have the relevant moral concerns.[14] For if these ends

[12] Cf. H. A. Prichard, 'Does Moral Philosophy Rest on a Mistake?', *Mind*, 21
(1912); repr. in *Moral Obligation* (Oxford: Oxford University Press, 1949).

[13] Hume's considered view is that, while the feeling of humanity or sympathy
is universal to the human species, so rooted in our nature is it, yet under certain
conditions it may be unactualized or even destroyed. Thus human beings in social
conditions such as savagery lack the opportunity for the enlarged reflections
which provoke such feelings; and individuals in mental and physical conditions
such as derangement and imbecility may have the capacity for the feeling destroyed (*Enquiry*, IX, §223, n. 1; *Treatise* III. i. 2, 474). But he supposes it universal
in healthy humans with well-disposed minds in civilized society. This is
unsurprising given the close tie between the feeling of humanity, or sympathy,
and the emergence of society in that full sense, which affords opportunity for these
enlarged reflections. (Compare Hume here with Aristotle, both as regards humans
generally in bestial conditions and individually in pathological conditions:
Nicomachean Ethics 7. 1 and 7. 5–6.) Early Foot too discounts the mad from counting as relevant exceptions to the universality of self-interest (122). But her 'thousand tough characters' (128) are presented as not necessarily either insane or
savage. However, she says nothing to allay a Humean suspicion that they are the
products of deprived environments or psychopaths of some kind.

[14] There are further issues over what exactly the empirical matter is. For example: (1) does 'everyone' cover past and present and future? Does it cover all times
of each individual's life? (2) Is it a matter of their actual desires, concerns, and
interests, or of those they would have if in possession of full 'factual' information?
And what is that? Is 'full information' relative to a historical time and place? Are
all sciences completable? etc. (3) The empirical facts are facts about how human
beings happen to be. But is this to be understood as contingent facts about the
psychologies of individuals, i.e. about what individuals happen to desire, or as
contingent facts about human nature, about how the human happens to be? These
are very different 'contingencies' (I pursue this elsewhere).

are universal, then moral considerations are necessarily reasons for every agent, on pain of rational error about what constitutively serves one of his ends. Much the same seems true for the instrumentalist, where the contingent matter is whether everyone happens to have the relevant non-moral end that moral action or morality serves. For if this end is universal, then moral considerations are again necessarily reasons for every agent on pain of rational error about what instrumentally serves one of the agent's ends.[15] On both views then the *necessity* of moral considerations being reasons for everyone on pain of rational error is that of means–end error.

If so, neither view captures what, one feels, was the intended thrust of the orthodoxy—the sense that the deontologist seeks to capture in claiming that, as Foot put it, everyone has reason to act morally *whatever their interests and desires*. We feel vaguely that the reason-giving force of morality must surely lie outside the realm of such contingency, that it is not dependent on what desires, interests, and concerns the individual agent merely happens to have (158). That we have this feeling may be conceded, but responded to in the form of a challenge. Both Humean and instrumentalist, it may be said, give the second orthodoxy, whether true or not, at least a readily intelligible sense, according to which its truth depends simply on that of the premises of the contingent universality of the end and of moral considerations non-accidentally serving that end. But if this is not the sense—if the 'ordinary' connection with agents' interests and desires is not to be viewed as the source of morality's universal reason-giving force—it needs must be made clear what is. That is the challenge. And until it is met, so far from the orthodoxy's being true, we do not yet understand its sense, or what would have to hold for it to be true. Yes, it is the expression of our wishful thinking, our anxiety, that

[15] I have in mind a global instrumentalism. This shares with Humean naturalism (and indeed with many deontologists) the assumption that (ultimate) ends are a matter of contingent desire, outside the realm of rational justification, but differs from naturalism in viewing morality as an instrument, not an end. It differs also from moral instrumentalism—the specific claim that morality is an instrument, but which leaves open the possibility that the non-moral end morality serves may be itself rationally necessary, i.e. one that an agent would be irrational not to have. Foot seems at one point to suppose this with prudence or self-interest (cf. J. McDowell, 'Are Moral Requirements Hypothetical Imperatives?', *Proceedings of the Aristotelian Society*, supp. vol., 52 (1978), 13–29. See further my n. 36.) This latter view too is open to the charge of providing the wrong justification for morality.

morality be somehow specially inescapable—but the intelligibility of this 'how', this special connection between morality and reason, remains completely obscure, and thus what exactly it could be that is being asserted.

I wish to pick up this challenge, though not as a deontologist.[16] I argue that the journey of Early and Middle Foot is dogged by a failure to attend to a very different conception of practical reason, the traditional one of Plato, Aristotle, and Aquinas. According to the traditional conception, the ordinary connection that makes something into a reason for an agent is not a connection with his desires or interests, but with the practicable good—with what the agent must do to be acting well—and this is generally independent of an individual's actual desires (though not in the way an intuitionist would have us suppose). In short, it is a good-dependent conception as against a desire-dependent one. It is, moreover, in this direction that Recent Foot has been moving, and I think rightly. I aim to articulate enough of this alternative conception to begin to make clear what *sense* it gives to the second orthodoxy. But although I believe the second orthodoxy, so understood, to be true, I shall not argue for this.

2. Early Foot: Self-Interest and the Instrumentalist Defence

2.1. *Clarification of the Second Orthodoxy*

Let us start again with Foot's original argument for the rationality of morality. Early Foot infers this second orthodoxy (henceforth 'O2') from two premises:

(P1) There is at least one (and perhaps only one) universally held end, *E*.

---

[16] The challenge is reminiscent of Hume on cause (*Enquiry Concerning Human Understanding*). This is not to say Foot is right and one should be put off exploring the deontological alternative. See e.g. C. Korsgaard, 'Skepticism about Practical Reason', *Journal of Philosophy*, 83/1 (1986), 5–25. There are important issues over how far a subtle deontologist may approach or mimic the traditional theory; or whether indeed they can be viewed as offering an even more abstract schema for a conception of practical reason, within whose terms the traditional conception is merely a specific version. However *in so far* as it is characteristic of a deontologist (1) to locate rational errors in irrationality, and (2) to view irrationality simply in terms of some kind of inconsistency, the outlook for such a view is not good.

(P2) The virtues, or their exercise (i.e. acting virtuously), are necessarily connected with, or serve, *E*.

This is schematic in leaving *E* unspecified and in using 'serve' to cover constitutive as well as instrumental relations. The defence poses several questions. The most important for our purposes concerns its principle of inference and Foot's commitment to a Humean conception of practical rationality. I consider this in Section 3.

Two brief comments. First, why demand a universally held end in P1? Granted P2 and the principle of inference, P1 certainly suffices for the conclusion, but all that seems necessary is a universal *spread* of ends each of which the virtues necessarily serve— i.e. that all have some end that the virtues serve, not that there be at least one such end that all have. Second, P2 is a modal claim, to the effect that the connection between the virtues and the end they promote should be non-accidental. Presumably the grounds of such non-accidentality differ according to whether the connection is instrumental or constitutive. But the point of claiming it at all needs some explanation (I suspect Foot's reason is connected to the 'interior' strategy I attribute to her in Section 2.6).

But what exactly is O2, the thesis being argued for? As perhaps already apparent from Section 1, Foot's formulations of O2 are opaque. The following remarks, perforce somewhat telegraphic and stipulative, must suffice. First, I doubt whether O2 expresses an orthodoxy common to Foot and her deontological opponent; as hinted in Section 1, I suspect that Foot's 'defence' of O2 takes the form of a reinterpretation of it. O2 is a modal claim. One formulation claims that moral judgements necessarily give reasons to each and every man.[17] I suspect that for Foot's deontological opponent this necessity is supposed conceptual, or essentialist—springing from the concept, or nature, of moral judgement. It is of the very nature, or conception, of a moral judgement that it gives a reason: being a moral judgement it thus 'automatically' gives a reason. (It is by means of such a conceptual or essentialist connection that the deontologist ensures the satisfaction of a commonly alleged requirement that morality be practical, where a Humean would look for an empirical connection).

---

[17] Foot omits the modal word in O2 at least once (130); but that passage can still be read with the modal force.

By contrast, for Foot, I think the necessity, if it is not simply a necessity of entailment that has crept in, is best viewed as a rational necessity: the agent *has* to find C a reason, *on pain of rational error*. (This also suits O2's other formulation, that 'no one can be indifferent to morality without error'). The talk of 'judgements' too is opaque. The deontologist's concern may seem to be with an agent's actually making (and receiving?) a moral judgement—that anyone *doing* this is thereby given a reason. This invites queries about people who refuse to employ moral concepts (cf. 126), and about whether there can be incorrect moral judgements, and if not why not (which leads on to questions about how 'moral' is being defined). For Foot, by contrast, the gloss given 'moral judgements' seems, as with 'Fregean thoughts', to be the content, indeed the content of any moral judging that would be true—and so, in other words, with moral considerations or moral facts. (Such facts as that φ'ing is the moral or virtuous thing for the agent to do, or is what virtue requires of them.) So for Foot I take O2 to unpack as the double claim that (1) moral considerations satisfy the conditions for *being* reasons in the case of each and every agent, and (2) thus any rational agent must take or accept them as such, on pain of being in some (possibly nonculpable) rational error. The necessity in question thus springs from moral considerations actually being *reasons*, and not from the considerations' nature as moral ones (though this may explain why they are reasons, depending on one's theory of practical reasonhood).

Second, the argument's aim is not to justify the thesis that for every action (or omission) that the virtuous person would do (or that is required by virtue or morality), there also happens to be some other non-moral, e.g. prudential, reason to do it—something that might be thought securable by the imposition of sufficient, strategically placed, external sanctions. Nor is it to show there is some other, e.g. prudential, reason to *appear* to do what the virtuous do *as* they do it, that is, from virtuous motives—something for which the external rewards of virtue might give everyone a reason. An agent who acted for such reasons would not count as virtuous, nor be acting virtuously. As Foot herself notes, morality 'concerns itself with a man's reasons for acting as well as with what he does' (164); to act simply from ulterior motives undercuts its counting as virtuous (Early Foot 129;

Middle Foot 154, 164–5). To count as virtuous, or as acting virtuously, one must do moral actions for their own sake, and not
solely for some ulterior motive (cf. Aristotle, *Nicomachean Ethics* 2.
4). This too is the import of Kant's example of the 'honest' trader.
So, although the success, and even the coherence, of Early Foot's
instrumentalist project may be queried, the thesis to be justified is
indeed that there is prudential (or *E*) reason actually to *be virtuous*,
and to *act virtuously*.[18]

Third, Foot gives two versions of O2:

(O2A) Everyone has got to find considerations of morality or
virtue reasons: these must, of rational necessity, engage
the will;

(O2B) Everyone has got to be virtuous or moral: virtue and
morality must engage the will.[19]

She apparently treats these as equivalent, and initially they may
seem so. If someone must have moral concerns on pain of rational
error (i.e. O2B), then it may seem they must find considerations
that speak to those concerns, i.e. moral considerations, reasons, on
pain of rational error (i.e. O2A). Anyone denying these were
reasons would seem in rational error (perhaps non-culpable
ignorance) over constitutive means to an end they either have or
at least ought to have. And conversely, in the light of the second
clarification above, it may seem that the sense in which moral
considerations must be reasons (O2A) *requires* that the agent be
moral or virtuous (for the agent to find 'that's just' the moral
reason it is, he must view its reason-giving force as stemming
from his concern, or rational need, to be just, and not from some
other concern). However, even if this latter is roughly correct, it
does not amount to the claim that O2A implies O2B. Indeed the
latter implication is false, at least under a Humean conception of
practical reason. For O2A would be true simply if everyone *happened* to have moral ends. But the simple happenstance universality of moral ends obviously does not suffice for the truth of

[18] Cf. G. Kavka, 'The Reconciliation Project', in D. Copp and D. Zimmerman
(eds.), *Morality, Reason and Truth* (Totowa, NJ: Rowman & Allanheld, 1985), 298.

[19] O2A: 'moral judgements necessarily give reasons to each and every man' (p.
xiii; 130). O2B: 'each man necessarily has reason to be just' (p. xiv; 127) (and to be
virtuous generally: cf. 166; 170); 'every man must have reason to act morally' (p.
xiii); 'no-one can be indifferent to morality without error' (p. xiv), i.e. all ought to
have morality as a concern.

O2B. Moral ends may be universal without there being any 'ought' about it. O2B requires that morality—having moral concerns—*ought* to be universal, i.e. that it is rationally necessary. So O2A can be true and O2B not.[20]

If morality, or being virtuous (having virtuous concerns) is to be rationally necessary as O2B requires, then either (1) it is rationally necessary *per se* ('for itself', or 'as an end' as a non-deontologist would say), or else (2) it is instrumentally related to some other non-moral end (or spread of ends), and it is this end that is either rationally necessary *per se* or else simply universal (setting aside possible complexities about this further end). So O2B requires either (*a*) the notion of rational necessity *per se* ('of ends', whether moral or non-moral), or else that (*b*) morality—having moral concerns—can itself be instrumentally justified in terms of some universally possessed non-moral end (or spread of ends). Those embracing a Humean conception of practical reason abjure (*a*). Their defence of O2B is then perforce the instrumentalist (*b*). This faces at least two problems: the logical problem of how an instrumentalist defence of an end *qua* end is even possible, and the problem of how such a justification, if possible, could be relevant or appropriate. Faced with these, a clear-thinking Humean naturalist might well wish to distinguish O2A very clearly from O2B, to abandon O2B, and to rest the case for O2A simply on the happenstance universality of moral ends (in effect the position described in Section 1).

---

[20] i.e. two conditions independently suffice for the truth of O2A: C1, that moral concerns, or ends, are universal; C2, that moral concerns ought to be universal (i.e. O2B). C1 is consistent with the falsity of C2, and so the truth of O2A with the falsity of O2B. The non-equivalence escapes both Early and Middle Foot. One reason may be that both suppose moral ends evidently not universal. For under this empirical assumption about the falsity of C1, it can seem that C2 is not only sufficient but necessary for O2A. If so, equivalence is restored. Another reason may be that Foot is focused on a deontological opponent. Given our second point of clarification, the crude deontologist too accepts that the object of justification is acting virtuously, and not for ulterior motives. But they do not construe acting virtuously as acting for morality as an *end*: for then they would consider it an empirical, or 'arbitrary', matter whether everyone has it. Being moral is for them rather a matter of abiding by moral rules, or being so disposed. If so, there may seem no great difference between O2A and O2B—between reason's demanding that the deliverances of a rule weigh with you, and its demanding that you be so disposed for them to weigh with you.

2.2. Early Foot's Version of the Argument in Terms of Self-Interest

So much by way of general clarification. Early Foot in defending O2 takes this to involve defending O2B, and clearly pursues the instrumentalist option, (b) above. Self-interest is offered as an end that is plausibly universal and non-moral; and it is this which, Foot argues, being virtuous instrumentally serves.[21] The attraction of such an instrumental justification is severalfold. It speaks to the feeling that morality must somehow tie up with human good and harm, or at least with what individuals actually want and care about (p. xii); morality cannot be left free-floating, as a kind of magic force or an irrelevance. It speaks also to the more particular feeling that the questions 'why want that?' or 'what's the good of it?', asked of morality, make sense and demand an answer, in a way that they may seem not to with pursuing pleasure or avoiding boredom, pain, etc. (cf. 126–7): morality after all is not obviously something everybody wants or cares about. Finally, in appealing to self-interest, it appeals to something that appears unproblematic and uncontroversially desirable—uncontroversial precisely because all parties to the dispute, moral and amoral alike, plausibly acknowledge self-interest as among the things they want or care about. No one is puzzled by it, because all have it as a concern. And so, if the requisite connection can be made out between it and morality, it can be used in a seemingly clear, Archimedean way to lever everyone into taking some heed of moral considerations, on pain of means–end irrationality.

2.3. Two Immediate Difficulties

Foot's argument, however, faces considerable difficulties. For a start, she defends P2 by arguing for a necessary instrumental

---

[21] Foot's instrumentalist justification is individualist, not social: the end served by moral considerations is each agent's own (non-moral) good, and not the common (non-moral) good. But Early Foot is no psychological egoist (127; 156; p. xiii). Reasons of self-interest are not the only reasons: e.g. many have benevolent interests, both local and extended (127–8; cf. 156). But, if one grants the argument's need for an interest that can be universally appealed to, even in the case of 'a thousand tough characters' (128), then that must be non-moral, and the only plausible common denominator is, she thinks, self-interest. So if morality must afford reasons to all, the justification must be egoist—in terms of 'individual utility maximization' (David Gauthier *Moral Dealing* (Ithaca, NY: Cornell University Press, 1990), 209).

connection between the four cardinal virtues and self-interest. And she is prepared to drop justice as a virtue if it fails to have this connection (125; p. xiii). But this makes it look as though the connection is being taken as criterial for, or even constitutive of, being a virtue. If so, P2 risks being no longer open to counter-example: any 'virtue' failing here can be dismissed as thereby not really a virtue. So, for Foot's argument to be substantial, we need to be assured that the virtues are not already surreptitiously defined in terms of the connection Foot is arguing for—but this is precisely what is threatened by her preparedness to abandon justice's claim to virtue.

Again in arguing the connection between self-interest and the particular virtue of prudence, she says only: 'obviously any man needs prudence' (123; 125). But prudence, as a *cardinal* virtue, is traditionally the virtue, or excellence, of practical reason—practical wisdom. If so, its nature is a function of how practical reason is conceived. And on the traditional conception of Plato and Aristotle, this excellence involves having correct ends as well as correct means. But if so, it is *not* obvious that prudence always promotes the agent's self-interest, since this, at least in the non-moral way Foot conceives of it, is not obviously always the wise end. On a Humean conception, by contrast, the excellence consists more narrowly in excellently working out means to ends not determined, or assessable, by reason. If so, then, given that self-interest is a universal end, the connection of prudence with self-interest will seem obvious. For the promotion of virtually any end, including wicked ones, needs prudence so conceived. But now it is not *obvious* why prudence so conceived should be regarded as a moral virtue, let alone a cardinal one. It seems simply an executive ability, the talent of 'fixing'—something in virtue of which Aristotle would call an agent 'smart' rather than 'wise', a natural virtue at best.[22] Moreover, what connection is there between prudence and the prudential? If prudence works out means, instrumental or constitutive, to the agent's own self-interest, and the latter is a non-moral end, once again it is unclear why prudence is so obviously a moral virtue (or else why self-interest is non-moral).

---

[22] Hume's answer is that prudence has the quality of being useful to self, which, on his theory, is one of the four general moral qualities (cf. *Enquiry Concerning the Principles of Morals*, VI, esp. §§199, 198).

2.4. Major Difficulty 1: The Moral–Prudential Distinction

There are further major problems. First, as just intimated, the very notion of self-interest is unclear in Foot, as in many others.[23] She talks variously, but apparently equivalently, of a man's 'advantage' (129; p. xiv; cf. 125), of what is 'profitable' to him (125; 126; 129), of 'well-being' (p. xiii), of 'what a man wants' (127), and of 'happiness' (p. xiv; 154). As I understand her, self-interest is (1) plausibly a *universal* object of interest. It is (2) *selfish*, comprised of concerns that are prudential in some Kantian contrast with moral ones: it is after all supposedly an interest that all, even the amoral, have, so that if morality can be shown to serve it, the amoral will stand convicted of error in their means–end reasoning. Moreover, given it is universal, this selfish interest must be (3) *general*: that is, it cannot include any interest or desire that is idiosyncratic, or culturally parochial (p. xiii).

Now there are two ways to understand this—both problematic. On the first, such general self-interest would consist in those rather general things that anyone, moral and amoral alike, would arguably need for any idiosyncratic project—things such as basic well-being (e.g. health), and freedom from injury, and from 'boredom, loneliness, pain, discomfort and certain kinds of incapacity' (127). Such seems, at times, Foot's view (e.g. p. xiii). But self-interest so conceived comprises the necessary conditions for an agent's happiness rather than that happiness itself. For it is surely in the satisfaction of an agent's own, often idiosyncratic or parochial, concerns that his happiness might be thought rather to reside. Moreover, general self-interest understood this way no longer looks like an ultimate end at all: each individual has *reason* to have such self-interest, because, and perhaps only because, it serves the idiosyncratic projects that comprise his indi-

---

[23] Self-interest is contrasted sometimes (1) with 'enlightened' self-interest, the contrast being between a so-called pathological mode of interest and a rational one (e.g. Kurt Baier, *The Moral Point of View*, abridged edn. (New York: Random House, 1965), ch. 5 sect. 3). Living *kata pathos* one follows the self-interest of the moment; living *kata prohairesin* one plans to maximize the attainment of self-interest over a lifetime. This may require one to resist an immediate satisfaction in return for a greater one later, and thus require quasi-virtues. (2) Self-interest is sometimes conceived narrowly as comprised of selfish, or self-directed desires, and sometimes broadly as comprised of all the interests that the self in question has (cf. Gauthier, *Moral Dealing*, 220). Here the contrast with the moral becomes progressively obscure.

vidual happiness. (Indeed its position seems little different from that of certain moral factors that are equally plausibly in the set of such necessary conditions, like liberty and friendship, and not obviously something in terms of which the latter are to be justified.)

Perhaps then we should understand this general self-interest differently, as the *form*, but not the material content, of idiosyncratic interests. That is, it is at least part of each persons' self-interest to satisfy his own particular, or parochial, 'non-moral' interests whatever these happen to be (folk-dancing, gambling, helping others, or killing them). But understood this way, why regard self-interest as selfish as against moral? For many individuals, though indeed perhaps not for all, the material idiosyncratic constituents of their happiness include 'moral' concerns, such as the more or less extended care for the welfare of other humans, as a substantial part.[24] And there is in any case nothing obviously amoral about some concern with oneself. So, while more needs saying, I do not find the supposed distinction between morality and prudence clearly articulated in Foot, nor in fact see any reason to suppose 'it' even can be (especially when deprived of the thesis of hedonism which might have given it some sense). This problem equally affects the correlative notion of 'moral'.

2.5. Major Difficulty 2: The Particular Case Problem

The second major difficulty arises over the 'particular case'. For an instrumental justification even to seem initially plausible, morality must at least have some *general*, or 'for the most part', instrumental connection with the candidate end, *E*, in the statisti-

[24] That is, happiness may be allowed to extend beyond crude self-interest, so that, for those with moral ends, the satisfaction of these ends, in acting virtuously, is constitutive of their happiness. (The connection may be psychological—acting virtuously becoming *associated* with the agent's happiness, as Hume and Mill suggest; or it may be logical or internal.) But in fact both Early, and more surprisingly Middle, Foot persevere in the Kantianesque split of prudential and moral, and the identification of happiness with the satisfaction purely of prudential interests. Middle, more explicitly than Early, Foot, allows that some humans have moral concerns as ends; but they have them not as *part* of their happiness, but as another independent basic interest alongside a basic interest in their own 'nonmoral' happiness. These are, for her, two independent sources of reason for those with these interests.

cal sense of promoting E in the majority of cases. But even so, as we saw with Hume over justice, there remains an apparent problem with the particular case. For to count as possessing some, or perhaps any, virtue, it may be that one is required by that virtue to sacrifice the advancement or attainment of E on some particular occasion (or even merely required to be so disposed should such a case arise). But if so, the justification for being virtuous that E provides in general seems lacking in the particular case. The source of the problem seems to lie in instrumentalism's foundationalist structure: for the 'particular case' problem arises whether one is trying to justify all the virtues in terms of some non-moral E like self-interest, or the other virtues in terms of some prime one like benevolence. The instrumental justification of morality in terms of individual self-interest faces then, over each virtue, the question 'who benefits?' (125; 123), and, for P2 to be true, each and every exercise of virtue (potential as well as actual) must, it seems, promote the self-interest of its possessor (whether or not it also benefits others). But how can this be true of justice? For, as Early Foot says, to count as just one has to be prepared 'in the event of very evil circumstances, even to face death rather than act unjustly'.[25]

By her own account, it was this problem over justice that led Middle Foot to suppose her earlier instrumentalist defence of O2

[25] Foot 129. Kavka rightly points out that 'in a substantial number of cases the sacrifice of one's life for moral ends may be consistent with the requirements of prudence because it constitutes the lesser of two extreme personal evils' ('The Reconciliation Project', 308), but, as he also says, this need not always be the case. Early Foot, however, mistook the extension of the particular case problem. P2 is in difficulty over any virtue that is either wholly directed to the good (or self-interest) of others, or that encompasses particular occasions where, of its nature, it requires the agent to sacrifice their own self-interest. Early Foot supposes justice alone of the cardinal virtues faced the problem (125). But courage equally requires a person to be ready to run the risk of sacrificing, and so, it may be, actually to sacrifice, their own self-interest: taking a reasonable risk to save a child drowning. Foot concedes that courage may be the cause of (possibly foreseen) 'incidental' harm to the agent (125). But it is unclear exactly why the incidental nature of such harm evades the particular case problem. Moreover, it is unconvincing to claim, as Foot does (125), that all such harm as may accrue to the agent in the other virtues is merely incidental: the soldier saving comrades by taking the blast of a grenade. Nor is the problem confined to cardinal virtues. People may act for reasons of benevolence, as Early Foot allows (127). Such considerations are not a matter of the agent's self-interest, but may be to their considerable disadvantage—and any benefit to their self-interest would be incidental (165). So benevolence, or charity, is at least as problematic as justice, as Middle Foot later acknowledged (154; 3; 165). Further consideration may reveal that all virtues face this problem.

could not be sustained, and hence to abandon O2 (p. xiii). She no longer felt she had to say 'that justice and advantage coincide, because I no longer think that each man, whatever his desires and whatever his situation, necessarily has reason to be just' (p. xiv; cf. 130–1).[26] But Early Foot had already acknowledged the particular case problem for justice (129). So why didn't *she* abandon O2? It is not enough to say: rather than that Early Foot would have given up justice as a virtue. For she didn't think that necessary. Instead she claimed to have a solution, one reminiscent of Hume's.[27] The mistake is to 'consider in isolation particular just acts'—in isolation, that is, from the practice, or disposition, of which they are an expression. A man 'could not have it both ways and while possessing the virtue of justice hold himself ready to be unjust should any great advantage accrue' (129). Dub this 'the generality defence'. In other words we must take seriously our earlier point that the object of prudential justification is being just and acting justly. And to count as just, one cannot be ready to 'take advantage of all the exceptions': that would show one hadn't really been just after all. So if a prudential justification can be given for being just, it is a justification for a practice or disposition that in principle already incorporates within it an element of prudential risk.[28] That it does so has already been taken into account in the justification of it as the character trait it is prudentially best to have as against other ones (which, it will be claimed, incorporate

[26] The remark is puzzling, since Early Foot never did think each man had reason to be just *whatever his desires*. That is the position of her deontologist.

[27] Hume, *Enquiry*, app. III, §§256–7.

[28] One will run some risk of paying a huge prudential price. But this doesn't mean prudential justification is impossible. Thus one may find mountaineering, or being a stuntman, athlete, or dancer, either themselves so engrossing or else prudentially rewarding in other ways, or both, that the *deformation professionelle* is worth enduring, and the risks inherent in the activities worth running. There is a reasonable enough expectation that the situations calling for these costs to be paid won't arise, or at least not in an extreme form. One may be unlucky (which is not to say the costs are 'incidental' to the activity). But that's life—no free lunch. So too with justice and perhaps the other virtues. Your being just may end in prudential disaster, but the adoption of no alternative policy would have been reasonable: there are no grounds for expecting any other policy to pay as well. The point could be made by asking after the supposed 'general' connection between virtues and *E*, or after Hume's 'general rule'. Is this a statistical remark? Or is it a claim about virtue as itself something essentially general (a disposition or practice): its *tendency* must be to serve *E*? The latter is compatible with its inherently inhibiting the pursuit of *E*, or disserving *E*, in particular circumstances; and with its accidentally not paying off as a 'policy' in the case of some, even all, individuals.

greater prudential risks). So justice, and the other virtues, can still be prudentially good bets, despite their prudential risk.

The original problem was that there are particular actions which, while required by virtue *V*, do not serve *E*, and are thus counter-examples to P2. For these to be counter-examples, P2's 'necessary connection' must be understood as:

(NC1) For there to be a necessary connection between a virtue *V* and *E*, that virtue must not, of its nature, or in principle, *ever* require the agent to go against *E*, not even in a particular, even 'exceptional', case.[29]

But the generality defence in effect reinterprets this connection in P2 as:

(NC2) For there to be a necessary connection between a virtue *V* and happiness, the practice of that virtue need not necessarily redound to the agent's benefit in every particular case, nor indeed overall in the agent's life, but it must, as things are, be the best bet for maximizing the agent's overall self-interest (a better bet than not having the virtue).

That is, given what justice is and the facts of human existence, the chances are that a life of injustice will not redound to your self-interest—and if this happens sometimes, it is an accident. It would be unreasonable to bank on it. For it is the practice of justice that is 'for the most part' connected with self-interest, in the non-statistical and normative sense that it is its essential tendency so to promote self-interest (or more so than any rival policies).

This latter instrumentalist project is a very different one: acts that are required by virtue *V* but do not serve *E* are no longer immediate counter-examples to P2. Foot, I believe, is confused here. For Middle Foot apparently abandons her earlier instrumentalist defence of justice on the grounds that justice fails NC1 (p. xiii).[30] But the earlier defence had been in terms of NC2. And

[29] More strictly, acting virtuously must on each occasion benefit its possessor more than any act other than the virtuous one—whether that of the corresponding vice, or indeed any other possible act. For the differential in benefit could count as 'loss' to the agent's self-interest.

[30] The connection between virtue and happiness (the agent's self-interest) is now held to be not 'necessary', but merely 'general', or 'close' (154; p. xiv; 80).

Middle Foot doesn't argue that *this* defence fails: indeed perhaps she even thinks it succeeds (3). Moreover, Middle Foot explicitly allows that the subscripted claim that 'you ought$_{\text{prudentially}}$ to have moral ends, to be virtuous' makes sense (169). And, for all that she says, it remains quite possibly true under NC2. Of course, for Middle Foot, this gives everyone a reason to be moral only if all desire the goal of the prudential system, self-interest. But Early Foot supposed that all do, and there is no sign that Middle Foot disagrees. If so, O2 *may* still be true, at least in the sense Early Foot attached to it: that anyone denying he has some reason to be virtuous and to act virtuously will, as things are, be mistaken in his means–end reasoning. So, *pace* pp. xiii–xiv, Middle Foot does not really give up O2. What she gives up is the claim that it is necessary to show that it holds. She is now prepared to accept, and not be frightened by, the possibility that it does not, and that, to the contrary, not everyone has reason to be moral—and to go on from there; Early Foot, like the deontologists, was not. But Middle Foot nowhere argues that this possibility is in fact realized and that her earlier generality defence is wrong; nor, in particular, does she question whether such a justification, were it forthcoming, would be an appropriate one.

2.6. *Major Difficulty 3: Problems for the Generality Defence*

However, the generality defence itself faces considerable difficulties, especially when the justifying base is the narrow one of self-interest. Many of these are familiar from disputes between rule and act utilitarianism, where social utility maximization takes the place of our instrumentalist's individual utility maximization, *re* the same non-moral utility (cf. Section 1). Thus it may be directly challenged whether the virtues are the prudentially good bets the defence claims. Other variant practices, or dispositions, may tend to a higher prudential yield. And even if some have higher risks, they may promise higher yields, and it is not obviously a rational error to opt for a high-risk strategy.

What seems denied is NC1. It is unclear whether the new 'general' connection is merely statistical (cf. 'co-incide', p. xiv), or a remark about a tendency. If the latter, the position is virtually that of Early Foot's NC2. (The point is unclear partly because it is unclear whether the contingencies on which the connection depends are supposed those of individuals' circumstances or of humanity's.)

Indeed it may be argued, mimicking an act utilitarian, that that disposition whose only principle is simply to hug the contours of prudential utility (or E) as close as possible is thereby guaranteed to secure the prudential (or E) justification. Moreover, it can be doubted whether the best prudential bet is the same for all: the strong may be prudentially better off with different dispositions than the weak, the clever than the stupid. Again there are difficulties when the facts determining the best bet include facts about how many others will, or are likely to, have the same dispositions or engage in the same practices: perhaps it is prudentially worth being just only when many others are, or, conversely, perhaps that is the very point at which to free-ride.

Again, while obligations may reach out into the future, how can the rationality of fulfilling them do so, and not become mere rule worship or blind conventionality? At t_1 policy A with its attendant risks may be a better bet than B, given the general facts of the human condition; but when at t_n that risk is realized, how can past commitment make it rational for someone caught in those particular circumstances and whose motive is self-interest now to pay the debt, or keep the promise? Appeal can be made to the benefits to his self-interest derived from the existence of the practice, and the dangers of undermining it. But for a specific agent *in extremis* how can these be guaranteed to outweigh those deriving from reneging on his commitments? Indeed the very need for, and presence of, external sanctions at such points testify to the vulnerability of the connection with self-interest, which these sanctions attempt to bolster and manipulate. And if a self-interested agent can see this, how can it be possible, let alone rational, for him sincerely to continue in his allegiance or even to make the initial commitments?

Finally, even with the generality defence, our instrumentalist is in trouble. For, as said earlier, it is problematic whether the strategy of providing an instrumental justification for an end *qua* end—and in particular for morality and being virtuous—is coherent, and, if so, whether it yields the appropriate justification for morality. What is to be shown is not that something is both an end and also a means to a further end; but that the pursuit of some end is itself justified as a means to a further end. And for a Humean who supposes that there are ends and means and no *tertium quid*, and that an end is something ultimate which cannot be justified, such a task seems logically impossible. Further it is sometimes objected that any attempt to justify morality will either be obviously circular, if the reason given is in terms of a moral end, or else irrelevant, if it is in terms of a non-moral end such as self-interest is supposed to be. Our naturalist concedes there is no justification; our deontologist argues that morality is not to be justified in terms of its relation to ends at all, but in terms of the formal constraints of 'pure' reason. Our instrumentalist, embracing the dilemma's second horn, must find a way to solve the logical problem while evading the charge of irrelevancy. Now, as we said, this instrumentalist project is not the crude one of finding any old instrumental reason to do what the virtuous do; but to justify doing what they do for the reasons they do it, that is, as an end in itself—'because it is the virtuous thing to do'. The crude instrumentalist justification is irrelevant because not addressed to the right object. But that the object of justification is the end of being virtuous serves only to emphasize the logical problem of giving an instrumental justification for an end.

If we assume the questionable distinction between morality and prudence, there are two main ways to try and carry out the project. These differ over whether the alleged prudential connection with virtue must be *transparent* to the virtuous as such, usable by them, indeed a central part of their ordinary justification for acting virtuously, or whether it must be *opaque* to the virtuous as such, representing 'a thought too many' for virtue, and so if not actually hidden from them then one that is viewed as irrelevant by them, *qua* virtuous. The first, adopted by Early Foot, demands that the prudential connection be shown to be interior to a virtue: that a virtue, being what it is and given the conditions of human life, of its nature instrumentally promotes the agent's (non-moral) self-interest. If so, to act justly in order to secure one's self-interest is not to act for an ulterior motive but out of a proper understanding of justice. The second demands that morality be mistaken as end if it is to fulfil its real function as means. Morality's real prudential justification needs not to be available to the virtuous as such. This requires a distinction between justification *within* a practice and *of* a practice, between how things strike us from within a practice (in the street), and how they seem when reason reflects on them from outside (in the study). On some versions the trick is turned by social and cultural conditioning; in others by nature and evolution. (Thus Humean naturalism and instrumentalism may combine. Nature has made us creatures with moral ends and feelings, whether we take these as constitutive of our happiness, or as a separate basic interest; reason reveals to us nature's secret instrumentalist purpose in doing so—that having such altruistic, or co-operative, concerns tends to serve each individual's self-interest better than if all were by nature to pursue only their own crude self-interest.) Whether reflection can free us from, or undermine, practice, or whether it is somehow insulated, is then a pressing question for such theories. But neither the first, nor the second, strategy is, I believe, convincing.

2.7. Conclusion

The issues above are complex, and it is unlikely that all, or any, can be satisfactorily resolved within the confines of a prudential justification—not least because of uncertainty about what that is (cf. Section 2.4). But they are not my basic concern. For *even if* morality could be shown to serve some non-moral end that is universally wanted, this fact would, I hold, be neither necessary nor sufficient to establish its rationality—not even to show that there is *a* reason for everyone to be virtuous. The whole viability of this kind of instrumentalist justification hangs on some Humean conception of practical reason, and this is a thin thread.[31] But isn't it now I who am making scandalous claims? Even Korsgaard, not exactly a friend to Humeans, concedes, I think *in propria voce*, as regards the sufficiency that: 'the consideration that such and such action is a means to getting what you want has a clear motivational source; so no one doubts that this is a reason'.[32] But I do so doubt.

3. The End-Relative Account, and Foot's Fork: Early Foot and Middle Foot

O2 claims that each person must be virtuous and have moral concerns, and/or must find moral considerations reason-giving.

---

[31] Kavka ('The Reconciliation Project', 315, and his n. 31) agrees in the fundamental *role* played by this assumption about the nature of practical rationality in this kind of instrumentalist project. But he finds the assumption itself plausible.

[32] Korsgaard, 'Skepticism about Practical Reason', 11.

The 'must', we are supposing, is that of rational necessity: that is, each person has to, or ought to, do so on pain of rational error. But what is the range of error here? Interpretations of O2 will differ according to the range they envisage. And this is a function of the interpreter's conception of practical reasonhood—of the conditions which constitute a consideration's being, and not being, a reason for an agent. For instance, if deontologists suppose ends are a matter of an agent's contingent desires, and take O2 to claim that moral considerations necessarily give everyone a reason whatever their ends, then they must employ a conception of practical reasonhood which characterizes the mistake of someone who is indifferent to morality as neither means error nor end error. (A favoured candidate is some form of inconsistency.[33])

So what is Foot's conception of practical reasonhood? That Early prefigures Middle Foot in assuming some Humean conception is evident when we ask after the principle of inference in her argument for O2. She argues for O2 on the basis of:

($P1_{si}$) Self-interest is at least a, and perhaps the only, universal end.

($P2_{si}$) Morality—being virtuous and acting virtuously—is necessarily connected with self-interest: it instrumentally promotes it.

What evidently follows from $P1_{si}$ and $P2_{si}$ is:

Morality non-accidentally serves an end, self-interest, that everyone happens to have.

But this, like its premises, says nothing about reasons. To infer O2 Foot needs the following principle of inference, understood as a constitutive principle of practical reasonhood:

(S) If agent A has some end (concern, interest, or desire) that consideration C non-accidentally serves, then C is a reason for A (or gives A a reason).

For then by $P1_{si}$ everyone has self-interest as an end, and by $P2_{si}$ this is served by moral concerns or considerations, and so by (S)

---

[33] Cf. 161–2; 152. If it is a 'logical' inconsistency, then this seems more a mistake of theoretical, than practical, rationality. If so, the deontologist risks losing any conception of practical rationality—much as the purely naturalistic exponent of ER does (see below). But perhaps the inconsistency is a 'practical' one.

the latter just are reasons for everyone, and any indifference to them an error of one kind or another.

For (S) to be such a constitutive principle, Foot needs to, and apparently does, hold the converse of (S), namely,

> (N) If C is a reason for agent A, then A has some end, or concern, that C serves.[34]

(S) and (N) together constitute a conception of practical reasonhood, which promises to explain in an intuitively appealing way the interdependent puzzles of why and when something is a reason for an agent, and of why and when it is not. Dub this the 'end-relative' (ER) account:

> (ER) A consideration, or type of consideration, C, is a practical reason for an agent A if, and only if, and because, it non-accidentally connects with, or serves, instrumentally or constitutively, something the individual agent happens to care about or value.[35]

ER's appeal lies partly in its own apparent obviousness, but partly in the mysteriousness of the only apparent alternative, the deontologist's. Suppose a consideration, or type of consideration, C, is taken to constitute a reason for acting for an agent: that in the light of C, he ought to, or should, φ. For example: 'you ought to drive: that's the quickest way to London', or 'you ought not to tease: that is unkind' ('because' could replace the colon). There seems a question of the *source* of the reason-giving force of the considerations, of the *logoi*, given for the 'oughts': in virtue of what are these *logoi* reasons for the agent? What makes them into reasons, or have the force of reasons? Here we seem to find a dilemma:

> *Foot's Fork*: What makes considerations reasons for an agent is *either*, as ER claims, their connection with some interest or

[34] Foot's commitment to both (S) and (N) is apparent in 'Moral Beliefs', 127: 'In general, anyone is given a reason for acting when he is shown the way to something he wants . . . (i.e. (S)). . . . 'It's unjust' gives a reason *only if* the nature of justice can be shown to be such that it is necessarily connected with what a man wants. (i.e. (N)).' Her commitment is evident also in the logical shape she assumes a defence of O2 must take.

[35] Adherents of ER often concede a certain variety among kinds of desires (appetites, projects, etc.), and tend to view evaluations as one kind of desire among these others, namely one for the good.

desire of the agent; *or else* some automatic reason-giving force that the consideration possesses.

For what *tertium quid* can there be? Yet even the *secundum quid* seems magical: for how can considerations have a genuine reason-giving force for the agent if they are totally unconnected to anything the agent wants or cares about? If so, we must embrace the first horn, ER. The source of the reason-giving force of any consideration must lie in the so-called 'ordinary' connection, instrumental or constitutive, with the individual agent's desires or interests. ER simply spells this out.

The commitment to ER, implicit in Early Foot, is explicit in Middle Foot.[36] She challenges her deontological opponent to produce a sense for the categorical imperative that would be distinctive to morality, showing moral considerations to have a distinctive reason-giving force, irrespective of the agent's desires and interests. For unless that challenge is met, we must, she

---

[36] For example, 'Morality as a System of Hypothetical Imperatives' and 'Reasons for Action and Desires'. Is Middle Foot consistently committed to ER? The postscript to 'Reasons for Action and Desires' (156) stands out: 'I myself incline to the view that all such reasons [namely for acting] depend either on the agent's interests (meaning here what is in his interest) or else on his desires. I take these to be independent sources of reasons for action, so that the fact that a man is indifferent to his future welfare does not destroy the reason he has for paying attention to it, but this particular thesis is not one on which I place any importance' (156; cf. 179). By 'agent's interests' Foot here means what is prudent for the agent (their self-interest, future welfare, health). She says that such things are reasons for agents to act even if they are *indifferent* to them. By 'indifferent' Foot may mean: (1) that the agent has neither interest in nor desire for these things (cf. 172); or (2) she may mean simply that pathological coldness one may have towards one's interests or projects which signifies lack merely of occurrent *desire* or inclination, and not of long-term *interest* (cf. 155; 158). On (1) those who are indifferent to prudential concerns would be mistaken or irrational, and this is a commitment to rational end assessment re prudential goals: they are concerns an agent *ought* to have. (1) is thus inconsistent with Foot's commitment to ER and with her conception of prudence as, like morality, a system (169). (2) is not. Charity favours (2). But Foot tells me that the remark was a recantation over prudential reasons, and an intended step away from Humeanism. The point was not clearly made (the postscript is un-dated, and inconsistent with other added footnotes)—and why does it have no 'importance'? It is, moreover, unclear what her concession to the realm of reason amounts to. For if prudence or self-interest is general in the first of the ways distinguished in Section 2.4, then having such concerns is a necessary means to satisfying the idiosyncratic wants agents are likely to have—outside an asylum (cf. the injury parallel, 122–3). If so, an agent's failure either to desire or be interested in prudence is simply a means–end error. Foot's concession in making it a require-ment of reason to have prudential concerns would not then step outside Humean bounds, and not succeed in being a recantation.

claims, take it that they engage the agent's will in the 'ordinary' ways as captured by ER, via serving the agent's desires.

Importantly, this does not make morality subjective. Just as it is not up to you—your interests, desires, and attitudes—whether x is rude or not, so it is not up to you whether x is the moral thing or what you ought$_{morally}$ to do. (The thrust of her earlier rejection of the first orthodoxy is preserved.) Morality is, so to speak, an autonomous system with its own rules for the application of its predicates, quite independent of the will of individual agents (172). And morality—like any other system—is in that sense inescapable: if you behave a certain way, then you just are cruel, whether you accept this or not.[37] But—and this is the important point in understanding Middle Foot—while morality is not subjective, its power to offer reasons is: like a game, it seemingly cannot from inside compel itself, or give reasons for itself, to be played. For whether moral considerations are reasons for the subject depends on the individual subject's having the requisite interests and desires. So morality's objectivity does not imply its rational necessity: that one ought$_{morally}$ to φ does not imply that one ought to φ (that morality ought to engage every agent's will).

What are the requisite desires and interests? ER leaves two possibilities. The first is that the agent have a non-moral interest that being moral serves, the second, that he have moral interests *per se*.

Thus ER circumscribes the senses that O2 can have. To recapitulate. On the first possibility—the focus of Early Foot—if all agents have some non-moral interest that being moral serves, then all ought to have moral concerns (O2B) and to find moral considerations reasons (O2A). On the second—the focus of Middle Foot—there is no sense in which anyone, let alone everyone, ought to have moral concerns; this is a contingent matter, not one of rational necessity. The immoral may not have standard desires and interests, but are only statistically unusual, and can-

---

[37] For Foot, the same is true of the thin predicates, like 'good' (or 'morally good'), as of the thick. On this Williams differs (*Ethics and the Limits of Philosophy*). I argue elsewhere that Foot is right on this (cf. also Warren Quinn, 'Reflection and the Loss of Moral Knowledge: Williams on Objectivity', *Philosophy and Public Affairs*, 16/2 (1987), 195–209). But it is another matter whether Foot is correct in her views of the criteria for the application of the predicate 'good' (or 'morally good').

not be said to be defective or mistaken in having the lousy ends they do (167). For on ER there is no sense to claims about what ends agents ought to have, except that provided by the first possibility.[38] That possibility aside, O2B is false, and the truth of O2A turns on the empirical contingency of whether all happen to have moral concerns.

Middle Foot does not believe moral concerns universal, and seems to reject both O2A and O2B. But, as noted in Section 2.5, she does not in fact show that the possibility of a prudential defence of being moral is ruled out.

The picture packs a tremendous punch, powered by Foot's Fork and the seeming ineluctability of the Humean 'end-relative' conception of practical reasonhood.[39] But it is, I believe, radically

[38] Middle Foot concludes that ' "One ought to be moral" makes no sense at all unless [A] the "ought" has the moral subscript, giving a tautology, or else [B] relates morality to some other system such as prudence or etiquette' (169). The idea in [B] may be that the 'ought' is subscripted to some non-moral system. If so, it is not a reason-giving use, but a rule-stating one, relating the system of morality to that, for example, of prudence: (i) one ought$_{prudentially}$ to be moral (or have moral ends). But then if (ii) someone has prudential interests, it follows for Foot that: (iii) they ought, unsubscripted, to be moral. For this unsubscripted 'ought' of reason is that of means–end rationality, and not some categorical or external usage. But this means that even for Foot 'one ought, unsubscripted, to be moral' can have a sense. Perhaps then in [B] the 'ought' was intended to be this unsubscripted means–end one. If so, it is misleading to assert that her theory 'disallows the possibility of saying that a man ought (free unsubscripted "ought") to have ends other than those he does have' (170): what it disallows is certain possibilities of saying this. Nor is [A]'s option of a tautology in 'One ought$_{morally}$ to be moral' perspicuous. One might suppose it not a tautology at all. 'You ought$_{prudentially}$, that is, as a matter of prudence, to be prudent (have prudential goals)' can be taken as an empirical claim, that prudence is not self-obstructing. For it might have been that prudential goals were better achieved by not being prudent. Or should we compare it with 'and the final club rule is to abide by the club rules', or 'you ought, from the point of view of chess-playing, to play according to the rules of chess'? It is not clear what use or sense such sentences have (though perhaps one can imagine some). Likewise, it is not obvious what sense 'one ought$_{morally}$ to be moral' could have (the notion of tautology is difficult).

[39] The key element is ER. From this Foot takes it to follow that immorality does not *necessarily* involve irrationality (162), and that, while there is indeed a categorical usage of 'ought', this has no genuine reason-giving force but relies on illusion (167). The same three elements are in Williams's explicitly neo-Humean 1980 paper 'Internal and External Reasons' (in *Moral Luck*). Admittedly he avoids the terminology of categorical and hypothetical imperatives, and in so doing presents Foot's three theses in a form generalized away from a particular concern with morality. Where Foot is concerned with the 'categorical' usage taken as distinctive of the moral, Williams is concerned with any external reason usage—with the general problem of how anything could have a reason-giving force for an agent, if it is external to what they happen to care about.

wrong, because ER is radically wrong. In a certain light nothing seems more obvious than that something can be a reason for agents quite irrespective of their actual desires and interests—so manifest indeed that the outrageous novelty of Hume's suggestion leaves one almost speechless. But not quite. Let us pick up the challenge, and sketch an alternative, traditional, conception of practical reasonhood, which will yield a very different sense for O2.

4. The End-Relative versus the Traditional Account

4.1. *ER as a Proper Account*

ER is basically an instrumentalist account that has been extended in various ways. But what range of possible errors does it allow? To answer this we need to distance ER as I understand it, and take Foot to do so, from certain other broadly 'Humean' theories (including perhaps Hume's own). In particular there are empirical theories to the effect that when human agents want X, and believe M the most efficient available means to X, then, *ceteris paribus*, they are by nature motivated to pursue M. Agents just do, or are motivated to do, what they calculate is the most efficient available means to what they most want. There is only this ordinary *theoretical* reasoning about means, and then the causal effect such reasonings by nature have, or tend to have, when conjoined with desiderative states of the agent. There is no distinctively practical reason, no genuinely practical, unsubscripted, 'ought'. Thus there is no sense in which an agent who fails to act as the account predicts is *defective* in point of practical rationality or 'practically irrational': his failure shows either that he did not really have the relevant desire or belief, or that the theory requires further refinement.[40] This is in effect a 'no theory' of practical

---

[40] Thus the theory may be elaborated to allow that under certain conditions, for example, of tiredness, agents tend not to put two and two together. The theory takes itself to be describing a natural mechanism, where a certain input has a certain output. It may allow in normativity at this lower level—allow that there is a way the natural mechanism *ought* to function—or it may, in a more full-bloodedly empiricist mode, strive to exclude normativity altogether as a bogus metaphysical glue. (The theorist must also face the question whether there is 'proper' *theoretical* rationality and irrationality, or whether this too must be purged of all normativity.)

reasonhood by contrast with a 'proper', non-reductive or non-eliminative, one.

I characterize a proper theory roughly as follows.

(A) Such a theory offers a normative principle as constitutive of practical reasonhood. This principle spells out what it is for there to be a practical reason for an agent—what conditions have to be satisfied. In conjunction with the facts of the particular case, this principle determines what there is reason for the agent to do in the sense of what the agent *ought* unsubscripted (that is *qua* rational) to do—whether the agent realizes this or not (unless, of course, such realization is itself built into the very conditions).

(B) The principle also functions as the principle of practical inference. Unsurprisingly, for what an agent takes in taking it that there is a reason for him to φ is precisely that the conditions for there being a reason for him to φ are satisfied in his case (and *pari passu* for his taking it that there is not a reason). Looked at one way, the principle thus dictates the form and nature of the premises needed for the inference—they consist in the con-ditions of practical reasonhood. Looked at the other way, it li-censes the agent to infer from such premises the conclusion that there is reason for him to φ.

(C) The principle is also determinative of practical rationality—of when the agent ought to, and ought not to, take it that there is reason for him to φ. The determination, however, is not the straightforward:

> *Qua* practically rational, *A* ought to take it that *C* is a practical reason for him iff *C* is a practical reason for him.

Practical rationality does not directly track the existence of practi-cal reasons. Rather the connection is mediated by the principle's role as principle of practical inference. For there are cases where, while there is reason for the agent to φ, we nevertheless do not think that *he* ought to take it there is reason for him to φ: for, relative to what he believes (reasonably or not) about the situ-ation, he would be practically irrational to do so. That is, to do so would require him to violate the principle of inference, in the application he supposes, albeit mistakenly, that it has to his case. And conversely there are cases where, while there is in fact no reason for him to φ, we hold he ought to take it that there is: for relative to what he believes, he would be practically irrational not to do so. (Cf. Aristotle, *Nicomachean Ethics* 7. 2. 1146ª31–ᵇ2.) If so, the biconditional is:

> *Qua* practically rational, *A* ought to take it that *C* is a practical reason for him iff *A* holds those conditions are satisfied whose satisfaction would mean there was such a reason for him. (*Pari passu* for the negative case.)[41]

That is, to be practically rational, the agent must conform to the principle in the application he believes it to have in his own case: that is, he must reason and act in the light of it. But so doing, while it ensures that he is practically rational, does not guarantee that he is correct about what reasons there are and aren't. That depends on his premisses, on whether the conditions for there being (or not being) a reason for the agent are as the agent supposes. So one can be practically rational (in one's reasoning and actions), but be mistaken in supposing that there is a reason. And one can be both mistaken and practically irrational (e.g. Aquinas on the erring conscience; or, within ER, if one is indifferent to what one, mistakenly, believes is the most efficient means to what one most wants).

So now we can see that in a proper theory there are at least these two rather different kinds of possible error that may be at issue in someone's being indifferent to a consideration—comparable to the archer's error in trying but failing to hit the target, and the error in not even trying to hit it. The agent may be materially mistaken in his premisses: he may believe the conditions of practical reasonhood to hold when they do not, and vice versa. (The case of the agent not believing that the conditions hold may be aligned with that of believing that they do not.) These are errors *within* practical rationality. But the agent may also violate practical rationality: he may take it that there is a reason when he should not, or fail to do so when he should, and thus impugn his practical rationality. The failure may be to draw (or acknowledge) the inference when he should, or a failure to reason and act in the light of the inference once drawn—'yes I ought to φ, but so what'. Such errors are ones of practical irration-

---

[41] An agent may be unwilling to draw a practical inference, but, if they are not to violate their practical rationality, this should lead them to query their belief in the conditions whose satisfaction would mean there was a reason for them.

ality: they are not within, but defeat the very point or purpose of practical rationality.[42]

And (D), what this is—the final and formal object of practical rationality (i.e. that which it aims at, and aiming at which makes it what it is)—is also enshrined in the principle the theory takes as constitutive of practical reasonhood. Thus, on ER, for example, the final and formal object is the efficient attainment of what the agent (most) wants.

The specific range and nature of both kinds of error—mistakes and practical irrationalities—will be a function of the particular proper theory of practical reasonhood that is adopted.

ER, in the way I understand it and take Foot to do so, is such a proper theory. So what is its range of errors? Here again it helps to differentiate it from another, this time proper, theory with which it can be confused. This, BER, claims that the conditions of there being a reason for an agent are that the agent have a belief that he (most) desires X, and a belief that M is the most efficient available means to X (other variants would alter only one of ER's conditions). BER is a proper theory in that any agent holding these conditions to be satisfied—who believes he has these beliefs—ought to hold that there is practical reason for him, on pain of practical irrationality. ER and BER offer rival accounts of the conditions of practical reasonhood. Crudely:

ER	BER
(1) A wants X.	(1*) A believes A wants X.
(2) M serves X.	(2*) A believes M serves X.

(3) There is a reason for A to M.

As accounts of practical reasonhood, on ER (1) and (2) are the conditions for (3), on BER (1*) and (2*). These schemata can also be taken as ones of practical inference. An agent infers (3)—that there is reason—from (1) and (2), with ER as his principle of inference. For him to make the inference requires of course that he believes that he wants X and that M serves X, but his inference is not from the facts of his having these beliefs, as it is on BER, but

---

[42] One may label these two sorts of error 'material' and 'formal'. But the topology of error here is complex, and I do not claim that all errors in practical reasoning can be neatly assigned to one or the other. All I need is that at least we level these different charges—that of having mistaken premisses, and that of being practically irrational (i.e. of violating practical rationality in some way).

from their content. Similarly with BER as principle of inference an agent infers (3) from (1*) and (2*); and to make this inference, he must believe (1*) and (2*), but his inference is not from his beliefs that he has these beliefs, but from the latter beliefs, that are the content (namely (1*) and (2*)).

An agent may be mistaken about the matters at issue in both (1) and (2), matters whose truth is seemingly independent of the agent's beliefs about them. That is, *re* (2) he may make means errors. He may be mistaken over the availability, adequacy (instrumental or constitutive), or comparative efficiency of means to ends. And *re* (1) he may make certain kinds of end error. He may make mistakes in the integration of his ends, for instance in their consistency, or priorities.[43] And he may be mistaken about what desires and interests he really has, believing he wants something when he does not, or vice versa; or mistaken about the degree of his desire or interest. (He can be alienated from his true self, whether by lack of self-knowledge, or by self-deception (169), or that of other individuals or his culture.) Now, *both* ER and BER allow that the agent may be materially mistaken in these matters.[44] But only on ER do such mistakes affect whether there really is a reason for the agent. For only on ER are these the very conditions of practical reasonhood. If the agent is wrong about the serving, or about his wanting X, then he is wrong about there being a reason for him: there is not; he only thinks there is. Or, *pari*

---

[43] Cf. Williams, 'Internal and External Reasons', 104. Given agents have many ends, questions of integration, both synchronic and diachronic, inevitably arise. The agent may live driven by the strongest desire of the moment ('living *kata pathos*', in Aristotle's phrase). One might think of that as a natural principle of 'integration', but integration proper implies a desire on the agent's part to arrange the attainment of his various ends so as to achieve maximum satisfaction. If so, the question arises for a neo-Humean whether the aim of integration is itself just another desire or interest *among* the others (albeit one with a certain second-order complexity due to its object), or whether, *pace* Hume, it is a principle of practical rationality, and it is more rational to go for the greater good or satisfaction.

[44] There is a difficulty here for empirical versions of the Humean theory. These view the agent's ends as a source of motivating power rather than as rationalizing (as what constitutes its being reasonable for the agent to act in a certain way—according to ER the considerations that they want *E* and that *M* serves *E*). Suppose the agent doesn't really have the desire in question: then if they act under the false belief that they do, it would seem to be the agent's belief that they have a certain desire that is the real source of motivational power, rather than their actual desire, which in this case they don't have. Empirical theories might deny this possibility and argue that agents have infallible access to their desires, or else claim that to think you desire something is to desire it. Neither response seems plausible.

passu, there is; he only thinks there is not. On BER by contrast, the truth or falsity of the agent's beliefs on these points doesn't affect whether there is or is not a reason for him. For it is the fact of the agent's having these beliefs, not their truth, that constitutes there being a reason for him (and his not having them there not being a reason). So if the agent doesn't really believe he wants X (or believes he doesn't want X), or else doesn't really believe that M serves X (or believes it doesn't), then there *isn't* a reason for him— even if in fact he does want X, or M really does serve X. And it is if he mistakenly believes that he has these beliefs when he doesn't that he may take it that there is reason for him when in fact there is not.

4.2. *The End-Relative and Traditional Conceptions*

Although I shall not argue this, I take ER, understood as such a normative principle of practical reasonhood, and so as a 'proper' theory, to be a theory of the right kind, and one more plausible than BER. Nevertheless it is, I think, false. It contrasts starkly with the traditional conception of practical reasonhood, a rough stab at whose constitutive principle is:

> (TC) A consideration C is a reason for an agent iff (and be-
> cause) it constitutes, or suitably connects with, the practi-
> cable good, i.e. with what the agent must do to be acting
> well.

Here the point, or formal object, of practical rationality is that the agent does what is best, or acts well, in the situation. Practical deliberation is directed at securing this. From the perspective of this conception, moralist and amoralist differ in that they offer rival accounts of what actually constitutes the best thing for the agent to do (in general and in particular).

The traditional conception, TC, is thus good-dependent where ER is desire-dependent. While for ER the source for something's being a reason for the agent lies in a connection with his desires, for TC it lies in a connection with what would be the good, or best, action for the agent to do. For example, suppose that were a child presently to visit grandparents, this would be kind, or that if he doesn't, the grandparents will be upset. These considerations *are* reasons for the child to visit—reasons why he ought to visit—iff (and because) it is a, or the, good thing for him to do, and a bad one for him not to: that is what his acting well and acting badly are here. If I were to *tell* a child: 'you ought to, you must, visit—because that's the kind thing to do, because otherwise they'll be upset', then in presenting these considerations in the form, and with the force, of reasons (in the *logos* position) I am presenting them as respectively good and bad: namely that he would be acting well in visiting, and badly in being the cause of upset to his grandparents. For taking the feelings of others into account is something a human needs to do. That I so regard them is what is *shown* in my presenting them as reasons. Their correctness may be challenged on point of fact and on point of reason.[45] Thus it may be queried whether the visit really is kind, and whether they will be upset; or it may be queried whether these things are really good or bad, either in general or in the particular situation—whether humans really do need to take such account of the feelings of others, or whether this child needs to take such account of the feelings of these grandparents (perhaps the consideration would generally be a reason but is not in this particular case). And I may then have to explain wherein the goodness of kindness in general consists, or wherein the goodness of being kind in this particular way consists in this particular situation.

ER theorists may agree that reasons are often given in the form 'you ought to φ: *C*'.[46] The difference is in their explanation of the source of *C*'s force as a reason. For them what makes *C* a reason, if it is, is its efficiently serving what the agent (most) desires (the so-called 'ordinary' connection). And so what is shown by my presenting *C* as a reason is that I take it that it efficiently serves some desire of the agent's (though this may be a bluff). Thus where on TC the child may query what is so good about being kind, on ER he will query instead why it is supposed that he has

---

[45] These two types of criticism may suggest a fact–value distinction. They should not. The questions whether the grandparents will be upset and whether it is bad to upset them are equally determined by the facts of the situation. Perhaps they are over-demanding and touchy. This means it is indeed likely they will be upset; and it may also mean that it's not so bad to let them be upset.

[46] The ER theorist may regard this as merely an elliptical presentation, where the desire in question is supposed too obvious to mention. Or it may be a variant, where they wish to view the agent's belief that they desire X not as coming in to practical inference as a premiss, but rather as operating as principle of inference, and to be something shown by the agent's inference.

a desire to be kind, or else what other desire it is he is supposed to have that is served by his being kind.

To say that TC is good-dependent and not desire-dependent does not mean that desire (the fact of the agent's desiring) cannot feature as a reason: it can. As also can the fact that a thing is a means to something you want.

> I must go and buy an ice-cream: I really want one and buying is the easiest way to get one.

But the source of the desire's *being* a reason, if it is, lies not in itself—its psychological presence—nor in some further desire of the agent's, not even a desire to do what is best. Rather for TC it is in its being a good, or the good, thing to do to satisfy the desire in the situation. (And the source of the agent's *taking* his desire to be a reason lies in the agent's supposing that the good thing to do is to satisfy this desire. That he so takes it is what is shown by his taking it as a reason.) Equally, the absence of desire can be a reason. If sexual desire is absent, then marrying someone is (let us suppose) not a good thing to do. So the absence of such desire is then a reason not to. Note first that while desires can feature as reasons, it is not the case that all reasons consist in desires. If I had said in the grandparent case above: 'You must visit them: I really want you to', or 'I really want you to be kind', this would have been to present a quite different reason. For, taken strictly, what I now present as good is that the child satisfy one of my (perhaps altruistic) desires, that he do it to please me. Note second that on TC a desire can feature equally well as a reason against, as well as for, an action that would serve it. Thus:

> I must not go and buy an ice-cream: I really want one.

Here the agent takes his desiring an ice-cream to be a reason not to buy one, and in doing so shows that he takes satisfying his desire (or at least doing so that way, by buying)—to be something bad and to be avoided.[47] The point is particularly clear with disgraceful desires. That someone desires, and would enjoy, sex with

---

[47] Taking the desire for ice-cream as a reason not to buy, rather than to buy, is more puzzling only because in the latter there is an obvious end that an agent may be supposing good (namely eating it). But if in fact this is not the agent's end in buying it, the case would be no more or less puzzling than the former. In both the agent's end, and why they suppose it good, would be as yet off-stage.

a child is a reason for him to avoid the company of children, and will, if he is right-thinking, be taken as such. It is not a reason to go for it, albeit one outweighed by other reasons against it. (The point is tied to that monstrous reversal of ordinary evaluation wrought by utilitarianism, whereby the fact that a torturer also enjoys his labours, while doubtless not sufficient to exonerate him, supposedly mitigates, rather than exacerbates, the awfulness of his action—that it is something to be said *for* it!)

Similar points hold of means. That some means M (buying an ice-cream) would efficiently satisfy one of the agent's wants can be a reason for the agent to take it. But the source of its being a reason lies not in the simple fact of this relation to one of the agent's desires, but in its being good for the agent to satisfy that desire in his situation, and good to do so that way—that is, in so far as efficiency, and buying, are good things in the situation (cf. Sections 5.2–3).

4.3. The Different Range of Possible Errors

The difference between ER and TC conceptions of practical reasonhood emerges in the different range of errors they permit. On TC, the practicable good, and so what there is reason for an agent to do, is a function of what it is best to go for, and how best to go for it, in the situation. That is, an agent's doing what is best consists in his taking the means he ought to take to the end he ought to have in the situation (or at least not to an end he ought not to have). Ends as well as means are assessable. The mere fact that some end is desired by the agent is neither necessary nor sufficient for there being a reason for him. Contrary to its sufficiency, even if a consideration serves an end the agent desires, it will not be a reason for the agent, if the end is not something good to pursue, or not in these circumstances, or not by him. (Of course, if he believes it good to do, it may be that, on pain of practical irrationality, he should take it, falsely, that there is reason for him.) And, contrary to its necessity, a consideration will be a reason for an agent even though he doesn't desire (or else desires to avoid) the end the consideration serves, if that is something good that the agent pursue—if that would be his acting well. (Again, if he believes it not good, it may be that he should, falsely, take it there is not a reason for him.) In short, agents can make mistakes over their ends, over what there is reason for them to pursue or avoid.

On ER by contrast there is no conceptual room for this kind of material mistake: there is simply no question of whether an end is good or worth pursuing, or of whether it ought (unsubscribed) to be pursued. One can be mistaken about what ends one has (about what one desires, or desires most), but not about what one, unsubscriptedly, ought, or ought not, to desire. There is no rational end assessment: the rational unsubscripted "ought" is confined to the rationality of taking efficient means to the ends the agent happens to have. For since, on ER, it is a necessary condition on a consideration's being a reason for an agent that it serves an end of his, no consideration can be a reason why he should, or should not, pursue some end as such. For any such reason would, on ER, have to consist in showing that the pursuit of this supposed end served some other further end of the agent's. So if reasons are end-relative, then on pain of infinite regress, the agent must pursue something as an end, and for which, *qua* end, they have not merely no further reasons (i.e. reasons in terms of some further end), but no reasons at all. On this conception all reasons are 'further reasons'. So on ER ultimate ends must as such be arational, or rationally contingent, in the sense that the agent happens to desire that end or have it as an interest, a connection between object and attitude that is not mediated by reason. There is no reason why they should, or should not, have it: they just do, or don't.

So on TC, unlike ER, agents can be materially mistaken about what end is good to, or worth, pursuing, whether in general or in their particular situation (whether taking what is not good as good, or what is good as not, or over comparative worth). Such are the mistakes of the light-minded and the wicked. But the difference in the constitutive principle of practical reasonhood affects not only the range of possible material errors, but also the range of practical irrationality—of possible violations of the principle. Thus over ends there is, for example, the practical irrationality of akrasia, viewed as the irrationality of agents' pursuing an end, whose efficient attainment they may indeed calculate, but which they believe (truly or falsely) they ought not to be pursuing in the first place—since, they suppose, the good thing for them to do is something else. This description of akrasia essentially involves the idea of a kind of rational end assessment which the ER conception rejects. Akrasia so characterized would then not be a possible practical irrationality on ER; indeed notoriously those ER theorists wishing to allow akrasia's existence have faced considerable problems in giving a description of it that both intuitively captures the phenomenon and preserves some sense of its practical *irrationality*.

4.4. Conclusion

Clearly, Foot's Fork is precipitate. Deontologists will doubtless feel given short shrift. But the traditional conception, TC, is, as yet, an unaddressed option. And on this conception, one possible mistake in an agent's being indifferent to considerations of morality consists in a material failure to have an *end* that *ought* to be had—a failure to have correct views about what is good and worth pursuing; and another lies in a formal failure to act rationally, that is, in the light of what the agent holds it best for him to do. Unlike a deontological defence, this defence is in terms of an end, but, unlike naturalism, one that it is rational to pursue. For if indeed it is correct, it is so because, being the creatures we are in the conditions of our world, it, and not amoralism, constitutes the good way for a human to live (the way that there is reason to live). What one views as good (or bad), one can be called on to describe the point of: one cannot call just anything good and there thereby be something there to understand. And nothing, I think, has been done convincingly to undermine this conception as precisely the correct conception of our practical rationality.

5. The Traditional Conception:
The Good as the Formal Object of Practical Reason

5.1. The Traditional Conception

Plato expresses a key point in the traditional conception when he says that, in contrast with what is just, everyone seeks what is really good, never what is merely apparently so. That is, if rational, we seek things under the description, or in the belief, that they are really good, not under the description, or in the belief, that they are merely apparently good. *That* mistake is not possible with good.[48] Of course when we pursue the good, we can pursue only what appears to us to be good or the good. And if our views of this are false, then we shall not be materially pursuing what in a formal sense we really seek. So mistake is possible here, but it is not one of seeking the apparent good as such rather than the real good, but the mistake of having a false view of what is really good. This allows the following remark to have sense:

(R) You ought not to pursue X, but Y, for that is what is really good.

Whether or not the agent agrees, he can see the force, or sense, of the charge—that he has false views about what is the really good thing to pursue. And if he cannot rebut, or defuse, the charge, then he must change accordingly, on pain of practical irrationality.

The traditional theory, as I view it, claims:

(T1) *The Formal Object and Point, of Practical Rationality*. The central, or defining, question of practical reason is: 'what should I do?' Its formal answer I take to be: 'do what is best' or 'act well'. To put this another way. The formal and final object of practical reasoning is the practicable good: it is this that makes practical reasoning what it is, and reveals what its point is. (Compare: 'winning is the formal object of playing a game' or 'food is of eating').

If so, there is no room for a certain kind of error here. One can mistakenly hold that appearing just, rather than being just, is what is good and so what there is reason to be, or do. But one cannot mistakenly hold that something's appearing good to do, rather than its being good, makes it that there is reason for it.

This point about the formal object, and thus the nature, of

---

[48] *Republic* 505D–506A. That is, one cannot be mistaken about goodness being a desirability characteristic as one can about justice. This is unsurprising, if, as I claim, to take something as a practical reason shows that something is being regarded as good: e.g. if you take φ'ing's being just as a reason to do it, you are thereby taking justice to be good. This does not mean that there is no sense to taking something's being good as a reason to avoid it, or its being bad as a reason for it. But here 'good' and 'bad' would not be formal occurrences but refer to certain material conceptions of what is good or bad (e.g. 'he thinks the good life is the good life', where the first occurrence refers to that lowest common conception of the good life as one of 'wine, women, and song').

practical reasoning needs to be supplemented by a theory, or at least a clarification, of the practicable good, or acting well. This is more than I can do here. But on the traditional conception, two elements of this are:

(T2) *The Objectivity of Good.* One cannot call just anything good or bad, worth pursuing or not, and make sense. 'Thin' predicates just as much as 'thick' ones are rule-governed. And what is the good that the agent should achieve, or the bad he should avoid, is determined by the facts of human nature and the world we live in, and the situations in which the individual is placed.

(T3) *The Extension of Good.* What the facts determine as good and bad include what ends are good and bad for the agent to pursue or avoid, as well as what means, and thus ends too can be rationally assessed.

The first thesis, T1, is a formal principle constitutive of practical rationality, linking the practicable good with reason, and practical evaluation with rational motivation. What there is reason for the agent to do is constituted by the practicable good (by how acting they would be acting well); and what the agent *qua* rational ought to take it there is reason for him to do is what he believes or calculates to be the practicable good. This, barring a reappraisal, is what the agent must (try to) do, in so far as he is rational. That is, his practical evaluation necessitates that he (try to) act accordingly; but the 'must' here is not one of causal or logical necessity, but of rational necessity—of what the agent has to (try to) do *on pain of irrationality*. Neither on this, nor indeed on any, proper theory is it required that the agent have a *desire* to be practically rational, or to do what he judges best for him to do, in order to motivate him: he *is* by nature practically rational, and this consists in being motivated by reasons—or acting in the light of the reasons the agent takes there to be (on pain of irrationality).[49] He does not need a desire either as a further reason to go for the good, or as an extra-rational element, giving him some supposedly

---

[49] Practical rationality is not a problem-solving system whose deliverances about what it is best for the agent to do require something else in order to be motivating. Thus no more on ER, as a proper theory, does the agent need a further desire in order to be motivated to take the means they believe they have reason to take (owing to its efficiently serving what they most want).

necessary oomph. This is not to say that to exhibit his practical rationality, the agent may not need certain interfering factors to be absent; nor that there couldn't be a special case in which desire did come in as a needed extra element—as it would if I found I couldn't move except when the appetite for ice-cream was upon me, and then rushed wildly around trying to catch up on things before the desire faded.

So if you take something as a reason for φ'ing—for instance, the fact the 4.15 train will get you to London by 6, as a reason to take it—that *shows* that you regard something as good to attain, e.g. being in London by 6. (Why this is good, or why it is held good by you, may or may not be obvious to others.) And, as T2 claims, there is a real question about whether you are right, and it is something good to pursue here and now. T2 connects facts with the agent's evaluations, and in particular with his evaluation of what it is best for him to do (in general and in particular). The facts determine what is good and bad for the agent to do, and so also the truth and falsity of his evaluations—his beliefs about what in the light of his conception of the facts is good and bad, and best, for him to do.[50]

T3 reflects the point that ordinarily we understand the central question 'what should I do?' to raise questions about ends as well as means. We suppose *ends* to be things that can be good and bad as well as means, and we spend time and effort on arguing about and assessing their goodness and badness, taking this to be determined by the facts. So, on the traditional conception, the practicable good—for the agent to act well—is determined by at least two things, what end it is good that the agent pursue in the circumstances, and what means (if any) it is good that the agent employ to that end. What ends and means are good in the situation will in turn depend on 'the facts'. Which facts? Let us add here the claim:

> (T4) *The criteria for the determination of good and bad action.* What ends and means are good or bad depends on what sorts of ends and means are good generally—that is, on human

---

[50] The facts fix this regardless of the agent's opinion. It is not determined by what facts the agent may choose to regard as relevant, but by what facts are relevant (of course these are likely to include facts about the agent). The facts, in thus determining evaluations, are therefore not supposed 'inert', since evaluations are not inert either.

goods and bads—and on the particular features of the situation and the agent, diachronic as well as synchronic. (You cannot call just anything you like a human good, or bad, and make sense.)

That '*A* should or ought to φ' (or that 'the best thing for *A* to do is φ') is, we could say, *doubly assessable*: it is false if either the end or the means are not the correct ones for the agent in the circumstances. Thus, 'I ought to say something comforting to them' might be false because the end of comforting is not one that should be pursued in the circumstances, or not by me (they need rather to be braced, or for someone else to be the comforter); and it might be false because what they need is a hug, not sympathetic words. What an agent, *qua* practically rational, should take it that he should do depends on his beliefs about what is good *re* ends and means. Of course if these beliefs are mistaken he will be mistaken about what he should do (or at least about its goodness), about how he must act if he is to act well. These mistakes may be ones of non-culpable ignorance where the agent could not have been expected to know better, or they may be culpable ones and, if based on a generally mistaken view of what is good or bad, may amount to wickedness.[51] Excellence in practical reasoning, or practical deliberation, consists primarily in having a generally correct understanding of what is good and bad in human life, and bringing it to bear correctly on, or rather realizing it correctly in, the situation in hand so as to act well—to get the correct end and means.[52] So to engage fully in practical reasoning one must have views about human goods and bads, about what is worth pursuing in life and what not, which one then brings to the situation in hand—for this is required if the agent is to be able to view his acting as his acting well; and to engage well in practical reasoning, one's views about human good and bad must be correct, as also must be one's deliberation about its application or realization in the particular situation. So, it seems, only the good can do it well. For only they will successfully fulfil the proper function of practical reasoning (the wicked by contrast, by being practically rational, will get for themselves 'a great evil').

[51] Cf. G. E. M. Anscombe, 'Two Kinds of Error in Action', in *Collected Papers*, iii (Cambridge: Cambridge University Press, 1981).

[52] Cf. Aristotle, *Nicomachean Ethics* 6. 9. 1142^{b}17–26; ^{b}31–3; cf. 7. 2. 1146^{a}21–31; 7. 8. 1151^{a}15–19; *Eudemian Ethics* 2. 11. 1227^{b}19–22.

In brief T1 introduces the possibility of practical irrationality, T2 that of mistakes within practical rationality, and T3 fills out the possible extent, or location, of such errors (irrationalities and mistakes).

5.2. Differences between the Traditional and ER Conceptions

The traditional and the ER accounts tend to differ over what they take as the point, and formal object, of practical rationality (cf. Section 5.6). The most striking difference is over the rational assessment of ends. The traditional theory holds both that we can sensibly talk of ends being such as an agent ought or not to pursue, and that this is something of which a rational understanding is possible. (It doesn't immediately follow that everyone is in a position to achieve this understanding.)

But TC and ER differ also over how means contribute to there being a reason for an agent, and so over what it is for a means to be correct, and thus in what goes into the practical deliberation of means and their assessment as correct. Both broadly agree over one criterion of correctness in means—what we can call their 'technical' merits, or 'technical' goodness or badness—that is, their availability, adequacy, and comparative efficiency (and their bearing on the attainment of other ends). Agents can go 'technically' wrong over means to their ends. On ER, the only criterion seems a 'technical' one of this sort, and the only sort of mistakes an agent can make 'technical' ones. By contrast, TC is concerned also with another sort of correctness or goodness in the means. The means may be bad because they are the means to an end that is bad (in general or in the particular circumstances), and thus one the agent ought not to have in the first place: and in this sense, there are no correct means to employ to murder someone, though certainly there are effective and ineffective ones. Furthermore, means are not automatically made good by a good end: there can be reasons not to take such means, either in general or in the circumstances, because of other ways they themselves connect up with human good and bad. Thus the goodness of the end of pleasing a child on his birthday does not, typically, counter the badness that attaches generally to stealing other people's bicycles: so there is reason not to take such means. Means can be bad in all three ways: stealing a toy gun to murder someone.

On ER, if a means is technically correct, then there is a reason for the agent to take it (provided the end served is what the agent most desires). Whereas on TC, that there is reason for one to φ (or that one should φ)—that in φ'ing one would be acting well—is, or can be, false either if the end φ'ing serves is bad, or if φ'ing is bad as means through its connection with other human goods and bads, or if it is 'technically' bad. Badness on any of these scores can suffice to undermine there being (a) reason for you to φ. Where badness in any suffices to undermine, then goodness in all is required for there to be a reason for you. (There are also corresponding differences in irrationalities between ER and TC.)

In short, on TC there are more aspects to talk or argue about—more possible conversations—in assessing the correctness of means than on ER. Thus on ER, the assessment turns on the technical questions of (1) the adequacy and efficiency of the means *re* the end in question, and (2) its impact on the attainment of other ends of the agent, on whether it furthers or hinders them. But on TC, the assessment not only draws on such issues, but also concerns the goodness and badness of the means as regards (1) the goodness of the end in question, i.e. whether the agent ought to be pursuing that end; and (2) whether the means is good or bad with respect to other ends that the agent *ought* to have (or ought not to have), whether they do or not.

So on TC it is very much *not* the case that the consideration that M efficiently serves something you want thereby amounts to there being a reason for you to pursue M. Take, for example, the hungry ascetic. He knows that a visit to friend F will produce an immediate invitation to dinner, one so pressing it would be rude to refuse. That a visit would serve his hunger he takes to be a reason, but a reason *not* to visit. For he supposes it bad to satisfy his hunger. He doesn't consider the fact that a visit would serve his hunger even a reason to visit. The fact may indeed make the visit attractive to him, but it is perhaps the fact of this very attraction that he takes to be reason to avoid the visit: for it is a sign that his psyche is not in that state of detachment from the power of things physical, which state he believes is the good state to achieve.

5.3. A Problem for TC: A Kind of Akrasia as a Counter-example

But can this be right? Take an akratic killer, or seducer, who, after the considerable deliberation and calculation often required in attempting such ends, concludes not merely: 'So I'll send them chocolates' but perhaps even 'So it's best for me . . .', or 'So there is reason for me to . . .', or 'So I should . . .'. And his apparent reason (the *logos*) for this is: (L) 'for doing that is the way to convey the poison' or 'to enamour her of me'. This puts the TC theorist in a quandary. For (1) it is natural to suppose (L) gives the reason the akratic takes there is for him to send chocolates. (2) But, on TC, his taking (L) as a reason for him to act *shows* that he views the poisoning or emotional entangling of the recipient this way as something good. (3) But, given he is akratic, he precisely doesn't regard this end as good (or the good thing for him to do); indeed he may disvalue it highly, and possibly even in that very aspect by which he finds himself attracted. So, it seems, either TC is wrong, or (L) doesn't give the *reason* he thinks there is for acting as he does, or there is no such akrasia. Humeans may take heart: for if they have their difficulties with akrasia, so, it now appears, do TC theorists.

One response would be that the akratic's irrationality is to be located precisely in this tension between (1), (2), and (3). But this seems to make his irrationality a matter of inconsistent beliefs, of the agent's believing that something is good to do and believing it not good to do. But, on TC, intuitively the akratic's irrationality is that of pursuing an end he holds he should not. It may be suggested that the akratic's real judgement is somehow occluded, allowing him temporarily to proceed to a best judgement that does not represent his real, or considered, view of what it is good and bad to do in the situation. But even if this sometimes happens, there seem other cases where the akratic doesn't at any point regard what he is doing as good—and to suppose that he must be so judging smacks of philosophy. The nub of the problem seems to be whether the notion of a reason attaches simply to intentional action or to the notion of an action's making full practical sense for an agent.

Full discussion is not possible here. But note first that if the akratic claims that he ought to, or should, without qualification (*haplos*), send the chocolate, or that in so acting he is acting well, the reply, as to someone who mistakenly held the killing or seduction good to do, is 'oh no you shouldn't, for whether or not that's an efficient means, you shouldn't even be going for this end'— only with the akratic we can add 'and you know it'. For he already accepts that he shouldn't, and is being irrational, not mistaken. This is the full practical 'should' (or 'ought' or 'best'). It has its place formed by the question what it is best that the agent do *haplōs*, of how he must act if he is to act well: and the pain in 'should . . . on pain of . . .' is that of failing, through some rational error, to act well, and as before the error may consist in a false belief, or some practical irrationality.

One kind of akratic, we allowed, may, at least temporarily, fool himself into holding that it really is best that he φ—that he should φ, where the 'should' is the full practical 'should': that this is what he must do to act well. But the problematic case for TC is the akratic who says:

> I know I should not pursue *E*, but I am going to; and *given* that this is what I am going to pursue, I *should*/it's best that I/there is reason for me to φ.

However, that the latter 'should' judgement occurs *within* the concession is all important. This akratic concedes he is going to make one error—he is going to pursue an end he holds he should not, and so is going to act irrationally. His concession sets the assessment of his judgement that he should φ in this respect to one side—we are to understand it as not vulnerable to falsification in this respect. So this 'should' is not the unqualified practical 'should' which presents what the agent (takes it he) should do *haplos* (i.e. if he is to act well). But, as we said, there are other ways in which practical calculations can go awry. The akratic agent can still err over the technical means, and he can still err over what means are best in not flouting other things that are of value, beside those already flouted in going for the akratic end. He can err in judging mistakenly about them; and he can err by irrationally not taking the means he judges, whether rightly or wrongly, to be technically correct, or best given his akratic pursuit. So, I suggest, our akratic's 'should' is a 'should' on pain of *these* mistakes and irrationalities, which unlike the full practical 'should' excludes from consideration mistakes and irrationalities over what it is best *haplos* to pursue in the situation. Of course avoidance of these other errors does not suffice to mean that he should *haplos* take those means, as something whereby doing which he would be acting well: not even he holds that, and not holding that could not act well in taking them.

This point about the qualified force (and sense) of the akratic's 'should' can also be expressed by noting that the concession marks a change in the practical problems the akratic is addressing. His problem is no longer 'the' problem of practical reason, that of what he ought *haplos* to do in the circumstances, or of what he must do if he is to act well. The agent knows he is not going to do that (or what he holds to be that): it's not now on that he may seek advice. His reasoning and deliberation focus instead on two other issues, and it is over these he may seek advice: that of not making a hash over the technical means to his akratic end, and the more subtle one of damage limitation in his selection of the means that are best given his akrasia. For given that the agent is going to pursue an end he holds bad, it doesn't follow that the only criterion left for establishing the best means is the technical one. There is reason even for the akratic agent to choose means that are not bad in that they flout other things that actually are of value, besides those already flouted in going for the akratic end. So, considerations from other things the agent (mistakenly or not) holds of value, which were irrelevant to what he took to be the badness of the akratic end, should be taken by him to constrain the means he is prepared to adopt in furtherance of this end (and perhaps even stymie it). The akratically relapsing smoker may hold he should not *steal* a packet, and if this is the only means (he believes) available, it may stymie his akrasia, without thereby rectifying his character (or his rationality). And even the reasons that the agent took for the badness of the akratic end in the first place can, and should, reappear to constrain the means the agent holds he should adopt, mitigating rather than exacerbating his fault: thus the relapsing smoker may think he should choose a low-tar brand, and the adulterer discretion. (Here too the akratic project may be stymied.) Admittedly akrasia may break out again, when the akratic, deciding to take means M, and not M^*, then takes the latter (buys a high-tar brand). And if the reasons the agent saw favouring M draw on other things he values, then more and more of his character can become compromised, as the original passion asserts itself to overturn or subvert more of what the agent stands by (as a would-be adulterer may find himself now contemplating murdering the obstacle to his passion).

These are different practical problems from the focal one of what best to do *haplos*, and their qualified 'should's are correspondingly sensitive to different considerations and errors. Our akratic doesn't see his sexual attraction as rendering the end of the attempted seduction of practical sense. Such reason—such sense—that sending chocolates has for him is to do with its technical appropriateness to a seduction (or that one in particular) and its relative innocuousness both as regards its compromising other things the agent holds of value, and as to its sensitivity to those aspects of badness the agent holds there to be in his akratic project. The akratic agent thus does not view his action as conforming fully to the form of practical sense—which is not to say it is entirely a practical nonsense (like the antics of a mad person, so bizarre we may not know even where to begin to describe what is going on); we can understand how sexual temptation can derail an agent into doing something that doesn't make full sense for him to do, even in the face of his agreement that it doesn't. TC, as I understand it, regards reasons as things that feature in an account of what it is best that the agent do—of what he should do *haplos*; and the reasons the agent takes there to be will be what feature in his account of what is good in doing what he does—of why that constitutes acting well, or is what it makes full practical sense for him to do.

5.4. *Another Problem for TC: Rational Indifference*

A different challenge to TC may seem posed by the 'So what?-ers', those who when told that φ'ing is what they ought to do, or what would be best for them, or what it befits a human to do, or doing which they would be acting well, etc. say, or think, 'So what? It doesn't serve any purpose I care about'. The TC theorist must press a division into two types of case here. In the first type someone thinks 'So what?' to the claim that his φ'ing would be his acting well, where he understands the claim already to presuppose or embody a specific material conception of acting well, say, a certain ordinarily respectable way of going on, or acting virtuously (i.e. justly, etc.). But he himself has a different conception of acting well (of how best to go on), such that 'acting well, i.e. respectably, or virtuously' is not acting well at all. So the fact that 'φ'ing would be acting well', i.e. respectably or virtuously, is not for him a *practical evaluation*. It is not something he wishes to challenge: it's just a fact to which he is completely indifferent, since he doesn't regard so acting as good. Had he understood the claim to be without such a presupposition, as one about what constitutes acting well 'formally' understood—that is, as a practical evaluation—he would not have brushed it aside with a 'So what?' but objected to it with a 'No, it's not'. This 'So what?-er' *is* then operating as a practically rational agent, aiming to act well, albeit with what the virtuous would argue is a mistaken conception of what that is. So the challenge here is not to TC but within TC, over the correct views of what is good and bad for an agent to pursue and avoid, over what he must do if he is to act well.

In the second type of case the indifference is to practical rationality itself. There is a vast range of cases.[53] Such agents may meet the full practical 'oughts' and 'shoulds' and 'act wells' with stark incomprehension. Or, more disturbingly, they may have views, even correct ones, about human goods and bads, and of what they ought to do, etc., but claim to have, and have, no concern with any of this: it leaves them cold. Such an agent may be adrift—so *déraciné* perhaps that even knowledge that he should not, or even that he should, kill himself ceases to have its proper force, his loss of any sense of self-value being such as to make it seem it hardly matters what happens. Or the agent may be full of purpose. He is going to φ—whatever the cost, to himself or to others: to survive in the trenches, or the concentration camp; or rising from unimaginable poverty, never again to be cold, hungry, or pushed around, never again to be the one to lose out; or falling into depression, to make away with himself; or to paint, or to be the one who discovers the cure to cancer; or out of sheer perversity and bloody-mindedness to do what he acknowledges he should not. To achieve his end he will do whatever it takes: and he will reason (technically) about how to secure it, for this is what he will have by hook or by crook. It is not that he takes this end to be of supreme value, nor even of supreme value 'to him': he is, or has become, indifferent to the question of its value, and may indeed think it is not good, or not good for him, to pursue (and may even regret that life has made him as he is, or as he takes himself to be). Like the akratic, such a commitment often seems to stem from passion, even obsession; and as we can understand an akratic's temptation, so too we may understand how a concatenation of

---

[53] I am much indebted to conversations with Philippa here.

certain experiences, as in a blighted childhood, might naturally take a person this way. And, while he may not, equally he may, like an akratic, admit that he is being practically irrational in not doing what he should do, that he is defective in not using, or properly using, a human faculty he possesses. But unlike the akratic he is indifferent to his error: it is not one that matters to him. For him it is not, or not usually, a question of temptation and regret; he simply doesn't care, or is beyond caring.[54] (It might be more illuminating to view akrasia simply as a particular species of rational indifference.)

But what threat do such cases pose for TC? Perhaps it is that, even more than akrasia, they indicate that TC is committed to an externalism that is unacceptable in permitting, in Nagel's words, 'someone who has acknowledged that he should do something and has seen *why* it is the case that he should do it, to ask whether he has any reason for doing it'.[55] Put like that, this would, on TC, be a grammatical misunderstanding of the relation of the notions of 'should *haplos*' and there being a reason: the agent sincerely judging that he should φ is thereby judging that there is reason for him. But the objection can be recast: TC apparently allows that some indifferents may understand that they should—that there is reason for them to—φ, yet not be motivated at all by this: yet reason is here supposed to be practical. That is, what TC offers as the rationalizing light—as the form of practical sense, as what constitutes the sense that it makes for the agent to do the action— is not sufficient: for here we have agents who see certain courses of action lit up in this light, yet are not thereby motivated to do

[54] Under the pressure of conversation agents may shift. They may begin by claiming that what they are doing is acting well, i.e. virtuously. They may then concede that it is not acting virtuously, but claim that it is, nevertheless, what it is to act well—the best thing to do. Finally they may concede that too is not so, but declare that it is what, goddammit, they are going to do, no matter what.

[55] Thomas Nagel, *The Possibility of Altruism* (Princeton, NJ: Princeton University Press, 1970), 9. The sentence is unfortunately very ambiguous. If I understand Nagel aright, both uses of 'should' are, for him, not 'should *haplos*' but 'should$_{morally}$'. If so, the TC theorist will disagree with him. For, on TC, someone can acknowledge that they should$_{morally}$ φ, and see why it is the case that they should$_{morally}$ φ—in the sense of why it is that morality requires this, and not something else—and still sensibly ask whether they have any reason for doing it. That would be to ask after the very point of being moral—what's so good about it? However, if by 'seeing why it is the case they should$_{morally}$ φ' is meant they see why it is practically good that they φ—that is, they see the reasons for acting morally— then they can't sensibly wonder whether they have any reason.

them. If so, those who favour some naturalizing 'no-theory' of practical rationality will suppose this shows the need for a psychological item of a different kind from belief to supply the motive power in those cases where the agent appears motivated by his practical evaluations; and those looking for a 'proper' theory may take it to show we need a different conception of practical sense, a different proper theory.

Against the latter, it can be immediately objected that there is no reason to suppose that there cannot be comparable cases of such rational indifference to what are practical reasons on their favoured 'proper' theory. And against the former, the obvious line of reply for a proper theory to make—obvious from the way the case is described—viz. that such indifference is in some way practically irrational, is equally open to TC. Whereas Type-1 'So-what?ers' were in rational error because mistaken in their views of good and bad, those of Type-2 are in rational error because, like the akratic, they violate the principle constitutive of practical reasonhood, in that they fail to reason and act in its light. With these indifferents their defect lies in their possession or mastery of the practices of practical reason. Perhaps they have not been properly, or fully, trained in these practices (taught the use of 'should'), or not responded fully to that training, or else their dire or deprived circumstances have generally distorted or declutched this training: in the presence of much unreason, it is difficult not to be alienated from the practices of reason.[56] I have not been supposing that they are wholly untrained or unhinged: they may technically calculate that ϕ'ing is the efficient means to what they want, and then take this fact—that it is such a means—as reason why they should ϕ *given the pursuit of their end*. This shows them as partial possessors of the practices of practical reason, where 'should' or 'reason' have only qualified senses.[57] But their in-

---

[56] The failing seems to betray a lack or inhibition of adult development, whether due to the psychopathology of the individual or their social and familial circumstances. Thus the extremity of their circumstances—dire poverty, complete disintegration of the ties of society, friendship, and family, slavery and abuse, or the terrors of the concentration camp—may simply prevent the agent from reflecting on their own situation, and on the questions how best to go on or live well, and what is worth while or of value in life; or else make such reflections seem quite irrelevant, a bitter joke. Like the question how best to occupy leisure, they may seem entirely problems of the well-to-do, or more fortunately circumstanced, as in Maxim Gorky's *Lower Depths* or Varlam Shalamov's *Kolyma Tales*.

[57] Like a 'Humean' reasoner (cf. Aristotle on *deinotes*). There is then the question

ability to comprehend, or their disinterest in properly acknowledging or engaging with the full practical 'should', with its double assessability, reveals them as in some way deficient. (That they are indifferent to this deficiency doesn't affect whether it is one: it is not a deficiency only on the condition of their caring.) The full practical 'should'—the 'should *haplos*' of practical evaluation—is properly an expression of the agent's will (or choice). If so, to say '(I know) I should φ, but so what' is puzzling—and reveals the agent as not using the 'should' with its proper force, as in effect estranged from their will. Such indifference, as with akrasia, betokens some 'disease' of the will, some practical irrationality. The practical rationality of such agents is defective by the standard of the proper practice of practical reason by adult humans in fit human circumstances or environments.

However, the cases of Type-2 indifference seem so varied that they may have to be replied to, and the defectiveness established, case by case. Perhaps no general reply will be convincing. But my main point is simply that the existence of such cases is not a knock-down objection to TC (or to proper theories generally). The TC theorist has a line of reply, and I see no reason to suppose that it cannot be made out convincingly. So neither Type-1 nor Type-2 indifference need threaten the correctness of the TC account.

5.5. Misunderstandings of TC: (1) TC as a Special Version of ER

But is TC really so completely different from ER? ER theorists may query both (1) whether TC isn't *au fond* just a special version of ER, or conversely (2) whether ER isn't just a special version of TC. *Re* (1), they may suggest that on TC too what there is reason for an agent to do is relative to his motivational set, but the

of the sense of these qualified 'should' judgements of means, of their truth-conditions. Thus that the agent *ought* to φ simply because it is the most efficient means to something they want may be viewed as itself constitutive of this defective fragment of practical rationality. Or it may be claimed that something's being an efficient means to what the agent wants is a reason to take it because it is *good* to take efficient means to the satisfaction of desires. If so, some explanation is owed of why this is good. (Is the good of it just that it leads to the satisfaction of their desire? But why should that be supposed always good, especially given that their desire may be bad, as even they may admit? Or is it supposed generally a human good for people to take means to whatever ends they happen to want most, as though a sense of frustrated desire were the prime human ill?)

peculiar twist TC gives to this is to make reasons relative to one special desire therein, the desire to act well and be a good human. The TC theory emphasizes that there is much constitutive deliberation in settling the content of this desire, of what it is to act well, or be a good human. Moreover, it considers this desire special, both in that it occurs in all (or almost all) humans, and also in that it is one that is, at least usually, accorded central importance and greatest weight in agents' deliberations. Indeed the TC theorist marks this by reserving the term 'reason' for considerations that serve this desire, while considerations that serve other of the agent's ends are not so dignified. But it is a mistake to think that this marks a radical departure from ER, rather than a terminological or conceptual one.[58]

Such a theory is a complete misunderstanding of TC. (1) An appetite for the good would not have the relevant constitutive connection with being rational; if everyone has it in their motivational set, this would be a contingent matter, and there would be no failure, or violation, of practical rationality were someone not to. (2) Both TC and ER theorists suppose agents have other desires, like an appetite for ice-cream. Their wish to act well, as they constitutively conceive this, may require them to avoid ice-cream. On TC, properly understood, the fully rational agent will not then take his appetite for ice-cream as a reason at all. But on ER the case thus far is one simply of competing desires, for the good and for ice-cream. Yet that seems to leave no room for a distinction between full rationality and continence (*enkrateia*), or else the wrong room, where the distinction comes out as one between a rout and a hard-won victory. Above all, on ER there is no sense in which the victory *should* go to the one desire rather than the other (provided that the agent is not deceived about the relative strengths of his desires). While it will not be 'good', there is nothing irrational in the ER agent giving preference to the appetite for ice-cream. (3) Finally, if both TC and ER theories agree there is no reason why agents *should* aim at the practicable good, or have acting well as an end, they will offer quite different explanations of this. On ER, there would be no reason because it is supposed an ultimate end,

---

[58] Thus the ER theorist may suppose that the TC theorist proclaims a conceptual connection—that it is part of the meaning of being 'practically rational' that an agent has this desire to act well; and so if they lack the desire, they would not count as 'practically rational'. This too would be a misunderstanding of TC.

and so outside the realm of practical reason. There is no rational explanation why agents should have this, or any, end. It is merely a matter of their desires. On TC, by contrast, the explanation is that humans are by nature practically rational and the practicable good's being the formal object or aim constitutes what it is to be practically rational—and so that's why there's no reason to aim at the practicable good. (There's no practical reason why humans, as a species, should be practically rational. Whether on TC it is meaningful to claim in certain contexts that individual agents should aim at the practicable good on pain of irrationality is something we can leave unresolved.) On TC then, unlike ER, the practicable good is not one end among others. As the formal object of practical rationality it is rather the form of rational ends—the form, or idea, of what it is for an action to make full practical sense for the agent, or to be what he should do (*haplos*).

So on TC, unlike ER, reasons are external to agents' actual concrete desires and interests. Agents may fail to act well because they have mistaken views about what reasons there are for them, about what they must do if they are to be acting well (mistakes which may or may not be censurable); and they may do so through various forms of practical irrationality, such as akrasia and rational indifference.

5.6. Misunderstandings of TC: (2) ER as a Special Version of TC

Thus far we have assumed that from the start ER views the formal object of practical reason not as the practicable good but as the efficient attainment of what the agent most desires (i.e. that ER denies T1, in Section 5.1). But ER may be presented instead as a special version of TC. ER advocates may concede that something's being a reason for an agent is a function of its connection with the practicable good, and that an agent's taking it as a reason is his taking this connection to hold. But thus accepting T1 (and that (R) makes sense), they then diverge from our TC in their theory of the practicable good—of what makes an action a good or bad one to do. Roughly, they confine practical evaluation, the assessing of what it is good or bad to do, to means, and to questions of their adequacy or efficiency. The good of ϕ'ing consists simply in its serving some end desired by the agent. So they reject the T3 claim that ends too are assessable as good or bad *haplos*. For them the practicable good that is the formal object of practical reason in T1 consists in the most efficient means to the agent's dominant end. (They can agree also to the criterial claim, T2, that the practicable good, in the limited way they conceive it, is settled by the facts of human nature and the world.)

But such a rejection of T3 is highly revisionary of our use of "good" and "bad", and of our ordinary practices of practical evaluation, as regards both ends and the criteria we use to assess the goodness and badness of means. Given this, ER theorists may well fight shy of conceding T1's claim about the formal object of practical reason.

5.7. Conclusion

ER is, I believe, false, and lacks the resources to make proper sense of ordinary practical evaluation. But it has not been my purpose to argue this so much as to distinguish TC from it, and to give some characterization of what the TC alternative amounts to.

6. Conclusion: The Traditional Conception and the Sense of the Second Orthodoxy

And what sense does TC give to the second orthodoxy, O2? Suppose we can show TC's claim of a formal connection between *practical rationality* and *goodness*, such that

(A) Everyone *qua* rational aims at the practicable good—at being good, or excellent, humans, and doing what is best to do, or acting well (excellently).

'Being good (excellent)' and 'acting well (excellently)' are here formal notions, and do not presuppose any particular material account of what it is to be good or act well, or what the excellences are—so that both a moralist and an immoralist, like Thrasymachus, could thus far be in agreement. (Just as seemingly it involves only a mastery of the concepts to answer the question 'Do you think it reasonable to go for a good holiday or a bad one?', in advance of disputes about what this consists in, with 'A good one, of course'; so too with a good or bad life, living well or ill.) Suppose next that we can show a connection between *goodness* and *morality or virtue*, such that

(B) What it is for a human to be good (excellent), or act well (excellently), is to be virtuous and act virtuously.

That is, what we ordinarily recognize as morality and the virtues drop out as the correct answer to the questions how best to live, or what best to do. Then we can derive the connection that O2 claims between *rationality* and *morality or virtue*, that

(C) There is reason for everyone to be virtuous and act virtuously. Everyone must find considerations of virtue reasons on pain of rational error.

And it is, I suggest, the possibility of this argument that gives a proper *sense* to the second orthodoxy. It avoids making the truth of O2 depend on the contingencies of what individuals happen to desire or care about. And it avoids reliance on some unexplained mysterious connection between morality *per se* and reason. It is because acting virtuously turns out to be the correct answer to the question how it is best for one to live or go on that there is reason for each so to act. Those who have an incorrect view need not be irrational, but they are mistaken in their view, and will live badly—and their confident illusion that it is they who are making a success of their lives is a final twist that locks them in their error.

My aim has been to suggest a sense for the second orthodoxy that does justice to the hold it exercises over us. This I have claimed is provided by the traditional conception. To argue that so understood it is true is another matter—a matter of defending (A) and (B). Yet 'is this impossibly difficult if we consider the kinds of thing that count as virtue and vice' and 'the facts of human existence' (p. 123)? Like Early Foot, I believe not.

6

Two Sorts of Naturalism

JOHN MCDOWELL

1. Philippa Foot has long urged the attractions of ethical natural-ism. I applaud the negative part of her point, which is to reject various sorts of subjectivism and supernaturalist rationalism. But I doubt whether we can understand a positive naturalism in the right way without first rectifying a constriction that the concept of nature is liable to undergo in our thinking. Without such prelimi-naries, what we make of ethical naturalism will not be the radical and satisfying alternative to Mrs Foot's targets that naturalism can be. Mrs Foot's writings do not pay much attention to the concept of nature in its own right, and this leaves a risk that her naturalism may seem to belong to this less satisfying variety. I hope an attempt to explain this will be an appropriate token of friendship and admiration.

2. I begin with a claim about how not to read Aristotle, whose ethical outlook is obviously naturalistic in some sense. There is an Aristotelian notion of what is necessary as that without which good cannot be attained.[1] It can be tempting to suppose that when Aristotle relates human virtue to nature he is, in effect, exploiting that notion in order to validate the appeal of ethical consider-ations to reason. The idea is that the appeal is validated on the ground that the virtues are necessary in that way, with the necess-ity founded in independent facts, underwritten by nature, about what it is for a human life to go well. But I think any such reading of Aristotle's intentions is quite wrong.

It is striking that that notion of necessity does not figure in Aristotle's own talk about the virtues. A quick reading of Aristotle's ethics may give the impression that this is only a verbal absence. Surely he represents happiness as a good unattainable

---

[1] *Metaphysics* Δ. 5. 1015[a]22–6.

without the virtues? But if we are to ground the appeal of ethical considerations to reason by exploiting the claim that the virtues are something without which good cannot be attained, the grounding must invoke a dependence within the sphere of the practical. The good in question—what figures as 'happiness' in our translations—must be independently recognizable as such. But Aristotle explains 'happiness' as 'acting well', with 'well' glossed as 'in accordance with the virtues'.[2] The good he represents as unattainable without the virtues just is virtuous activity. And we obviously cannot help ourselves to the thesis that virtuous activity is a good while we are suspending judgement as to whether ethical considerations really appeal to reason, as we must if we are to exploit nature to establish that the appeal is genuine. There is no promise here of founding the rational appeal of ethical considerations on a claim of natural necessity.

Of course decent people (like us) think acting in accordance with the virtues is, as such, a good. So we can say we need the virtues, since without them we cannot attain that good. But if we say that, we are not pointing to any dependence within the sphere of what has a claim on practical reason. To say 'We need the virtues' is just to say that ethical considerations constitute genuine reasons for acting, not to give the outline of a grounding for that claim.

I think the reading of Aristotle I am rejecting is mostly held in place by inability to see any alternative. I hope the rest of this essay will help to dislodge it.[3] But I can mention a couple of exegetical points in advance.

The reading makes it difficult to place an attractive thesis of Aristotle's, to the effect that virtuous actions are—presumably rightly—seen by a virtuous person as worth performing *for their own sake*.[4] On the reading I am rejecting, when Aristotle says the good for human beings is a life of activity in accordance with the virtues, he must mean that a life of virtuous activity is recognizably good, as such, only derivatively; it is non-derivatively recognizable as good not under the description 'a life of virtuous activity', but under some description that displays an indepen-

---

[2] See *Nicomachean Ethics* (henceforth *NE*) 1. 7.

[3] See also my paper 'The Role of *Eudaimonia* in Aristotle's Ethics', repr. in Amélie O. Rorty (ed.), *Essays on Aristotle's Ethics* (Berkeley, Calif.: University of California Press, 1980).

[4] See *NE* 2. 4. For the idea that a virtuous person gets this kind of thing right, see e.g. *NE* 3. 4.

dent appeal to reason—an appeal we can see that the life so specified has, even while we are suspending judgement on whether reason requires virtuous activity. But how can this cohere with the suggestion that virtuous action as such recommends itself to a rational will?

Similarly, consider the thesis that a virtuous person acts 'for the sake of the noble'.[5] A virtuous action's appeal to reason—which a virtuous person gets right—consists in the action's being noble. This goes well with the suggestion that virtuous action appeals to reason in its own right, not as needed to secure some good whose status as such can be recognized independently of whether virtue's demands on reason are genuine. A virtuous action's appeal to reason is captured by an evaluation, 'noble', which is internal to the standpoint of someone who already accepts that virtue's demands on reason are real. Accepting that, and accepting that 'for the sake of the noble' gives a reason for acting, are the same thing.

3. Just how convincing a grounding for the appeal of ethical considerations to reason is available anyway, from the claim that human beings need the virtues if their life is to go well? Would this claim be like the claim that wolves need a certain sort of co-operativeness if their life is to go well?

Suppose some wolves acquire reason. I mean this as something one might say in Greek with the word '*logos*'. What the wolves acquire is the power of speech, the power of giving expression to conceptual capacities that are rationally interlinked in ways reflected by what it makes sense to give as a reason for what.

I have spoken of wolves rather than of a lone wolf, and this bypasses one of the difficulties one might have about whether the supposition is really intelligible. Other difficulties remain: Wittgenstein's aphorism 'If a lion could talk, we could not understand him'[6] is very much to the point, and we should add that if we could not understand him, that ought to undermine our confidence that we were entitled to suppose talking was what he was doing.[7] But for my purposes, it does not matter whether it is

---

[5] See e.g. *NE* 3. 7.

[6] *Philosophical Investigations* (Oxford: Blackwell, 1953), 223.

[7] See Donald Davidson, 'On the Very Idea of a Conceptual Scheme', repr. in his *Inquiries into Truth and Interpretation* (Oxford: Clarendon Press, 1984).

genuinely intelligible that wolves (or lions) might acquire *logos*; it will be enough if we can get as far as pretending that it is.

A rational wolf would be able to let his mind roam over possibilities of behaviour other than what comes naturally to wolves. Aside from the fact that it comes within the scope of our pretence, that may seem obvious, and indeed it is. Even so, it reflects a deep connection between reason and freedom: we cannot make sense of a creature's acquiring reason unless it has genuinely alternative possibilities of action, over which its thought can play. We cannot intelligibly restrict the exercise of conceptual powers to merely theoretical thinking, on the part of something whose behaviour, if any, flows from a brutely natural aspect of its total make-up, uncontaminated by its conceptual powers—so that it might conceive 'its own' behaviour if any (it could not be its own in any very strong sense) as just another phenomenon in the world it conceptualizes. An ability to conceptualize the world must include the ability to conceptualize the thinker's own place in the world; and to find the latter ability intelligible, we need to make room not only for conceptual states that aim to represent how the world anyway is, but also for conceptual states that issue in interventions directed towards making the world conform to their content.[8] A possessor of *logos* cannot be just a knower, but must be an agent too; and we cannot make sense of *logos* as manifesting itself in agency without seeing it as selecting between options, rather than simply going along with what is going to happen anyway.

This is to represent freedom of action as inextricably connected with a freedom that is essential to conceptual thought. The physical make-up of the animal who is the thinker and agent sets limits on these freedoms, and contingent deficiencies of imagination (inborn or conditioned) may restrict their actual exercise more stringently yet. No doubt the question how imaginative a rational wolf might be is too wildly counterfactual to be worth bothering with. But that does not matter. The point is that something whose physical make-up left no free play in how it mani-

---

[8] This formulation fits representations of states of affairs in the world apart from the subject, entering into the aetiology of action aimed at bringing them about; and also representations of the subject's projected interventions themselves. It is a question over which I shall not pause whether a conceptual scheme could have no concepts of the exercise of agency except those constructed out of the concept-schema *bringing it about that* . . .

fested itself in interactions with the rest of reality, or something whose physical make-up, although it left such free play, somehow precluded the development of the imagination required to contemplate alternatives, could not acquire reason. This does not depend on pretences about lions or wolves.

Suppose now that a rational wolf finds himself in a situation in which some behaviour would come naturally to him: say playing his part in the co-operative activity of hunting with the pack. Having acquired reason, he can contemplate alternatives; he can step back from the natural impulse and direct critical scrutiny at it. We cannot allow ourselves to suppose that God, say, might confer reason on wolves, but stop short of his giving them the materials to step back and frame the question 'Why should I do this?'

But once this critical question has arisen, how can it help to appeal to what wolves need? 'Why should I pull my weight?', says our reflective wolf, wondering whether to idle through the hunt but still grab his share of the prey. Suppose we respond, truly enough: 'Wolves need to pool their energies, if their style of hunting is to be effective.' If our wolf has stepped back from his natural impulse and taken up the critical stance, why should what we say impress him?

A statement to the effect that wolves need such-and-such is what Michael Thompson calls 'an Aristotelian categorical'.[9] The logical powers of such statements are peculiar. Consider the example 'Human beings have thirty-two teeth'.[10] There is a truth we can state in those terms; but from that truth, together with the fact that I am a human being, it does not follow that I have thirty-two teeth. (In fact it is false.) Similarly, from 'Wolves need such-and-such' and the fact that he is a wolf, our wolf cannot conclude that he needs such-and-such. Of course this logical weakness of 'Aristotelian categoricals' raises no practical problem for an ordinary non-rational wolf: the way what wolves need impinges on its behaviour is not by an inference to what *it* needs. But the point makes a difference when we imagine a rational wolf wondering what to do.

One difference reason would make is to bring the facts about what wolves need to conceptual awareness, and so make them

---

[9] See his contribution to this volume, p. 281.
[10] Discussed by G. E. M. Anscombe in 'Modern Moral Philosophy', *Philosophy*, 33 (1958), 14.

available to serve as rational considerations. But what converts what animals of one's species need into potential rational considerations is precisely what enables a rational animal to step back and view those considerations from a critical standpoint. So when they become potential reasons, their status as reasons is, by the same token, opened to question. And now it matters that the predicate of an 'Aristotelian categorical' about the species cannot be deductively transferred to its individual members. The deliberative question reason enables our wolf to ask is not about wolves in general but about himself: 'What should I do?' And the deductive impotence of the 'Aristotelian categorical' brings out that what wolves need is not guaranteed a rational bearing on his question; and this even if he never forgets that he is a wolf. Reason does not just open our eyes to our nature, as members of the animal species we belong to; it also enables and even obliges us to step back from it, in a way that puts its bearing on our practical problems into question.

With the onset of reason, then, the nature of the species abdicates from a previously unquestionable authority over the behaviour of the individual animal. We are supposed to be looking for a grounding for the genuineness of the demands that virtue purports to make on reason, and while the search is on we may not appeal to those demands. This can easily leave the individual interest of the deliberator looking like the only candidate to take over the vacant throne. It would not be surprising if the deliberating wolf thought reason requires him to transcend his wolfish nature in pursuit of his individual interest, exploiting the less intelligent wolves who continue to let their lives be structured by what wolves need. No doubt the transcendence can be only partial, since the idea that free-riding might be a good plan depends on its being a way to secure things that naturally matter to wolves, such as plenty of meat to eat, not having to exert oneself if one can avoid it, and so forth. But a deliberating wolf might still take large parts of the natural pattern in the life of wolves to have no rational bearing on what he should do.

He might adopt a Calliclean or Nietzschean stance, regarding the less intelligent wolves whom he proposes to exploit as degenerate. This involves reconceiving the project of partially transcending his nature as a project of properly realizing his nature. After all, he has not stopped being a wolf, and reason, which seems to him to dictate the project, has become part of his nature.

(It is part of our nature.) The concept of nature figures here, without incoherence, in two quite different ways: as 'mere' nature, and as something whose realization involves transcending that. This wolf has no need to deny those facts about the nature—the 'mere' nature—of wolves that underlie the claim that a good wolf is one who pulls his weight in the hunt. In fact he must agree that most wolves had better not behave as he proposes to; but that is all right, because he is not preaching to the herd, or rather, in this case, the pack. There is nothing he is denying or overlooking about the natural patterns of life among wolves. Of course he may be quite wrong in thinking his project is workable, or in thinking it will be satisfactory to him, wolf that he is. But perhaps he is not wrong; and if he is, we cannot show him he is by reaffirming the facts about what wolves need. There is nothing there that he needs to dispute.

So even if we grant that human beings have a naturally based need for the virtues, in a sense parallel to the sense in which wolves have a naturally based need for co-operativeness in their hunting, that need not cut any ice with someone who questions whether virtuous behaviour is genuinely required by reason.

4. It would be a mistake to think Aristotle might be invulnerable to this point, because he has a thick 'pre-modern' conception of nature. The point is structural; it does not depend on the content of any particular conception of the needs that nature underwrites. As soon as we conceive nature in a way that makes it begin to seem sensible to look there for a grounding for the rationality of virtuous behaviour, the supposed grounding is in trouble from the logical impotence of 'Aristotelian categoricals'. Reason enables a deliberating agent to step back from *anything* that might be a candidate to ground its putative requirements. This is a problem for Aristotle on readings like that of Bernard Williams, who thinks Aristotle had a conception of nature, no longer available to us, in which it would serve as an Archimedean point for justifying ethics.[11]

Perhaps Aristotle missed this. But it is surely better to try out the thought that his naturalism simply does not promise to validate putative rational requirements. That he is not concerned about grounding is anyway strongly suggested by the fact that he

[11] See ch. 3 of Bernard Williams, *Ethics and the Limits of Philosophy* (London: Fontana/Collins, 1985).

addresses his ethical lectures only to people who have been properly brought up.[12]

We find it difficult not to want a foundation, but that is because of a location in the history of thought that separates us from Aristotle. To understand his naturalism correctly, we need to achieve a willed immunity to some of the influence of our intellectual inheritance, an influence of which Aristotle himself was simply innocent. That way, we can stop supposing the rationality of virtue needs a foundation outside the formed evaluative outlook of a virtuous person.

5. The most striking occurrence in the history of thought between Aristotle and ourselves is the rise of modern science. I want to suggest that a dubious philosophical response to that has made it difficult for modern readers to take the measure of Greek naturalism.

It is a commonplace that modern science has given us a disenchanted conception of the natural world. A proper appreciation of science makes it impossible to retain, except perhaps in some symbolic guise, the common medieval conception of nature as filled with meaning, like a book containing messages and lessons for us.[13] The tendency of the scientific outlook is to purge the world of meaning—the object of reason, in an old sense that is threatened by just this development.[14]

Hume is the prophet *par excellence* of this tendency, although he is quite unconscious of the historical explanation for it. Reason, Hume insists, does not find meaning or intelligible order in the world; rather, whatever intelligible order there is in our world-picture is a product of the operations of mind, and those operations are themselves just some of what goes on in nature, in itself meaninglessly, as it were.

From this standpoint, Kant looks like a desperate reactionary. He insists that intelligible order is found in the world, but he makes this out only by reconstruing the world as partly constituted by mind. This looks like an image of Hume's picture in a

[12] *NE* 1. 4. 1095^{b}4–6.

[13] For an elaboration of this, see ch. 1 of Charles Taylor, *Hegel* (Cambridge: Cambridge University Press, 1975).

[14] With an eye to what is to come, let me remark that the relevant notion of reason includes what Kant calls 'understanding'.

distorting medium. It looks inferior, by the lights of what seems a merely sane naturalism, in that it takes the meaning-yielding operations of mind to be transcendental rather than part of nature. And it looks unconvincing in its insistence that the order is there to be found; it seems to undermine that by suggesting that we constitute the order ourselves.

This view of the Kantian alternative provokes an understandable recoil. The usual response is to retain Hume's picture of the meaning-yielding operations of mind, but to discard his responsiveness to scepticism, which keeps Hume himself from a scientistic realism. According to the sort of outlook I mean, reality is exhausted by the natural world, in the sense of the world as the natural sciences are capable of revealing it to us. Part of the truth in the idea that science disenchants nature is that science is committed to a dispassionate and dehumanized stance for investigation; that is taken to be a matter of conforming to a metaphysical insight into the character of reality as such. (The fact that the natural sciences reveal the world as intelligible has to be glossed over somehow; I shall return to this in Section 7 below.) Any candidate feature of reality that science cannot capture is downgraded as a projection, a result of mind's interaction with the rest of nature.[15]

Against this background, it will seem that a putative operation of the intellect can stand up to reflective scrutiny only if its products can be validated on the basis of the facts of nature, on the disenchanted conception of nature yielded by modern science. For if we are to conceive what is in question as an operation of the intellect at all, we must make room for objectivity: for there to be a difference between being right and seeming right.[16] And science has presented itself as the very exemplar of access to objective truth.

This will go for practical reason as much as any other putative operation of the intellect. Hume himself does not officially recognize practical reason; but we can graft a notion of practical reason into the neo-Humean position I am describing if we can make out a notion of correctness in practical thinking that is suitably

---

[15] This Humean image has been recommended by Simon Blackburn in a number of places; see e.g. *Spreading the Word* (Oxford: Clarendon Press, 1984), chs. 5 and 6.

[16] See Wittgenstein, *Philosophical Investigations*, § 258.

grounded in facts of nature. Hume himself suggests that correctness in practical thinking can be grounded only in individual wants and likings, conceived as brute unassessable facts; that is why he cannot see any substantial practical role for reason. But in the neo-Humean position there is no need for this subjectivistic conception of the possibilities. The basic picture is that putative reasons need to be grounded in facts of disenchanted nature (nature no longer construed as addressed to us). And those facts can include such things as what animals of a particular species need in order to do well in the sort of life they naturally live.

6. It can easily seem, now, that an appeal to such facts is the only way to try to make out that ethical considerations make real demands on reason. Given the conception of nature we have arrived at, we have a forced choice between this and an unpalatable dilemma.

If we confine ourselves to the realm of nature, the only alternative to this appeal to needs (or interests) is some version of the subjectivism we can find in Hume himself. But in its pure form that gives up the project of certifying that ethical considerations genuinely constitute reasons. It is true that there are descendants of the Humean outlook, like prescriptivism, that purport to execute the project. The idea is to superimpose some quasi-Kantian formal or structural requirements of reason on pro-attitudes (or something to that effect), conceived as in themselves—were it not for the superimposition of reason—capable of fastening on anything at all. But Mrs Foot has argued, convincingly, that the underlying conception of pro-attitudes (or whatever) in this picture makes no sense.[17] The envisaged superimposition of reason yields an appearance of objectivity, but it comes too late to make any difference to that.

Perhaps we need not confine ourselves to the realm of nature? But then we are conceiving reason as a foreign power, ordering our animal nature about from outside the natural world. Our lives are mysteriously split, somehow taking place both in nature and in some alien realm in which reason operates.[18] This sort of overt

[17] See esp. the first part of 'Moral Beliefs', repr. in *Virtues and Vices* (Oxford: Blackwell, 1978).

[18] In 'Plato's heaven', perhaps. In fact I believe it is quite unfair to Plato to represent him as a supernaturalist about reason in this way. Plato is a naturalist of the Aristotelian sort, with a penchant for vividly realized pictorial presentations of his thought.

supernaturalism is of course hard to take seriously. It, too, has been a target of effective polemic from Mrs Foot: no one has done more than she to expose the uselessness of a conception of reason as somehow authoritative over us from outside our natural attitudes and inclinations.[19]

What I have sketched here can look like a cogent argument by elimination, forcing us to try to ground the rationality of ethics in something like what it is for the life of the species to go well.[20] Williams's reading of Aristotle fits here in a way, as a response to the fact that such a grounding has its own problems (Section 3 above), which means that the framework of available options is under stress. It is as if, barring subjectivism, the appeal to the supernatural has to show up somewhere, and only in a primitive conception of nature could it pass unnoticed that something supernatural is being smuggled into nature.[21]

But there is still the option of looking for a position that disclaims any need for foundations. Following this through, we shall see that we do not need to accept the conception of nature that organizes this inventory of available positions.

7. The neo-Humean outlook I have described (Section 5 above), freed from Hume's subjectivism and sympathy for scepticism, can seem sheer common sense, if the only alternative is the mysteries of transcendental idealism. But this assessment misses an essential Kantian insight.

Empiricist realists insist on the intellectual respectability of certain cognitive states: those that register direct observation, how-

---

[19] See esp. 'Morality as a System of Hypothetical Imperatives', repr. in *Virtues and Vices*.

[20] See 'Hume on Moral Judgement', repr. in *Virtues and Vices*. That paper recommends the thesis that 'moral virtues are qualities necessary if men are to get on well in a world in which they are frightened, tempted by pleasure and liable to hurt rather than help each other', on the basis that this is the way to preserve Hume's opposition to a supernatural conception of reason, while avoiding his lapse into subjectivism.

[21] This is the context in which to understand David Wiggins's remark that 'Aristotelian Eudaemonism' attributes an 'unconvincing speaking part' to nature: 'Truth, Invention, and the Meaning of Life', *Proceedings of the British Academy*, 62 (1976), 375. (See also *Sameness and Substance* (Oxford: Blackwell, 1980), 187, with pp. 183–4.) The 'speaking part' Wiggins thinks Aristotle assigns to nature must be either the role for ordinary nature considered in Section 3, which is unconvincing for the sorts of reasons canvassed there; or a role for a supposed special Aristotelian super-nature, such as figures in Williams's reading, which is unconvincing because we know now that nature is not like that.

ever that is conceived, and those that result from however much natural science they allow to derive intellectual respectability from that of observation. We need not bother with the different options; the essential point is that, whatever the details, an acceptable world-picture consists of articulable, conceptually structured representations. Their acceptability resides in their knowably mirroring the world; that is, representing it as it is.

Well and good; I do not believe that thought need attract our suspicion.[22] But note that if we retain it, we cannot suppose that intelligible order has completely emigrated from the world we take to be mirrored by intellectual states in ground-level good standing, the standing on the basis of which the standing of any other intellectual states is to be established. We have to suppose that the world has an intelligible structure, matching the structure in the space of *logos* possessed by accurate representations of it.[23] The disenchantment Hume applauds can seem to point to a conception of nature as an ineffable lump, devoid of structure or order. But we cannot entertain such a conception. If we did, we would lose our right to the idea that the world of nature is a world at all (something that breaks up into things that are the case), let alone the world (everything that is the case).[24] Hume himself, innocent of the very idea of conceptual articulation, is oblivious of this point; his modern successors lack his excuse.[25]

Kant has this point, but his picture contains a version of the fully disenchanted item that lies at the end of Hume's path, something brutely alien to the space of *logos*. Thus the thesis that the

[22] Compare Richard Rorty, *Philosophy and the Mirror of Nature* (Oxford: Blackwell, 1980). Rorty suggests that mirror imagery is suspect in its own right; but I think what follows accommodates his good point without jettisoning such imagery.

[23] I am deliberately being very unspecific here. Kant himself claims to have been nudged into transcendental philosophy by a recoil from Hume's treatment of causation in particular. But a thought of the general shape I am describing might cohere with a quasi-Humean disbelief that causal connections are an aspect of the way *logos* as it were permeates the world; this possibility finds expression in Wittgenstein's *Tractatus Logico-Philosophicus* (London: Routledge & Kegan Paul, 1961).

[24] See Wittgenstein, *Tractatus*, § 1.

[25] There is a temptation, which presumably issues from an inkling of the trouble this point makes, to suppose empiricism can dispense with mirroring or accurate representation, and make do instead with an idea like that of organizing. This would be congenial to the thought that intelligible order is, across the board, imposed rather than found. On this, see Davidson, 'On the Very Idea of a Conceptual Scheme'.

world of nature cannot be constitutively independent of the space in which thought operates becomes the thesis that the world of nature is, transcendentally speaking, a joint product of the structure of subjectivity and an ineffable 'in itself' that is fully independent of that structure. This is quite unsatisfying: it looks like a displacement of the objectivity we wanted in the world of nature to a place in the overall picture where it is no use to us—for the ineffable 'in itself' is, by Kant's own showing, nothing to us. About the world of nature, we are fobbed off with idealism; and it is really no consolation to be told (with at best questionable intelligibility anyway) that it is only transcendentally speaking that that world is in part a product of subjectivity.[26]

This is what makes it seem common sense to detranscendentalize Kant's structure of joint determination by subjectivity and the 'in itself'. The perfectly describable empirical world takes over the role played in Kant's structure by the ineffable 'in itself', the role of objective member of a pair of determinants. It is not now intelligible order as such that is jointly produced by such a pair of determinants, since the empirical world already has that, of itself as it were. But all other intelligible order, all other meaning or value, beyond what is required for the natural facts to be articulable, is conceived as partly a reflection of our subjectivity. In such a position, it is natural to say, in Humean style, that the surplus of meaning or value is projected on to objective reality from its subjective source. So transcendental idealism triggers a recoil, representing itself as common sense, into an empiricistic realism about nature, with any other features of a world-view conceived as projections.

But mirroring cannot be both faithful, so that it adds nothing in the way of intelligible order, and such that in moving from what is mirrored to what does the mirroring, one moves from what is brutely alien to the space of *logos* to what is internal to it. That is no reason to give up the idea that empirical thought can mirror the natural world.[27] But if we keep the idea of accurate representation, we cannot shirk the consequence, which we might put by saying that the natural world is in the space of *logos*. The ineffable

---

[26] For an eloquent expression of this point, see Barry Stroud's contribution to the symposium on 'The Disappearing "We" ', *Proceedings of the Aristotelian Society*, supp. vol., 58 (1984), 243–58.

[27] See n. 22 above.

'in itself' in Kant's picture performs the function of satisfying a felt need to recognize something wholly alien to subjectivity; and Kant's insight is that the natural world, just because it is not ineffable, cannot take over that function.

It may now seem that we are trapped between a rock and a hard place: between Kant's insight and the repulsiveness of the sort of idealism that says we make the world. But that is not so. The insight degenerates into that sort of idealism only because Kant keeps a role in his picture for the ineffable 'in itself', the item that lies at the terminus of the process of expelling intelligibility from the world for which Hume acts as cheerleader. In fact Kant goes beyond Hume here, in extrapolating from the disenchantment of nature. The insight saves him from supposing there is a viable conception of nature as what we are left with when all intelligibility has been expelled, but he does find that terminal item another role, and that is what introduces idealism. The thesis that the world of nature is internal to the space of *logos*, in which thought has its being, becomes an affirmation of idealism only because the structure of subjectivity is conceived as a joint determinant of the intelligible structure of the world of nature, along with the 'in itself'. If the 'in itself' drops out, the thesis that the natural world is in the space of *logos* need not seem to be a form of the thesis that thought makes the world.

This puts us in a position to focus on the insight, without being distracted by the fear of picturing nature as our creation. We should not conceive the disenchanted natural world as a satisfyingly detranscendentalized surrogate for the 'in itself'. Since it is a world, the natural world is not constitutively independent of the structure of subjectivity. It is a mistake to conceive objectivity in terms of complete independence from subjectivity. We miss the point if, retaining the hankering that that idea expresses, we nod in the direction of Kant's lesson that the 'in itself' is nothing to us, but think we can fasten on the disenchanted natural world as the next best thing. Kant's own thinking comes to wreck because of a vestige of the hankering; what it is after is repositioned but not dislodged by the insight, which cannot achieve its proper form in an environment in which the hankering persists. The real lesson is that we ought to exorcize the hankering. It is a splendid thing to find out the facts of disenchanted nature, but not because that is as close as we can come to knowing the 'in itself'.

Why is our wish to acknowledge a role for the 'in itself' so obstinate? I am suggesting, in effect, that it kept Kant himself, who almost saw through it, from a proper appreciation of his own insight. The role of science in our culture is not immediately the explanation. Science does not itself lay claim to enshrining metaphysical truth; it takes philosophers to make such claims on its behalf. More to the point is an intelligible wish to avoid responsibility. If something utterly outside the space of *logos* forces itself on us, we cannot be blamed for believing what we do.[28] Our position in history makes available to us the idea of the world as science reveals it; that means that in our case the wish to disclaim responsibility has a concrete and determinate object to fasten on. (The rise of modern science would also be central in an account of why we are especially prone to feel the responsibility of thought as a burden.)

There is no need to deny that what science reveals is special, in a way that is brought out by the point about disenchantment. In discarding the medieval conception of nature as a book, science indeed unmasked projective illusions, and it is essential to how scientific investigation rightly conceives its topic that it should be on guard against such illusions. The investigative stance of science discounts for the effects of features of the investigator, even his humanity. That is why the world as science reveals it does not contain secondary qualities. More generally, what science aims to discover is the nature of reality in so far as it can be characterized in absolute terms; the content of the view from nowhere, in Thomas Nagel's evocative phrase.[29] And the practice of science is not a mere quirk of our culture, on a par with, say, chess. Thanks to science, we know far more about the world, and understand it far better, than the medievals did, and it does not undermine the fact that this is an objective improvement to say (true though it is) that we make these assessments from our present standpoint,

[28] Rorty, *Philosophy and the Mirror of Nature*, has suggestive things to say about this.
[29] Thomas Nagel, *The View from Nowhere* (New York: Oxford University Press, 1986). On 'absolute', see ch. 8 of Bernard Williams, *Descartes: The Project of Pure Enquiry* (Harmondsworth: Penguin, 1978); also ch. 8 of his *Ethics and the Limits of Philosophy*.

which includes the hard-won idea of disenchanted nature as the province of scientific understanding.[30] But it is one thing to recognize that the impersonal stance of scientific investigation is a methodological necessity for the achievement of a valuable mode of understanding reality; it is quite another thing to take the dawning grasp of this, in the modern era, for a metaphysical insight into the notion of objectivity as such, so that objective correctness in any mode of thought must be anchored in this kind of access to the real.[31] And it is simply a confusion if one is encouraged in this thought by the idea that what science uncovers is the nearest we can come to the 'in itself'. The detranscendentalized analogue of Kant's picture that empiricist realism amounts to is not the educated common sense it represents itself as being; it is shallow metaphysics.

8. I have been trying to explain how an understandable recoil from Kant's philosophy of nature encourages the idea that all intellectual respectability, including whatever intellectual respectability can be possessed by exercises of practical reason, must in the end be grounded on correctness about the disenchanted natural world. The upshot is that the philosophy of nature, which aims to deal with how the world comes to expression in *logos*, as it were swallows up the philosophy of practice, which aims to deal with how *logos* comes to expression in the world.

Kant's own philosophy of practice is of course a separate enterprise, in a way we can perhaps understand as reflecting the thought that I have been representing as having a debilitating effect on his philosophy of nature. He keeps something wholly alien to subjectivity in the picture, and that means the philosophy of nature has to take this general shape: although empirically speaking we find meaning or intelligible order in the world, transcendentally speaking we co-operate with the 'in itself' to make it.

---

[30] See Williams's reaction to Rorty, at pp. 137–8 of *Ethics and the Limits of Philosophy*; compare *Descartes: The Project of Pure Enquiry*, 248 n. 21. To undermine the metaphysical pretensions of 'the absolute conception of reality', one need not say, as Rorty likes to, the sort of thing that provokes this response.

[31] See Charles Taylor, 'Theories of Meaning', in his *Human Agency and Language: Philosophical Papers*, i (Cambridge: Cambridge University Press, 1985), 248–92, esp. at pp. 290–1.

The idea of making meaning fits action, so perhaps we can understand Kantian philosophy of practice as shaped by the thought that there is a general lesson to be learned here: all making of meaning has a transcendental aspect. Meaning is not in nature, on the disenchanted conception, and transcendental philosophy attempts to show us how to live with the thought that the disenchanted conception of nature is indispensable to what has become our paradigm for intellectual respectability. In the philosophy of nature, we have the idea that behind an empirical transaction in which a fact impresses itself on a knowing subject, perhaps causally, there lies a transaction between subjectivity and the 'in itself' that constitutes the fact: a transaction that cannot be causal, since causation operates within the constituted empirical world. In the philosophy of practice, we have the roughly corresponding idea that behind the causal goings-on involved in an action, there is a transcendental injection of meaning into the world from outside: necessarily not a causal transaction for the same reason. The correspondence is only rough, because the meaning injected by the transcendental operation involved in action is as it were a second dose; what this meaning is injected into is not the 'in itself', but the empirical world, to whose constitution subjectivity has already made a transcendental contribution.

If the meaning that action has by virtue of being the expression of *logos* is injected into the natural world from outside, the *logos* that expresses itself in action cannot be part of the natural world. So Kant's philosophy of practice needs to reject naturalistic ways of giving substance to practical reason. The central concept must be the concept of pure practical reason, constrained only by considerations of form. If we supposed that correctness in practical reason might be non-formally determined, that would deprive practical reason of its capacity to be the transcendental originator of the meaning of action.

Rehearsing these features of Kant's philosophy of practice may reinforce the temptation to think a recoil into a neo-Humean naturalism is common sense: if we want to recognize practical reason, we must construct the requisite idea of getting things right out of the facts of disenchanted nature. But none of this further detail undermines the fact that that sort of naturalism loses Kant's insight. I have suggested how we can extricate the insight from transcendental idealism in the philosophy of nature;

what happens if we extend the implications into the philosophy of practice?

The recipe was to rid ourselves of the hankering to acknowledge something brutely alien to subjectivity. If we can manage that, we can stop supposing that behind the finding of meaning in the empirical world with which the philosophy of nature deals, there is a transcendental making of meaning. But then the philosophy of nature no longer contains grounds for insisting that the making of meaning with which the philosophy of practice deals must be transcendental. We can go on conceiving action as the making of meaning, as practical *logos* expressing or realizing itself, but we no longer need to think of practical *logos* as external to nature. But we should now be past the idea that we must construct a notion of correctness in exercises of practical reason out of facts available to natural science. So we bring practical reason back into nature; but it is practical reason conceived in a somewhat Kantian fashion, as something that does not need certification from outside itself.

A good way to begin to appreciate the shape of the possibility that opens up here is by reflecting on the concept of second nature, which is all but explicit in Aristotle's account of the acquisition of virtue of character. Virtue of character embodies the relevant proper state of practical *logos*, what Aristotle calls 'phronēsis'—'practical wisdom', in the translation of W. D. Ross.[32]

---

[32] See *NE* 2. Many modern commentators separate *phronēsis* from the formed character—second nature—that is Aristotle's concern in that book: they take his view to be that *phronēsis* (an intellectual virtue) equips one's reason to issue the right orders to one's formed character, the point of character-formation being that it makes one's second nature willing in its obedience to reason's commands. (For a very clear example of such a reading, see John M. Cooper, 'Some Remarks on Aristotle's Moral Psychology', *Southern Journal of Philosophy*, 27, supp. (1989), 25–42.) But *NE* 2. 4, with the requirement that the virtuous person chooses virtuous actions for their own sake, suggests that Aristotle conceives the topic of book 2, officially the moulding of character, as already including the proper shaping of the practical intellect. And *NE* 6. 13 does not compel the idea that character takes orders from reason, as opposed to the idea that the moulding of character *is* (in part) the shaping of reason. The architectonic device of 1. 13, dividing the virtues into virtues of character and intellectual virtues, leaves open the possibility that Aristotle means it to become clear, as the doctrine unfolds, that the division is not exclusive. The contrary reading of Aristotle is shaped, I believe, by the anachronistic importation of a quasi-Kantian extra-natural conception of practical reason. (Cooper would object that the conception of reason as autonomous, constituted independently of the natural motivational propensities that are moulded into virtues of character, is not modern, as I am suggesting, since, even if its presence in Aristotle is disputable, its presence in the Stoics is not. I think this reflects a philosophical misreading of Stoicism, but I cannot go into that here.)

The concept of second nature registers that we do not need to conceive practical reason as subject only to formal constraints. What it is for the practical intellect to be as it ought to be, and so equipped to get things right in its proper sphere, is a matter of its having a certain determinate non-formal shape, and a practical intellect's coming to be as it ought to be is the acquisition of a second nature, involving the moulding of motivational and evaluative propensities: a process that takes place in nature. The practical intellect does not dictate to one's formed character— one's nature as it has become—from outside. One's formed practical intellect—which is operative in one's character-revealing behaviour—just is an aspect of one's nature as it has become.

9. In Kant, the critique of pure reason and the critique of pure practical reason are somewhat separate enterprises. The former yields a picture of how the world comes to expression in *logos*; the latter handles the way *logos* expresses itself in the world. But we are now equipped to consider a version of the upshot of the first critique that fits both these topics.

Consider again the thesis that the world is not constitutively independent of subjectivity, which has its being in the space of *logos*. So far I have discussed this thesis exclusively in connection with theoretical reason. But the very idea of thought—the exercise of intellect—presupposes a notion of objectivity that we can gloss in terms of a distinction between being right and seeming right.[33] And the idea of the world, as it figures in that vestigially Kantian thesis, need not amount to more than an expression of that notion of objectivity. Practical thought aspires to objectivity in that general sense no less than theoretical thought does; it could not be thought, as opposed to, say, attitudinizing, if it did not. If we let the vestigially Kantian thesis embrace that point, our conception of the world, in the sense of what *logos* aims to represent accurately, expands to include features that practical *logos*, if equipped to get things right in its proper sphere, takes to justify its expressings of itself in action—rightly, since it is equipped to get things right.[34]

One supposed ground for doubt that practical thought should be allowed its aspiration to objectivity, in that general sense, is

---

[33] See n. 16 above.

[34] I believe this is the sort of framework within which we should start to understand Aristotle's difficult notion of practical truth: see *NE* 6. 2.

that practical thought does not aspire to a kind of truth that one could conceive in terms of mirroring the disenchanted natural world. An empiricistic naturalism restricts us to the following options for ethics: deny that ethical truth would have to be practical, or, if we hold on to the idea of ethical truth, if any, as a species of practical truth, either force practical truth into the form of mirroring disenchanted nature or else—for those who doubt that that is feasible—renounce the aspiration to ethical truth: for instance embrace a position like emotivism, but there are more sophisticated ways of taking this last option.[35] But I have insisted that this empiricistic naturalism is metaphysically shallow.

This expansion of the notion of the world is the point of at least one version of what has come to be called 'ethical realism'. One misses the point if one takes the position to represent ethical investigation as a kind of para-science, as in J. L. Mackie's 'argument from queerness',[36] or (more subtly) in Bernard Williams's idea that ethical realism would have to suppose—what is indeed implausible—that there is a prospect of convergence on ethical questions that could be explained in the sort of way we can explain convergence on scientific questions.[37] That is how the rhetoric of ethical realism would need to be understood if someone produced it in the context of the sort of empiricistic naturalism whose shallowness I am trying to bring out. But that is simply the wrong environment for the idea. The only similarity there needs to be between ethics and science, for ethical realism properly understood to be acceptable, is that in both of them it can be rational to say of a conclusion that *logos* itself compels it (to echo Plato's Socrates).

There is no need to deny that *logos* compels conclusions in science in a special way: the conclusion that *logos* compels is not

[35] See Williams, *Ethics and the Limits of Philosophy*, 170–1, on confidence rather than knowledge as a model for ethical conviction. Williams's idea that a knowledge model is unavailable reflects his adherence to the empiricistic naturalism I am attacking. He does not suggest that practical thought needs to renounce an aspiration to get things right; and he is rightly concerned with the fragility of that aspiration in our modern intellectual milieu. But he never considers the role, in bringing about that fragility, of the empiricistic naturalism he himself continues to take for granted.

[36] See ch. 1 of J. L. Mackie, *Ethics: Inventing Right and Wrong* (Harmondsworth: Penguin, 1977).

[37] See ch. 8 of Williams, *Ethics and the Limits of Philosophy*.

only that things are thus and so, but also that investigation has led to that conclusion because of the causal influence of the fact that things are thus and so. There is no analogue to that in ethics. But this cannot exempt scientific truth from the need to establish its status by recommending itself to *logos*. And *logos* has, everywhere, only its own lights to go by; the role of causation, in scientific thought's well-grounded conception of itself, does not rescue scientific thought from Neurath's boat. Empiricistic naturalism misses the significance of the fact that the Neurathian 'predicament' is quite general. If one protests that science is in the same boat, that tends to be misconceived as expressing a relativistic refusal to accept that science is objectively special.[38] Science is indeed objectively special, and ethical realism does not require us to unlearn its lessons, as if we were to try to regain the medieval conception of nature as a book. But it is a mistake to think we cannot show proper respect for science unless we suppose that truth about disenchanted nature is the sole context in which the material good standing of an exercise of intellect can be directly apparent, so that any good standing that is not that must be either merely formal or indirectly grounded on such truth. Good standing is, everywhere, for *logos* to pronounce on, using whatever standards it can lay hands on; nothing but bad metaphysics suggests that the standards in ethics must be somehow constructed out of facts of disenchanted nature.

I have insisted that the point involves no debunking of the scientific way of understanding nature. And it is part of my correction to Kant that exercises of the practical intellect do not impinge on nature from outside. So there can be nothing against looking for a scientific explanation of the place of, say, ethical discourse in disenchanted nature. There might be a question whether the disenchanted conception of nature contains the resources to recognize the topic as discourse, as expressive of thought. But we need not worry about that; in any case the availability of such an explanation would not compete with inquiry into how well supported by reasons a particular bit of such discourse is. The sheer possibility of doing science here cannot show

[38] See n. 30 above. At p. 218 of *Ethics and the Limits of Philosophy* Williams finds it 'revealing' that, in 'Virtue and Reason', *Monist*, 62 (1979), 331–50, I trace scepticism about objectivity in ethics to a 'philistine scientism'. I think his point is that he takes me to share the anti-scientific relativism he finds in Rorty.

that there is no room for a mode of assessment that might certify what is expressed as a thought that is simply correct, without needing to base that correctness on the thought's relation to extra-ethical reality.[39]

10. Holding firm to the thought that the second nature acquired in moral education is a specific shaping of practical *logos*, we can register the point I made by means of the parable about rational wolves (Section 3 above). Moral education does not merely rechannel one's natural motivational impulses, with the acquisition of reason making no difference except that one becomes self-consciously aware of the operation of those impulses. In imparting *logos*, moral education enables one to step back from any motivational impulse one finds oneself subject to, and question its rational credentials. Thus it effects a kind of distancing of the agent from the practical tendencies that are part of what we might call 'his first nature'.

Nature controls the behaviour of a non-rational animal. It seemed that reason compels nature to abdicate that authority, leaving a void that self-interest seemed fitted to fill. But now we can see that the way reason distances one from first nature need not invite a *coup d'état* from self-interest. In acquiring one's second nature—that is, in acquiring *logos*—one learned to take a distinctive pleasure in acting in certain ways, and one acquired conceptual equipment suited to characterize a distinctive worthwhileness one learned to see in such actions, that is, a distinctive range of reasons one learned to see for acting in those ways. If the second nature one has acquired is virtue, the rationality of virtue simply is not in suspense, though it is always open to reflective questioning. The dictates of virtue have acquired an authority that replaces the authority abdicated by first nature with the onset of reason. (It cannot be the same authority, because everything is now open to reflective questioning.) It is not that the dictates of virtue fill what would otherwise be a void; they are in position already, before any threat of anarchy can materialize.

---

[39] Simon Blackburn has persistently argued as if the sheer possibility of asking scientific questions about ethics would establish the correctness of a neo-Humean projectivism. See e.g. 'Errors and the Phenomenology of Value', in Ted Honderich (ed.), *Morality and Objectivity* (London: Routledge & Kegan Paul, 1985). This is just one more expression of the empiricistic naturalism I am attacking.

The alteration in one's make-up that opened the authority of nature to question is precisely the alteration that has put the dictates of virtue in place as authoritative.

Any second nature of the relevant kind, not just virtue, will seem to its possessor to open his eyes to reasons for acting. What is distinctive about virtue, in the Aristotelian view, is that the reasons a virtuous person takes himself to discern really are reasons; a virtuous person gets this kind of thing right.[40] Aristotle himself is notably unconcerned to defend, against potential competitors, the way things look to the kind of person he thinks of as virtuous. And we should not play that fact down; one thing it reflects is his immunity to the metaphysical sources of our modern diffidence about such things. But, without abandoning a fundamentally Aristotelian outlook, we can let the question arise whether the space of reasons really is laid out as it seems to be from the viewpoint of a particular shaping of practical *logos*. What we must insist is that there is no addressing the question in a way that holds that apparent layout in suspense, and aims to reconstruct its correctness from a vantage-point outside the ways of thinking one acquired in ethical upbringing. This allows for radical ethical reflection, as Aristotle himself seems not to. But, like any reflection about the credentials of a seeming aspect of *logos*, it must be Neurathian; we cannot escape the burden of reflective thought—the obligation to weigh, by the best lights we have, the credentials of considerations purporting to appeal to reason—by a fantasy of having some suitable first-natural facts force themselves on us in a way that would bypass the need for thought.[41]

Of course first nature matters. It matters, for one thing, because the innate endowment of human beings must put limits on the shapings of second nature that are possible for them. This is not

[40] See n. 4 above.

[41] In *Aristotle's First Principles* (Oxford: Clarendon Press, 1988), Terence Irwin reads Aristotle as a 'metaphysical realist', as opposed to an 'internal realist', and takes him to have the idea of a kind of dialectic that somehow breaks out of inherited conceptual schemes into contact with the real. My phrase 'by the best lights we have' reflects the sort of thing Aristotle says about ordinary dialectic, which I believe is the only sort of dialectic Aristotle envisages. We cannot but start from what we find ourselves already thinking, and any thoughts of others that we can understand. 'Metaphysical realism', and the doubt Irwin ascribes to Aristotle whether a procedure so described could attain objective truth, make no sense except as a confused response to Kant. The anxiety about objectivity that Irwin attributes to Aristotle makes no sense before the modern era, in which it can seem to be alleviated by a scientific metaphysic.

just because a shaping of second nature involves a moulding of prior motivational tendencies. It also involves the imparting of practical reason; and reason is inherently open to reflective questions about the rational credentials of the way it sees things. Not that people do not often embrace without reflection a conceptual organization of the sphere of ethical conduct that has been imparted to them by their elders; but if what is in question really is something conceptual, it is essential to it that reflection can break out at any time. People come unstuck from a traditional ethical outlook when reflection does break out, and they come to think, rightly or wrongly, that they have seen through the outlook's pretensions of rational cogency. If something is to be an intelligible candidate for being the way second nature should be, it must at least be intelligible that the associated outlook could seem to survive this reflective scrutiny. And there are limits on the courses reflection can intelligibly take, which come out in limits on what can be intelligible in the way of statements that purport to express part of such reflection. We can vividly bring out the bearing on reflection of these limits on intelligible speech if we conceive reflection as a communal activity; but even if one engages in reflection by oneself, one must be able to convey one's thought to others (which is not the same as convincing them of it), on pain of its being in doubt whether what one has engaged in was really thought at all. And one source of these limits on intelligibility is first nature.[42]

First nature matters not only like that, in helping to shape the space in which reflection must take place, but also in that first-natural facts can be part of what reflection takes into account. This is where we can register the relevance of what human beings need in order to do well, in a sense of 'doing well' that is not just Aristotle's 'acting in accordance with the virtues'. Consider a rational wolf whose acquisition of practical reason included being initiated into a tradition in which co-operative behaviour in the hunt is regarded as admirable, and so as worth going in for in its own right. What wolves need might figure in a bit of reflection that might help reassure him that when he acquired a second nature with that shape, his eyes were opened to real reasons for

[42] This is Wiggins's point, in 'Truth, Invention, and the Meaning of Life', in writing of the 'enabling role' which he contrasts with the 'unconvincing speaking part'.

acting. The reflection would be Neurathian, so it would not weigh with a wolf who has never acquired such a mode of valuation of conduct, or one who has come unstuck from it. And there would be no irrationality in thus failing to be convinced. But this need not undermine the reassurance, if the reflection that yields it is self-consciously Neurathian. The point stands that what members of one's species need is not guaranteed to appeal to practical reason. But the point is harmless to the genuine rationality of virtue, which is visible (of course!) only from a standpoint from which it is open to view.

It is important that when the connections between virtue and doing well—in a sense that is not Aristotle's 'acting in accordance with the virtues', a sense that is not itself shaped by ethical concerns—do figure in a reflective reassurance about an ethical outlook, they operate at one remove from the subject's rational will. What directly influences the will is the valuations of actions that have come to be second nature. This point helps us to cope satisfactorily with the fact that virtue sometimes requires self-sacrifice. Mrs Foot considers this matter with special reference to justice;[43] but the point is not restricted to specifically other-regarding virtues, and I shall discuss how it arises in the case of courage.

The connection of courage with doing well, in the relevant sense, is that human beings need courage if they are to stick to their worthwhile projects, in the face of the motivational obstacle posed by danger. Something on those lines belongs in the reflective background for a second nature that values courageous actions.[44] But we should not try to picture such a consideration as what directly engages the will of a courageous person. If we do, we risk losing our hold on how it can be rational to face danger, even in the interest of something one values deeply, if one's own death is a possible upshot. The point of courage was supposed to be that one needs it to ensure that one sticks to one's projects. How can this point not be undermined by a probability, even a slight one, that if one acts courageously one will no longer be around to have any projects, let alone stick to them?

[43] See part II of Foot, 'Moral Beliefs'. (In that paper, she thought she had to argue that justice is something anyone needs in his dealings with his fellows; but see the renunciation in the added note, pp. 130–1.)

[44] This helps explain why there is nothing morally admirable in facing danger for its own sake, with no independently sensible project thus protected from abandonment.

Transposing Mrs Foot's discussion of justice to this case suggests the response that courageousness is primarily a matter of being a certain kind of person. One cannot be that kind of person but stand ready to rethink the rational credentials of the motivations characteristic of being that kind of person, on occasions when acting on those motivations is in some way unattractive; part of what it is to be that kind of person is not to regard those credentials as open to question on particular occasions. That response is exactly right. But it works only in the context of my point that the general human need for courage stands at one remove from the rational will of a person engaged in courageous behaviour. Without that context, the response looks like a recommendation to abandon reason—which surely does examine the rational credentials of actions one by one—in favour of blind adherence to a policy. Within that context, the damage that acts of virtue can do to one's interests is unproblematic: the point of a particular courageous action lies not in the fact that human beings in general need courage, focused, as it were, on the circumstances at hand, but in the fact that this action counts as worth while in its own right, by the lights of a conceptual scheme that is second nature to a courageous person.

11. Finding a way to preserve Kant's insight leads, I have claimed, to a conception of reason that is, in one sense, naturalistic: a formed state of practical reason is one's second nature, not something that dictates to one's nature from outside. But the conception is not naturalistic in the sense of purporting to found the intellectual credentials of practical reason on facts of the sort that the natural sciences discover.

To use the rhetoric of ethical realism, second nature acts in a world in which it finds more than what is open to view from the dehumanized stance that the natural sciences, rightly, adopt. And there is nothing against bringing this richer reality under the rubric of nature too. The natural sciences do not have exclusive rights in that notion; and the added richness comes into view, not through the operations of some mysteriously extra-natural power, but because human beings come to possess a second nature.

Nature, on this richer conception, is to some extent autonomous with respect to nature on the natural-scientific conception. Correctness in judgements about its layout is not constituted by the availability of a grounding for them in facts of first nature; it is a matter of their coming up to scratch by standards internal to the formed second nature that is practical *logos*. Of course the autonomy is not total; facts about what human beings need in order to get on well, on a first-natural conception of what getting on well is for human beings, figure in the reflective background of specific shapings of second nature (see Section 10 above). This should be seen as a case of a relation that Wittgenstein draws to our attention, between our concepts and the facts of nature that underlie them. The concepts would not be the same if the facts of (first) nature were different, and the facts help to make it intelligible that the concepts are as they are, but that does not mean that correctness and incorrectness in the application of the concepts can be captured by requirements spelled out at the level of the underlying facts.

Nature, on the neo-Humean conception, can be pictured as the content of the view from nowhere. This conception can find goodness in nature, provided it is not goodness visible only to a human subject. What doing well is for a tree, or a wolf, are topics that a neo-Humean naturalism can embrace; they are not erased from nature by discounting the effects of a specifically human perspective, because the relevant assessment of good and bad is not relative to human projects and interests. (For my present purposes, we can ignore a physicalism that refuses to count plant or animal flourishing as a subject for natural science.) When this kind of naturalism considers what doing well is for a human being, a human perspective can no longer be irrelevant, but that is a mere peculiarity of the topic. The metaphysical rules do not change; the account of what doing well is for a human being can be shaped by a human perspective only in so far as what shapes the perspective can be supposed to figure in nature as seen from nowhere, or from God's point of view. So in forming a suitable conception of what doing well is for a human being, one must discount any valuations and aspirations that are special to one's historical or cultural situation: anything one cannot regard as characteristic of human beings as such. To work one's way back to endorsing a historically concrete ethical outlook, with its specific sense of what is a reason for what, one would have to hope that the concrete detail can be represented as an application, suitable for just these cultural circumstances, of prior truths about what it is for human beings as such to do well.

Contrast the naturalism that makes play with second nature. Any actual second nature is a cultural product; this is no less true of outlooks informed (as Aristotle's is not) by a lively sense of alternative possibilities for human life, lived out in cultures other than one's own. The more putative ethical reasons for acting one can represent as enjoining only a culturally specific realization of what doing well is for human beings as such, the less vulnerable one will be to a certain kind of loss of confidence. But there is nothing to suggest that confidence in a particular region of an ethical outlook is misplaced unless it can be given that treatment. Whether confidence is in order or not is for second nature itself to assess, exploiting whatever materials for critical reflection are available: including, so long as they stand up to Neurathian scrutiny, concepts that are part of its specific cultural inheritance.

Radical critical reflection is open-ended, and confidence is inherently fragile. But there is also a peculiarly modern threat to confidence, posed by neo-Humean naturalism itself. Neo-Humean naturalism requires confidence to be grounded in facts of first nature, and it is not difficult to make the materials available for such grounding look inadequate: in effect, to make the sheer fact that ethical thinking is not science into a problem for the rational credentials of ethical thinking.

It is true that Callicles, for instance, in Plato's *Gorgias*, exploits the notion of nature, but that is no problem for my claim that the threat I am talking about is peculiarly modern. Callicles exemplifies only the standing fragility of confidence. He does not invite us to realize that first nature cannot ground a conventional ethical outlook. Rather, he disputes the conception of second nature embodied in a conventional ethical outlook, on grounds internal to practical *logos*, such as that a life of conventional virtue is slavish.

The presence of Callicles in Plato's work shows Plato's interest in people who have come unstuck from an inherited ethical outlook, even to the extent of becoming confident that it is a manipulative fraud. Aristotle, by contrast, gives no sign that he is so much as aware that the fragility of ethical confidence is fragile, let alone concerned about the fact. He simply stipulates, in effect, that he is addressing only people in whom the value scheme he takes for granted has been properly ingrained.[45] In Williams's reading, this reflects a conviction on Aristotle's part that the virtues he lists are necessary for proper realization of human nature as it would figure in an accurate depiction of the view from nowhere—a thesis that Williams rightly says we cannot now believe, about any list of virtues, even ones we ourselves admire and aspire to. (See Section 4 above.) I think the only interesting thing it reflects is rather Aristotle's enviable immunity to that peculiarly modern threat to confidence. If it is a fact that Aristotle did not share the concern of Plato (who had that immunity too) with the perennial fragility of confidence, it is a superficial fact: the result of a propensity towards smugness, perhaps. And by my lights, Williams's reading is a historical monstrosity; it attributes to Aristotle a felt need for foundations, and a conception of nature as where the foundations must be, that make sense only as a product of modern philosophy, and then represents him as trying to satisfy the need with an archaic picture of nature.[46] According to Williams, modernity has lost a foundation for ethics that Aristotle was still able to believe in.[47] But what has happened to modernity is rather that it has fallen into a temptation, which we can escape, to wish for a foundation for ethics of a sort that it never occurred to Aristotle to supply it with.[48]

12. There is no purely formal notion of practical reason such as Kant envisaged: something that could enforce the claims of virtue on the rational will of anyone at all, no matter what his motivational make-up. That is one way of putting the point of 'Morality as a System of Hypothetical Imperatives'. This impotence of

[45] See n. 12 above.

[46] I find ironic the superior note Williams sounds when he remarks, of my use of a non-Aristotelian virtue in discussing an Aristotelian conception of virtue, in 'Virtue and Reason', that it shows that I am 'unconcerned . . . about history' (*Ethics and the Limits of Philosophy*, 218). I am unabashed about abstracting from Aristotle's substantive ethical views; it seems obvious that if anything in Aristotle's ethics can still live for us, it is his moral psychology, as a potential frame for a more congenial list of virtues. Where lack of concern with history, or getting history wrong, matters is in a reading of the moral psychology.

[47] See p. 53 of *Ethics and the Limits of Philosophy*, where Williams says that this supposed loss is the state of affairs on which the argument of his book is going to turn.

[48] Williams's book is an attempt to show us how to live with the lack of foundations. It cannot be ultimately satisfactory, by my lights, because he does not

Kantian practical reason leaves untouched virtue's grip on the rational wills of volunteers in the army of duty,[49] those who care about the goods achieved by virtuous conduct. So far, so good. What was disquieting about Mrs Foot's position in that paper was the further suggestion—implicit in putting the anti-Kantian point by reversing Kant's own terms—that virtue's appeal to reason, when it has any, is on a par with the appeal to reason of the actions necessary to achieve any goal one happens to care about, say building the biggest ever matchstick model of St Paul's. This suggestion seemed to be simply a corollary of the negative point, because the thought that one *should* care about the goods achieved by virtuous conduct seemed to involve the elusive notion of a practical application of reason that would speak to anyone whatever he cared about.

The neo-Humean naturalism I have been considering in this paper might seem exactly suited to respond to this discomfort. It promises to underwrite the thought that one should care about the ends achievable by virtuous conduct, not in the mysterious purely formal way that Kant envisaged, but in a way that bases the rational appeal of virtue on material facts. But my point in Section 3 above can be put by saying that, even though this picture has no truck with the Kantian idea that a rational motivation could be spun out of formal requirements without material motivational input, it still runs foul of a version of the admirable negative point of 'Morality as a System of Hypothetical Imperatives'. This picture loses the good point that is made by speaking of volunteers in duty's army; it suggests that reason does after all order all human beings to join up, just as Kant thought, even if some are deaf to the command. But the material base of the construction is not guaranteed to appeal to reason; practical reason distances an agent from his natural motivational impulses.

Aristotelian naturalism satisfies all the desiderata that are in play here. Those who serve in duty's army do not just happen to care about certain ends; we can say that reason reveals the dictates of virtue to them as genuine requirements on a rational will. The reason that effects this revelation is their acquired second nature.

unmask the modern philosophy that makes the lack of foundations look like a problem in the first place; his own conception of the metaphysical status of science (see ch. 8) is a version of that very philosophy.

[49] For this image, see Foot, *Virtues and Vices*, 170.

That this opens their eyes to real reasons for acting is argued not formally but materially, on the basis of Neurathian reflection that starts from the substantive view of the space of reasons opened up to them by their ethical upbringing. This makes it obviously wrong to expect right reason to be capable of issuing commands to just anyone, whatever his motivational make-up. On these lines, we can have it that those who serve in duty's army are kept loyal not by goals they happen to pursue but by reason's dictates as they rightly see them; but this talk of rightness does not require us to invent a way in which reason can be conceived as imposing these dictates on just anyone—neither Kant's formal way nor the material way offered by neo-Humean naturalism.

One might be tempted to object that this represents the soldiers in duty's army as conscripts, not volunteers. But reason did not order them to join up; they were not in a position to hear its orders until they were already enrolled. It is their continuing service that is obedience to reason's categorical demands. I put it this way to emphasize that the position has a distinctly Kantian flavour, though it is entirely free of formalism and supernaturalism.

I relish the fact that what I am urging in this paper can be put by saying that it takes reflection on Kant, of all people, to show us the way to an acceptable picture of the relation of reason to nature: to show us the way to an acceptable naturalism. Naturalism of the neo-Humean variety seems doomed to oscillate between the idea that the attractions of virtuous conduct just happen to appeal to some people, like the attractions of stamp-collecting, and the idea that the appeal of virtue to reason can be grounded on first nature, which I have claimed is unsatisfactory. It might be objected that we do not need reflection on Kant to see our way past this; by my own showing, reflection on Aristotle should suffice. But modern readers will always be prone to misinterpret Aristotle if they read him without first immunizing themselves against the damaging effects of modern philosophy; and I do not think we can do that without working our way through Kant's thinking, realizing what went wrong, but recognizing what was right.

7

Putting Rationality in its Place

WARREN QUINN

One kind of metaethical debate between realists and antirealists is about the character of ethical truth, with realists asserting and antirealists denying that truth in moral thought transcends our capacity to find reasons in support of our moral judgments. The antirealist in this kind of debate, no less than the realist, thinks that there is objective moral truth and knowledge. And the truth in question is not merely disquotational. Both parties think that a true moral claim corresponds, in some way or other, to the way the world is. Their disagreement, like that of their counterparts in mathematics, is about the nature of this correspondence. The antirealist sees it as a relation between the claim and the publicly available facts that could be adduced as good reasons to accept it, while the realist sees it as a relation to what he thinks of as the truth condition of the claim—a state of the world that may transcend our ability to detect its presence by way of reasoned argument. This issue is surely an important one, but it is posterior to the more fundamental question that has dominated metaethics in the last half-century. This is the question whether what lies at the heart of moral thought are beliefs capable of genuine truth or noncognitive attitudes that cannot be so assessed: feelings, emotions, desires, preferences, prescriptions, decisions, and the like.

This essay originally appeared in R. Frey and C. Morris (eds.), *Value, Welfare and Morality* (Cambridge: Cambridge University Press, 1993). It is reprinted here with the kind permission of Marion Quinn and Cambridge University Press. It was written during 1987 and delivered in the fall of that year at the University of Washington and the University of Rochester. It was revised in 1988 with the very helpful comments of Tyler Burge, Bob Adams, and Philippa Foot, and delivered in that form to a conference at Bowling Green State University. It benefited later from elaborate comments by Joseph Raz, and interesting criticisms from Chris Morris, Mark Greenberg, and Ruth Chang.

Let's use J. L. Mackie's terms 'subjectivism' and 'objectivism' to name the opposing camps in this older debate.[1] In this essay (in Section 2) I will argue against a certain common and influential version of subjectivism as it bears on the nature of reasons for action and practical rationality, and then (in Sections 3 and 4) try to sketch out part of the defence of a vaguely neo-Aristotelian version of objectivism. But first I will try to bring out some important features of the contrasting conceptions.

1

The earlier subjectivists, notably Charles Stevenson and R. M. Hare, argued that the primary function of ethical thought and language is emotive or prescriptive rather than descriptive. Stevenson thought that the job of ethical language is to express moral feeling and so to influence the feelings and behaviour of others.[2] Hare thought that a person's morality consists in the universalized principles he decides to try to live by and therefore prescribes to himself and others.[3] These authors were, in short, noncognitivists about ethical judgement. To say or think that an act was good or bad might, in a secondary way, imply certain facts about it, but its goodness or badness could never consist in such facts. Ethical concepts and judgements are on this view quite special. The concepts do not have the function of picking out properties or relations, and the judgements do not have the function of ascribing them. Their job is rather to enable us to express to ourselves or others the noncognitive attitudes mentioned above.

[1] J. L. Mackie, *Ethics: Inventing Right and Wrong* (Harmondsworth: Penguin, 1977), ch. 1. Mackie's introduction of 'objectivism' (p. 15) as the view asserting that (intrinsic or categorical) moral values are 'part of the fabric of the world' could at first suggest evaluative realism. And if so, subjectivism, which is introduced as the denial of objectivism, would be compatible with moral antirealism of the truth-admitting kind. But as Mackie gives content to the notions in the following discussion, it turns out that his subjectivism denies that moral evaluations of the relevant kind *can* be true. So the salient contrast turns out, after all, to be over truth.

[2] The nub of the theory is clearly presented in Charles Stevenson, 'The Emotive Meaning of Ethical Terms', repr. in his *Facts and Values* (New Haven, Conn.: Yale University Press, 1963).

[3] R. M. Hare, *The Language of Morals* (Oxford: Clarendon Press, 1952), 69 ff.

J. L. Mackie himself rejects this noncognitivist version of subjectivism in favour of an 'error theory'.[4] According to him, our ethical concepts and judgements have the same descriptive function as their empirical counterparts. The trouble is that there are no moral properties or relations answering to the concepts and no moral truths answering to the judgements.[5] For such properties and truths would be unacceptably 'queer'. They seem real only because we mistakenly project our own attitudes on to the world. But Mackie wishes not simply to do away with morality, but to reconstruct it. And if this reconstruction is to be done along metaphysically respectable lines, it will have to avoid the vulgar projective error. This is what he must have in mind when, speaking of the honest ethics that is 'not to be discovered but to be made', he says that 'the morality to which someone subscribed would be whatever body of principles he *allowed* ultimately to guide or determine his choice of action'.[6] So Mackie's reconstructed morality looks something like Hare's version of noncognitivism.

This is not surprising. The subjectivists I want to consider are not, in Mackie's terms, 'first-order' moral skeptics.[7] They want to be able to make and 'defend' moral claims. So, given that the point of *belief* has so much to do with the acquisition of truth, morality—conceived as a set of false beliefs, or beliefs that can be neither true nor false—seems needlessly defective. The natural remedy is to reconceive, or remake, it along expressivist lines. So, following this line of thought, I will treat all error theorists who think, like Mackie, that what lies behind and animates each sincere moral belief is a corresponding noncognitive attitude as potential noncognitivists.

But there is another aspect to typical subjectivist thought that is as essential as its noncognitivism. *It is the idea that an agent's moral judgements can and must, despite their noncognitive character, rationalize the moral choices that he makes in accordance with them.*[8] The

---

[4] Mackie, *Ethics*, 35.
[5] Mackie admits that certain claims of instrumental value can be true, but only because those claims are naturalistically reducible (ibid. 50–9). Judgements of instrumental value that presuppose judgements of intrinsic value must be just as badly off as the judgements of intrinsic value they presuppose.
[6] Ibid. 106. The emphasis on 'allowed' is mine.   [7] Ibid. 16.
[8] This use of 'rationalize' is an old one that completely lacks the modern psychoanalytical idea of finding false but self-comforting reasons for what one does or feels.

objectivist agrees, at least when the moral judgements are reasonable. But the agreement is superficial. For we find two very different conceptions of how the rationalization comes about. The subjectivist of the kind I am imagining adopts a broadly instrumentalist (or derivativist) theory of practical rationality that includes finding suitable means to one's determinate ends, suitable determinations of one's indeterminate ends, and suitable applications of one's chosen principles.[9] If, for example, an agent has a moral pro-attitude toward helping the poor and believes that something he can now do will relieve someone's poverty, he then has a perfectly objective instrumental *prima facie* reason to do it. And if he subscribes to the principle of keeping his promises, then he has a perfectly objective *prima facie* reason to keep this particular promise.[10]

Moral pro- and con-attitudes, whether directed to goals or to principles, thus have the power to rationalize choice. And this power is essential. For it is extremely uninviting to suppose that an agent's moral judgements—or, on cognitivist accounts, an agent's reasonably correct moral judgements—could fail to provide reasons for action. For subjectivists, these reasons are provided only with the help of the noncognitive attitudes that moral judgements express. In this respect modern subjectivists have extended Hume's idea that morality produces motives only through its noncognitive content to the idea that it produces reasons only in the same way.[11]

---

[9] For an example of a very broad conception of instrumental rationality see Bernard Williams's 'sub-Humean model' in 'Internal and External Reasons', in his *Moral Luck* (Cambridge: Cambridge University Press, 1981), 102.

[10] David Gauthier, who certainly holds that moral preferences and self-prescriptions give instrumental reasons, also accepts a kind of reason applying to certain important moral situations that cannot be counted as instrumental. On his view, *if* it is instrumentally rational for me to be disposed to honour personally advantageous agreements (as it might be if enough people could see through any insincerity) *then* I thereby have a special moral reason to comply with the terms of one that I made with the honourable intention to comply. See David Gauthier, *Morals by Agreement* (Oxford: Clarendon Press, 1988), ch. 6. Of course, if I retain my earlier honourable disposition then I have, in my broad sense, an instrumental reason that flows simply from that. For complying instantiates a pattern of behaviour that I personally value. This is a typical subjectivist reason that presumably remains present in Gauthier's system. But, given the other parts of his complex view, I would still have a reason even if I had lost the disposition. This latter reason does not fall under the present discussion of subjectivism.

[11] Stevenson was, admittedly, strangely silent about reasons for action. But Hare makes it clear that moral reasons come from preferences, which he certainly

This shows up in Bernard Williams's 'Internal and External Reasons', where he includes 'dispositions of evaluation' in an agent's 'subjective motivational set' (S-set), the set from which all the agent's reasons for action derive through various acts of deliberating.[12] The evaluations that an agent's S-set disposes him to make presumably include the moral evaluations that he has internalized and made part of his way of life. But the practical reasons afforded by these moral evaluations do not derive from his recognizing them to be true. Even if he could come to see that they were false and others not flowing from his S-set true, he would not, on Williams's view, have any reason to follow the latter. For he would have no rational method of transferring the motivation present in his existing dispositions to the better ones.[13] Indeed he would be caught in such a bizarre dilemma (forced to accept his self-acknowledged false evaluations as reasons and unable to act on their true alternatives) that the overall position can be saved, I think, only by denying that the evaluations that flow from his motivational set can be rationally assessed as true or false. And, by our criterion, this not only makes Williams, at least in 'Internal and External Reasons', a subjectivist about what must be an important class of moral evaluations, but also one who thinks that reasons follow from their noncognitive force.

Objectivists—at least of the kind I am considering—see things very differently. They agree that moral thought, at least when it is correct, provides reasons for action. But they think it does so only because of its cognitive content. What rationalizes or makes sense of the pursuit of a goal, they assert, is some way in which the goal in question seems *good*. And what rationalizes or makes sense of

---

regards as noncognitive dispositions to choose, exposed to facts and logic. See e.g. R. M. Hare, 'Another's Sorrow', in his *Moral Thinking: Its Levels, Methods, and Points* (Oxford: Clarendon Press, 1981), 104–5. Something similar holds, I believe, for Mackie, although his discussion of reasons in ch. 3 of *Ethics* makes things a bit tricky. He there distinguishes three categories of reasons or requirements: merely external and conventional ones (like the rules of a game or social practice seen from the outside), those that spuriously purport to bind categorically and intrinsically, and those that, depending on an agent's own attitudes, bind hypothetically. The latter might be called natural reasons. And it is these that, on his account, a properly 'made' morality would give the agent whose morality it was.

[12] Williams, *Moral Luck*, 101–13.

[13] According to Williams, deliberation is always *from* existing motivations, bringing *them* to bear upon the possibilities of action. See ibid. 109.

strict conformity to a principle is some way in which it seems that one can act *well* only by following it.

According to this kind of objectivism, practical rationality is not as different from theoretical rationality as the subjectivist supposes. Practical thought, like any other kind of thought, requires a subject matter. And for human beings the subject matter that distinguishes thought as practical is, in the first instance, human ends and action in so far as they are good or bad in themselves. The branch of practical thought that is usually called practical reasoning is the determination of how something desired as good can be obtained. In practical reasoning, thus defined, one does not critically examine the desired good to see if it is genuine or, if it is, to question whether something in the special circumstances forbids its pursuit.

These important questions belong to a more fundamental kind of practical thought that might be called ethical. Here one tries to determine what, given the circumstances, it would be good or bad in itself to do or to aim at. These questions are referred to larger ones: what kind of life it would be best to lead and what kind of person it would be best to be. The sense of 'good' and 'best' presupposed in this noncalculative form of practical thought is very general. In an Aristotelian version of objectivism these notions attach to actions, lives, and individuals as belonging to our biological species.

The object of this kind of thought is not in the first instance morality or prudence as these are commonly understood. For most people think that a human being may be prudent without being good, and many think that there is room for Nietzschean or Thrasymachean skepticism, according to which the best kind of human life might be immoral in one or another way. An objectivist of the kind I wish to defend sees practical thought as deploying a *master* set of non-instrumental evaluative notions: that of a good or bad human end, a good or bad human life, a good or bad human agent, and a good or bad human action. Practical reason is, on this view, the faculty that applies these fundamental evaluative concepts. If there is no truth to be found in their application, then there is no point to practical reason and no such thing as practical rationality.

I have already indicated a way in which subjectivists who hold an instrumentalist conception of practical rationality can be objec-

tivists about practical reason and rationality. While they deny that
ends, principles, and actions are objectively good or bad in themselves, they hold that a person acts rationally in trying to realize
his own ends or maximize conformity to his own principles. On
the plausible assumption that acting rationally is a natural and
not merely conventional form of acting well (and acting irrationally a natural form of acting badly), and in the apparent
absence of grounds for other not merely conventional forms, instrumental rationality thus becomes the one objective virtue and
instrumental irrationality the one objective vice.[14] In contrast, my
objectivist regards instrumental rationality, in this sense, as mere
cleverness—something that may or may not be a good to its
possessor or make her a better agent. If, on the other hand, someone's practical reasoning is necessarily constrained by appropriate ends and principles, and a sense of the fine and the shameful,
then his cleverness constitutes a real virtue—part of his overall
practical rationality.[15]

[14] Note, however, that some subjectivists have backed away from this theoreti-
cally odd hybrid—either, like Richard Brandt (in *A Theory of the Good and the Right*
(Oxford: Clarendon Press, 1979), 10–16), by adopting a descriptive account of
practical rationality that does not require it to be regarded as an objective excellence or, like Allan Gibbard (in *Wise Choices, Apt Feelings: A Theory of Normative
Judgment* (Cambridge, Mass.: Harvard University Press, 1990), e.g. 45–6) by applying an expressivist–prescriptivist account of rationality itself. For Gibbard there is
no fact of the matter whether maximizing the satisfaction of one's preferences is
rational, and argument can break down about fundamental questions of rationality in much the way Stevenson thought it could about fundamental questions of
goodness. That such argument breaks down as rarely as it does (that there is
mutual argumentative influence over even such basic matters) is a result of the fact
that we have been biologically selected to be conversationally cooperative creatures. While I suspect that the substance of my antisubjectivist argument could be
applied to these authors, I must postpone the complexities of that discussion for
another occasion.
[15] A review and minor elaboration of this quasi-Aristotelian vocabulary might
be helpful. *Practical reason* is the generic faculty of which *practical thought* is the
characteristic generic activity and *practical rationality* the generic virtue. *Practical
reasoning* (that is, *instrumental reasoning* in my broad sense) and *ethical thought* are
the two main species of practical thought. If practical reasoning does not presuppose a correct evaluation of the ultimate suitability, whether in general or in the
circumstances, of the desired goal or chosen principle, then its virtue is *cleverness*.
For the neo-Humean, cleverness exhausts the virtue of practical rationality. If
practical reasoning does rest on a correct assessment of the present suitability of
the goal or principle, its virtue is, let us say, *real instrumental rationality*. And
wisdom is the virtue of ethical thought. *Prudence* and so-called *moral goodness* are
conspicuous but controversial candidate characteristics that wise ethical thought
may deem the chief virtues of action.

According to the objectivism I will defend, the primary job of practical reason is the correct evaluation of ends, actions, and qualities as good and bad in themselves. And what it is for something to be a reason for action follows from this. *On this view, a reason to act in a certain way is nothing more than something good in itself that it realizes or serves, or, short of that, something bad in itself that it avoids.* To the extent that one realizes or serves some such good one acts well. To the extent that one realizes or serves some such bad one acts badly. An objectivist therefore sees moral obligation as giving an agent reason to act only because, and only to the extent that, the agent will act well in discharging it or badly in neglecting it. Moral skepticism therefore comes to nothing more than the doubt that acting morally is a genuine form of acting well.[16] This is the kind of doubt with which moral philosophy began. And, on this view, it is the most important doubt for moral philosophy to resolve.

The subjectivist has a very different account of how moral judgement provides reasons for action. He obviously wishes to avoid bringing in any of these allegedly grounding concepts of actions, lives, ends, and agents as good or bad in themselves. He proposes instead an appeal to basic and therefore cognitively uncriticizable *attitudes*. And this is what, as I shall now try to argue, he cannot do. As unpromising (or even 'queer') as the objectivist picture may seem (and I shall be examining some objections to it later), I wonder if it is not our only hope of retaining the idea of practical rationality that we want.

2

The problem lies, I think, in what the subjectivist must take these noncognitive pro- and con-attitudes—these emotions, desires, aversions, preferences, approvals, disapprovals, decisions of principle, and so on—to be.[17] So far as I can see, a reasonably up-to-date subjectivist would present them as functional states that,

---

[16] Alternatively, that the so-called moral virtues are real human virtues.

[17] I use the term 'noncognitive attitude' here broadly to cover all of these mental states. A decision of principle includes a pro-attitude toward the standard of behaviour one has chosen and a con-attitude toward behaviour that violates the standard.

inter alia, tend to move an agent in various practical directions and therefore help explain why his having certain beliefs and perceptions makes him choose, or feel inclined to choose, one course rather than another. They underlie his *tendencies* or *dispositions* to form and express feelings, and to choose certain practical actions in the presence of various perceptions and beliefs. To say in the intended sense that someone has a pro-attitude toward world peace is to say, among other things, that his psychological set-up disposes him to do that which he believes will make world peace more likely. And to say that keeping his promises is one of his principles is to say that, among other things, he is set up to do that which he sees as required by the promises he has made.

But how can a noncognitive functional state whose central significance in this context is to help explain our tendency to act toward a certain end, or in accordance with a certain principle, *rationalize* our pursuit of the end or our deference to the principle? How can the fact that we are set up to go in a certain direction make it (even *prima facie*) rational to decide to go in that direction? How can it even contribute to its rationality? Even if a past decision is part of the cause of the psychological set-up, there still remains the question whether to continue to abide by it. It is not, according to the view we are considering, the specifically moral aspect of the noncognitive attitude that gives *it* the power to rationalize. Moral attitudes, whatever their special moral earmarks, rationalize because they are dispositive functional states and not because they are moral. The underlying neo-Humean theory of rationalization is completely general. So in testing its plausibility we are free to turn to nonmoral examples. Such examples also free us from the distracting worry whether a given functional-dispositional state rationalizes in a distinctively moral way. *The basic issue here is more fundamental: whether pro- and con-attitudes conceived as functional states that dispose us to act have any power to rationalize those acts.*[18]

Suppose I am in a strange functional state that disposes me to turn on radios that I see to be turned off. Given the perception that a radio in my vicinity is off, I try, all other things being equal, to get it turned on. Does this state rationalize my choices? Told

---

[18] My skepticism about this and related matters is shared by others in recent ethics, perhaps most thoroughly by E. J. Bond in *Reason and Value* (Cambridge: Cambridge University Press, 1983), esp. 56.

nothing more than this, one may certainly doubt that it does. But in the case I am imagining, this is all there is to the state. I do not turn the radios on in order to hear music or get news. It is not that I have an inordinate appetite for entertainment or information. Indeed, I do not turn them on in order to *hear* anything.[19] My disposition is, I am supposing, basic rather than instrumental. In this respect it is like the much more familiar basic dispositions to do philosophy or listen to music.

I cannot see how this bizarre functional state in itself gives me even a *prima facie* reason to turn on radios, even those I can see to be available for cost-free on-turning. It may help explain, causally, why I turn on a particular radio, but it does not make the act sensible, except in so far as resisting the attendant disposition is painful and giving in pleasant. But in that case it is not the present state that is the reason but the future prospect of relief.[20] Now at this point someone might object that the instrumentalist subjectivist does not or need not regard basic noncognitive pro-attitudes as rationalizing their *objects*, but rather as rationalizing actions that are the *means* to them. So, of course, my odd pro-attitude gives me no reason to turn on radios.

The picture here is of practical reason as a cognitively criticizable mechanism for transferring motivation from the objects of attitudes to that which is 'toward' them.[21] Since the ultimate objects are rationally uncriticizable, no reasons are produced for them—no reasons to have those ends or principles or to do those things that are wanted or chosen for their own sakes. But since it is possible to reason well or badly about what will enable one to have or do those objects, reasons are produced for ancillary actions. So if, for example, one loves to listen to music—a contingent taste unassessable by reason—one's attitude does not give a reason actually to listen, but only, in the context of further intentions, to get a record down from the shelf and put it on the turntable.

[19] There are several variations on what the object of my pro-attitude might be: (*a*) the *act* of my turning on radios, (*b*) the *state of affairs* in which I turn them on, (*c*) the state of affairs in which they are turned on (by anyone), and so forth. For my purposes it doesn't matter how my state is conceived, although I will tend to use (*a*) for simplicity. Note that, on all three interpretations, hearing something coming from a radio may be evidence that the object of my pro-attitude has been achieved, even though hearing something is not in itself the object of that attitude.

[20] We will be coming back to the question of rationalization by the prospect of pleasure or pain.

[21] This possible objection, to whose subtleties I may not be doing complete justice in the following remarks, was raised by Joseph Raz.

I find this construction of instrumentalism, while possible, unattractive. If my basic love of listening to music doesn't give me a reason to listen, then it doesn't, I think, give me a reason to take the record down. The appeal of the view, apart from suggesting a line of escape from my argument, may come from conflating two distinct points: (*a*) that, on an instrumentalist view, a person's ultimate preferences are uncriticizable (except by reference to their compatibility) and (*b*) that a person's ultimate preferences do not mark off their objects as, given that he has those preferences, rationally appropriate for him. The first point is essential to instrumentalism, but the second does not follow from it. Nor is it a particularly plausible part of that view. But even if it were, my counter-example still works. For my basic noncognitive pro-attitude (conceived as a dispositive functional state) toward turning on radios seems not only to give me no reason to turn on radios but also no reason to take the necessary steps, such as plugging them in. Both seem equally senseless.[22]

But surely my disposition must strike me as odd, if only because it must strike others as odd. Perhaps then I regard it as an embarrassment and wish to be rid of it. And this might seem to make a difference that the subjectivist can exploit. It is not any old functional-dispositional state that rationalizes action, but only one that an agent is ready to stand behind or is at least not alienated from. A second-order endorsement (or the absence of a second-order rejection) is the missing ingredient.

It will be admitted, of course, that an unwelcome first-order attitude can provide the actual point of someone's doing something. A pyromaniac may hate it that he takes pleasure in setting fires, yet set another fire for that very pleasure. But perhaps the subjectivist will say that in such a case the pyromaniac's pleasure fails to give him a genuine reason to set the fire. For that he would need to approve it, or at least not disapprove it, at some higher level.

Now I think it very doubtful that a subjectivist can legitimately attach this significance to the existence or nonexistence of opposing higher-level attitudes. Here, as elsewhere, he is presupposing

---

[22] Since turning on radios and taking the steps thereto (for example, plugging them in) seem to me to stand or fall together, I will continue, for reasons of economy, to apply the question of rationalization to the former. If the reader disagrees, he may, whenever I speak of turning radios on, substitute some mere means to that end.

a significance that depends not on level but on content. An objectivist would take the pyromaniac's higher-level disapproval seriously because he would see in it an evaluation of the pleasure as bad,—for example, perverse or shameful. And this would be relevant simply because someone who thinks that an attraction is bad in some such way can scarcely think that he will act well by giving in to it. So the higher-level disapproval shows that the *positive evaluation* that would normally attach to an action as pleasure-producing is cancelled. The self-disapproving pyromaniac would not see the prospective pleasure as something that tends to make the torching choice-worthy. But the subjectivist, in rejecting the idea of choice-worthiness as the subject matter of practical reason, can see nothing in the higher-level disapproval except more complexly structured psychological *opposition*, and such opposition would seem to leave the lower-level attitude securely in place with its own proper force.

This point is perhaps worth emphasis. Higher-order attitudes pro- and con- lower-order attitudes will presumably be treated by the subjectivist as further noncognitive states of the same generic functional type—states grounding, among other things, dispositions to choose one thing rather than another in the face of certain percepts and beliefs. Rather than grounding dispositions to seek certain first-order ends such as pleasure or health, they ground dispositions to seek to be or not to be a person who has or acts toward those ends. What this picture does not explain, however, is the *authority* of the higher-level attitudes.

If the pyromaniac regards his fascination as sick and reprehensible, then he will not see it as giving him a reason to set fires. He may succumb to it as a temptation, but as he looks back on his choice he will not regard the pleasure he took as at least something positive to be credited to his choice. But on the subjectivist's view, it is hard to see why he shouldn't be consoled in just this way. For the subjectivist sees the pyromaniac as having two practical attitudes at odds with each other. His lower-level attraction moves him toward the act of pouring the kerosene, and his higher-level aversion moves him away from it. If he goes ahead he satisfies one of these attitudes, if he refrains he satisfies the other. There is therefore something to be said for and against each alternative. Without the thought that the appetite for fires is bad and therefore *without power to rationalize choice*, there seems no way to keep it from counting.[23]

Even setting this point aside, I cannot see how the subjectivist can insist that I *must* have some higher-level disapproval of my odd disposition to turn on radios. Perhaps, upbeat person that I am, I positively like my first-order attitude. But even if I do, this still doesn't seem to help rationalize my behaviour. Turning on radios still seems perfectly senseless.

Perhaps a subjectivist should simply reject the example as too bizarre. According to this objection, we can make sense of someone's behaviour as revealing pro- and con-attitudes only if the attitudes are ones we share to some considerable extent. So if my allegedly basic pro-attitude toward turning on radios is not rendered in one way or other familiar, it may have to be rejected. Attempts to undermine the neo-Humean theory by way of outlandish examples are thus doomed to failure.

Subjectivists may hope by means of some such argument to bring the actual implications of their theory of rational action more in line with those of objectivists, who think that we make sense of an action only when we find something that seems good about it—some advantage, pleasure, boost to the ego, or the like. For the objectivist, the state disposing me to turn on radios fails for want of a point. Neither acts of turning on radios nor the state of affairs in which radios are on can intelligibly be seen as goods in themselves. But since the pro-attitude is stipulated to be basic, it cannot be rationalized by being referred to any further good, such as entertainment or knowledge.

Perhaps subjectivists can rule out motivational interpretations that are very strange. But it is difficult to see how. For I do not see how they could rule it out that I might actually engage in the odd behaviour in question and that the best functional explanation would be that I had a correspondingly odd pro-attitude understood in their favourite functionalist terms. Indeed, I do not see how they could rule it out that someone might have basic pro-attitudes (conceived as such favoured functional states) toward

[23] In case one is tempted to think that the force of the higher-order attitude derives from its taking account of the lower-order attitude, note that in typical cases the lower-order attitude also takes account of the higher. That is, it remains in existence despite its recognition of opposition from above. Even though the pyromaniac may hate himself, he still wants to set fires.

very many bizarre things (disease, pain, poverty, or the like). This is easiest to imagine in someone who desires to communicate reasonably truthfully,[24] is aware of her own eccentricity, has a reasonably accurate picture of the world, deliberates well about means toward and constituents of her largely bizarre ends, and acts accordingly. Such a person would be intelligible as desiring these strange things *if* desires were the things subjectivists took them to be.[25] And she would not be incapable of recognizing her odd ends and counter-ends for what they were, and for their oddity. A person does not have to be set up to strive for health to know what health is, a gloomy ascetic temperament does not rule out the knowledge of pleasure, perverse drives frequently recognize (indeed revel in) their own perversity, and so on. Such odd psychologies might, of course, be determined by an anomalous brain state. We might even come to recognize the neurological causal factors. But then the rest of us could imagine that we too might (unhappily) come to have these attitudes.

So I do not think that subjectivists can rule out the possibility of my radio case. Nor can they rule it out that, if I perform my odd routine cheerfully and without regret, my first-order attitude is unopposed by higher-order attitudes of disapproval. So they ought to see it as having the power to rationalize. But that is exactly what it seems to me *not* to have. It may in some way explain the fact that I turn on another radio, but it does not, in my view, go one step toward showing it to be sensible.

---

[24] That and other familiar pro-attitudes (about communication and learning) are certainly necessary when so many others are lacking.

[25] It is sometimes said that some interpretations of preferences, conceived along subjectivist lines, will simply be ineligible on the ground that neither we nor the subject will be able to justify the interpretation. For example, that while the subject might, on perhaps frivolous aesthetic grounds, prefer normal oranges to red apples but green apples to normal oranges, she could not, for example, be understood to prefer normal oranges to red apples on high shelves but red apples on low shelves to normal oranges (at least not unless there was something more to the story—highness and lowness of shelf could simply not be an ultimate object of attachment). But again this seems to confuse the question of causation and justification. If preference is conceived along subjectivist lines as a pre-evaluative functional state causing one to feel and act in various ways under various conditions of belief and recognition, then there is no reason why this odd 'preference' could not emerge. Indeed, the person might be bemused by her own highly unusual internal psychological economy. And to say this in no way implies that either the subject or anyone else is infallible about her 'preferences'—we might come to see that it was something other than shelf-height after all.

I have chosen a bizarre example to make my point as sharply as possible. But the argument applies, I think, with complete generality. No noncognitive, dispositive functional state of the kind under consideration can, by itself, make the contribution to rationalizing action that subjectivist instrumentalists suppose it to make. This is true even if the state points toward something good like pleasure or health. For pleasure or heath provide a point to their pursuit that does not consist in the fact that they are pursued. A noncognitive pro-attitude, conceived as a psychological state whose salient function is to dispose an agent to act, is just not the kind of thing that can rationalize. That I am psychologically set up to head in a certain way cannot by itself rationalize my will's going along with the set-up. For that I need the *thought* that the direction in which I am psychologically pointed leads to something good (either in act or result), or takes me away from something bad.

Someone might object that I am imputing to the subjectivist too narrow a conception of desire, aversion, preference, approval, disapproval, commitment, and the like—that I am focusing too exclusively on their role in explaining tendencies to *act*. These states may have other characteristic noncognitive features that better account for their rational force. Chief among these would be the pleasing light that positive attitudes, and the unflattering light that negative attitudes, cast on their objects.[26]These hedonic colours may also be lent to the idea of doing that which will make the pleasant or painful prospect more likely. And perhaps it is here that we find the rationalizing force of pro- and con-attitudes.

But how is this to be spelled out? It might be said that pleasure or pain in the prospect of having or doing something makes pleasure or pain in the reality more likely. So a person with a basic pro-attitude can expect pleasure in achieving his object and frustration in failing to achieve it, just as someone with a basic con-attitude can expect unpleasantness in getting his. And it is this that rationalizes pursuit or avoidance.

---

[26] Here I return to a point that I explicitly put aside earlier. It may be more plausible with respect to desire and aversion than to commitment to principle. But it might also be thought that commitments (whether moral or personal) lend the prospect of their fulfilment a pleasing aspect of self-consistency and personal integrity, and their violation a disturbing aspect of incoherence and failure.

There are at least two problems that stand in the way of this solution. To the extent that a present basic pro-attitude rationalizes by virtue of a promised pleasure, then rationalization should also be present—and just as strong—in the case where the agent expects the pleasure but oddly lacks the present motivation. If I believe that I will get just as much pleasure from this piece of candy, which tempts me, as from that piece, which oddly does not, then it is hard to see, at least as far as gustatory pleasure is concerned (the typical reason for buying candy), how I could have more reason to choose the first. That I now find pleasure in the *thought* of eating or buying the first piece but not the second seems irrelevant. Or if I believe that I will feel as much psychic pain in violating a rule (in the sense of a possible rule) that I have deliberately not subscribed to (perhaps because I feel its pull on me is irrational) as in violating a rule that I have adopted, it is hard to see how the prospect of pain can give me more reason to observe the second than the first.

But there is an even more serious problem with supposing that a basic pro-attitude rationalizes by reference to the pleasure its fulfilment promises or the pain its frustration threatens. For the objects of many basic desires do not include the subject's pleasure or pain at all. Suppose, for example, I want to see famine ended in Ethiopia. I therefore take pleasure in the very idea of famine relief (and perhaps also in the idea of working toward it) and feel pained when politics stands in the way. But if I attach basic value to the end to famine, then it is the thought that doing such-and-such will help feed people that gives me my basic reason to do it—not the thought that doing it will bring me pleasure or save me pain. These might give me *additional* reasons, but they cannot be my basic ones.

It seems, moreover, that the pleasure one expects in getting (or working toward) what one basically wants and the displeasure in failing to get it are themselves rationally assessable. It generally *makes sense* to be pleased or frustrated in these circumstances. What more sensible thing to be pleased or displeased about? But surely the subjectivist will want to say that this good sense depends entirely on the attitude. It is rationally appropriate to be pleased at getting what one wants or displeased at failing to get it *because* one wants it. So, again, the pleasure or displeasure cannot provide the basic reason to pursue the object.

In any case, it seems to me a mistake to think of the concepts of pleasure and displeasure as purely descriptive, psychological concepts. To call an experience pleasant or unpleasant is already to bring it under an evaluative concept.[27] That is why purely psychological accounts of pleasure seem to leave it utterly mysterious *why* we should pursue the pleasant and shun the unpleasant. On one such account, a pleasant experience is, roughly speaking, one whose intrinsic character makes an agent want to prolong it. When we combine this with a subjectivist account of wanting, we conclude that a pleasant experience is one whose intrinsic character creates a functional state grounding, among other things, the disposition to prolong it. But why should anybody want to be in such a state? Suppose I tell you that if you start scratching your ear the experience will strongly dispose you to keep on scratching. Does this by itself give you reason to want to scratch? Conceived as a kind of psychological inertial force, pleasure takes on a somewhat sinister aspect. This is because the account leaves out the salient thing: that an agent wants to prolong a pleasant experience precisely because it is pleasant—because it feels good. Pleasantness is not merely that which brings about a prolonging disposition, it is what makes sense of it.

So far, I have urged that neither the dispositional nor the hedonic aspect of pro-attitudes can provide what we want in the way of reasons for action. The subjectivist might respond by taking a somewhat different tack. He might claim that noncognitive attitudes may be formed in a rational or irrational way, and that *rationally formed* attitudes can provide reasons. This might, of course, mark a considerable retreat from the familiar subjectivist position that *any* pro- or con-attitude can give a reason for action. But if the requirements of rational attitude formation turn out to be weak, the retreat may be limited. If the requirement were merely one of reasonably adequate information, then many noncognitive attitudes would provide reasons. If, on the other hand, the requirement were as demanding as Kant's generalization test, far fewer would qualify.

My response to this strategy is to deny that the kinds of noncognitive state the subjectivist means to be talking about can

[27] In *The Varieties of Goodness* (London: Routledge & Kegan Paul, 1963), 63–85, Georg Henrik von Wright argued that pleasure is not merely good but is itself a kind of goodness.

be made rational or irrational by the way in which they are formed. This is because I cannot see how, in the absence of objective prior standards for evaluating ends or actions as good or bad in themselves, a state disposing one to act can be any more rationally criticizable than a state disposing one to sneeze. Any factor (like having a perfectly regular character or being caused by true rather than false beliefs or valid rather than invalid reasoning) could be just as true of sneezing as acting. It's true that the disposition to sneeze can be irresistible, while dispositions to turn on radios, or read philosophy papers, typically are not. But space for the voluntary seems to me in itself devoid of rational significance unless it is in the service of an agent's values.

It is often said that an attitude formed in light of true beliefs has more power to rationalize than one formed in error. And while there is something right about this, it is not something that the subjectivist can obviously make use of. Suppose, liking canned chop suey and believing it to be a typical Chinese dish, I am moved to seek more Chinese food, and in particular to try out my local Szechwan restaurant (where my bland tastes are likely to be shocked). Such examples are often taken to show the need for some informational constraint on rational desire and preference.

But surely what is ultimately bad about my motivation here is not that it is based on false belief, but that it is a very uncertain guide to food that I will find good-tasting. To the objectivist, information is relevant because without it I won't be pointed in the direction of good things, like innocent pleasure. But the subjectivist must reject the cognitive claim that pleasure is a good. For him, liking something is just another non-cognitive pro-attitude. And his account of pleasure, in omitting the idea that what is liked is found experientially good, removes the sting from the criticism of my motivation to patronize the Szechwan restaurant. For if we ask the subjectivist why it's too bad that my desire for Chinese food was rooted in error, he can say only that it is because the functional state in which my desire consists will probably extinguish itself once I get real Chinese food. But this seems to miss the point. Why should cultivating a functional state that will extinguish itself be less rational than cultivating one that won't? What is so important about resistance to extinguishability?

One might agree that an informational constraint is not enough, but think that adding some other conditions will do the trick.

Hare, for example, has argued that if we are going to give our-selves certain kinds of prescriptions, we must give ourselves perfectly universal ones.[28] (He thinks that moral language is analytically cut out to express just such universal commands or norms.) Yet why should someone who sees himself as choosing in a cognitive void where there is no prior truth about good or bad action insist on giving himself universal commands? Of course *we* wish to give ourselves such commands, because we think there is a subject matter of good and bad action which, like all genuine subject matters, is to some considerable extent regular. Since we think that certain *kinds* of action are bad—for example, sticking one's hand in a fire—we tell ourselves not to do actions *of that kind*.[29] But if we thought there were no such knowledge of good and bad action to be had, I do not see why we should want our self-prescriptions, or some set of them, to be universal. And it would make no difference if there were, which I think there is not, some special vocabulary exclusively dedicated to making such commands. Why should we use this vocabulary? Or why shouldn't we subvert it?

Of course it may be said, plausibly, that we need to cooperate and coordinate, and so need to find common norms.[30] But I do not see it as a point to subjectivists. For, on their reading, this need must consist in something like the fact that with the cooperation bred of common norms we will get more of what our pro-atti-tudes—either independent, norm-permitted ones (for example, my morally innocuous pro-attitude toward turning on radios) or new, norm-generated ones—point us toward. And if the preced-ing argument is correct, we have no reason to care about *this*. I suspect that the theoretical appeal to the importance of coordi-nation works because we think that without common norms (or serviceable and just common norms) life with each other would be pretty bad—indecent, painful, suspiciously on guard, and too short to be meaningful. We need good common norms to live well together. If human beings didn't need to be thus coordinated, the selection of such norms would be pointless. Since they do need it, norms that make it possible, especially those that help us make the most of our human potential, have something objective in their favour.

<hr>

[28] Hare, *Moral Thinking*, 1–24.
[29] With perhaps an escape clause for very unusual situations.
[30] A point stressed by Gibbard, *Wise Choices, Apt Feelings*. See e.g. pp. 26–7.

3

But am I really claiming that desire and preference can't rationalize choice? Not at all. I am claiming instead that the subjectivist's account of desire is impoverished, leaving out precisely that element of desire that does the rationalizing. I have been careful not to raise the question whether my odd functional state *is* in fact a basic desire to turn on radios. That is, I have been careful not to raise the question whether the existence of a noncognitive dispositive functional state of the kind subjectivists would take desire to be is sufficient for desire. I have not raised it because I am not at all sure of the answer. What I feel sure of, and what I have argued, is that, whether or not the mere functional state is sufficient, it cannot ground reasons for action. What does that is another element (of necessity) typically present in basic desire, namely some kind of evaluation of the desired object as good— as, for example, pleasant, interesting, advantageous, stature-enhancing, decent, and the like. I am not saying, however, that desire is in general nothing more than positive evaluation. In some cases we would not speak of desire if the implicit positive evaluation did not provoke or were not accompanied by some kind of appetite that prods the will toward the object for the good that it seems to offer.[31] What seems amiss in standard neo-Humean subjectivism is the way it runs together the ideas of explanation and rationalization. The noncognitive attitude present in many cases of desire may sometimes be part of the causal account of why the desired object is pursued, but the pursuit is rationalized not by the attitude but by the apparent

---

[31] This kind of motivating state—one that has influence *on* the will—must be distinguished from dispositive states *of* the will, forms of executive rationality (steadfastness, courage, prudence, and the like) or irrationality (distraction, cowardice, weakness, and the like) that enable or disable the will in its natural pursuit of the best course of action. On my anti-Humean conception, which has been greatly influenced by discussion with Philippa Foot and by Thomas Nagel's *The Possibility of Altruism* (Oxford: Oxford University Press, 1970), ch. 5, much rational human action comes about *without* the influence of motivational pushes and pulls. I see that it is a convenient time to get needed service for my car and I simply proceed to do it. All that is required is the perception of overall advantage (the safety and comfort of having a well-running car and the convenience of present service) and a reasonable degree of executive rationality. In such a case we may also speak of my desire for the advantage, but this desire is nothing more than my will's healthy recognition of its availability. Such a desire is not something the will *takes account of* in determining a rational choice.

value that attaches to its object or to the pursuit of it. Without the appearance of the value, the attraction would be empty, as it is in my counterexample.

It might seem, however, that the view that desires and preferences rationalize only because of the value judgements they involve can scarcely be correct. Aren't there rationalizing desires and preferences that point to no real or apparent good? To answer this question I need to make some distinctions between different types of goods to be attained in action and the different types of rationalization that they involve. First, and most obviously, an action may promote goods that speak in its favour *as a good action* and therefore one that ought to be done. It is in this way that considerations of health and pleasure typically support visits to the supermarket and the doctor. A good such as this—one that in the circumstances tends to make its pursuit good—may be called *choice-worthy*. Some choice-worthy goods are in particular circumstances *conclusive*—they provide decisive reasons for acts that would bring them about—while others are *contributory*, providing reasons that may be overruled. Choice-worthy goods give full-fledged reasons for action. So here we may speak of rationalization in the fullest sense.

But we must also consider goods that are *not* choice-worthy. These are goods that do not, ever, or at least in some particular circumstances, speak in favour of their pursuit. A plausible example is the pyromaniac's pleasure in watching a building burn. The pleasure of parent–child incest is another. No right-minded person who is capable of these pleasures would suppose that he had good reason to seek them. They are clearly not goods in the full-fledged sense, for they do not contribute to the goodness of action or life. Yet, *contra* Plato and Aristotle, these pleasures do seem genuine. We can imagine a prospect which has nothing in it to attract us but which, oddly, sets up in us a strong impulse to seek it. But the prospect of these pleasures, to one who can experience them, is not like that. They present such a person with a real temptation. It therefore seems plausible to regard them as some kind of experiential good. We might say that they *make intelligible*, but do not rationalize, a choice to pursue them.

Perhaps we should also briefly consider goods that are *merely apparent*. These are objects that appear good in some choice-worthy or non-choice-worthy way, but are not. Some present simple illusions, like vanilla, which smells delicious but tastes bad. Some involve symbolic connections with real goods, as in the case of someone who anxiously avoids stepping on cracks. Other cases are less psychiatric. At some emotional level all of us invest certain minor successes and failures with a significance they really lack. Such 'goods' and 'evils' cannot, when they fail to take us in, rationalize pursuit or avoidance. Nor can they make pursuit or avoidance intelligible, at least not in the way in which the special class of goods and evils just considered can. Yet to the extent that we are taken in, they can, in a sense, do both.

With these distinctions in mind, we may consider cases in which an inclination unadorned by any prospect of objective value might seem to rationalize or make sense of action. What about whims, for example? Can't people have whims to do that which serves not even an apparent value? I think we should not assume that they can. Philosophers' examples might, in this regard, be misleading. What we would do on whim is usually something whose value (or apparent value) can either be discerned or made the object of intelligent speculation. In some cases only the timing or means is capricious. One flies off to London for a haircut. One gets up at midnight, dresses, and goes out to seek pie *à la mode*. Anscombe's example of wanting to touch a spot on the wall or Davidson's example of wanting to drink a can of paint may not, I think, be all that typical. But they do count, so what can I say about them?

It seems to me a mistake to say that your wanting to drink paint counts as a whim only if there is no answer to the question what you see in it. We often, of course, put off that question by saying that it's just a whim. But putting off the question and there being no answer are different. The smooth and creamy paint might, after all, look delicious. And the allure of this appearance might be reinforced by a perverse curiosity. You might wonder what the paint tastes like.[32] The whim might have other explanations. It might be an odd desire to do something really, if trivially, *original*—to break the fetters of convention if only in some silly way. Adolescents are famous for this kind of desire, and there are

[32] When one is curious about something, the knowledge one seeks *seems* interesting and perhaps even important, even if at some level one knows that it is not. And it is this impression of significance (or urgency) that makes the curious behaviour intelligible.

outbreaks of adolescence even in the apparently mature. It might have a related but even more primitive significance. Children are continually performing actions which might at first glance seem pointless, but which may well aim at the demonstration, however symbolically, of what they wish to be unlimited powers of independent agency in the physical world. They empty out drawers, pick up sticks and run them along fences, skim stones on the water, and so forth. Given the vicissitudes of the human predicament, all this makes a certain sense. And adult whims might sometimes be like this. They might reflect a curiously displaced need to demonstrate the power to act outside our rutted ways.

There are other diagnoses of very odd whims that have a more exclusively psychiatric significance. The odd desire to drink the paint might focus some unconscious need of rebellion. Perhaps you drank some paint as a child and were severely reprimanded by your frightened parents. Or perhaps the drinking has a hidden sexual significance. Doesn't everything?

I think we are very reluctant to rest content with the whim as a state that merely disposes you to drink the paint. This is because we wish to treat the whimsical urge as at least marginally intelligible. And to do this we need to see the whim as pointing to something that might be or at least seem attractive from your point of view. If we can find no such value—if there is nothing that you see or seem to see, consciously or unconsciously, *in* drinking the paint—then, however effective its causal influence, the dispositive state gives no support to your choice to drink the paint.[33] Perhaps we should treat such a disposition as a limiting and degenerate case of desire. Or perhaps we should treat it as merely resembling genuine desire and preference. But, on either view, I am inclined to see whims as no exception to the general rule that desires can rationalize only by reference to the conscious or unconscious evaluation that is (typically) at their core.

But here another perhaps more difficult objection arises. Even if some kind of value judgement is always, or almost always, present in desire and preference, a desire or preference is often, as I have indicated, more than a value judgement. We may see the availability of certain good things but be unmoved by them, and if we are unmoved then surely we may lack at least a certain kind

---

[33] Unless of course it is unpleasant to resist.

of reason to seek them. Some good things that leave us cold (for example, our future health) still give us strong reasons for action, but in other cases an absence of felt attraction may affect our reasons. Both X and Y may offer the prospect of equally witty and intelligent conversation, but you may be much more attracted to the kind offered by X than to the kind offered by Y. Surely then you have much better reason to spend time with X.

According to this objection, at least some good things are rationally pursued only to the extent that they attract us. But then, contrary to what I have been urging, our being moved must itself be *part* of our reason for pursuing them. If mere pro-attitudes are not sufficient to rationalize, they are in some cases necessary. But if so, then surely some doubt is thrown on the claim that they lack any kind of rationalizing force.

I cannot here try to consider all the kinds of case in which reasons might seem to depend partly on attraction as well as on expected value. In cases that involve personal taste, such as taste in company, the significance of attraction might lie in its containing a foretaste of pleasure or satisfaction. Attraction to people, or for that matter to novels and paintings, promises a kind of personal pleasure in our future interactions with them. And that anticipated pleasure can give a perfectly respectable reason to seek them out.

Someone might object that such pleasure is nothing more than the consciousness of having got that to which one's noncognitive pro-attitude propelled one. If so, the pleasure would be a mere logical reflection of the earlier pro-attitude. But this picture seems wrong to me, although it may be encouraged by an easily missed ambiguity. An inclination might, in one sense, be said to be satisfied when its object is obtained. But it is a sad truth that this kind of technical satisfaction may lack any element of real pleasure or fulfilment. The anticipated pleasure that is part of ordinary attractions to people or art is, however, real pleasure. It might, as a matter of empirical fact, be pleasure partly caused by the previous inclination. And if it were, the existence of the inclination could be evidence for it. But even so, it is only the pleasure itself that makes sense of acting on the inclination.

There are many other cases in which we would have to look closely to see whether noncognitive attitudes were themselves providing reasons. Let me just mention one of the most puzzling.

Two people may be equally supportive, kind, admirable, beautiful, pleasant to be with, and so on, but we may, because of some
other difference of quality that in no way reflects well or badly on
either, be fonder of the first than of the second. And when this
happens most of us suppose, at least in practice, that we have
greater reason to pursue the good of the first. Why? Someone
might say that the greater fondness is simply constituted by a
stronger altruistic disposition. But I think the answer must be
more complicated. Human beings can thrive only in various private connections of concern and identification—as with family,
friends, colleagues, or acquaintances. Some of these connections
are thrust upon us, but many are not. And some people simply fit
better than others into the highly personal sympathetic world we
have already created for ourselves. These people belong in our
story and so their good is especially important to us. I cannot
claim to understand fully the nature and operation of such judgements of importance. But I feel it would be a travesty to interpret
them as nothing more than functionally grounded tendencies to
go for some people's good over that of others.

4

My claim has been that noncognitive analyses of desire, preference, commitment, and the like cannot capture their *reason-giving*
force. In depriving pro-attitudes of any evaluative thought,
noncognitivism reduces them to functional states that, upon reflection, may show what we will do under certain conditions but
not what we should do. Practical rationality, I have argued, requires a subject matter of the values to be achieved or realized
in human action—a subject matter that only cognitivism can
provide.

Even if I am right about this, there remains room for evaluative
skepticism, which, if correct, might remove actions altogether
from the authority of reason. As noted earlier, Mackie and others
have argued that certain evaluative judgements, while genuinely
cognitive, cannot be *true*. There are in evaluative thought the
concepts appropriate to a genuine subject matter, but the world
does not, indeed cannot, furnish the corresponding properties
and relations. Evaluative facts would be unacceptably queer in

two ways: first, in providing motivation—in effect exercising a power over the will—and second, in providing reasons for action that do not depend on subjective inclinations. Mackie objects to the idea of motivation or rationalization (he speaks of the latter as prescriptive authority) that is not wholly explained in a neo-Humean manner. Like Hume, he thinks that genuine thought is by itself powerless to cause or make good sense of action.

Now I think an objectivist should be more or less unperturbed by the part of the argument that concerns motivation. To say that someone recognizes a value (say a moral value) that can be achieved in action is not to say that the recognition must be a spur to his will. To recognize that justice or decency requires us to do something is, in my view, to recognize that we shall act badly if we do not do it. The connection with motivation is indirect and conditional. To be unresponsive to the genuine badness of an action is to have a will that is unmoved by a conclusive reason for not doing something—a will that is, to that extent, irrational or unreasonable. If we were more reasonable, we would care more about the quality of our actions. And since most of us are not wholly unreasonable, we do to some extent care. That, I think, is what the motivational force of unconditioned value comes to. And that does not require value-facts to have any 'queer' power over the will. It requires instead a conception of the will as the part of human reason whose function is to choose for the best.

The other skeptical argument questions whether objective value could have rational authority. Let's begin with the objective value of ends. Why, it will be asked, should we care whether or not our ends have objective value? Why is such a concern rational? If, as I think, practical rationality chiefly consists in correctness of thought about human good and evil, a concern is rational just in case reason determines that it is a good concern for us to have. And if a concern belongs to real human virtue—the qualities that make us and our actions good—then it can hardly be denied that it is a good concern. So, on this conception of rationality, to show that we have reason to be concerned with the objective goodness of our ends it is enough to show that such concern is essential to human excellence. And while showing this may present many difficulties, it does not seem to be ruled out in advance as an unacceptably 'queer' task. Something similar can be said about reasons given by the objective goodness of action itself. If, as I think, the reasons for doing an action just *are* the good-making features it has either in itself[34] or that it derives from the good ends it serves, then the mystery of how the goodness of action can provide reasons seems to disappear. Mackie's problem depends on supposing that we start with an idea of practical rationalization or prescriptive authority that is prior to our idea of good and bad action. If that were true, and if goodness weren't in some way reducible to rationality, then we could raise the question, and so make it seem mysterious, how the mere recognition of something good about an action could give us a reason to do it. But I am skeptical of this prior conception of reasons, and therefore suspect that the real mystery that Mackie and others are circling around is how actions can have objective goodness in the first place. They suggest that the problem is how, if there were such a thing, it could give reasons. But, if I am right, the problem must be more fundamental.

In much of contemporary moral thought, rationality seems to be regarded as the basic virtue of action or motivation, one that grounds all the other virtues. This, I have been arguing, is a mistake. Practical rationality *is* a virtue of a very special kind. But it is not special in being the most fundamental merit of action or motivation. It is special by being the virtue *of* reason as it thinks about human good. A virtue isn't a virtue because it's rational to have it. A good action isn't good because it's rational to do. On my view, the only proper ground for claiming that a quality is rational to have or an action rational to do is that the quality or action is, on the whole, good. It is human good and bad that stand at the centre of practical thought and not any independent ideas of rationality or reasons for action. Indeed, even in its proper place as a quality of practical reason, rationality is validated only by the fact that it is the *excellence*, that is the *good* condition of practical thought. Even here the notion of good has the primary say.

But note that I have not here argued against the possibility that practical rationality makes demands on practical thought that should be understood antirealistically as requirements on the

---

[34] Either directly (for example, its pleasantness) or because of the virtue or right principles to which it conforms (for example, its fidelity).

construction of a picture of human good and bad.[35] On such a constructivist view, we might have to begin practical philosophy with a critique of practical reason as it thinks about human good. Here I have been arguing only that the primary questions are not what it is rational or irrational, but what it is good or bad to be, seek, or do—that is, protesting the confusion that arises when the notions of rationality escape their proper place and become themselves the primary objects of practical thought.

[35] The evaluative realist thinks that every constraint on practical reason has the function of maximizing the likelihood of correspondence to a transcendent, and therefore possibly unapproachable, reality. The constructivist, in the perhaps special sense I have in mind, thinks that there are constraints, which, coming from the nature of practical thought itself, must set limits on where the truth can lie and on how much truth there can be. The method of reflective equilibrium as discussed by John Rawls in *A Theory of Justice* (Cambridge, Mass.: Harvard University Press, 1971) can be given a constructivist interpretation not as the best method for descrying an external or internal moral reality, but as the only systematically acceptable method of moral thought, the applications of which determine, in so far as such determination is possible, where the' moral truth is to lie. Such constructivism might come, however, in two varieties. In one, the rational constraints would lead first to the identification of actions and ends as rational and *therefore* good. In the other, the constraints would be from the very start constraints on rational thought about the good. It is only the first kind of constructivism that I have been attacking.

8

Notes on Unfairly Gaining More:
Pleonexia

DAVID SACHS

Philippa Foot, more than any other prominent philosopher of our time, has reinvigorated the fundamental topic of virtues and vices. She brings to the topic not only many of the insights of Aristotle and Aquinas; she casts a penetrating and modern light on it. Thus in the title essay of her collection *Virtues and Vices*[1] she gives fresh support to a number of crucial claims. First, she makes intelligible and convincing the complex relations between persons' wills and wishes and their virtues and failings. Next, she shows how nothing less than the habits of choice that manifest the virtues can defeat the temptations and forestall the kinds of neglect to which human nature is prone. Third, she unravels the puzzle as to whether or not an act that exhibits a virtue can also display a vice.

Those are the three chief accomplishments of 'Virtues and Vices' but the essay stakes out further and by no means minor positions. Among the latter there is one with which I take issue, but I should underscore the fact that my disagreement has no bearing on any of her major claims about the virtues and vices. Instead it is a question of doing justice to Aristotle's account of justice. Unlike a raft of recent and more or less hostile critics of Aristotle on justice, among them Hardie, Urmson, and notably Bernard Williams, Foot does not attack Aristotle's view of that virtue. Her opposition to it is largely tacit; in the remarks to follow, I hope to move her and perhaps some of Aristotle's less friendly critics to reconsider his view.

David Sachs worked to finish this paper while he was dying in 1992, and was just able to hand it to Philippa when she flew over to the States to say goodbye to him.

[1] *Virtues and Vices, and Other Essays in Moral Philosophy* (Oxford: Blackwell, 1978).

1. The Programme

To rebut recent critics of Aristotle on justice and especially injustice, one has to show that human beings have a natural or at least typical tendency which, if not moderated, eventuates in the vice of injustice, the vice Aristotle called *pleonexia*. But that in turn requires showing that the trait, when unmoderated, supplies the motive of injustice in the various circumstances in which the vice betrays itself. Once that is shown, it will follow that injustice has as much unity as other vices, say, intemperance or cowardice.

A defence of Aristotle's doctrine should also support his insistence that justice, unlike other virtues, has only one vice opposed to it, i.e. *pleonexia*, or as I shall at times call it, aggrandizement.

2. The Main Objection: Aristotle's Awareness of the Fact on which it Depends

A criticism which, if successful, would undo Aristotle's doctrine is one Bernard Williams stresses: 'there is no particular motive which the unjust person, because of his injustice, necessarily displays'.[2] More forcefully he says: 'it must be basic to this vice, unlike others, that it does not import a special motive, but rather the lack of one'.[3] Though she did not deploy them against Aristotle, Foot made similar claims: Justice does not correspond 'to any particular desire or tendency that has to be kept in check'.[4] Justice is unlike 'a virtue such as courage or temperance . . . which overcomes a special temptation'.[5] 'There is no moderation of a passion implied in the idea of justice.'[6]

A point both Foot and Williams state in favour of their view is that, in her words, 'Almost any desire can lead a man to act unjustly, not even excluding the desire to help a friend or to save a life, whereas a cowardly act must be motivated by fear or a desire for safety, and an act of intemperance by a desire for

---

[2] Bernard Williams, 'Justice as a Virtue', in Amélie O. Rorty (ed.), *Essays on Aristotle's Ethics* (Berkeley, Calif.: University of California Press, 1981), 198.
[3] Ibid.   [4] Foot, *Virtues and Vices*, 9.
[5] Ibid. 8.   [6] Ibid. 9.

pleasure . . . '.[7] Williams's examples of possible motives for unjust acts support what Foot says about their diversity. Among others he lists anger, fear, malice, lust, and laziness, and adds 'or whatever'.[8]

Williams also repeatedly suggests that Aristotle was 'strongly disposed' to deny the variety of possible motives for unjust acts and to hold that 'each unjust act must have the same motive as the unjust acts that are the product of an unjust character'.[9]

That unjust acts vary in their motives is undeniable. But for Williams to suppose that Aristotle probably thought otherwise is baffling—baffling because Aristotle is explicit about the diversity of motives for unjust acts. Thus, after noting that one can act unjustly without being an unjust person, Aristotle defends that commonplace with the truism that many unjust acts are due to passion rather than deliberate choice.[10] He there means by 'passion' (*pathos*) any of the gamut of ordinary human feelings. Later he spells it out, saying that persons can act unjustly because of 'anger or the other passions necessary or natural to human beings'.[11]

Aristotle acknowledged the diverse motives of many unjust acts. But unlike Foot and Williams he did not think that diversity told against the vice of injustice being traceable to a particular tendency or trait. Of course neither Foot nor Williams asserts that Aristotle is inconsistent thereby, and surely his allowing various motives for different unjust acts is compatible with his characterizing the vice of injustice and the unjust person in terms of acts due to a particular trait. Indeed he could have claimed that the unjust man may at times act unjustly out of diverse desires; even so, he would not have contradicted his view that a particular tendency characterizes the vice of injustice.

---

[7] Foot's claims about cowardly and intemperate acts should be qualified. Motives ranging from little more than social agreeableness to a strong desire for group approval can at times account for a cowardly act or a profligate night.

[8] Williams, 'Justice as a Virtue', 193; see pp. 192–4.   [9] Ibid.

[10] See *Nicomachean Ethics* 1134ª17–23. (My references to Aristotle's text are to the Bywater edition (Oxford: Clarendon Press, 1894).) Aristotle's examples of the commonplace are at 1134ª21–2: 'a man is not a thief though he stole, not an adulterer though he commited adultery'. Of course he held that unjust acts should be rectified. See *Nicomachean Ethics* 5. 4 *passim*.

[11] See 1135ᵇ19–24.

Missing from the critical literature on Aristotle on justice is a line of reasoning based on the fact that diverse motives—e.g. fear, respectability, ambition, etc.—account for the performance of many just acts. By parity of reasoning with the objection of Foot and Williams, the diversity of motives for just acts would argue as little or as much against there being a virtue of justice as the variety of motives for unjust acts tells against there being a vice of injustice. (I take it that to deny on that basis that justice is a virtue—or that there are just persons—would have been unwelcome even for Aristotle's more hostile critics.) Aristotle, it should be noted, mentions acting justly but unwillingly and out of fear. He reasonably says that conduct thus motivated cannot be characterized, except incidentally (*kata sumbebēkos*),[12] as doing what is just or acting justly.

In any case, it may be thought that the diversity of the motives for many unjust acts constitutes a prima-facie case against ascribing the vice of injustice to a particular tendency. And it may be held that Aristotle's failure to confront that seeming difficulty was a signal omission. In what follows, I shall argue that once one is reminded of certain everyday matters of human rearing, the prima-facie case against Aristotle's view dissolves, and with it the charge of omission.

Before that, however, a word on Aristotle's formulation of the trait in question and an account of one of the operative terms in it.

3. The Trait in Question: Aristotle's Seemingly Odd Conception of Gain

Aristotle was especially terse when he stated that pleasure in gain—or attraction to it—is the trait that prompts *pleonexia*, or aggrandizement.[13] Aggrandizement, to be sure, that is unfair to others. But he helpfully delineated three features of his conception of gain.

First, what are the possible objects of unfair aggrandizing? What kinds of objects, that is, can one unfairly gain? Aristotle's list is short but compendious: 'honour or possessions or security

---

[12] See 1135^{b}1–6.   [13] See 1130^{a}14–^{b}5.

or that which includes all these, if we had a single name for it'.[14] Aristotle's first sort of justice, the distributive, concerns the allocation of honours, goods, and other things which may be apportioned among those who belong to the polity.[15] Again, the 'other things' would include provisions for the security of the polity's members, 'security' (*sōteria*) comprising, I take it, the safety and preservation of both person and property.

The role of Aristotle's second sort of justice, the corrective, is to rectify unjust conduct on the part or members of the polity, whether distributors or anyone else, toward other members of it. Unjust conduct unfairly deprives someone of a measure of honour or goods or security.

Second, one may unfairly *gain* the lesser evil, that is, unfairly shift the larger burden of loss or harm or dishonour to someone else. Of the unjust man, Aristotle says his unfairness extends alike to his pursuit of the greater good and the lesser evil.[16] Even in the absence of the vice of injustice, unjust acts will aim at either the greater good or lesser evil.[17]

Persons can, then, unfairly *gain* lesser evils; also, they may fairly *gain* them. If they can fairly *gain* them, of course they should pursue them.[18] But why, in either case, the obvious oddity of speaking of 'gain'? (It's rather like a late twentieth-century merchant advertising the *saving* you will accrue if you purchase an item he has on sale.) In cases of the lesser evil, whether unfairly or fairly sacrificing some negotiables, or being to some extent dishonoured, one *loses* something instead of *gaining* anything. Likewise, if one is in some measure harmed, one suffers a *loss* of capacity or ability or so. Aristotle's use of 'gain' in connection with lesser evils may well seem, so to put it, a topsy-turvy one.

---

[14] 1130[b]2–3. The phrase 'that which includes all these' could conceivable embrace anything that can be gained and that in itself (*haplōs*) was fortunate; opposed to it would be any loss which, in itself, was unfortunate. See 1129[b]1–8 and 1137[a]26–30; but cf. also 1130[b]31–2.

[15] See Charles Young's succinct account in 'Aristotle on Justice', *Southern Journal of Philosophy*, 27, supp. (1988), 239–40. Among goods to be allocated, Aristotle probably included distributions of public monies. Hardie, following Vinogradoff, suggests that Aristotle also had in mind the payment of citizens for jury duties, the distribution of foreign corn, of land when founding a colony, and of assistance for the elderly, the ill, and the disabled. See W. F. R. Hardie, *Aristotle's Ethical Theory*, 2nd edn. (Oxford: Clarendon Press, 1980), 190, 185.

[16] See 1129[b]6–11.   [17] See 1134[a]5, 33–4; 1132[a]16–17, [b]19–23.

[18] See 1131[b]20–3.

The difficulty, however, proves superficial. For he who gets the lesser evil instead of the greater one—fairly or unfairly—thereby *has more* of what is not evil than he otherwise would have. It is as though Aristotle kept the etymons of *pleonexia* before his eyes and let their sense determine his usage of 'gain'. That there is a point involved which is not a matter of usage will emerge in the next section. First, however, Aristotle's most vexing use of 'gain'.

Speaking of an assailant unjustly striking or killing someone, Aristotle says that the assailant's action and the victim's suffering are discriminated as unequal, and that the rectifying judge tries to equalize the victim's loss by taking away the assailant's *gain*.[19] Aristotle allows that in, for example, such cases as striking a blow and suffering it, the words 'gain' and 'loss' may not be at home, but he claims that once the victim's suffering was estimated, one spoke of the victim's loss as well as the assailant's *gain*.[20]

But what conceivably could constitute the *gain* the assailant gets just by striking or killing his victim? What is the gain which is got *thereby*? Precisely the unjust, involuntary loss suffered by the victim at the assailant's unjust, voluntary hands. The rectifying judge will justly see to it that at least a comparable loss is suffered by the assailant.[21]

One can of course rightly enough speak of the victim's loss and of his assailant compensating or indemnifying him or his survivors. Also, the assailant will have seen, even if only briefly or mistakenly, his unjust and violent attack as somehow desirable. But so seeing it could not constitute anything he automatically gained by it.

Perhaps the now rather archaic term 'spoliation' can be of some help here. Legally, a meaning it has is the spoiling of evidence. What the assailant automatically *gains*, only to spoliate, is a measure of one of the society's divisible goods, i.e. security (*sōteria*). For as long as his violent unjust action goes unrectified, he will have *had more* of that good at his disposal and despoiling than fellow citizens of the polity who conducted themselves justly when violent and were otherwise peaceable.

In sum, Aristotle predicates 'gain' or 'having more' not only of the getting of honours or possessions or security, but also of

[19] See 1132ª4–10.
[20] Later, Aristotle remarks that the words 'loss' and 'gain' come from situations of voluntary exchange.
[21] See 1132ᵇ28–30.

having more than one would otherwise have, and of the despoiling of a measure of the good of security.

4. Some Everyday Facts of Life Prefigured in the Rearing of Children

In his treatment of just and unjust persons and acts, Aristotle focuses on adults. The ways, however, in which adults try to inculcate justice in a child are instructive. Their aim is not only to suppress the child's attraction to more than his just share but also to subdue his aversion to burdens, and to moderate inclinations he may have to violence.[22] As with other virtues and many other disciplines and practices, trying to instil justice is complicated. One has to convey an understanding of justice, which is given by the reasons distinctive to it, and at the same time illustrate both it and violations of it by examples. The training and teaching of temperance, importantly different from that of justice, provides a useful comparison.

In the first phases of trying to instil temperance in a child one often says and at times backs up forcibly: 'that's enough' or 'no more now'. Almost unavoidably one begins too early to use some of the pairs of modals: 'can't' and 'can', 'mustn't' and 'must', 'shouldn't' and 'should', 'ought not to' and 'ought to', and so on. At the start the modals may perplex a child, especially 'can't', when he is literally able to go on eating or drinking or nestling and being caressed. The 'can't' and 'must' may first be regarded by him as indicating or threatening that one is going to compel him to stop doing something or to do such-and-such. Though they vary in strength, some of the modals are used interchangeably, and negative, stopping modals are often employed instead of positive, forcing ones, and conversely.[23]

Efforts to instil temperance are soon supported by adding reasons such as '*x* is not—more of *x* is not—good for you'. Also, one

---

[22] Such efforts of course vary between cultures and subcultures and households and extended families. The variations are often rightly criticized in the name of justice, in the name, that is, of *to whom* goods and burdens are to be fairly allocated, and privileges and security justly provided.

[23] Particularly in the foregoing para. I am indebted to essays by G. E. M. Anscombe, esp. 'The Question of Linguistic Idealism' and 'On the Source of the Authority of the State'. They are in vols. i and iii of her *Collected Philosophical Papers* (Minneapolis: University of Minnesota Press, 1981).

urges or insists 'you need more *y*' or ' . . . more *y* if you are ever going to . . . ' etc. These are of course just rubrics of reasons one gives when trying to instil temperance. Not all of them are unique to that effort but they are especially appropriate to it. Importantly, they are of no help in trying to specify the kinds of reason given when attempting to inculcate justice.

When one tries to impart justice, one uses the same modals employed in instruction in the other virtues and elsewhere. But in the giving of reasons for being just, pronouns and pronominal adjectives come to the fore. They become prominent, of course, because justice is a virtue that has to express itself in conduct toward others.[24] Thus in reference to a child's siblings and play-mates or parents and other persons who tend him, one says, 'That's hers' or 'It's his toy or turn or place'. Or, referring to some onerous chore: 'You should do it today, I did it yesterday'. Or 'Leave him alone; it's not for you to strike—or discipline, or punish—him. Who said you could?'

Those examples are typical of the kinds of reason one gives when trying to inculcate justice. Like other examples, they con-cern the kinds of item Aristotle thought could be justly or unjustly gained: possessions, privileges, burdens,[25] and violence against persons and property. Aristotle's account of just gain, it would appear, is not unlike 'the virtue of justice, take in the old wide sense in which it had to do with everything *owed*'.[26] 'Owed', it should be noted, was another figure of speech taken from situ-ations of voluntary exchange.

The last few paragraphs may suggest, among other questions, the following: to what extent can one ascribe to those responsible for children's rearing an understanding of the virtues and a con-cern to impart them? (In answer, I confine myself mostly to justice and temperance.) Of course, both the understanding and the con-cerns vary, and vary more or less interdependently. Moreover, which virtues are emphasized, and in relation to which children,

---

[24] Aristotle observes that just persons also wish for things that are just and that unjust persons wish for unjust things. (See 1129ᵇ6–10.) A possible but unlikely construction, given by R. A. Gauthier and J. Y. Jolif on 1129ᵃ7, *L'Éthique à Nicomaque* (Louvain: Publications Universitaires de Louvain, 1970), vol. ii, pt. 1, p. 330, restricts the just man's wishes to matters that concern only himself.

[25] The limiting case of placing the entire burden on another person was open to Aristotle, though he did not mention it.

[26] Philippa Foot, 'Utilitarianism and the Virtues', *Mind*, 94 (1985), 205.

also varies.[27] But even if it is partial and less than ubiquitous, some comprehension of justice and temperance, and of efforts to instil them, can be met with everyday. One has to avoid children and persons busy raising them if one is going to avoid those phenomena. Consider, again, how mundane the phenomena are of being taught to take no more than one's fair share, and of behaving peaceably.

Some measure of understanding of the virtues is available to almost everyone. Only pedestrian observation is usually needed to tell a sot or glutton or lecher, or one who is averse to, or by policy committed to abstaining from, ordinary human pleasures. Nor is perspicacity required to identify a person as one who unfairly aggrandizes himself at the expense of others. Those who rear children are usually alert to signs that prefigure the vices of intemperance and injustice and try to discourage them.

To be sure, among the interests one may have in trying to effect virtuous conduct, there are relatively inferior ones, such as avoiding future trouble or the neighbours' disapprobation. But even those interests can play a part in steadying one's comprehension of the virtues and in reinforcing efforts to instil them.

A further word about children, the modals, and the reasons given in support of their use. Though at the outset there is some mimicry on the children's part, and though their early uses of them may falter, children rapidly pick up on the modals and the reasons that account for their employment. Repeatedly hearing both from adults and older or precocious children and learning that their function is rationally to prevent or induce behaviour, the young soon employ the same instruments for the same purposes. They come to use them, that is, to shape and assess the conduct of peers and also parents, themselves, and others. Gradually and more or less successfully, the modals, together with the reasons that support them, displace force and thoughtless protest.

[27] See n. 22 above.

9

Fear of Relativism

T. M. SCANLON

1. Introduction

Relativism is a hot topic. By this I do not mean merely that it is now much discussed but, rather, that its discussion always arouses certain passions. From some, relativism provokes passionate denial, the passion and haste of these denials suggesting a kind of fear. Others are eager to affirm it, and often do so with a particular exhilaration and sense of satisfaction, perhaps even of superiority. The question that I will begin with here is, what gives the topic this heat? Since my own reaction to relativism has generally been one of opposition, I will approach the question mainly from that side, by asking why we should want our judgements of value in general, or our moral judgements in particular, to have some property that relativism would deny them. As will become clear, my thoughts about this topic have been in large part shaped by Philippa Foot's writings.

2. What is Relativism?

Before addressing this question I want to say something about what I take relativism to be. Relativism is sometimes described as the view that conflicting judgements can be equally correct or equally justified.[1] How could this be so? As a first step, it would seem that part of what the relativist is claiming must be that there

The work on relativism from which this paper is derived has been presented in various forms, long and short, to many audiences. I am grateful to participants in all of these occasions for their comments and criticisms, and also to Derek Parfit and Hilary Putnam for their detailed comments on earlier drafts.

[1] What Gilbert Harman calls 'metaethical relativism'. See his 'What is Moral Relativism?', in A. Goldman and J. Kim (eds.), *Values and Morals* (Dordrecht: Reidel, 1978), 143 and 146–8.

is no single standard of 'correctness' or 'justifiability' by which all judgements of the kind in question are to be judged, no matter who makes them or to whom they are applied. Accordingly, I will take it to be a *necessary* condition for an account of judgements of a certain kind to be relativistic that it must hold that the cardinal virtue for judgements of that kind (whether this is being true, being justified, or some other property) cannot be assigned absolutely, but only relative to certain conditions or parameters. These parameters can vary, and a relativistic view must hold that particular ways of setting these parameters are not subject to appraisal (e.g. as true, or justified) by the standards appropriate to judgements of the kind in question.[2] I will call this necessary condition for relativism Condition R.

An account of moral judgements can satisfy my Condition R without falling prey to the kind of incoherence that often troubles relativist views. I have in mind the problem that arises, in its simplest form, when one person says, 'Every judgement is relative. What is true for you need not be true for me' and someone else replies, 'So is *that* judgement just true for you?' The assertion of relativism seems to deprive relativists of the ability to make the very claim they want to assert.[3] Condition R allows for at least two possible routes of escape from this problem. First, it is formulated as a claim about judgements of a certain kind, and the assertion of relativism for judgements of kind *A* may not itself be a judgement of that kind. An assertion of moral relativism, for example, may not itself be a moral judgement, hence not a judgement to which the asserted relativity applies. Second, suppose that some thesis of relativity (perhaps a higher-order thesis) applies to the claim that judgements of type *A* are relative to certain

---

[2] This amounts to what Harman has called 'moral judgment relativism' (ibid. 143). My characterization leaves it open how the parameters governing a given moral judgement are set or constrained—whether, for example, they are determined by facts about the speaker's attitudes, or the agent's, or by facts about the societies to which they belong. It is therefore left open whether or not the relativism in question is 'normative relativism' in Harman's sense, that is to say, relativism which holds that different agents are subject to different ultimate moral demands. Harman's own view (as expressed in this article and others, such as 'Moral Relativism Defended', *Philosophical Review*, 84 (1975), 3–22) is that moral judgements of the 'ought to do' variety are relative to attitudes shared by the speaker, the agent, and the intended audience of the judgement.

[3] This problem is forcefully presented by Hilary Putnam in ch. 5 of his *Reason, Truth and History* (Cambridge: Cambridge University Press, 1981).

parameters. Then the question can be asked, 'With respect to what system of parameters is your thesis of relativism for judgements of kind *A* supposed to be justifiable?' But the relativist may have a reply to this question that is not embarrassing because it does not undercut the claim he or she wishes to make. For example, one possible reply[4] would be to say, 'it is justifiable with respect to every evaluative standpoint that I can imagine taking seriously. You are welcome to try to convince me that, given the parameters that describe your situation, the mode of justification for judgements of this higher-order kind that is appropriate for you is one with respect to which the thesis of relativism for judgements of kind *A* is not justifiable, but I doubt you will succeed in anything except possibly convincing me that your outlook is a very strange one.'

What might an account of evaluative judgements satisfying Condition R be like? In formulating R I have referred to the 'cardinal virtue' in question as that of 'being true or being justified, or some other property', rather than just as 'being true', in order to allow for the possibility that the distinction between relativism and non-relativism about a class of judgements can cut across the distinction between non-cognitivist and cognitivist accounts of these judgements. So consider first a non-cognitivist account of some class of evaluative judgements, that is to say, an account according to which these judgements are not to be understood as making factual claims but only as expressing some attitude or emotion.

On such an account, even though these judgements appear to have the form of declarative statements they are not the kind of thing that can be true or false, but only appropriate or inappropriate, justified or not justified. Such a view need not satisfy Condition R. For even if the judgements in question are not properly assessed as true or false, the attitudes they express may be assessable as justified or unjustified, and it may be that there is a single standard of justification for such attitudes, a standard applicable to all agents and societies. If there is, then the account in question is not relativistic, but if there is not—if the justifiability of the

---

[4] I take something like this to be the reason why Nietzsche thinks that he can square his 'perspectivism' with his apparently unqualified assertion of this and other doctrines. He would not, however, apply the term 'relativist' to his position.

attitudes in question is relative to some variable features of the individuals in question and their societies—then we may have an account satisfying Condition R. On such an account, it could be said that 'conflicting evaluative judgements of the kind in question can both be justified'. These judgements would not 'conflict' by making incompatible truth-claims. But they would conflict in a more practical sense by expressing conflicting attitudes that no one could live by at the same time.

Now suppose, alternatively, that the evaluative judgements we are concerned with are best understood as stating facts. The 'cardinal virtue' for these judgements will then be truth, so a relativistic account of them must hold that their truth-conditions vary, depending on certain 'parameters'. For example, a relativistic, but cognitivist, account of moral judgements might hold that 'right' and 'wrong' are relational in something like the way that 'is tall' is. According to a 'relational' view of this sort, an act can be called 'wrong' only relative to some norms or standards, of which there can be many, and a judgement using this predicate is intelligible only if, in the context, we can identify the norms that the person making that judgement intends to invoke. Alternatively, it might be held that what a judgement of the form 'X is morally wrong' asserts is that X is disallowed by norms that bear a certain relation to the person making the judgement (for example, norms that that person accepts or has reason to accept, or norms generally recognized in the society in which that person lives). Assuming that different norms can stand in this relation to different speakers, this 'indexical' account of the semantics of 'is morally wrong' will satisfy my Condition R.

On either of these accounts, the judgement 'Lying is always wrong', made by one speaker, and the judgement 'Lying is not always wrong', made by another, could both be quite correct; but if so then these utterances would not make conflicting judgements in the strict cognitivist sense: they can both be true, at the same time, so they are not incompatible. But there are at least two other senses in which the claims that these speakers make could be held to conflict. First, in so far as they invoke different standards of conduct which no one could live by at the same time, they conflict in the practical sense mentioned above. Second, we could say, following Gilbert Harman,[5] that these judgements

---

[5] Harman 'What is Moral Relativism?', 160.

make claims which would conflict if they were interpreted non-relativistically. I want to explore this idea more fully since it seems to me that something important lies behind it.

Consider the following example. I believe that there is nothing morally objectionable about sexual relations between adults of the same sex. That is to say, I believe that the kind of considerations that I think of as relevant to morality—the kind that back up my judgements that murder and exploitation are wrong, for example—do not support any objection to such conduct. But it is easy to imagine someone, a devoted member of a fundamentalist Christian community, for example, who would hold that homosexual relations are, in themselves, deeply wrong—that they are incompatible with and excluded by that form of life that we are all required to live according to the authoritative teachings laid down in the Bible, which are the basis of all morality. This disagreement fits the pattern of cognitivist relativism just described: I judge a certain form of conduct to be morally permissible, another person judges it morally impermissible, and our judgements refer, implicitly or explicitly, to different standards of conduct. But there is a further element: each of us regards the standards to which we refer as authoritative and binding—as standards which we have good reason to regard as outweighing all others, and whose violation is proper grounds for feelings of guilt and shame. If we did not so regard them then it would be questionable whether our judgements are properly called moral judgements. So here is, at least potentially, a new kind of conflict: we may disagree over which standards of conduct are authoritative—which have that distinctive importance which the term 'moral' entails. We disagree in part, perhaps, because we disagree about what that kind of importance is, or at least about what could or does confer it.[6]

If we are both non-relativists, then we will each hold that the standards which we have in mind have unique claim to this distinctive kind of importance, and our judgements about homo-

---

[6] This kind of disagreement would be one version of the phenomenon which David Wong describes by saying that the term 'adequate moral system' may have different extensions as used by different people. See his *Moral Relativity* (Berkeley, Calif.: University of California Press, 1984), 45. But some of the other forms of disagreement that I have described may also fall under Wong's description, since it is not clear that he means to restrict disagreement over the extension of 'adequate moral system' to disagreement over the source or ground of moral authority.

sexuality (which presuppose this claim) will thus conflict in this further way. This is a plausible interpretation of what Harman means when he speaks of judgements which would conflict if interpreted non-relativistically. On the other hand, if both parties to the dispute I have imagined are relativists, then both may hold that there is no unique set of standards that can claim this importance: it is not something that can be claimed absolutely but only given the setting of certain parameters, and, depending on how these parameters are set, many different standards may claim this authority.

It is this idea of the authority or importance of moral considerations which is, I believe, the central problem of relativism for non-relativists and for many relativists as well. It is the central problem for non-relativists because it is the thing which, above all, moral relativism seems to threaten. It is also a central problem for those relativists who do not see their relativism as a form of scepticism.

Relativism is often seen as a self-consciously debunking doctrine, a challenge which might be put in the form: 'Morality is merely a matter of social convention. After all, what else *could* it be about?' At least this is the way relativism is often imagined by non-relativists, and no doubt some relativists also have this kind of thing in mind. The proper response to this sceptical form of relativism is a positive account of what the authority of morality could amount to. But such a response might be successful while still leaving *relativism* untouched. That is, one might succeed in fending off scepticism—in showing that morality is not *merely* a matter of social convention, say—while still leaving open the possibility that moral requirements may vary in the way that Condition R describes. In fact it seems to me that many of those who speak in favour of relativism actually take themselves to be defending a view of this kind, a form of non-sceptical, or *benign*, relativism, according to which the requirements of morality vary but are not for that reason to be taken less seriously. Philippa Foot seems to me to put forward a version of benign relativism in the papers I will discuss below, and I believe that Michael Walzer also sees his view in this way. Outside philosophy, it seems to me that anthropologists, who are some of the most common proponents of relativism, are often best understood as having this benign form of the doctrine in mind: they urge us to respect the moralities of other cultures as 'just as good as ours', the suggestion clearly being that both 'ours' and 'theirs' should be respected. The question that most interests me about relativism, and that I will be mainly concerned with below, is whether and how a form of benign relativism could be true.

I have claimed that Condition R is a *necessary* condition for an account of a class of judgements to count as relativistic. Is it also a *sufficient* condition? This seems unlikely, at least if the line between relativistic and non-relativistic doctrines is supposed to distinguish between those that do and those that do not give rise to fears and objections of the kind that relativism has generally provoked. In order to do that, a definition would have to rule out, more clearly than I have so far done, forms of what might be called 'parametric universalism'. By this I mean, in the case of morality, views which hold that there is a single standard of validity for moral principles but which leave open the possibility that what valid moral principles allow and require can vary, depending on certain variable conditions. To take the most trivial example, it might be a valid general principle that governments' policies should be responsive to the needs of their citizens, among which is the need for protection against the climate. But this requires different measures in arctic, temperate, and tropical zones. A less trivial example is the general principle that where a just scheme is established to provide an important public good, it is wrong to take advantage of that scheme while ignoring the requirements it imposes on one.[7] This principle also has the consequence that what is morally required of a person will depend on facts about that person's society and its customs, but no one, I think, would call either of these doctrines relativistic. And neither of them satisfies Condition R, since the two principles just described (and the standards of justice alluded to in the second of these principles) are presumably held to be valid on some 'universal', non-parametric basis.

Now consider a third example. I have maintained elsewhere[8] that an action is wrong if it would be disallowed by any set of principles for the general regulation of behaviour that no one suitably motivated could reasonably reject. As I will say later, it

---

[7] Essentially John Rawls's principle of fairness. See *A Theory of Justice*, 111–14.

[8] In 'Contractualism and Utilitarianism', in A. Sen and B. Williams (eds.), *Utilitarianism and Beyond* (Cambridge: Cambridge University Press, 1982).

seems to me that what one can 'reasonably reject' may well vary, depending on, among other things, those features of a society that determine which goods and opportunities are essential for the kind of life most people will want to live. Is this a form of relativism? One might argue that it is not, since the contractualist formula just stated is a substantive, universal moral principle, on a par with the two I have mentioned, but more general. But this formula could as well be seen as a characterization of the idea of moral wrongness and of the kind of justification appropriate to claims that certain acts are wrong. As such, it could be seen as on a par with avowedly relativistic claims that acts are wrong simply in virtue of being disallowed by principles that are generally accepted in the society in which those acts are committed. If one of these doctrines is to be counted as relativistic in the sense that people are inclined to fight about it and the other not, this cannot be because one of them, but not the other, makes arguments about wrongness dependent on 'parameters'—features of the society in question which are not themselves right or wrong. The difference must lie in what these 'parameters' are held to be, and perhaps one cannot tell whether the contractualist account of wrongness is relativistic in a controversial sense until one knows what the features of a society are that are supposed to affect what it is 'reasonable to reject'. We need to know whether dependence on *these* features is something that we have reason to fear or object to. Let me turn, then, to consider some reasons why relativism has seemed to many people a doctrine that is to be feared and resisted.

3. Why Resist Relativism?

Three kinds of reason for fearing or resisting relativism occur to me. First, relativism can be threatening because morality is seen as an important force for keeping people in line, and keeping the rest of us safe from potential wrongdoers. For those who take this view, relativists will seem dangerous in something like the way that Locke thought atheists were. Near the end of his *Letter on Toleration* (1689) after a firm condemnation of seventeenth-century practices of religious intolerance, and a stirring endorsement of toleration, he mentions some exceptions, ending with this one:

'Lastly, those are not at all to be tolerated who deny the being of a God. Promises, covenants, and oaths, which are the bonds of human society, can have no hold upon an atheist. The taking away of God, though but even in thought, dissolves all . . .'.[9]

Similarly, by claiming that familiar moral requirements may fail to apply even to cases that seem to us the clearest examples of wrongdoing, relativists may seem to announce that people are free to treat us in ways that these requirements forbid, and they encourage others to believe this as well. This would explain the element of fear in responses to relativism, and to that extent at least would seem to fit the facts. Describing such reactions to relativism, Philippa Foot says, for example, 'We are, naturally, concerned about the man who doesn't care what happens to other people, and we want to convict him of irrationality, thinking he will mind about that.'[10] She does not say exactly what the nature of this 'concern' is, but a natural hypothesis is that it is, at base, a desire to restrain others for the sake of our own protection. This hypothesis is supported by Foot's suggestion, later in the same paragraph, that it would be more honest 'to recognize that the "should" of moral judgment is sometimes merely an instrument by which we (for our own very good reasons) try to impose a rule of conduct even on the uncaring man'.

In order for the 'should' of moral judgement to be successful in this task (and not merely by deception), it needs to give reasons to (and thus, at least potentially, to motivate) every agent, whatever that agent's desires may happen to be. In addition, that 'should' has to have the right content—it has to forbid at least those actions by which we are most clearly threatened. Relativism is a threat on both scores: it threatens to exempt some agents from moral requirements altogether, and it threatens to allow the content of those requirements to vary—even, some fear, to the extent of permitting what we now see as the most heinous crimes.

The prospect of people in general giving no weight to even the most basic moral demands is indeed a frightening one. But relativism, as a philosophical doctrine, does not seem to me likely to lead to this result. So I am not much moved by this reason for

---

[9] John Locke, *Letter on Toleration* (1689). Quoted from p. 52 of the Library of Liberal Arts edn. (Indianapolis: Bobbs-Merrill, 1950).

[10] Philippa Foot, 'Morality and Art', *Proceedings of the British Academy*, 56 (1970), 143.

resisting relativism. I mention it mainly in order to distinguish it from a second reason, which I take more seriously.

This second reason is grounded in the confidence we have or would like to have in our condemnations of wrongful conduct and of those who engage in it. For example, when Gilbert Harman told us[11] that 'ought to do' judgements do not apply to people who lack relevant reasons, and that we therefore cannot say that it was wrong of Hitler to murder the Jews or that he ought not to have done it (even though we can condemn him in other ways), this claim seemed to deprive us of something important. It does this even if we believe that the thought that he was behaving wrongly, in the sense that we want to preserve, would not influence Hitler or others like him at all. What relativism threatens to deprive us of in such a case is not a mode of protection but rather, I would suggest, the sense that our condemnation of certain actions is legitimate and justified.

It may of course be asked why one should care so much about condemnation. This concern is sometimes ridiculed as an idle and self-righteous desire to be able to pass judgement on every agent, even those at great cultural or historical distance from us. So portrayed, it may seem unattractive. But if we give up the idea that an agent can be properly condemned for his action then we must also withdraw the claim, on his victims' behalf, that they were entitled not to be treated in the way that he did, and that it was therefore wrong of him to treat them that way. One need not be excessively judgemental or self-righteous to feel that conceding this would involve giving up something important, and I believe that this feeling, rather than a concern with self-protection or a self-righteous desire to pass judgement, is what lies behind most people's reluctance to accept Harman's claim about Hitler. But while the accusation of self-righteous moralism on the one side and the appeal to the perspective of the victim on the other have a certain rhetorical power, neither captures exactly what is at stake in this reason for resisting relativism. The essential point is that certain moral judgements seem to us clearly true and important (focusing on cases in which there is a clear victim just helps to make this apparent). Relativism is a threat in so far as it would force us to withdraw those judgements, or would undermine their claim to importance.

---

[11] In 'Moral Relativism Defended'. Harman does allow that we can condemn Hitler in other ways, for example by saying that he was evil.

Different forms of relativism can have these threatening effects to different degrees and in different ways. What Harman calls normative relativism, the view that different agents are subject to different ultimate moral demands, can be threatening in the first way, since if moral demands that we take seriously do not apply to an agent then judgements based on those demands must be withdrawn. What he calls moral judgement relativism is in this respect less threatening. This is the view that moral judgements are to be assessed not absolutely but only relative to the particular standards that they presuppose, and that different judgements (like different utterances of 'is tall') presuppose different standards. Recognizing that your favourable judgement of a certain action and my unfavourable one presuppose different standards does not require me to withdraw my judgement. But it may be threatening in another way in so far as it requires me to accept the idea that our judgements are 'equally correct'. This form of relativity (to the 'choice' of standards) may undermine the importance attached to our judgements of right and wrong. Whether it does so or not will depend on the kinds of reason that one can have for adhering to one set of standards rather than another. I will return to this question in Section 4.

Given this account of the interests that lie behind these first two reasons for resisting relativism, let me turn now to consider what would be required to satisfy these interests. If our opposition to relativism were based on the hope that morality will restrain others, then what we would want would be for there to be reasons to be moral which, if presented in the right way, would motivate even a 'bad' person, and would be available to restrain the rest of us, should other motives fail. But motivation is less central to the second reason for resisting relativism, which I have just considered. If what we are concerned about, in the first instance, is merely that our moral judgements 'apply to' those to whom we take them to apply, even, or especially, when these people care nothing for morality, then we need not be concerned with motivation *per se*. Motivation becomes an issue only if it is true, as Harman and others[12] have held, that 'ought' judgements of the relevant sort can apply to an agent only if he or she has a reason to behave accordingly. 'Ought' judgements that are not so

---

[12] Harman, ibid.; Bernard Williams, in a slightly more qualified way, in 'Internal Reasons and the Obscurity of Blame', *LOGOS: Philosophic Issues in Christian Perspective*, 10 (1989), 1–11; see esp. pp. 6–7.

grounded are, Williams claims, inappropriate, since, lacking any basis in what the agent cares about, they could not sincerely be offered as advice. But these claims are controversial. Unless they are accepted, the possibility that some agents might not have reasons to care about certain moral judgements, e.g. reasons grounded in their 'subjective motivational set', does not mean that those judgements must be withdrawn.

In order to get a clearer view of this problem it will be helpful to consider a related point about the plausibility of a response to relativism put forward by Philippa Foot. She has argued that an unrestricted moral relativism could not be correct because there are 'definitional criteria' which limit the content of anything that could be called morality, with the result that, for example, nothing properly called 'morality', or 'a moral system', or 'a moral code' could permit what Hitler did.[13] From the point of view of restraint this may seem small comfort, since it matters little whether Hitler's action can be *said* to be wrong if that judgement will in any event have no motivational effect for people like him. But things look different when we consider the importance of the judgements themselves, as embodied, for example, in the claims of victims. It adds insult to injury to have to admit that the person who attacked you did no wrong, and relativism may be resisted precisely because it seems to force this admission. From this point of view, then, Foot's appeal to definitional criteria has more substance: it preserves the judgement that the victim was wronged, and the further observation that the agent is one who cares nothing for moral considerations may take nothing away from this judgement, or from the importance it has for us. (Whether it does so is something I will consider at length below.)

Let me turn now, finally, to the last of the three reasons for resisting relativism that I said I would consider. Some may fear and resist relativism because it seems to threaten their sense that they have adequate grounds for believing their way of life is justified, and for preferring it to others. Like a concern with condemnation, this reaction to relativism may be regarded with scepticism. Indeed, it is open to attack from two opposing directions. Relativists may see it as involving an inappropriate attitude towards others—an unseemly desire to see other ways of life as inferior. Others (Nietzscheans, I might call them) may see it as involving an inappropriate attitude towards oneself: why, if one finds a certain way of life appealing and wants to live that way, must one need to believe, in addition, that it is 'correct' in some deeper sense? Why should one need the support of 'objectivity'? Why, Nietzsche asks in a notebook entry,[14] do people think that they can have an ideal only if it is *the ideal*? To think this, he says, is to deprive one's ideal of its own special character. On the contrary, he suggests, 'One should have [an ideal] in order to distinguish oneself, not to level oneself.'

With respect to those elements of a way of life that might be called 'traditions and customs', both of these criticisms seem correct at the same time. Suppose that I attach importance to eating certain foods, dressing in a certain way, observing certain holidays, playing certain sports, supporting a certain team, listening to a certain kind of music, and singing certain songs, all because these are part of the life I have grown up in and I see them as elements of my continuing membership in that life and connection with its, and my, past. This provides me with ample reason for doing these things and for preferring them to others. Perhaps I might like to think that in some way this way of life is 'better than all others', but there is no need for me to think this in order to have good reasons for following it. Why think that there is some notion of 'getting it right' which is what we should strive for in such matters? To take this seriously would be a sign of insecurity and weakness (as the Nietzscheans would say) and a foolish desire for superiority (as the relativists would add).

This is the best example that I can imagine of clearly benign relativism—relativism that can be accepted without undermining the judgements to which it applies. Following one 'way of life' (one set of customs and traditions) is something I have reason to do not absolutely but only relative to certain parameters: in this case my being a person who was brought up in this particular way and for whom these customs therefore have a particular meaning. If I had been born in a different place and had a different life, then I would have had no reason to do the things just listed but would instead have had other, parallel reasons for following different customs. Moreover, acknowledging this para-

---

[14] F. Nietzsche, *The Will to Power*, tr. Walter Kaufmann and R. J. Hollingdale (New York: Vintage Books, 1968), sect. 349.

metric dependence does not undermine the force that these reasons have for me, or make these reasons merely a matter of preferences that I 'just happen to have'. The 'parameters' (being a person who has a certain past and for whom these customs therefore have a certain meaning) are mere facts which are themselves not up for justification, but they serve as *grounds* for my preferences, not merely as their causal determinants.

This parametric dependence explains not only why members of two different groups can have reasons for accepting different judgements as justified but also why they would be mistaken in applying these judgements to members of the other group: it would make no sense to say that I have reason to follow the customs of some group to which I have no connection, or that they have such reasons to follow mine.

This is not a case of 'parametric universalism', since there is no need to invoke an overarching principle of the form 'People whose life and history is of type A ought to live according to R(A)' and to claim that each of the groups I have imagined is an instance of this principle. The reasons that a person has to follow the traditions that are part of his or her way of life depend on the particular meaning that those actions and that history have for that person. They need not derive this importance from any beliefs about the value of 'tradition' in general. In fact, once one reaches that level of abstraction reasons of the kind in question largely lose their force. (When people start talking in general terms about 'the value of traditions' they are usually on the edge of ceasing to care about their own.)

It is easy to see why examples of this kind are emphasized by defenders of (at least a qualified) relativism, such as Stuart Hampshire and Michael Walzer.[15] These examples are convincing in themselves, and they illustrate what I take to be the relativists' main point: that those who think we must look to the idea of objectivity in order to account for the importance that our way of life has for us are in fact looking in the wrong place. Many relativists (including Walzer, but not Hampshire) urge us to extend this example, taking it as the model for understanding other modes of moral evaluation, including standards of justice.

---

[15] See S. Hampshire, 'Morality and Convention', in his *Morality and Conflict* (Cambridge, Mass.: Harvard University Press, 1983), and M. Walzer, *Spheres of Justice* (New York: Basic Books, 1983), esp. chs. 1 and 13.

How might this extension work? In the example just considered the model was this. We can describe, abstractly, a certain kind of importance, roughly the kind of importance that a form of behaviour has for a person if it defines a community of which he or she feels a part or expresses a connection with a certain history to which the person is attached. We can then see how it can be reasonable for different people, given their different histories and situations, to attach this kind of importance to quite different modes of behaviour. Applied to the case of morality, then, the idea would be first to characterize the kind of importance or authority that moral considerations have, the kinds of reason they give people, and then to show, in the light of this characterization, how different people could, quite reasonably, attach this kind of importance to different forms of conduct.

The kind of moral relativism that this strategy leads to will depend heavily on how the importance or authority of morality is characterized. One possibility is that this account will remain quite close to the example just given, that is that it will take the importance that moral considerations have just to be that importance that attaches to any standards that we are brought up to take seriously, that are part of the life of a community to which we feel attached, and that are enforced within that community by sanctions of approval and disapproval. This yields a form of relativism that has seemed to many people to be threatening in both of the ways I have mentioned above: it gives a deflationary account of the importance of morality and it allows the content of moral rules to vary widely, perhaps even to permit actions that now strike us as very clearly wrong.

Walzer has argued that his view should not be seen as threatening in this latter way, since there are good reasons why any set of standards that are generally accepted in a society will include a common core of basic prohibitions against such things as 'murder, deception, betrayal and gross cruelty'.[16] I want to focus here, however, on the first of these anti-relativist worries, and less on the fixed than on what is seen as the variable part of morality. In so far as moral standards vary, what kind of importance can they claim?

[16] M. Walzer, *Interpretation and Social Criticism* (Cambridge, Mass.: Harvard University Press, 1987), 24.

4. Contingent Principles

Some possible answers to this question are suggested by a form of relativism considered by Philippa Foot in 'Morality and Art' and in 'Moral Relativism'. According to this view, moral judgements, like judgements about who is tall or what food tastes good, always presuppose certain standards. A particular moral judgement is to be assessed as true or false by determining how the standards that it presupposes apply to the case in question. But these standards cannot have just any content. As I have said above, Foot holds that there are 'definitional starting-points of morality', considerations which must be counted as relevant and given a certain weight by any standards that can properly be called moral.

Relativism remains a possibility, however, because these definitional starting-points may underdetermine the content of morality. There may be 'contingent principles' on which different sets of standards could differ while still being fully entitled to be called moral standards. If two sets of standards differ in this way, then moral judgements which implicitly refer to these differing standards could give opposing views about the permissibility of a given action while both remain true. These judgements would not contradict one another, since they refer to different standards. But they would at least conflict in the practical sense I discussed above, and each would be true, since it makes a correct claim about how the standards to which it refers apply to this case. Nor could we claim that one of these sets of *standards* is true and the other false if they are each compatible with the 'definitional starting points' and there is no possibility of 'proving or showing' on the basis of 'criteria internal to the concept of morality' that one of them rather than the other is correct. Foot indicates at least some sympathy for Bernard Williams's claim that truth has no 'substantial' application in such cases.[17]

As I have stated it, this hypothesis leaves open the crucial question of where the fixed part of morality ends and the contingent part begins, and Foot expresses uncertainty on this point.[18]

---

[17] 'Moral Relativism', 8. She cites Williams's essays 'Consistency and Realism', *Proceedings of the Aristotelian Society*, supp. vol. (1966) and 'The Truth in Relativism', in *Moral Luck*, 132–43.

[18] See pp. 17–19 of 'Moral Relativism' and the 'Retrospective Note' added to the version of 'Morality and Art' repr. in T. Honderich and M. Burnyeat (eds.), *Philosophy As It Is* (New York: Penguin, 1979).

It is unclear, she says, how much is determined by the criteria internal to the concept of morality, and how much room is left for relativism. But the examples of possibly contingent principles that she cites in 'Morality and Art' give some guidance as to what she had in mind at least at that time.

The first of these is abortion. 'Thinking about the problem of abortion,' she writes, 'I come to the conclusion that there is a genuine choice as to whether or not to count as a human being, with the rights of a human being, what would become a human being but is not yet capable of independent life.'[19]

Second, she suggests that something similar may be true in some cases in which the interests of individuals clash with those of the community. 'We ourselves', she says, 'have a strong objection to the idea of *using* one person for the benefit of others, and it probably guides our intuitions in many cases. It does not seem clear, however, that one could rule out of court the principles of a strict utilitarian who would, at least if he were consistent, allow things that we will not allow in the interests of cancer research.'[20]

In another article,[21] Foot suggested that the solidarity shown by the people of Leningrad during the siege was 'contingent'. She was not there discussing relativism, and she may well have meant to suggest a different form of contingency. But since I find the example a helpful one I want to bear it in mind.

Foot remarks that she thinks it unlikely that many people will be willing to accept even the qualified relativism that this hypothesis suggests where ethics is concerned.[22] Why should this be so? I suggested above that relativism is threatening when it forces us to withdraw moral judgements that strike us as clearly correct, or when, while allowing our judgements to stand, it undermines the importance that they seemed to have. Would Foot's relativism have effects of this kind?

It is not obvious that accepting her hypothesis would require us to withdraw judgements which seem clearly true. To begin with, it would not have this effect where judgements based on 'definitional criteria' are concerned. So there would be no problem of the sort that arises with Harman's claim about Hitler. And

---

[19] Foot, 'Morality and Art', 133.   [20] Ibid.
[21] Philippa Foot, 'Morality as a System of Hypothetical Imperatives', *Philosophical Review*, 81/3 (July 1972), 305–16.
[22] Foot, 'Morality and Art', 139.

even in the case of contingent principles, the kind of relativity that is suggested does not, by itself, make it logically inappropriate to pass judgement (based on 'our' standards) on the actions of people who live in societies where quite different standards prevail.[23] A Sicilian tourist in Los Angeles who writes on a postcard to his family that almost everyone in California is very tall will be saying something true, even though it would be false by the standards of the Californians. So an analogous relativity would not be a bar to cross-cultural moral judgements. If such judgements are sometimes odd or inappropriate this must be for some further reason. For example, even when it makes sense to criticize the practices of another society—to say, for example, that they are unjust—it may sound odd to criticize an individual in that society for not doing what we would see as the right thing if such an action would have made no sense in that context.

Even if relativism of the kind Foot considers would not force us to withdraw judgements that seem clearly correct, it would require us to accept the idea that other, opposing judgements are equally correct and that there is no question of truth between our standards and the ones reflected in these judgements. As Foot says, this might be resisted on the ground that it involves a 'weakening of allegiance' to our own standards.[24] There are two problems here. The first is understanding how the 'contingent' part of one's moral outlook is supposed to be related to the non-contingent, or 'definitional', part. How can we see some of our principles as 'contingent' yet at the same time having the force of morality for us—the same kind of importance that the rest of morality has? Given an answer to this question, we can then go on and inquire whether it is compatible with this kind of allegiance to our contingent principles to say that there is no question of truth as between these principles and the different contingent principles held by others.

Before addressing these questions I need to say more about the status of Foot's definitional criteria. In speaking of the 'importance' of morality I do not mean to presuppose that it has the kind of special authority that Foot called into question in 'Morality as a System of Hypothetical Imperatives': that is, I do not mean to be

---

[23] What we have here is, in Harman's terms, a form of moral judgement relativism, not normative relativism.
[24] Foot, 'Morality and Art', 139.

assuming that morality 'gives reason for acting to any man'.[25] Whether it does this or not is a question I mean to be leaving open. The importance I have in mind is the importance that moral considerations have for those who take morality seriously. Even among those for whom it has such importance, however, there may be disagreement about its nature and basis.[26] Some people see morality as depending crucially on the authority of the will of God. For others, it may be based in one or another secular idea of human excellence. Still others may see it as grounded in what Mill calls 'the social feelings of mankind; the desire to be in unity with our fellow creatures',[27] or, in my terminology, the desire to be able to justify our actions to others.[28]

In so far as they are taken to mark the limits of applicability of the concept 'morality', Foot's definitional criteria must be common ground for people who disagree in this way. In discussing these criteria she says, 'A moral system seems necessarily to be one aimed at removing certain dangers and securing certain benefits, and it would follow that some things do and some do not count as objections from a moral point of view.'[29] Here the words 'aimed at' can be understood in a stronger or weaker way. On the weaker interpretation the claim that is being made is about the content of morality: anything that is to count as a moral code must recognize our need for protection against certain dangers and the importance for us of certain benefits. On the stronger interpretation, the claim would be that protecting us in these ways and securing these benefits must be the ultimate aim and source of importance of anything that could be called a system of morality. This stronger interpretation seems too strong. Taken strictly, it would rule out the possibility of a religious basis for morality, and even if one thinks religious accounts of morality mistaken it would be excessive to say that calling them 'moral views' involved a misuse of the term. On the other hand, the weaker

[25] See generally Foot, 'Morality as a System of Hypothetical Imperatives' and 'Morality and Art', 142–3.

[26] This distinction, between accounts of the content of morality and accounts of its nature and importance, is discussed at greater length in my paper 'The Aims and Authority of Moral Theory', *Oxford Journal of Legal Studies*, 12 (1992), 1–23. I am indebted to Angel Oquendo for many discussions of the bearing of this distinction on issues of relativism.

[27] J. S. Mill, *Utilitarianism*, ch. 3, para. 10.

[28] See my 'Contractualism and Utilitarianism', sect. 3.

[29] Foot, 'Morality and Art', 132.

interpretation, taken strictly, seems too weak. We would not count just any code with the relevant minimum content as a moral system, no matter what its rationale might be. (The dictates of a malevolent superbeing would not count as a moral system even if, for some reason related to that being's ultimate purposes but not at all to our good, they forbade us to kill or injure one another.)

So the rationale of anything plausibly called a morality must be related to some conception of how it is good for us to live. But this definitional constraint is compatible with a wide variety of different views of the nature of morality and its distinctive importance, including at least those I have listed above. It follows from this general constraint on its rationale that the content of a morality must include the definitional starting-points Foot mentions, but different accounts of this rationale will explain this content in different ways. Someone who believed that morality derives its importance from God's will could explain its content by arguing that, given the nature of God, any system of commands plausibly attributed to him would have to take account of the needs of human life, and they would offer a specific account of what these are. Millians, contractualists, or Aristotelians would offer other, quite different explanations, and these accounts, while agreeing in a general sense on the 'definitional starting-points of morality', are likely to lead to differing interpretations of their content.

Let me return now to the question whether, if we accept the idea that between different sets of contingent principles there can be no question of truth, this would undermine our allegiance to the contingent principles we accept—undermine our grounds for assigning them moral significance and the importance that goes with it. What, then, are these grounds? If we concede that a principle cannot be proved or shown to be correct on the basis of criteria internal to the concept of morality, what ground could we have for giving it the kind of importance that moral principles have as opposed to considering it merely a matter of shared reactions or of custom and tradition? There are a number of possible answers.

One possibility is that the moral standing of contingent principles depends on their relation to the 'definitional starting-points' of moral argument, but that there may be room for different sets of such principles because there may be different ways of understanding these starting-points. As Foot says, we may agree that murder must be counted a serious moral wrong, but disagree about exactly what counts as murder.[30] What kind of reasons might one have to accept one definition of murder rather than another as morally determinative? A person might take one definition (or one class of definitions) to be superior on the ground that the others all involved restrictions on the scope of 'murder' that seemed arbitrary. It is plausible to suppose that something like this is the reason some people have for thinking that abortion is always, or nearly always, murder. This is certainly not a proof. Is it 'showing'? Well, it is at least a consideration capable of determining the mind for a number of people. There are, of course, considerations that can be offered on the other side. Could a person who finds these counter-arguments insufficient, and therefore holds that abortion is nearly always murder, none the less accept the claim that there is no substantial sense in which this principle, but not opposing ones, can be called true?

Such a person could, at least, admit that there is a degree of uncertainty here. That is, they could, while remaining convinced that abortion is wrong, admit that there are reasonable grounds for holding the opposite view. But it is more difficult to see how someone whose reasons for believing abortion to be wrong were of the kind I have mentioned could admit that there is no substantial question of truth between this principle and opposing ones. To make this admission plausible we would need to move beyond mere uncertainty to something more like genuine underdetermination: it is not just that we cannot be certain which way of characterizing murder is in fact morally correct but rather that there is no fact of the matter as to which is correct; moral argument is underdetermined and does not settle this question.

There may be problems about how this idea of under-determination is to be understood. But, leaving these aside for the moment, there is the question of what reason we could have to regard one of two answers as having moral force if we saw the choice between them as morally underdetermined. It seems that we would have to appeal to reasons of some other sort, for example to considerations like those I discussed above under the head-

---

[30] Ibid. 133.

ing of 'tradition'. Suppose that a significant, but not conclusive, moral case can be made for each of two conflicting principles. If one of these principles has long been accepted in my community, then I can have strong reason to be guided by it rather than by the alternative principle for which, I recognize, an equally good abstract case can be made. In such a case I could, without undermining my allegiance to my principle, admit that it had no greater claim than the alternative to moral truth.

But there is, I think, a better explanation. The moral status of contingent principles might depend not on their logical ties to 'definitional criteria', understood as fixed points in the content of morality, but rather on their connection with different conceptions of the nature of morality and its authority. This suggests a more plausible understanding both of the nature of the underdetermination and of how it can be filled in in different ways that will seem, to the person who holds them, to be entirely continuous with the core or morality. As I have argued above, the limits on the application of the term 'morality' must leave open the possibility of different understandings of its rationale and basis. That the concept of morality underdetermines its content is hardly surprising. But particular understandings of the basis of moral requirements are more determinate. As I have argued above, different ways of understanding the basis of moral requirements can support different interpretations even of what Foot calls definitional criteria, and the case of abortion may be an example of this. Moreover, different moral outlooks may go beyond these definitional criteria in different ways and include different contingent principles because these outlooks are based on different conceptions of the nature and importance of morality, or on different interpretations of the same conception.

Foot's example of utilitarianism can be used to illustrate these two possibilities. Like some contractualists, some utilitarians may locate the ground of morality in what Mill called the desire to be in unity with one's fellow creatures. These contractualists and utilitarians may agree that any principles that can claim to be responsive to this desire must include Foot's definitional starting-points, but beyond this point they may disagree about the content of morality, the utilitarian allowing, as in Foot's second example, greater sacrifice to be imposed on individuals for the sake of the common good. To a utilitarian, a contractualist's interpretation of the 'desire for unity' may seem to be narrow and ungenerous and to fail to recognize the full force of this basic moral impulse. Someone might be a convinced utilitarian for this reason, and such a person would hold utilitarian contingent principles for the same reason: not because they follow from the definitional starting-points but because they are supported by the best account of the moral force of those starting-points.

Utilitarians of this kind could recognize contractualists' moral judgements as 'true relative to' (i.e. as genuinely following from) contractualists' contingent principles. They also have reasons for finding those principles unappealing. And contractualists have their own objections to utilitarian principles. Indeed, these reasons may be, from their point of view, more exigent, since they may see utilitarian principles as licensing actions that at least come very near to violating definitional starting-points if, for example, they allow medical treatment to be withheld from people who refuse to participate in medical experiments.

Must each of these parties think that the other's principles are *false*? At least they will think them mistaken in so far as they purport to represent the moral consequences of the idea of 'unity with one's fellow creatures'. Given that each side has these reasons for regarding the other not only as an inferior moral outlook but also as an inferior expression of the shared but disputed idea of 'unity with one's fellow creatures', and given that the judgements expressing these views seem to have the logic of ordinary declarative sentences, it seems natural to use the terms 'true' and 'false' to describe their disagreement.

So let us consider instead the possibility that utilitarians and contractualists are appealing to quite different conceptions of the ground and authority of moral requirements rather than making rival claims about the proper interpretation of the same ground. Some utilitarians see morality as following from a general demand of rationality, that one always chooses the action that one has reason to believe will yield the best consequences, objectively understood.[31] They might also claim that since actions that meet

---

[31] Sidgwick gave the classic statement of this rationale for utilitarianism in book IV of his *Methods of Ethics* (Chicago, Ill.: University of Chicago Press, 1962). Foot criticizes modern versions of the idea in her article 'Utilitarianism and the Virtues', in S. Scheffler (ed.), *Consequentialism and its Critics* (Oxford: Oxford University Press, 1988).

this requirement have the best possible justification they can certainly be 'justified to' others. But the idea of justifiability to others does not have the fundamental place in their outlook that it enjoys in contractualist or Kantian accounts of morality. So when utilitarians of this kind make judgements about right and wrong they could be seen as appealing not just to different contingent principles than Kantians or contractualists invoke but also to a conception of the importance and appeal of morality that is quite different from the idea of a 'kingdom of ends'.

Supposing that moral judgements made by a contractualist and by a utilitarian are understood in this way, could each of these parties admit, without undermining allegiance to his or her own outlook, that what the other says is equally true? At one level it would seem that they could do this, since each can see the other's judgements as being 'about' a different subject: what we owe to each other is one thing, what would produce the most valuable state of affairs is something else. But at a higher level, the two parties must see themselves as making conflicting claims about the same subject: about what considerations we have reason to give most weight to in governing our lives. The result is relativism about judgements of right and wrong (because these judgements have varying reference) but not about claims about reasons. This limited relativism does not seem to me to present a threat.

Might it be extended to a more thoroughgoing relativity, according to which the parties to a disagreement like the one I have just described might recognize their opponents' claims about reasons to be 'equally correct'? And could they do this without sacrificing allegiance to their own positions? I see two possibilities here. One would be a relativism about reasons, according to which all claims about reasons for action are relative to certain 'parameters'.[32] This could be threatening in so far as the relativity

[32] Bernard Williams's well-known claim that all statements about reasons for action are relative to the agent's 'subjective motivational set' would be an example. See 'Internal and External Reasons', in Moral Luck (Cambridge: Cambridge University Press, 1978). He appears to regard this as what I have been calling a benign view—one we have no good reason to fear. Foot has said (in the postscript to 'Reasons for Action and Desires', in Virtues and Vices (Oxford: Blackwell, 1978), 156) that she is inclined to the view that at least one class of reasons (those deriving from what is in an agent's best interest) are independent of desires, thus rejecting Williams's extreme position. But she seems there to remain agnostic on the more general question of the relativity of reasons.

in question seemed to undermine the force of reasons we take ourselves to have. But it would take me too far afield to explore here the questions whether some such view might be correct and whether it should be seen as threatening. A second possibility is that each of the parties could (without becoming relativists about reasons) recognize the others' outlook as a reasonable alternative worthy of respect, even though it is not one that they themselves would adopt. I believe that this is closer to what many benign relativists have in mind.

This possibility can be illustrated by a revised version of the Leningrad example, which I will take to involve a contrast between a form of liberal contractualism on the one hand and, on the other, what we may imagine to be the moral ideal of solidarity that, we may imagine, moved many of the people of Leningrad during the siege. I will suppose that this ideal demands a greater level of self-sacrifice than contractualism does, but does not license the use of coercion to extract these sacrifices. The people who hold this ideal, we may suppose, see that because of the sacrifices it requires it is something that others could reasonably reject. None the less, it represents the kind of life with others that they want to live. They would not be satisfied with less.

Foot's hypothesis seems plausible in this case. When a citizen of Leningrad says, of a particular act of sacrifice, 'This is what I must do', she says something true even though when I say, looking back, 'No one is required, morally, to do what they did', I also speak truly. Moreover, when we step back from the 'contingent principles' on which these judgements are based, and from the conceptions of morality from which they draw their force, there is much that might be said to explain the appeal of each, but the idea of truth does not seem to have a significant role to play in this discussion. Each can recognize, without sacrifice of allegiance, that the others act on good, respectable reasons.

Could the same be said about the disagreement between secular liberal and conservative Christian views about homosexuality that I mentioned in Section 2? The proposal would be this. When a conservative Christian says, 'Homosexuality is a sin', and I say 'There is nothing morally objectionable about sexual relations between two men, or between two women', I may hope that the Christian is mistaken even in his own terms, but it is conceivable that we may both be saying something true. The standards that

our judgements presuppose make conflicting claims to allegiance:
they conflict in a practical sense. Given the very different bases of
these claims, however, it might be suggested that the contingent
principles that they support are not plausibly understood as making conflicting truth-claims about the same subject.

I have expressed the Christian's claims in terms of 'sin' in order
to emphasize this divergence. There would be at least the appearance of more direct conflict if we were to imagine instead that he
urges on me the claim that 'Homosexual conduct is morally
wrong'. This claim could be understood in two different ways. It
might embody the claim that Christianity offers the best, perhaps
the only, coherent way of understanding what *I* mean by morality. If so, then the dispute has much the same form as the one
between the utilitarian and the contractualist as I first described it.
There is a single subject, an allegedly shared idea of morality,
about which conflicting claims are being made, and there seems
little reason to deny that these claims can be true or false. Alternatively, 'Homosexuality is morally wrong' may amount to the
same thing as 'Homosexuality is a sin', giving added emphasis,
perhaps, to the Christian's belief that *these* are the standards
worth caring about. In this case, as in the original version of this
example and in the case of the people of Leningrad, the question
of truth seems less relevant, and my reason for rejecting the Christian's claim is not that it says something false about morality but
rather that it expresses a conception of what is important in life
that I see no reason to accept (perhaps because it involves factual
assumptions which I see as mistaken).

Should we accept this proposal? In one respect there seems to
me to be something clarifying about it. We often speak, in moral
philosophy, as if there were one subject-matter, *morality*, the domain of one particular kind of reason for action, which we are
studying and to which everyone is referring when they make
judgements about right and wrong. The present proposal is helpful in suggesting, very plausibly I think, that this is not so, and
that different people may have quite different kinds of reason in
mind when they use the terms 'right', 'wrong', and 'morality'.
This much could, I think, be accepted without compromising our
allegiance to our own moral views. But it would be much more
difficult in this case for either party to accept the further idea that
the reasons backing the other side's conception of morality are

'just as good as' their own. This was possible in the version of the Leningrad example that I just discussed because the ideals in question there were ones that each side could recognize as alternatives deserving of similar respect. But in the present case we have conflicting outlooks that make stronger claims to unique authority and rest on premises which the opposing side is likely to see as false.

My conclusions are these. The concept of 'a morality' or 'a moral system' is broad enough to allow variation not only in the content of what is required but also in the reasons seen as supporting these requirements and their claim to importance. Variation of the latter kind explains the former: people who all recognize the same 'definitional' principles as morally required, can see different sets of 'contingent principles' as having the same status as these shared principles because they have different views about what this status amounts to. Recognizing other people's (definitional plus contingent) principles as constituting 'a moral system', and recognizing the judgements they make as true (relative to this system), need not be incompatible with allegiance to our own moral views. Despite the applicability to both of the term 'moral', their judgements and ours are properly understood as making claims 'about different things'. What is more difficult to see is how we might, without sacrificing allegiance to our own principles, regard the reasons others have for following their principles as just as good as our reasons for following our own. I have suggested that this would be possible if we accept the substantive evaluative judgement that both ways of life are worthy of respect and adherence. This seems to me the most plausible way for a benign moral relativism to be realized. So understood, it is not a possibility that there is any reason to fear.

10

The Representation of Life

MICHAEL THOMPSON

1. Introductory

1.1. Logic and Life

Among the many scandalous features of Hegel's table, or system, of logical categories, we would nowadays want, I think, to accord high rank to this, that he finds a place for the concept *life* on it. Hegel is of course not blind to the counter-intuitive character of his teaching on this point. In the so-called 'Greater Logic', the chapter headed 'Life' begins with the formulation of an objection to any specifically *logical* treatment of the notion. Something in the objection, at least, might still find favour today:

The idea of life is concerned with a subject matter so concrete, and if you will so real, that with it we may seem to have overstepped the domain of logic as it is commonly conceived. Certainly, if logic were to contain nothing but empty, dead forms of thought, there could be no mention in it at all of such a content as the idea of life.[1]

We may set aside the lyrical opposition of life's golden branches and poor grey lifeless theory, a favourite object of Hegelian ridicule. Even if there *are* special forms of thought allied to the concept of life, it is hard to see how they would be any more or less *dead* than those linked to the concepts of, say, being and quantity.

If the tendentious rhetoric is dropped, the implicit objection can be expounded in a series of apparent truisms. For logic, if tra-

---

[1] G. W. F. Hegel, *Hegel's Science of Logic*, tr. A. V. Miller (London: Allen & Unwin, 1969), 761. (I have omitted certain initial capitals.) Hegel's response to his objection is unfortunately of no value. He says that logic is concerned with cognition, and that cognition is life; therefore etc. This gets us nowhere unless the first premise means that *cognition* is one of the logical categories. But the premise is only uncontentious if it expresses the traditional view that the logical categories are the forms of thought or cognition.

dition can be trusted, relates to the *form* of thought—a form of inference, for example, or the 'logical form' of a judgement. 'Form' here is of course opposed to *content*, a distinction that begins to become explicit for us when we learn to use schematic letters of different types and to substitute other expressions for them. How the distinction is to be further elaborated, and how exactly logic is supposed to 'relate' to the associated notion of form, are admittedly matters for dispute. But let them be resolved as one likes: how can anyone pretend that thought about living things differs in any such respect from, say, thought about planets?

After all, living things, organisms, are just some among the concrete individuals we think about, marked off from the others in quite definite ways. The word 'life' is meant to capture these points of distinction. It therefore expresses one of those 'particular characteristics of objects' which, according to Frege (here following tradition), logic must 'disregard'.[2] We could hardly have said the same about the ultra-abstract, bare-bones distinctions of category that Frege himself introduces, for example that between *Begriff* and *Gegenstand*. If the former sort of thing were marked out within a wider class (the class of entities, as it is inevitably called) by the possession of some particular characteristic—which we express, maybe, by calling the things 'unsaturated'—then there would have been no problem about the concept *horse*.[3]

If, then, we conceive or judge or infer differently in connection with the living, it is just that we conceive and judge and infer different things. It is no use to affirm that life is an 'essential property' of whatever has it—or that maybe 'being' is a basic category of thought and *vivere viventibus est esse*. 'Metal' and 'monocotyledon' arguably express essential properties of whatever satifies them; and if 'to be, for living things, is to live', then presumably also being, for a cockroach, is being a cockroach, or living a roach's life. If any of these concepts sets the theme for a theoretical discussion, then the discussion must fall under one of the special sciences. A properly *logical* discourse would have to be

---

[2] Gottlob Frege, *Begriffsschrift*, tr. Stefan Bauer-Mengelberg, in Jean van Heijenoort (ed.), *From Frege to Gödel* (Cambridge, Mass.: Harvard University Press, 1967).

[3] See esp. Gottlob Frege, 'On Concept and Object', tr. Peter Geach; repr. in *Collected Papers*, ed. Brian McGuinness (Oxford: Blackwell, 1984).

carried on under some more abstract heading, e.g. 'individuals', 'relations', 'properties'—perhaps even 'being' or 'essential properties'—but 'life' and organism', never.

I propose to attack this sort of conception, and to make a beginning of what amounts to a logical treatment of the idea of life, and its near relatives, and their expression in language. Hegel, I think, was so far right. Thought, *as thought*, takes a quite special turn when it is thought of the living—a turn *of the same kind* as that noticed by Frege in the transition from object to concept, from 'Philippa is wise', to 'The wise are few'.[4]

1.2. Ethics and Life

But why treat such an abstract and extra-practical topic in a work of homage to Professor Foot? The answer of course is that an appeal to notions of life and organism and life-form is to be found throughout her works. Such thoughts are a part of her so-called naturalism, and have always formed a focus of attack on her own and similar views of her former colleague Elizabeth Anscombe.

We find such notions expressed, for example, in Professor Foot's treatment of the concepts of damage and injury;[5] in her account of certain appearances of the word 'good';[6]—and even in her discussion of euthanasia, where the suggestion is made that

there is a conceptual connexion between *life* and *good* in the case of human beings as in that of animals and even plants. Here, as there, however, it is not the mere state of being alive that can determine, or itself count as, a good, but rather life coming up to some standard of normality.[7]

---

[4] I have been advised to warn the reader that throughout this essay I take Frege's above-mentioned remarks on concept and object as a paradigmatic elucidation of a 'distinction of logical category'. It may be that this commits me to a somewhat eccentric employment of the phrase. It is one of the lessons taught by Ludwig Wittgenstein, if I understand him, that we must recognize many intuitively more determinate distinctions *of the sort Frege introduced*. Wittgenstein of course calls the corresponding sort of distinction among *signs* a 'grammatical difference'.

[5] Philippa Foot, 'Moral Beliefs', in her *Virtues and Vices* (Berkeley, Calif.: University of California Press, 1978), 115–18.

[6] Philippa Foot, 'Goodness and Choice', in her *Virtues and Vices*, 145–6.

[7] Philippa Foot, 'Euthanasia', in her *Virtues and Vices*, 42–3.

More recently such 'naturalistic' thoughts have appeared, and in still bolder formulations, in a series of lectures and unpublished essays aimed at revising the positive account of the rationality of morality put forth in 'Morality as a System of Hypothetical Imperatives',[8] which was itself a revision of the doctrine of the second part of 'Moral Beliefs'. It is this more recent appeal to ideas of life and organism that I am especially hoping to defend.

In those lectures, if I understood them,[9] the suggestion was made that practical reason be viewed as a faculty, akin to the powers of sight and hearing and memory; it was further maintained that an individual instance of any of these latter powers is to be judged as defective or sound by reference to its bearer's *species*; as, for example, a house cat's visual capacity is, one gathers, not to be remarked upon, if it cannot apprehend the ripening of a tomato, though that of a human being would be. This is not simply because the cat is unlikely to share its owner's interest in the ripeness of tomatoes, but because of the difference in kind or species, or because of what each of them is.

Now, in the work of practical reason we have to do with a movement in quite different categories, in some sense, from those of mere sensibility. But, then, sensibility seems to differ just as radically from the sub-psychical, merely vegetative aspects of life; and yet absolutely parallel remarks could be made about the criteria of defect in the parts and operations of individual plants. Why, then, should the novel character of rationality prevent our again according the *kind* or *species* some of the status it seemed to possess in respect of the 'lower' faculties?

And so, for example, if we care to contemplate kinds of reasoning animal other than our own, shouldn't we also imagine different shapes of practical reason, subject to different standards of defect—that is, of *irrationality*, as defect may be called in this sort of case? And similarly, moving in the other direction: whatever place is to be given the picturesque customs of the world and to peoples' 'projects' and the like, won't there be some larger more generic standard of rationality the same for all who are of our

---

[8] Foot, *Virtues and Vices*, 157–73.

[9] What follows is not intended as a record of these lectures, but as a coarse expression of a theoretical *tendency*—one which, I think, was also expressed in her remarks. What matters for the moment is the tendency only; I am hoping in what follows to supply some materials for its adequate expression.

same kind? And if something in the way of justice, for example, is a part of the life characteristic of humankind, then won't its presence in a person's thinking be among the marks of a sound practical reason that are associated with our kind? It will perhaps be impossible, after all, to effect the separation required to make a great question of it, whether morality in general is rational.

1.3. Ethics and Logic

This is all very crudely expressed, but one need not enter into details. The slightest movement in such a direction is enough to set off alarms in many quarters. Some of the likely objections are notoriously difficult to understand; for example, that when it comes to treat moral questions such a line of thought must inevitably commit the naturalistic fallacy, or pretend to supply materials for a would-be derivation of 'ought' from 'is'. Other types of resistance involve a wrong idea of the place of controversy— the tendency is thought, for example, to aim at an axiom from which particular practical principles (inevitably illiberal ones) would then be derived, and that the proponent's next step will be to prove that, say, usury and contraception are 'wrong' because 'unnatural'.

But the objection I think I understand and want to take seriously starts from the thought that in employing such notions as life and organism and species we introduce something *foreign*, in particular something 'biological', into ethical theory. Any such view, one thinks, must involve either a vulgar scientistic dissolution of the ethical, tending maybe towards an 'evolutionary ethics', or else the substitution of an outdated metaphysics for what we know to be empirical. Each path leads to its own absurdities. Together they may be thought to betray a yearning to view our practices 'from outside' or 'from sideways on' in hope perhaps of providing them with a foundation or an external grounding.

It is, I think, to be granted that ethical theory, in all its departments, is in a certain sense conceptually fastidious, and that there is here again a sin of 'overstepping' akin to that Hegel noticed in connection with logical theory, and that the formulation of ethical principles must be contaminated by anything that comes our way through a purely scientific development. This, if it is right, is not a consequence of some more general crime of struggling to 'get beyond our practices' or 'outside our language' or what you will, but a specifically ethical truth. It is what Rousseau meant when he said that one shouldn't have to make a man a *philosophe* before making him a man,[10] and what Kant presupposed in shrugging off the criticism that his *Groundwork* proposed no new moral principle, but only a new formula.[11] I will not defend the idea here, except to remark that, if we reject it, we will also have to reject the traditional asymmetry between ignorance of principle and ignorance of fact.

But suppose that the concepts *life, organism,* and *life-form* really are logical determinations, and that some such primitive practical concept as, say, *action* belongs to the sphere they govern, and is not itself to be castigated as a novelty or a foreign body or 'the latest revelation of wisdom'. Then the ethical employment of such concepts would merely make articulate something already present in *pensée sauvage pratique*—and it would seem that Professor Foot was looking at things head on, not sideways on.

2. Can *Life* be Given a Real Definition?

2.1. *'Signs of Life'*

I want to begin by raising difficulties for one of the thoughts I took for granted in articulating Hegel's objection to his own proceeding—namely, the apparently innocent idea that *living things are just some among the concrete individuals we think about, marked off from the others in quite definite ways.* If this is right, then the word 'life' expresses a 'particular characteristic of [those] objects', in Frege's phrase, and presumably not their logical category.

The question forced upon us by this thought—what the supposed characteristic marks of the concept *life* might actually be—is not one that much exercises contemporary philosophers as philosophers. We may say of the problem what Frege said of investigations into the concept *number*—another 'concept fundamental to a mighty science':

[10] J.-J. Rousseau, *Discourse on the Origin of Inequality* (1755), preface.
[11] 'Who would want to introduce a new principle, and as it were, be its inventor, as if the world had hitherto been ignorant of what duty is, or had been thoroughly wrong about it?', I. Kant, *Critique of Practical Reason*, preface, tr. L. J. Back (New York: Macmillan, 1993), 8.

Admittedly, many people will think this not worth the trouble. Naturally, they will suppose, this concept is adequately dealt with in the elementary textbooks, where the subject is settled once and for all. Who can believe that he has anything still to learn on so simple a matter?[12]

I want to consider just such an *Elementarbuch*, a typical college freshman's biology text.

In her book *Biology*, Helena Curtis supplies us with a special illustrated section, separated off from the main text and labelled 'The Signs of Life':

> What do we mean when we speak of 'the evolution of life', or 'life on other planets' or 'when life begins'? Actually, there is no simple definition. Life does not exist in the abstract; there is no 'life', only living things. We recognize a system as being alive when it has certain properties that are more common among animate objects than inanimate ones. Let us take a look at some of these properties.

Here the apparently innocent thought is frankly expressed, and the associated task of expounding *Merkmale* is gladly shouldered. There turn out to be seven of them. 'Living things', she tells us, 'are *highly organized.*' They are '*homeostatic*, which means simply "staying the same"'. They '*grow and develop*', and are '*adapted*'. They '*take energy from the environment and change it from one form to another*' and they '*respond to stimuli*'. Finally, of course, 'Living things *reproduce themselves.*'[13]

It may seem a bit odd to take casual remarks from the opening pages of a textbook and make them the starting-point for one's reflection, but consider Frege's remark quoted above, and his method throughout the *Grundlagen*. Curtis's discussion is not really casual. A random survey of college bookstores will show that her list is one of many, all of them apparently distant progeny of some *Ur*-list, a Q-document for which one searches in vain, but which we find repeated again and again, subject to whatever improvements occur to the immediate author.[14] A

[12] Gottlob Frege, *Foundations of Arithmetic*, tr. J. L. Austin (Oxford: Blackwell, 1980), p. iii.

[13] Helena Curtis, *Biology*, 3rd edn. (New York: Worth, 1979), 20–1.

[14] Moritz Schlick had produced such a list already in lectures of 1927, attributing it to 'Wilhelm Roux, the founder of so-called developmental mechanics [who] says: A body is living if it possesses the following characteristics: (1) Metabolism . . . (2) Growth; (3) Active movement . . . (4) Reproduction . . . (5) Inheritance . . .', but he unfortunately supplies no reference to Roux's works. The idea of such a list must have arisen during the vitalist–mechanist debates. See Schlick's

certain type of context, at once introductory and reflective, seems to attract this kind of thing. Perhaps there is no Q-document to uncover, but even if there is one, possession of it would only supply a superficial explanation of this peculiar tradition. We would still have to explain the fact that the list gets *repeated*, and that no one worries where the idea of such a thing came from, and that it all seems so obvious. The source of the repetition of such lists—a certain form of philosophical unconscious, I suppose—is the true original of any one of them, as also of the rare more learned account, and it is, I hope, the real focus of my remarks.[15]

But let us return to our token of this type, Curtis's list. Troubles begin even before we consider the several properties adduced: what does she mean to be saying about them? She is linking an expression for life or organism with a number of predicates in unquantified propositions: 'Living things are *F*'. What form of judgement is being expressed? One of the hints she gives us is clearly mistaken—*baldness, bad manners*, and *home ownership* are all 'more common among animate objects than inanimate ones', but presumably none was a candidate for inclusion. She seems to allow that the properties she retails are neither collectively sufficient nor severally necessary for the 'system' that bears them to count as alive; are they meant to illustrate a system of 'family resemblances'? And are we doing metaphysics or epistemology? She calls the properties 'signs' of life, and speaks of how we recognize a system as being alive; but the inner tendency of such a list is surely towards a real definition, a metaphysical analysis, a teaching about what life consists in—in any case, something on the order of criteria, not symptoms.

We may prescind from this obscurity: the reasons for it will emerge, I think, from a discussion of the individual members of the list.

Philosophy of Nature, tr. A. von Zeppelin (New York: Philosophical Library, 1949), 73 ff.

[15] The idea of employing this tradition of list-making as a clue to the typical contemporary *Lebensweltanschauung*, so to speak, is anticipated by Gareth Matthews, who rightly contrasts these lists with the familiar and seemingly similar list produced by Aristotle. See his '*De Anima* 2. 2–4 and the Meaning of *Life*', in M. Nussbaum and Amélie Rorty (eds.), *Essays on Aristotle's* De Anima (Oxford: Clarendon Press, 1992), 185–93.

2.2. Organization

Nothing is more common than to make life a matter of organization, order, structure, or complexity. Curtis will be no exception. She writes:

Living organisms are highly organized, as in this cross section of a pine needle. It reflects the complicated organization of many different kinds of atoms into molecules and of molecules into complex structures. Such complexity of form is never found in inanimate objects.

It is worth inquiring, though, how the intended notion of organization is supposed to work. Is it meant to cover the organization of parts in an animal, of parts in a car, of words on a page, of people in a factory, of molecules in a crystal? If the notion is so abstract, then I think we can have little reason to think that there is any one consistent measure of more-and-less in respect of it. Is the administration of the University of Pittsburgh more highly organized than, say, a Buick or the Hope diamond, or more complex than the rules of chess? Any of these would at best make an unhappy metaphor. But I suppose the lament of a 1950s auto mechanic, faced suddenly with a recent Volkswagen, would have straightforward content.

Now, Curtis mentions that atoms and molecules are among the elements organized, and later on that 'living things take energy from the environment' and so forth. This might suggest that we have to do with a determinate conception of organization after all, namely that sometimes said to be implicit in thermodynamical theorizing. This interpretation would perhaps supply a determinate scale; and we can happily allow that the physical contents of the regions of space occupied by terrestrial organisms tend to take on its higher values—I mean, in relation to other things we know of.

Is it perverse, though, to remind ourselves that fresh corpses are not alive, and yet have presumably lost little in the respect measured on the relevant physical scale? Suppose we freeze a bunch of camels' corpses, and arrange them for art's sake in a sort of flying wedge, hurtling toward Alpha Centauri; could the adventitious *arrangement* supply, for the whole, what the individuals lost with death? The thought seems perverse since, but for a camel's life, we have no camel carcass, and anyhow the additional arrangement sprang from the allegedly awesome degree of order or organized complexity exhibited within our skulls—a part, that is, of *our* life. Should we say, then, that living things are *sources* of thermodynamically highly organized lumps of stuff? The 'living body' of an organism would be just one such highly organized precipitate of its life processes, alongside the nest or honeycomb or house it helps to build, and the dry leaves, paw-prints, or corpse it leaves behind. We would be characterizing the life-process by its physicalistically intelligible and salient results.

But do we really know that nothing else can bring the results about, or that if something else can, it must be rarer, on a cosmic scale, than living things are? Even if we do know these things, or manage to find them out, it would be wrong, I think, to incorporate this knowledge into a list of the type we are hoping to construct.

To see the difficulty, it may help to consider another proposed list-occupant. Ernst Mayr, in a somewhat differently motivated 'tabulation' (as he calls it), puts our present topic, 'Complexity and Organization', just ahead of something he calls 'Chemical Uniqueness'. In explaining the latter the says:

These organic molecules [sc. those from which terrestrial organisms are composed] do not differ in principle from other molecules. They are, however, far more complex than the low molecular weight molecules that are the regular constituents of inanimate nature. These larger organic macromolecules are not normally found in inanimate matter.[16]

Now, it is true that if we were sending a probe to Mars to search out 'signs of life', we might have it test for the presence of 'large organic macromolecules'. But then, we might have it test for the like of DNA in particular. One supposes that 'Living things contain DNA' might hold good even on a cosmic scale—perhaps we could discover that there is no other way to get this sort of thing going, given the physical constitution of 'our universe'. But no one would hope to improve on the tradition by incorporating it into one of these lists. The judgement about DNA, if it were true, would only show how resource-poor the physical world really is. It could make no contribution to the exposition of the concept of life, or to a teaching on the question what life is—except perhaps

[16] Ernst Mayr, *The Growth of Biological Thought* (Cambridge, Mass.: Harvard University Press, 1982), 54.

as pointing to a few gorillas and turnips might. The ends of our sort of list, however obscure they may be, point to something more abstract and would clearly be contravened by it.

But does mention of DNA differ fundamentally from a sparer appeal to 'large organic macromolecules'? Appeal to what is, after all, a *particular physical quantity*, thermodynamical order or organization—though it be that much more abstract—is evidently in the same boat as either of them.

The point would be easier to make if we could say that God and the angels are 'living things' if they are anything, and that physical concepts hardly have a place in the analysis of *their* kinds of life.[17] But in the context of the present essay, and the relevant sort of list, 'living thing' means *organism*. This narrower focus does not, however, supply a pretext for the importation of empirical physical concepts—as a further narrowing to, say *mammal, primate*, or *gorilla* might. I do not know whether the proposition 'Not everything that lives is an organism' is really coherent; but on the tradition according to which it is, and is true, the specific difference of the organism was marked in a number of ways, hands left clean of the empirical. One said, for example, that organisms *are composite*, or *have parts*.

Let us return, then, to the thought from which we started—that the unsubscripted notion of order or organization is a very abstract or generic one, and that, left abstract, it does not make sense to think of a standard of more-and-less in respect of it. We have, on the one hand, the concept or idea of organization, and, on the other, a number of conceptions, determinations, types, or genera of it. If a remark of the form '*A* is organized' is to express a definite thought, it must isolate one of these. Which do we have in view, then, if not the allegedly thermodynamical one—and if it is 'quality' and not the 'quantity' of order that matters? The obvious answer is that the relevant conception is simply equivalent to the idea of life: to be alive is to be *organized*; to be alive is to be a subject of, say, 'vital organization'. Or if, as we were just imagining, a living thing needn't be an organism, then the thought should rather be that *organisms* are in that sense organized; or, equivalently, that if a life is a life-with-parts, then this sort of order must prevail among these parts.

---

[17] See e.g. Thomas Aquinas, *Summa Theologiae*, I, q. 18.

The formula 'Living things have parts', which has seemed a little too obvious to merit a career as a list-occupant, is evidently closely related to the thought that living things are organized: the parts are the elements that are arranged or ordered. But if the notion of order or organization is abstract, the notion of part is as much so: we need to supply a subscript before the suggestion that living things have either of them can express a definite thought. Our language, feeling this need, sometimes permits the subscripts to be supplied non-contextually through certain uses of the words 'organ' and 'member' and 'tissue'—though these terms are all perhaps most apt in connection with sensitive or animal life, as words for *partes animalium*.

I said that no one would append the like of 'Living things contain DNA' to a list of the sort we are considering, even given suitable physical hypotheses. No one would add 'Living things have parts, in the sense of organs' either, but for another reason. Will he or she follow the cautious Mayr and remark, in the scholium, that organs are 'not normally found in inanimate matter'? My suggestion will be that *every* candidate list-occupant must strike the sub-metaphysical Scylla of 'DNA' or else sink into the tautologous Charybdis of 'organs', and that every such list may as well be replaced by the empty list.

2.3. *Stimulus and Response*

Before pausing to reflect on these matters, I want to move on to some of Curtis's other criteria. Two of them seem to me to belong together. First, an underwater scene:

Living things respond to stimuli. Here scallops, sensing an approaching starfish, leap to safety.

And now the forest, as an owl descends open-clawed upon a mouse:

Living things take energy from the environment and change it from one form to another. They are highly specialized at energy conversion. Here a saw-whet owl is converting chemical energy to kinetic energy, thereby procuring a new source of chemical energy, in this case a white-footed mouse.

Again there is a problem of understanding. Are we to say, for example, that the asphalt on a summer day 'takes energy' from sunlight, and 'converts' it into heat? And is an avalanche, on the other hand, the 'response' of a snow-covered hillside to the 'stimulus' of, say, excessive yodelling?

But before considering what can be made of these rhetorical questions, I want to raise a few objections to the given formulations. First, it is clear that the notion of 'response' employed in the first criterion *must* apply not just to *the leaping of threatened scallops*, but also, for example, to *the effect of spring warming on the buds of maple trees*. Otherwise the notion will be left covering a phenomenon merely of sentient or animal life. It would thus acquire the standing of baldness and bad manners—it would be a property uncommon even among the living, but all the same 'more common among the living than the non-living'. And notice further, in connection with the second criterion, that there is nothing really special about taking *energy* from the 'environment'—she could as well have characterized the living as taking *stuff*, *matter*, from the environment, and converting *it* into other forms. Energy is after all just another physical quantity; if the considerations of the previous section are sound, then it is vulgar anyway to drag an expression for such a thing into the sort of account we are hoping to produce. Curtis's formulation of each criterion seems, then, to be defective. But what is the thought that tempts one to propound them, or anything like them?

Let us consider just the first criterion for the moment, the thought that living things 'respond to stimuli'. *The warming of an asphalt road-bed* and *the train of photosynthetical events in a green leaf* are both of them, in some sense, the effect of sunlight. And *the thawing of icy ponds* and *the opening of maple buds* are each occasioned by rising spring temperatures. It is natural, though, to think that the two vegetative phenomena belong together as instances of a special type of causal relation, or a causal relation with special conditions, distinct from any exhibited in asphalt or water. (The corresponding phenomena of sentient life, those most aptly described in terms of 'stimulus' and 'response', belong to a subdivision of this type which need not specially concern us.) On the other hand, though, the effect of a *hydrogen bomb* on a rose, and on a road-bed, will be pretty much the same—at least if they are both at ground zero. I mean not only that the effects will be similar, but that the type of causality will be the same. It is in a more restricted range of cases that we seem to see a difference, if the affected individual is an organism. I mean: sunlight makes the asphalt warm; moisture and cold make it crack; the H-bomb turns it to a vapour. These things are all on a level. The asphalt is in a sense passive in the face of any of them. But, in the familiar metaphors, the rose or maple is ready for certain of these 'influences'—rising spring temperatures, for example—it is already on to them, it takes advantage of them. Green leaves are not *subjected* to the light, if it is not too strong; they are not in the same sense passive in respect of it; the access of photons is not to be understood on a model of bombardment—that is, as it would have to be if we were discussing the fading of a book-cover or the warming of a stone. This, I think, is the contrast one is trying to register, in placing 'responsiveness to stimuli' among the characteristic marks of the concept *life*.

If we attempt to put the thought less metaphorically, in terms of a notion of process, we come upon some surprising appearances. The arrival of spring, on the one hand, and of the photon, on the other—these events are meteorological and physical, and we can trace them back to their antecedents in the relation of the earth to the sun. But they are also phases of larger processes *in the plant*, just as the replication of yeast cells is part of a larger culinary-technical process, if it takes place in some sourdough. The rose and maple are subjects of processes of their own, which the meteorological or physical events merely complete or continue: the formation of leaves of a certain character, come spring, and the fixation of carbon in those leaves, once illuminated.

In learning of the various cellular processes unearthed and described in biochemistry—photosynthesis, for example, or the Krebs cycle, or the replication of DNA—one is inclined to think, It's all getting boiled down to chemistry and physics, isn't it?, and in some sense of 'boiling down' this is of course true. But it is interesting that if the only categories we have to apply are those of chemistry and physics, there is an obvious sense in which none of these goings-on will add up to *a single process*. In a description of photosynthesis, for example, we read of one chemical process—one process-in-the-sense-of-chemistry—followed by another, and then another. Having read along a bit with mounting enthusiasm, we can ask: 'And what happens next?' If we are stuck with chemical and physical categories, the only answer will be: 'Well, it depends on whether an H-bomb goes off, or the temperature plummets toward absolute zero, or it all falls into a vat of sulphuric acid . . .'. That a certain enzyme will appear, and split the latest chemical product into two, is just one among many possibilities. Physics and chemistry, adequately developed, can tell you what happens in any of these circumstances—in *any* circumstance—but it seems that they cannot attach any sense to a question 'What happens next?', *sans phrase*. The biochemical treatise appears to make implicit play with a special determination of the abstract conception of a process, one distinct from any expressed in physics or in chemistry proper.

If these traditional though perhaps rather metaphysical meditations are sound, then it is not just that 'the rose and maple are subjects of processes of their own': they are also subjects of a special type of category of process—'biological' processes, if you like, or 'life-processes'. The possibility of a biochemical discourse uniting purely physical and chemical descriptions of things and events is enough to show that the illustrated 'life-processes' are not marked off from others by their *content*. Whether they share a *form* of the sort to interest us in a logical investigation is a matter to be considered later.

The list-occupying notions of stimulus and response (which, as I have said, must be construed broadly so as to cover phenomena in the life of maple trees and blue-green algae) can be explained in terms of this type of process. The simplest explanation would involve a prior idea of events as coming respectively 'from outside' and 'from within' the thing stimulated and responding. Let us leave this commonsensical distinction momentarily unanalysed. Then, roughly, events will add up to stimulus and response if the first comes 'from outside' and the other 'from within' the subject of the events, and they are joined as elements of *this* kind of process, a life-process, as I was calling it.

The receipt of photons and the formation of glucose, the rising temperature and the unfolding leaves, the apprehension of a starfish and the leaping away are all of them bound together in this sort of nexus—though the lattermost pair of events is also caught up in certain more determinate (psychical) categories. But the radiation cast off by the detonated H-bomb and the evaporation of a thing, whether it be asphalt or an organism, will not be so joined or united. This particular type of process or nexus, this *form of unity of events*—which by the way need not be sorted into those 'from without' and those 'from within': the phases of, say, the Krebs cycle are not—this is, I think, what is really at issue when 'stimulus and response' make it on to our kind of list. But, again, it is clear that a philosophical account of this form of unity, and a philosophical account of life, are at bottom the same: such processes are after all what goes on as life goes on.

2.4. *Vital Operation*

The same thought will perhaps be supposed to underlie that other list-occupying formula 'Living things take energy from the environment and convert it into other forms'. For it is in the nature of our sort of enterprise, I said, to recoil from words for particular physical quantities. If we cleave to this principle and delete the reference to energy, we are left with a general schema of 'taking and converting'. And this, it might be argued, is itself only worth mentioning as an illustration of *events as bound together in a life-process*.

But perhaps everything that follows the word 'energy' depends on it and should fall with it. The remaining thought would then simply be that *Living things take*. This is more a thought-fragment than a thought, but it suggests what is at least prima facie a different account of the idea that underlies the criterion we are mutilating: it is not that living things are the subjects of events falling into a certain form of process, but that they are subjects of a certain form of *agency*.—We have to do, that is, not with a special *nexus of events*, but with a special *nexus of thing and event*.

The topics are obviously closely related, and another of Curtis's criteria, 'Living things grow and develop', would seem to split itself between them. 'Development' is another word for process, and it can only be a life process that is intended. *Growth* involves a notion of increase in size, which, given certain very general but philosophically unmentionable facts of physical nature, would seem to be entailed by the demands of reproduction (a matter to be discussed later). The rational kernel of such a criterion is just the *difference* between the growth of a chipmunk or a pine tree and the growth of, say, a trash heap—which difference has of course nothing to do with growth. The relevant nexus of thing and event is the one we intended above in speaking of an event as 'coming from within' a thing.

Now, the tactic of marking off a class of things by the special relation they may bear to some of the things they do—which doings are *ipso facto* 'doings' in some restricted and italicizable sense—is a familiar one. Suppose, for example, that a certain thing can be said to will or intend some of what happens to it or some of what it does (in some broad sense), or that some of these happenings can be said to be 'caused by' its intention, desire, or judgement. Then presumably we can call the thing a *person* or an *agent*, and dignify the event too with a title of 'intentional action' or even 'action' simply.

The notion of an animal and the notion of 'behaviour' or 'animal movement'—*motus animalium*—might be given a parallel treatment. How does a bird's progress out of the stadium, where it has been mistaken for a fast ball, differ from a progress out in search of better food? It is usual to say that, in the one case, the bat moves the bird, and that, in the other, the bird *moves itself.* If this account of the difference is sound then we may perhaps go on in good conscience to introduce some new expressions, granting a title of 'animal' or 'self-mover' to whatever is such a source of things, and applying the words 'behaviour' or 'animal movement' to any event with that sort of source.

If, arguably, *person = subject of intentional action* and *animal = subject of animal movement*, then perhaps what the fragment 'Living things take' really means to tell us is that *living thing = subject of (say) 'vital operation'*; this is our 'deeper reading' of Curtis's intentions, or rather those of the tradition she represents.[18] And as persons and animals are forms of living thing, so presumably also intentional action and animal movement are forms of vital operation. The traditional hierarchy of forms of life appears to correspond to a hierarchy of forms of agency.

I don't want to object to any of these identities. The question, once again, is whether anything like the third of them can rightly

---

[18] Gareth Matthews quotes a list of so-called basic characteristics of living things which includes the *responsiveness* we have already discussed, but also—and at first glance completely mysteriously—*movement* ('De Anima 2. 2–4 and the Meaning of Life', 185). That the quoted author must have heard of the laws of falling bodies, on the one hand, and of deep-rooted trees, on the other, suggests the necessity of such a deeper reading; it is only the present broad form of 'agency' that can be intended. In the list Schlick quotes from Wilhelm Roux, the place of movement is thus taken by something called 'active movement' (see n. 14 above).

contribute to a real definition of its subject. As I have formulated them, the second and third equivalences would give an appearance of circularity if advanced as definitions, a fact which may be put down to my tendentious nomenclature. After all, we have an explanation of 'animal movement' as *self-movement*. But is the explanation any good?

There is no question that a misunderstanding about which of the two sorts of stadium-and-bird case one had intended can be cleared up with the words 'No, no, it moved *itself*'. If, however, we ask in philosophy what the difference is between the cases, then we mean to find the difference between such cases generally, and an appeal to 'self-movement' is not illuminating.[19] The reflexive is simply one of the means our language gives us for marking the different relation posited between subject and predicate, thing and event. It does not by itself tell us what this relation is.

It will perhaps help to see this if we remember that the relation of the bird to its movement was supposed to be somehow higher or more sublime in the no-bat case than in the other, and that, of course, the same sublime nexus of creature and event can bind a bird and the movement of *something else*, a piece of straw, for example.[20] And, more obviously, the sublime relation between a bird and the movement of its own parts need not be severed if the movement can be said in some sense to spring from something other than the bird, suitable prey up yonder, for example. And in general if *A* moves *B*, then the mereological sum of *A* and *B* in some sense moves itself, or some of itself. Some 'self-movement', then, is other-movement; some 'self-movement' is movement-by-another; and some non-'self-movement' is self-movement after all.

We are considering the special case of animals and animal movement for purposes of analogy, but in truth, I think, any attempt to mark the character of organisms in general by an employment of such prefixes as 'self-' or 'auto-'—as in, say, 'self-

[19] See a parallel remark in G. E. M. Anscombe, *Intention* (Ithaca, NY: Cornell University Press, 1963), 3.

[20] It may be objected that a bird never moves straw, except by moving itself— that is to say, parts of itself. But if we refuse to take the idea of the limits of an animal's body for granted, and ask how it is settled *what is a part of it*, and *what is just stuck to it* or *what it is just holding* or *what, come to think of it, is really on the other side of the room*, then we will, I think, be forced to import the notion of 'animal movement' as something already understood.

reproduction', 'self-organization', or 'auto-regulation'—is for the same reason completely empty. The phrase to which the prefix is attached is always a distraction, and the whole problem is already contained in the reflexive; it should be replaced in each case with some such transparently circle-making expression as 'bio-', 'biological', or 'vital'. The emptiness of a *philosophical* appeal to this reflexive is already shown by the fact that we incline to it in so many places—to distinguish the two types of growth, the two types of bird-flight, and even, in Kantian moral philosophy, two types of rational agency. At each link in the great chain of agency, activity, autonomy, or spontaneity we employ the reflexive to introduce another 'higher' link; it is a finger pointing upward, yes, but we want to know what's up there.

If we must drop the special emphasis on the reflexive then it is natural to explain the special nexus of animal and event by appeal to sensation or appetite. Our account of the concept *motus animalium* would then mirror the sort of account of the category of willed, voluntary, or intentional action which takes such notions as desire, intention, and judgement for granted, along with some abstract conception of cause.[21] Something must fall between the would-be agent and what it does—something which, as 'cause' of the latter happening, gives the whole ensemble the special character of rational agency or intentionalness in the one case, and of animal movement in the other.

Elizabeth Anscombe has attacked this doctrine of intentional action,[22] and one would want to reproduce her thinking in a more extended discussion of the broader category of animal movement. But we need not produce any analogous counter-argument in the case of our present quarry, the still wider category of 'vital operation', or 'life-functioning'. *The materials for constructing a Cartesian–Davidsonian account are simply unavailable in this more general case.* What individual happenings will 'fall between' a tree and its getting larger, thereby potentially distinguishing this nexus from that involved in a crystal's or flame's or trash-heap's getting larger? Well, no sap runs in a crystal, you might say, and there is no photosynthesis in a flame; but then no sap runs in an amoeba, and there is no photosynthesis in a human being. Noth-

---

[21] See esp. the first five essays repr. in Donald Davidson, *Essays on Action and Events* (Oxford: Oxford University Press, 1981).

[22] See e.g. Anscombe, *Intention*, sects. 5–15.

ing has the position in respect of organisms generally that sensation and appetite have among animals, and judgement, intention, and desire have among persons. There is no general *type* of event, X, of which we will be tempted to say: whenever an individual event is to be brought back to the 'vital operation' of an organism, there must be some other event of type X which pre-dates the attributed event and causes it—unless of course it be simply more vital operation. An account of *this* type of 'agency', 'activity', 'substance-causality', or 'spontaneity' in terms of a prior abstract notion of cause and a particular kind of state or event is thus I think impossible.

2.5. *Summary of Results Reached So Far*

A number of abstract categories—that of a concrete individual; of a thing's being a part of something; of order or organization; of one thing's following another in a process; of a thing's doing something—are all together determined or specified, or thrown into a higher gear, to yield the concepts: *organism*; *organ*, 'part' or 'member'; *vital order* or *organization*; *life-process*; and *vital operation*. The abstract notion of existence, in the sense of actuality (Frege's *Wirklichkeit*) evidently bears the same relation to that of *life*: 'to be, for a living thing, is to live'.[23] I will later suggest that this same shift of gear will turn the abstract notion of a kind or of a 'natural kind' into that of a *life-form*—the notion, that is, of a living kind, or of a species (on one reading of that expression).

These concepts, the vital categories, together form a sort of solid block, and we run into a kind of circle in attempting to elucidate any of them, a circle much like the one Anscombe found at a higher stratum of things:

Why is giving a start or gasp not an "action", while sending for a taxi, or crossing a road, is one? The answer cannot be 'Because the answer to the question "why?" may give a *reason* in the latter cases', for the answer may "give a reason" in the former cases too [e.g. where the "reason why" you gasped is that you misheard "It's satin" as "It's Satan"]; and we cannot say, 'Ah, but not a reason for *acting*'; we should be going round in circles. We need to find the difference between the two kinds of "reason" without talking about "acting"; and if we do, perhaps we shall

[23] Aristotle, *De Anima* 2. 5 (415ᵇ13).

discover what is meant by "acting" when it is said with this special emphasis.[24]

Our circle may of course be larger: 'Why is a taxi not an organism while a tarantula is one? The answer cannot be, "Because a tarantula has *members*", for a taxi has parts as well . . .' We might go on to explain the intended notion of part in terms of vital organization, say, but in the end the fly-paper will have to stick somewhere. It is of course useless to attempt a 'holistic' account, seeking to elucidate the several categories together by describing their interrelations: the relations that hold among the vital categories are presumably the same as those holding among the more abstract ones.

Anscombe escapes her circle by fixing on the relevant sort of *reason*, and then rejecting what may be called a purely metaphysical approach to it. It is the hope of giving a real definition which sends us reaching back into the circle and then from pillar to post. She takes refuge instead in the *representation* of 'reasons', 'explanations', or 'accounts' *in general*, in the asking and answering of questions 'Why?' If, now, she can isolate a certain particular 'sense of the question "Why?"', she will have exposed the more determinate kind of reason, and with it a whole ensemble of practical categories: action, intention, end, means, will, motive, etc.

Our method is meant to be the same. To apply it, though, we must first expand our circle to include the concept of a life-form or a species; this, I think, is the weak link. A species or life-form is just a certain kind of kind—the sort of thing to be the subject of a general judgement or a general statement; the sort of thing that is said of something and about which something can be said. Our problem will then reduce to one of isolating a particular form of general judgement or statement—a *natural-historical judgement*, as I will call it, or an *Aristotelian categorical*. What is fit to be the subject of such a thing we may call a species concept or a life-form word. A species or life-form, then, will be whatever can be conceived through such a concept or expressed by such a word—not a real definition, alas, but not a circular one, I think, and not egregious organicistic metaphysics either. It is because in the end we have to do with a special *form of judgement*, a distinct mode of joining subject and predicate in thought or speech, that I am emboldened to say that the vital categories are logical categories.

3. The Representation of the Living Individual

3.1. Reproduction and Homeostasis

This discussion has so far focused on the metaphysical ambition of the list-making approach to the question 'What is life?' But there is another hope evinced by that tradition, a hope bound up with a certain extreme 'individualism', as I think it can rightly be called. An acceptable answer to the great question is implicitly required to tell us *how things must be in a given region of space* if we are to say, 'A living thing is there'—or, perhaps better: what a *region of space-time* needs to be like if it is to be the 'time-worm' of an individual organism.

That Curtis is not managing to pull the trick off becomes painfully clear in the text for her final 'sign of life', which she illustrates with a photograph of a mature pair of ostriches and twenty head of little ones. It is a traditional favourite:

Living things reproduce themselves. They make more of themselves, copy after copy after copy, with astonishing fidelity (and yet, as we shall see, with just enough variation to provide the raw material for evolution).

Problems of understanding again arise, this time from the apparent accident that she has put her definiendum in the plural. It is not just that living things generally 'take energy from the environment'—I, Thompson, do this as well; and I, Thompson, 'react to stimuli', I suppose. What would it be, though, for me, Thompson, to make more of *myself*? We are not envisaging an increase in portliness.

Let us say that it means: to make a copy, indeed 'copy after copy'. We might forestall mention of it that I have not done this in all these years of seeming life, if we adopt a backward-looking formulation of the criterion, as, say, 'Living things *are made by* more of themselves', or 'Living things are copies of what they are made by'. This raises the problem of a beginning, but, putting that aside, the question must still arise: in just what respects am I supposed to be copied, or to be a copy? Or again: more of *what*? It is of course no use to say that the formula means simply that *living things come from living things*, so that the words 'living thing' themselves express the respect of sameness. This need not be circular; it might be an implicit definition, requiring us to solve the equation in order to arrive at the content of 'living thing'. But again *material object* will make as good a solution as *living thing* will.

The same difficulties must beset another of Curtis's properties, the last I will mention. 'Living things', she tells us, 'are homeostatic, which means simply "staying the same".' Now, of course, on one way of taking these words, they would formulate a fairly sound criterion of death. *What*, then, do we have to 'stay', if we are to 'stay the same' in the sense intended?[25] One is familiar, after all, with fairly radical phenomenal and physical alterations, 'metamorphoses' as they call them, in the typical life of various sorts of animal. It is clear that the concept of life is plastic enough to allow *such* 'changes of form' to be as thoroughgoing and frequent as one likes, consistently with the thing's being alive. What happens once in a typical butterfly's life might happen a hundred times in the typical life of some yet-to-evolve quasi-butterfly.

I want to say that in neither the case of reproduction nor that of so-called homeostasis is the requisite sort of sameness fixed or determined by anything in the individual itself: whatever else may come from a thing, and whatever becomes of the thing itself, the upshot will be in some respects the same and in other ways different from what we had before. If we call the relevant sameness *sameness of form*, then that a thing *has* a given such form will not be an 'individualistically' determinable fact about the thing; it will not, for example, be equivalent to any collection of physical or phenomenal facts about the thing. The imagined example of a sort of polymetamorphic butterfly makes this obvious in the second sort of case: the superficial, changing *morphē* may be taken in

---

[25] I take it that the word 'homeostasis' has been supplied with a rather extended sense in this context, so that it does not cover mere maintenance of body temperature or the ratios of things dissolved in cells, but the whole 'reproduction of the individual'. Her criterion is a form of the traditional slogan that substance has a tendency to keep itself in being.

by the eye, or registered by a physical apparatus—each of which trades in what is present here and now; the shape of things that must be *maintained*, according to the criterion, is realized differently at different times, or may be. But the case of reproduction bears some further discussion.

Since a thing needn't actually reproduce itself to count as alive, one wants to say that it must at least be able to, or have it in it to do so. Even this is not quite right, given any ordinary understanding of the words 'able to'; but let this pass. Our thought would seem to be that if a thing is to count as alive, it must fall under some universal U where (1) an individual's falling under U is an individualistically ascertainable fact about the thing, and (2) some general truth approximately formulable as 'From a given instance of U, another instance can come to be' holds. I have already remarked that this proposition will come out true if we substitute 'material object' for 'U'; but let us suppose we have a principle for ruling out such trivial readings.

Now, 'Another can come from it' doesn't mean: another can come from it, whatever the circumstances. We can at most require that we get 'another' in *some* circumstances. The necessary weakening must bring the whole naïve picture to ruin. One is acquainted, after all, with the astonishing works of some of the 'large organic macromolecules' that characterize terrestrial life, enzymes for example. Now there must be many chemical substances C such that, for some appropriate stew of *other* chemical stuffs S (some of them perhaps 'larger organic macromolecules'), the following holds good: if a bit of C is introduced into a vat of S, then a bit *more* C will be produced, and so later on a lot more C will have been produced, until in the end we face a parody of 'environmental collapse'. Perhaps this is true of every chemical substance. And why shouldn't it be true of *anything*, whether it be held together by chemical bonds or not, and under any of its physical descriptions, partial or complete?—there is some 'environment', also physically describable, in which, if there is one of that description, another will come to be. If it isn't so, then this is just another empirical fact about this vale of dross and tears, the 'physical universe'. From the point of view of physics, after all, a text in a scrivener's shop is like an amoeba in the sea, or a bacterium in my bloodstream. And so perhaps everything has 'reproductive fitness', and under any description, and all things are full of souls. It is just that most of them are starved for the circumstances that would express the trait.

What we miss, or miss most obviously, in the flat physicalistic picture of reproduction, is any conception of the unity of a thing and its circumstances as potentially *non-accidental*. An organism's coming to be in such circumstances as tend to its reproduction is itself typically a vital operation, a phase in a life-process, and therefore, in a certain sense, 'no accident'. A dandelion seed's falling on reproductively apt soil may seem fortuitous, but its parent, by a kind of ruse of vegetation, makes such an accident no accident, most obviously by producing so much seed. The reproduction and staying-the-same that are put down as 'signs of life' are really just 'self'-reproduction and keeping 'oneself' the same, where the reflexive expresses, not an abstract relation to the subject, but vital operation.

And so in the last analysis these criteria might be thought to take us nowhere we haven't been. It is enough that the thing should exhibit *any* vital process or operation—why should reproduction and 'homeostasis' in particular be among them? But though the conception of the relevant sort of 'form'-transmission or 'form'-maintenance is a notion of vital operation, it may yet be that a grasp of the category of vital operation, or of any conception of a particular vital operation, must presuppose a grasp of the appropriate category of form. And this, I think, is what really gets registered in criteria of 'homeostasis' and reproduction—that is, of the 'reproduction of the individual' and the 'reproduction of its kind'.

3.2. The 'Wider Context'

Rather dark, that, but let us make a fresh start, in hope of explaining it, with some quotations from Anscombe's discussion of contraception:

Acts that are pretty clearly defined biological events, like eating and copulation, may be said to be by nature acts of a certain kind. Eating is a useful example to illustrate further the concepts I am using; it is a biological example like copulation, but on the other hand we shall not here be confused by controverted moral judgments. Eating is intrinsically a nutritive act, the sort of act to be nutritive; this would be an essential mark of eating if we wished to identify it in an animal species differing very much from us in structure.

And she also says:

In the same way, we may say that . . . the eye is as such an organ of sight: consider how we would identify eating and the eye from one species to another. And it is in this sense that copulation is intrinsically generative—though there are very many copulations which in fact do not generate.

And best of all she says:

When we call something an acorn, we look to a wider context than can be seen in the acorn itself. Oaks come from acorns, acorns come from oaks; an acorn is thus *as such* generative (of an oak) whether or not it does generate an oak.[26]

Anscombe is mostly interested in the idea of an action's bearing an 'intrinsic nature'; having attained the conception, she puts it to work in a classification of sexual acts. But I am interested in the matter of a 'wider context', a matter she promptly drops: *When we call something an acorn, we look to a wider context than can be seen in the acorn itself.*

'Acorn', I suppose, means 'oak-corn' or 'oak-seed', and this might seem to make the point about the look to a wider context pretty trivial. In thinking of something as an acorn, we tie it up specifically with *oaks*, none of which need be present here, and so of course we 'look beyond' the individual lump of stuff. But the remarks about eating and the eye show that the point is not trivial: the 'look to a wider context' occurs already in thinking of the acorn as *seed*.

But that materially different things can add up to the same—be it seed, or eating, or eye—is not enough to vindicate an 'anti-individualistic' account of the thing that *is* the same; thus, for example, copper, iron, and silver are all equally metal. That the reverse is also true in our sort of case may, however, be seen if we expand on Anscombe's example of eating.

We can readily enough imagine the genesis of a novel kind of shark—one nourished, not by the flesh of smaller fish, but by

[26] All of these quotations are from pp. 85–7 of G. E. M. Anscombe, 'You Can have Sex without Children', in *Collected Philosophical Papers* (Minneapolis: University of Minnesota Press, 1981), iii.

plankton and the like. Certain elaborate structures have developed on their sides: these continuously filter the water and extract the nutritious elements. All the same, we may suppose, these newly developed sharks or quasi-sharks can sometimes be seen to chase after smaller fish and incorporate them. No part of this flesh ever enters the bloodstream, rather it makes a hideous brew and is spewed out occasionally to frighten predators. The operation looks very much like the hunting, munching, and swallowing that actually existing sharks go in for, and no doubt some of the genetic basis of the latter will have carried over to the former. Someone might take the movement for the same sort of thing, and call it eating; but it is clear that it isn't eating. When we call something eating, then, we appeal to something more than is available in the mere spectacle of the thing here and now. 'Philosophers can arrange', as Professor Foot would say, that the spectacle should be there with or without the eating.

Another example may be constructed from the familiar textbook facts about mitosis—the doubling, sorting out, and splitting up of chromosomal material. It may be happening here, under the microscope, in an amoeba; and there in a human being. In the first case, an event of this type will of course be a phase in a process of reproduction—one of the forms of generation available to that kind of thing. But in the case of the human it will rather be a part of growth or self-maintenance; reproduction is and has another matter among them. The distinction between the two cases of mitosis is not to be discovered by a more careful scrutiny of the particular cells at issue—any more than, as Frege said, the closest chemical and microscopical investigation of certain ink-markings will teach us whether the arithmetical formulae they realize are *true*.

It is pointless to say that, after all, the DNA will have a different structure in the different cases—as pointless as it would be to say that the quasi-shark's quasi-eating will not really *look like* that of a proper shark, what with the repulsive apparatus the quasi-shark carries about with it. Philosophers can arrange that the apparatus should have fallen off moments before in a lover's quarrel. The 'look to a wider context', then, is not a look to the left and right.

This will perhaps be more obvious if we consider another sort of case involving DNA. Lab technicians keep lines of human cells of certain types multiplying in vats for ages; suppose then a lake in South America, one maintained by nature in such a character as the lab solution is by art, and shaken perhaps by frequent earth-quakes; and now—it does not matter whether it be by a process of evolution from something else, or a quantum-mechanical acci-dent, or an act of God—something as like as you like to a human cell of the appropriate type appears in that sinister fluid. At some point we will have a race of one-celled vegetative creatures, to be given a Latin binomial name and investigated like any other. This kind is evidently not humankind, and its mode of reproduction is not the human sort. The division that takes place in the lake has a characteristic, *reproduction of the species*, not exhibited in the vat or flask. Moreover, in the one case we have a collection of *individual substances* and *organisms*, and in the other case nothing of the sort. Yet if we ladle up a bit of the lake and take it back to the lab in New York, no test, however subtle, will ever disclose the differ-ence. The example is maybe a bit wild, but it shows, I think, that the same sort of DNA can 'control' the operations of merely vegetative and of rational life. It follows that a proposition run-ning 'This DNA contains *in itself* all the information . . .', while perhaps sound enough in its place, cannot bear a metaphysical emphasis—and that the Human Genome Project will no more uncover the 'real essence' of the human than will a study of the anatomy of the hand.[27]

3.3. The 'Wider Context' and Vital Description

If a thing is alive, if it is an *organism*, then some particular vital operations and processes must go on in it from time to time—

---

[27] Perhaps a tamer illustration will be of some use in exposing the 'fetishism of DNA and its secret'. Distinct plants falling under the same species will of course often present quite dissimilar appearances if grown in different soils and climates, especially if these are in either case intuitively deficient in some respect. Let us then suppose *two* species to have evolved independently, one in the Arctic and one in Brazil. One kind has red flowers and one has white; one is compact and creeping and one is tall and upright; one is pollinated by bees and one by a special sort of moth; etc. The various segments of genetic material will thus carry widely different bits of 'information' in either case. It is of course consistent with this, and with every physicalistic slogan, that the *seeds* they form, and thus their *genetic material*, should be alike in every physical detail. The 'phenotypical' differences would then arise solely from the differences in soil and climate to which the two species are adapted. Although they are indistinguishable, the seeds are caught up in different sorts of life, or different 'wider contexts', and will thus necessarily attract different non-physical descriptions.

eating, budding out, breathing, walking, growing, thinking, reproducing, photosynthesizing; and it must have certain particular organs or 'parts'—leaves, legs, cells, kidneys, a heart, a root, a spine. But we have suggested, following up Anscombe's clue, that if any of these things *is there*, or *is happening*, then this is not something fixed or determined by anything in the organism considered in its particularity or as occupying a certain region of space. That they are there or happening, and thus that we have an organism at all, presupposes the existence of a certain 'wider context'; it is this that stamps these several characters on to things.

This is a purely metaphysical formulation of the thought; let us move on to the matter of representation. It is obvious that a language cannot contain any representation of *objects*, in the thin Fregean sense, unless it also contains predicative expressions. And, perhaps more generally, an intellect cannot have a power of apprehending objects unless it has a power of thinking something *of* them—that is, if you like, of apprehending Fregean concepts.

We may also say that a language cannot contain any representation of things in the narrower but richer class of *concrete particulars* unless it also contains some of a narrower but richer class of predicates—for example, verbs expressing special causal concepts possibly applicable to such particulars. 'A small selection: *scrape, push, wet, carry, eat, burn, knock over, keep off, squash, make* (e.g. noises, paper boats), *hurt.*'[28] And, again, an intellect cannot receive a power to judge of concrete particulars, unless it also receives, *inter alia*, some such special causal concepts.

Perhaps this last will not be accepted, but it is in any case only a model for what I want to say, namely this: if a language contains any representation of members of the yet narrower class of *organisms*, it must also include a battery of what we may call 'vital' or 'life descriptions'. Such would be, for example: representations of parts as organs or members; representations of particular sorts of going-on as vital operation—a subclass of that of which we had a 'small selection', just as organisms are a subclass of concrete particulars; and so forth. And, again, an intellectual capacity to think of individual organisms will have to involve possession of some of the corresponding concepts.

But, of course, what falls under such descriptions and such concepts will be different in different 'wider contexts'. And so, if

---

[28] G. E. M. Anscombe, 'Causality and Determination', in *Collected Philosophical Papers*, ii. 137.

Michael Thompson

there is to be thinking of organisms or a representation of life at all, then the thinking and speaking subject must have some means of apprehending the various sorts of 'wider context'—the various 'life-forms', as I will call them. Even the most pedestrian case of life description, say, that the cat is drinking the milk, must make an implicit claim about the relevant 'form' or 'context'—that *for it*, or *in it*, the events before us add up to drinking; or that what the creature is doing is drinking, *for such as it is*.

But still, what *is* this supposed 'wider context', this 'life-form', as I am calling it? The doctrine into which these ciphers enter has a structure in common with other more familiar ones: it is to be compared, for example, with that expressed by Rawls in the decisive passage of 'Two Concepts of Rules' (which is itself, of course, intended as an application of certain thoughts of Wittgenstein's):

Many of the actions one performs in a game of baseball one can do by oneself or with others whether there is a game or not. For example, one can throw a ball, run, or swing a peculiarly shaped piece of wood. . . . [But no] matter what a person did he could not be described as stealing a base or striking out or drawing a walk unless he could also be described as playing baseball, and for him to be doing this presupposes the rule-like practice which constitutes the game. The practice is prior to particular cases: unless there is the practice, the terms referring to actions specified by it lack sense.[29]

Rawls claims that the sort of 'wider context' intended in the description of an individual action as one of stealing a base or striking out is a *practice*; and we may say that Anscombe, by contrast, in her remarks on 'eating' and 'eye', implicitly claims that the 'wider context' at stake in particular applications of those words is a *species*.

This suggests, though, that we know what practices and species *are* before we come to advance such claims. Do we take the concepts over, maybe, from sociology in the one case and biology in the other?[30] But we are practising philosophy, or mean to be, and

[29] John Rawls, 'Two Concepts of Rules', repr. in Philippa Foot (ed.), *Theories of Ethics* (Oxford: Oxford University Press, 1967), 164.

[30] On practices see e.g. Max Weber's classification of 'empirical uniformities of action' in *The Theory of Social and Economic Organization*, tr. A. M. Henderson and T. Parsons (New York: Free Press, 1964), 120–3. On species, see Mayr, for example, *The Growth of Biological Thought*, 270–5. It is remarkable that contemporary moralists, many of whom uncritically employ notions of 'practice', 'social practice',

so if we accept the equation *the 'wider context' of vital description is the species*, then we must, in McDowell's phrase, 'enter it on the left side'. Vital description of individual organisms is itself the primitive expression of a conception of things in terms of 'life-form' or 'species', and if we want to understand these categories in philosophy we must bring them back to that form of description.

If this is right, then, of course, we are wrong to think of the concepts of the various life-forms as reached through abstraction from features of their particular bearers. *That* notion takes for granted a picture of the terrestrial biosphere as offering us a magazine of living individuals, which we then carve up in accordance with certain principles. The error is not overcome, but only complicated, by the realist notion that, after all, we 'carve at the joints'. What is wrongly called *carving* is already a part of thinking of things as alive, as organisms available for 'classification'.

This is not to say that the category we reach in the explanation of 'species' or 'life-form' as 'wider context of vital description' cannot be further specified or schematized with a view to empirical terrestrial employment. The thin category that is accessible to philosophy must, for example, leave many questions of sameness and difference of life-form unsettled, questions which might be decided by a 'definition' in terms of interbreeding populations. It may be that the word 'species' is best left to express this more determinate conception, but I will not so leave it. The resolution of these fine points of course presupposes an accretion of empirical content—so that, for example, the formula 'It is a merely empirical fact that organisms fall into species' will come out true on the empirically schematized reading and false on our own. But even this, I think, does not entail that in the central range of cases a sentence containing a word associated with the definition in terms of interbreeding populations must express a *thought* different from one expressed with a term that has been given a sparer, philosophical exposition. (The thought that it *must* entail that is perhaps just a Fregean prejudice: 'Differ-

'custom', and the like, yet view any notion of species or life-form with suspicion, as a sort of foreign scientific intruder. But each concept can seem to spring from empirical science; and where either emphatically does not, it can seem to involve a screwy metaphysic of 'inner *nisus*' and so forth.

ent concepts touch here and coincide over a stretch. But you need not think all lines are circles.'[31]) I think, then, that Anscombe was not wrong to import the word 'species' into this context, but at most a bit uncritical.

A species or life-form of course *determines* a class of individuals, its bearers. But if the only possible account of the concept of a species or life-form were in terms of ensembles of individuals bound together by certain relations, then our remarks about the 'wider context', read accordingly, would be completely absurd. We may see this if we consider a more radical illustration of those remarks.

What should we say about a creature who comes to be from sand or swamp-muck by the agency of lightning or by quantum-mechanical accident—a creature part for part the same as I am, standing nearby, and just considered physically? One wonders whether the limits of philosophical imagination have not been transgressed in such a fable, but let us waive the suspicion. Philosophers have doubted whether such a thing could have thoughts, or whether its thoughts would have content.[32] If you shout the name 'Thompson!', each will *turn his head*, it is supposed, but while I am *wondering 'What's N.N. doing here?'*, the newcomer will not be.

We must accept this scepticism and carry it further: the thing has no ears to hear with and no head to turn; it has no brain-states, no brain to bear them, and no skull to close them in; prick it, and it does not bleed; tickle it, and it does not laugh; and so forth. It is a mere congeries of physical particles and not so much as alive.

In the other cases we considered, physically or phenomenally similar events took place in different 'wider contexts'. The oppos-

[31] Ludwig Wittgenstein, *Philosophical Investigations*, 3rd edn. (New York: Macmillan, 1963), II. x. 192. So also, if Wittgenstein is right, and I understand him, his favourite signs, 'non' and 'ne' (where 'non non $p = p'$ and 'ne ne $p = $ ne p'), may each express the category of negation involved in, say, philosophical difficulties about not-being; here, and in the central cases of affirmation and denial, the thoughts expressed in either vocabulary will be the same, though of course the thoughts expressed by the doubling of the signs will differ. (See *Investigations*, sects. 547–57 and Ludwig Wittgenstein, *Remarks on the Foundations of Mathematics*, 2nd edn. (Cambridge, Mass.: MIT, 1978), 102–10.)

[32] Donald Davidson, 'Knowing One's own Mind', *Proceedings and Addresses of the American Philosophical Association*, 60 (1987), 441–58.

ing life-forms put divergent interpretations on these events, or sent them in different directions; and so different vital descriptions applied. Here we have no determinate form at all, and so the ground of all vital description is removed. We can say, in the light of *my* form, that *these* are arms—a bit weak maybe, but fairly together. Are *those*, which 'he' 'has', maybe *legs*, after all—only horribly deformed and not much good for crawling with? Or are they mutilated wings? Is his tail missing? It may be thought that these matters are settled by a look to 'his genes'. But suppose he has genes: are they defective? Or, again, suppose we are each now turned to jelly by a land-mine left from the last war: *those* micro-events, happening just before the blast, were the opening stages of (say) glycolysis in me—a process unfortunately left hanging, glucose unsplit. But in him? That the conditions were there for 'the next stage', considered chemically, is by hypothesis *accident*, in every sense, just as 'his' origination was; they have no more bearing on the description of what *has* happened than the bomb itself does.[33]

What is missing, the 'wider context' that would bring these things into focus, I have called a life-form. I have also called it a species, with some reservations, and would be happy to call it *soul*.[34] But each of these latter expressions carries a baggage of associated imagery—a picture to hold us captive, if you like. I mean: *what do I have that 'he' lacks, and by which I am alive?* Friends and countrymen? Or a *ghost*? Or perhaps, if we stress the word 'form' in our preferred 'life-form', the thing will even be sought in a platonic heaven, or in the mind of God. I think our question should not be: What is a life-form, a species, a *psuchē*?, but: How is such a thing described?

---

[33] Compare Wittgenstein, *Remarks on the Foundations of Mathematics*, 336. Wittgenstein is, alas, merely ambivalent about the description of denizens of his two-minute model of a part of England as, say, *adding* or *subtracting*. But it is important that he imagines a God in this connection, so that the case is like that of Adam in the Garden, and not sheer accident. Where the act of addition presupposes a practice—and it is hard to see how such a category can gain a foothold in two minutes—breathing and glycolysis presuppose a life-form (as of course any so-called practice does). Reflection on some of our earlier examples, especially the polymetamorphic form of butterfly, will I think show that two or even twenty years will fail to hook my *Doppelgänger* up with any determinate form.

[34] Aristotle, *De Anima* 2. 1.

4. The Representation of a Life-Form

4.1. Natural-Historical Judgement

Everyone is familiar with the characteristic *mood* of what was
formerly called 'natural history'—the supposed content of Aristotle's *Historia Animalium*, for example, and of dusty books bearing
such titles as *Conifers of the Central Rockies* or *Winged Creatures of
Western Pennsylvania*. The voice-overs on public television nature
programmes are characterized by propositions in the sort of
'mood' I am intending. We will see film footage depicting some
particular bobcats, taken perhaps in the spring of 1977; the voice-
over will include verbs and other predicates which were verified,
as the film shows, in the activities, parts, and environment of the
featured, or starring, individual bobcats. But the verbs and predicates we hear will not generally be combined with proper names
or demonstrative expressions—words that, as we say, 'make
singular reference'. It sounds like this: 'When springtime comes,
and the snow begins to melt, the female bobcat gives birth to two
to four cubs. The mother nurses them for several weeks.' (Here
perhaps we see and hear violent mountain streams, rioting birds,
blossoming alpine flora, and, say, three predictably adorable cubs
piled up against a perplexed but stoical mother—not just 'two to
four' of them, but exactly three.) '. . . As the heat of summer ap-
proaches, the cubs will learn to hunt.' (And here the viewer might
witness a thankfully inept attempt on a half-fledged California
condor.) The filmed individuals themselves are rarely mentioned.
Or, if they are, it will be for example to give a sort of personal
touch to the broadcast: 'Ah, this little one seems to have awak-
ened the neighbourhood rattlesnake . . .'—that sort of thing.

It is evidently irrelevant to the ends of this sort of employment
of film that it might sometimes be a different bobcat family that is
filmed later on in the summer. Why should the film-maker wait
until next year if the original crop of cubs falls to distemper?
There would be no dishonesty in the substitution, given what is
going on, and even though what is going on is documentary
production. It would be quite different, though, if she were attempting to film a biography—a sort of bobcat version of *28 Up*;
and someone might mistake the nature programme for such a
thing. The sameness presupposed is not that given by the words

'same individual animal'. Someone who does not grasp the other sort of sameness of animal will of course not understand the broadcast.

The peculiarity of this sort of employment of verbs and predicates comes out even better in the telegraphic style of a certain sort of field guide. Here we find a Latin binomial name, a common noun, and then some such text as 'Four legs. Black fur. Nocturnal. Lives among rocks near rivers and streams. Eats worms and fish. See plate 162.' It is important to see that these very predicates can as easily be attached to designations of individuals and to individual variables. Again, someone might mistake the grammar of our field guide for *such* predication, viewing it as something on the order of the FBI's Most Wanted List: 'Blond hair. Six feet tall. Lives in cheap hotels. Partial to Italian cuisine. Armed and dangerous. See photo opposite.'[35]

Let us call the thoughts expressed in the field guide and in the nature documentary *natural-historical judgements*. We may take as their canonical expression sentences of the form 'The S is (or has, or does) F'—'The domestic cat has four legs, two eyes, two ears, and guts in its belly', 'The Texas blue-bonnet harbours nitrogen-fixing microbes in certain nodes on its roots', 'The yellow finch breeds in spring, attracting its mate with such-and-such song', whatever. Such *sentences* I will call 'Aristotelian categoricals'. But our language of course permits the same judgements to be expressed in a number of other ways, for example, by 'Ss are/have/ do F', or 'It belongs to an S to be/have/do F', or 'Ss characteristically (or typically) are/have/do F', and a hundred others. The mere form of words, however, is in no case enough to show that the thought expressed is of our type. It is necessary that a common noun (S) and some other predicative expression (F) be present or in the offing; the other linking expressions—the definite article, the unquantified plural—are part of the context which may or may not show the nexus of signs to be of the sort that interests us. That I am making voice-overs for a nature documentary is just another part of the context, tending to force our sort of

---

[35] The field guide and the FBI list of course aim at supplying materials for *identification*. But the propositions employed in the FBI list record plain facts about the suspect persons; the further purpose they are meant to serve does not affect the kind of predication involved. Similarly, we should not suppose that the type of predication we find in the field guide or nature documentary must limit itself to the attribution of differentiae or 'species-specific' traits.

construction on to my remarks. But background knowledge, my alarmed tone of voice, and the predicate I use in saying 'The domestic cat has three legs' will show that here I am not making an attempt at natural history, that it is poor Tibbles that I am talking about, and that my statement has the 'logical form' of 'The cat is on the mat'.

Natural-historical judgements tend to be formulated in some type of present tense. If temporal designations enter into their expression, it is typically a matter of before and after—'in the spring', 'in the fall', 'in infancy', 'in adolescence'—and not of now and then and next spring and when I was young and so forth. The temporal indicators thus express a B series, in McTaggart's sense, and not an A series.[36] It is of Elsa, *hic et nunc*, that we say: she *bore* three cubs last spring. Of her kind we say: the mature female bears two to four cubs in *the* spring—employing a form of present tense even if we pass the information on in winter.

Of course, we ourselves do have means of throwing these propositions into an intelligible past tense, as when we describe life-forms now extinct—and so we are also able to describe changes in the characteristics natural-historically attributable to particular kinds of living thing. But it is clearly possible to enjoy a capacity for this type of sentence formation, and yet lack any past- or future-tense employment of the propositions so formed. By contrast, I think, we could not suppose a language to contain any description of concrete particulars if it did not contain a past- and perhaps a future-tense employment of them, in addition to the present. I mean: to know what it is for a person to walk or a raindrop to fall, one must know what it is for the walking or falling to be over; but to know what it is for a form, kind, or 'species' of bird to be crested one need not attach any significance to a notion of *its* ceasing to be crested.[37]

It may seem a bit absurd that a form of predication suggestive of field guides, dusty compendia, and nature shows should be supposed to be the ticket for a philosophy of organism. But I think

[36] J. M. E. McTaggart, *The Nature of Existence* (Cambridge: Cambridge University Press, 1921–7).

[37] Thus I think problems about the reidentification of species across geological expanses of time and through more or less massive alterations in natural-historically attributable traits—problems about 'cladism' and so forth—must fall outside our subject, as attaching to an empirically warranted specification of the concept of a life-form and of the form of judgement in which we represent it.

we can see that many of the specifically 'biological' propositions falling under such headings as anatomy, physiology, ethology, biochemistry, and so forth are themselves such statements or else, and more commonly, generalizations on the common-noun position in such statements. That is, in a properly *begriffsschriftliche* formulation of these more abstract propositions of terrestrial biology, the verbs and other predicates would be attached to a variable; substitution instances of the corresponding open sentences would be simple Aristotelian categoricals. When Aristotle says that some animals are viviparous, he does not give Helen and Penelope as *examples*, his examples are: *man, the horse, the camel.*[38] His thought may thus be canonically expressed as 'For some terrestrial life forms *S*, the *S* is viviparous'. And when he says that some animals shed their front teeth, but there is no instance of an animal that loses its molars,[39] he will not give up the sentence when faced with a denture wearer; denture wearers aren't the 'animals' he was talking about. Similarly—I want to say—when an introductory botany book says that photosynthesis, a process it will spend many pages of chemical formulae describing, is characteristic of flowering plants, among others, the exceptions it mentions will be, for example, *field dodder* and *Indian pipe*, and not this pitiful albino marigold seedling. Our mode of sentence formation must thus, I think, lurk at the bottom of even these abstract pages.

It might be suggested that a natural-historical judgement should be able to take some higher genus as its immediate subject—a judgement to be canonically formulated as, say, 'The flowering plant *is F*', or 'Flowering plants *are F*', rather than as, say, 'For every terrestrial life-form *S*, if *S* is a form of flowering plant, then the *S* is *F*' (as I would write it). It is a possible theory. My purposes do not, I think, require that I refute it. But we should remember that it is a merely empirical truth, an artefact of their evolution from earlier forms, that terrestrial life-forms admit of any interesting classification into higher genera. But if the thoughts advanced in Section 3.3 are true, then it is *not* a merely empirical fact, given that there are any organisms, that they fall under the particular items we were calling 'life-forms'. The received taxonomical hierarchy is a record either of history or of the

---

[38] Aristotle, *Historia Animalium* 489[b]1.   [39] Ibid. 501[b]1.

similarities that this history explains; but the simple 'classification' of individual organisms in terms of life-form precedes any
possible judgement of similarity or of shared historical genesis.
The real subject of a natural-historical judgement and of an Aristotelian categorical is, I think, inevitably a representation of *the
thing that must be there*—that is, of what was formerly called an
infima species. But even this description is impure and not properly philosophical: it retains the suggestion of higher 'species',
and thus of collateral *infimae species*, which, as I have said, need
not be there.

4.2. *The Irreducibility of this Form of Thought*

We have to do with a special nexus of concepts in a judgement, or
of general terms in a proposition, however it may be formulated—'The *S* does *F*', '*S*s do *F*', 'This is how things go with an *S*:
it does *F*'. One's first inclination, though, is to attempt to reduce
the connection to something more familiar.

So, for example, we might attempt to assimilate 'Man sheds his
teeth' to 'Each man sheds his teeth', or, equivalently, to 'For every
man *x*, *x* sheds his teeth'. On such an account the predicate 'sheds
his teeth' is caught up in the same sort of combination (but with
an individual variable) as it is in, say, 'When little Arthur sheds
his teeth . . .' The account is of course worthless: 'man' sheds all
'his' deciduous teeth, but some of us keep a few, and in any case
it isn't *shedding* if they are kicked out in a street-fight.

Does the sentence then rather amount to something on the
order of '*Most* men shed their teeth'? At first sight even Aristotle
appears to have made the identification. Something akin to our
mode of combination of terms is explicitly mentioned in his
account of accident, for example. He characterizes the propositions so formed as holding *hōs epi to polu*, a phrase typically
rendered 'for the most part'.[40] But, again obviously, although
'the mayfly' breeds shortly before dying, *most* mayflies die long
before breeding. And if the description of the 'life-cycle' of the
monarch butterfly told us 'what mostly happens', then it would
soon be unnecessary to visit that strange Mexican valley in order
to wade knee-deep among them. A natural-historical judgement

---

[40] Aristotle, *Physics* 2. 5. 196ᵇ10 ff.; see also Aristotle, *Posterior Analytics* A. 30.
87ᵇ20.

may be true though individuals falling under both the subject and predicate concepts are as rare as one likes, statistically speaking.[41]

Perhaps then our sort of proposition should be brought under the linguists' rubric *generic sentence*, and we should follow them in their attempt to supply a 'semantic' analysis.[42] Here, though, we meet with a different sort of problem. It is not that the suggestion is simply false. If the class of generic sentences is marked off by possession of some such outward form as the unquantified 'bare' plural '*S*s are *F*', then there is no question that a natural-historical judgement *can* be expressed in a 'generic' sentence. But is there any reason to think that the class of generic sentences, so understood, is not a rag-bag covering many forms of conjunction of subject and predicate—our own type just one among them? We have already seen that a similarly identified class of 'statements with a definite description as subject' would have to constitute a merely surface-grammatical category: it is clear that the words 'The domestic cat has four legs' contain a syntactical ambiguity, and that the natural reading is not the one Russell attempted to explain.

It is implicit in Aristotle's remarks that inferences involving judgements *hōs epi to polu* should mirror those involving universal judgements.[43] And it does seem true that, just as 'All *A*s are *F*' and 'All *A*s are *G*' together entail 'All *A*s are both *F* and *G*', so also 'The *S* is *F*' (or '*S*s are *F*') and 'The *S* is *G*' (or '*S*s are *G*') together entail 'The *S* is both *F* and *G*' (or '*S*s are both *F* and *G*')—if it is our sort of combination that is expressed. The inference would obviously be invalid for any sort of statistical generalization. And it would be too bold to claim that it holds for generic statements or bare plurals generally, if only because the bare plural can presumably express a form of statistical generalization. The validity of such inferences is, I think, one of the reasons why we incline to express natural-historical judgements by means of a definite article—after all, inferences involving proper names and definite descriptions mirror those involving universal

---

[41] See the remarks on the number of teeth 'man' has, in G. E. M. Anscombe, 'Modern Moral Philosophy', in *Collected Philosophical Papers*, iii. 38.

[42] A standard treatment is Gregory N. Carlson, *Reference to Kinds in English* (New York: Garland, 1980).

[43] Aristotle, *Posterior Analytics* 87ᵇ23.

generalizations in a number of ways, as was traditionally noticed. A typical page of biochemical exposition exhibits none of the inferential anxiety that would be called for if the propositions it contains expressed mere statistical generalizations or if they were to admit only the inferences holding generally among so-called generic propsitions.

A similar recommendation would be that our propositions be taken as Fregean universal propositions after all, but qualified by something one calls a *ceteris paribus* clause. 'The bobcat breeds in spring' will thus, I suppose, amount to something of the form 'For all *x*, if *x* is a bobcat, and spring is approaching, and . . . *x* . . . , then *x* will soon be breeding'. How one completes the ellipsis will depend on one's understanding of these *ceteris paribus* clauses. The added condition will either be 'normative' or not; if it is, I will come to it later; if it is not, then the suggestion will be either that conditions are normal or standard or ordinary in some non-'normative' sense, or else that nothing intervenes that might prevent the breeding.

Let us consider the case of intervention first. I object: the question what *counts* as that is surely to be answered, in any given case, by appeal to the system of natural-historical judgements with the relevant kind as subject. And so we cannot simply take such a category for granted and then employ it in an account of our form of thinking. If the mother bobcat leaves her young alone, then they will wither and rot; if she nurses them they will develop thus and so. In which case, though, do we find 'intervention', and in which rather 'what happens, *ceteris paribus*'? No one will insist that the mother's nursing be viewed as the intervention of something alien, from without, into an otherwise inviolate cub-system set to evolve in its own direction. But to *deny* it is just a more stilted way of expressing the thought that bobcats are not to be compared with caterpillars—they do not strike out alone and set themselves straightaway to munching. No, 'the mother nurses them for several weeks'; I heard about it on a nature documentary.

The same sort of objection may of course be raised against any appeal to 'normal', 'ordinary', or 'standard' conditions. Let us take the simplest sort of judgement to which such an account might reasonably be applied. If I say 'Water is a liquid' or 'Oxygen is a gas'—and who will not?—I do seem to presuppose what are sensibly called 'normal conditions'. And so, 'In normal conditions, water is a liquid' is a more precise and strict formulation of my thought. If, now, I go on to spell these conditions out, I will mention, for example, room temperature. What is 'normal' or 'standard' is here evidently judged by reference to myself. The 'normal conditions' presupposed in such a statement as 'Water is a liquid' are not *normal conditions for water*—continuous bits of it will indifferently occupy any of the three states of matter—and to articulate them is not to articulate any truth about water.

Now suppose I say, 'Bobcats breed in spring': it is again obvious that this isn't going to happen in any particular case unless certain conditions are satisfied. Perhaps a special hormone must be released in late winter. And perhaps the hormone will not be released if the bobcat is too close to sea-level, or if it fails to pass through the shade of a certain sort of tall pine. But, now, to articulate *these* conditions is to advance one's teaching about bobcats. It is not a reflection on the limited significance of one's teaching. The thought that *certain hormones are released*, or that *they live at such-and-such altitudes and amid such-and-such vegetation*, is a thought of the same kind as the thought that *they breed in spring*. The field guide and the nature documentary assign an external environment to the intended life-form, after all, and in the same 'voice' they elsewhere employ in describing its bearers' inner structure and operations. These conditions are thus 'presupposed' by the life-form itself, and not by the poor observing subject with his low-resolution lens. If Q is simly *true*, then 'P on condition that Q' does not supply a more 'precise' or 'strict' formulation of anything that P might 'loosely' formulate—though it may of course be an interesting truth in its own right. All of this must, I think, distinguish our natural-historical judgements from the so-called hedged generalities or *ceteris paribus* laws said to be employed in certain of the 'special sciences'.[44]

It is worth noticing that by repeated application of our appar-

[44] See e.g. the exchange between Stephen Schiffer and Jerry Fodor in *Mind*, 100 (1991), 1–34. This particular dispute is in any case over judgements linking event-types with event-types, and not judgements like our own, which link individual-substance-types with all manner of things—parts, features, *and* events. It is clear, by the way, that on Fodor's account of his super-abstract category *ceteris paribus* statement, the things will not support the Aristotelian form of inference I mentioned—see esp. the diagram on p. 139 of his 'Special Sciences', repr. in *Representations* (Cambridge, Mass.: MIT, 1981).

ently unexciting rule of inference—'Ss are *F*', 'Ss are *G*', *ergo* 'Ss
are both *F* and *G*'—we will presumably always be able to produce
a true statement of our form involving a complex conjunctive
predicate that is not true of *any* member of the kind denoted by
its subject, living or dead. I mean: nobody's perfect. (Will
anyone say, by the way, that anything is, *ceteris paribus*, what it
never is?)

This may seem to cut our propositions entirely free of 'the
facts'. But consider the ensemble of true natural-historical judgements with a given kind, *S*, as subject; call it *the natural history of
Ss*. I do not doubt that many of the features attributed to *S* itself in
this imagined 'history' will also have to be attributable to many of
the individual *Ss* (attributable, that is, in the more familiar 'When
little Arthur sheds his teeth . . .' sort of way). To deny it would in
any case make for a bold expression of Platonism. But the affirmation alone tells us nothing about the relation that any *particular*
judgement in the 'history' must have to the class of individual *Ss*
and the facts about them.

The unity of subject and predicate realized in an Aristotelian
categorical 'The *S* is *F*', and the act of mind expressed in it, are
thus not to be compared with those realized and expressed in the
English forms 'Some *S* is *F*', 'All *Ss* are *F*', and 'Most *Ss* are *F*'. The
latter, we may say, relate directly to features of the class of individuals covered by the subject term. The former rather express
one's *interpretation* or *understanding* of the life-form shared by the
members of that class. This understanding may of course be shallow or deep, extensive or narrow, mostly true or largely mistaken.
It is itself the 'look to a wider context' which we said governs the
description of the individual organism *hic et nunc*: what is implicit
in the tensed description of an individual organism is explicit in
an Aristotelian categorical. But in truth the lyrical opposition 'an
understanding of the life-form' versus 'a mere survey of the class'
is itself just a more abstract rewrite of the concrete opposition of
natural-historical judgement and, say, statistical or Fregean universal thinking.

4.3. Is Natural-Historical Judgement 'Normative' Judgement?

But perhaps I have overlooked a possibility of reduction. Frege
himself, in his dispute with Kerry, considers the sentence 'The

horse is a four-legged animal', clearly intending it to be taken in our sense. He says that it 'is probably best regarded as expressing a universal judgement, say "all horses are four-legged animals" or "all properly constituted horses are four-legged animals" '.[45] The first alternative is obviously wrong; the second raises the possibility of what we may call a normative analysis.

I should say that I do believe that our natural-historical judgements are closely related to a range of judgements that one would want to call 'normative'. I will object rather to the idea that we can give anything to be called an analysis or elucidation in terms of them; the reverse is closer to the truth. As for sentences of the form 'A properly constituted S is F', my own view is that, in them, the words 'properly constituted' do not restrict the common noun, S. Rather, the words 'A properly constituted —— is——' move together and are just another sign that the judgement expressed is a natural-historical judgement.

But Frege wants to construe the original sentence as expressing a universal judgement in his sense. This presupposes that in his substitute sentence the words 'properly constituted horse' act as a unit, and designate or express the concept *properly constituted horse*. How is this concept supposed to be explained? If it is a veterinarian's or horse-breeder's notion, so to speak, then presumably a horse will fall under it if it meets a certain limited range of conditions. But many of the features we would want to attribute to 'horses' or 'the horse' in a natural-historical judgement will have to fall outside this range; there is no reason to think that all 'properly constituted horses' have them.

We might instead try to explain the concept in something like the following terms: a properly constituted horse is a horse that is as a horse should be (or 'ought to be', or 'is supposed to be') in every respect. Here, though, we should notice, first, that there is every reason to think that we now have an empty concept, and thus that our proposition would come out true whatever we put in the predicate place. Moreover, such an analysis forces us to believe that the quotidian sentences printed in the field guide and voiced over the nature documentary involve an implicit second-order quantification over 'respects', which is absurd.

But the best objection to this last account is that it ends up

[45] Frege, 'On Concept and Object', 185.

attaching the 'normative' expression to the *predicate*, or rather to a variable for which predicates are to be substituted. Why not try that with the original? Let 'The horse is a four-legged animal' amount to 'It holds good of every horse that it ought to have four legs'. But, now, what are we to make of the subsentence 'it ought to have four legs'? Here the norm word falls between a predicative expression and a variable ranging over individuals, which is what Frege really wants. But this norm word is so far left too abstract to supply us with a complete account of the original proposition. There is, after all, a way of hearing the word 'ought' which might have us assent, in certain moods, to something like 'It holds good of every cockroach that it ought to be killed'. This 'ought' evidently pertains to 'human ends and projects' and is thus out of the question. What we want is a so-to-speak intrinsic, or non-relative, oughtness—we want, for example, 'It ought, *as far as its merely being a horse goes*, to be four-legged', or 'It is supposed, *by its mere horse-nature*, to be four-legged', or 'It ought, *considering just what it is*, to be four legged'. There are, no doubt, other ways of bringing off this specification of the 'ought'. Some may be more elegant, but each must bring the common noun back into the expression for the relation between the individual and the property. Or, if it does not reintroduce the common noun directly, then, as in the lattermost case, it must inevitably employ a pronominal expression—in this case 'what it is'. But this pronoun is one for which the common noun can be substituted; it is as it were a pro-common-noun.

In order to control the shapeless 'ought', then, we are forced to join the predicate and the common noun (or its pronominal representative) together *immediately*—though in the presence of a 'normative' expression and an individual variable. But what a given horse is 'supposed by its mere horse-nature to be' must presumably be the same for every horse. The individual variable, and the quantifier that binds it, are thus wheels turning idly in such a formula as 'For every x, if x is a horse, then x is supposed by its mere horse-nature to be four-legged'. (It is as if one were to replace the proposition 'Two and two make four' with 'For all times t, two and two make four at t' with a view to rendering the philosophical problems about the former more tractable.) What we are really saying, then, is 'Horses are supposed to be four-legged'. All we are really working with is a common noun, a predicate, and 'something normative'. We are thus no further on than we were with 'A properly constituted horse is four-legged'.

But, finally, it was only a hope of reducing our kind of generality to the familiar Fregean sort that had us reaching for anything normative in the first place. On reflection, the move was a desperate one, and did violence to the transparently 'factual' or 'positive' character of the teaching of the field guide, the nature documentary, and the biochemical treatise. In the end, I think, all we are *really* working with is a predicate and certain sort of common noun; the appearances are *bene fundata*.

4.4. Conclusion: Goodness and Life

In natural-historical description, we meet, I think, with a logically special form of appearance of predicative expressions, one to be distinguished from the essentially tensed connection they may have with representations of individuals, including individual variables. We may say that a common noun has the 'grammar' of a *life-form word* if it is suited to be the subject of such predication—that is, if this is among the powers of combination with other words that go to fix its sense. Or, equivalently, a word is a life-form word if the capacity to express natural-historical judgements in terms of it is a part of the mastery of its employment. It is here, I think, as it was with Frege's 'concept words', which may be said to supply the apt predicates for the more familiar form of predication. An expression 'F' or 'is F' has the 'grammar' of a concept word if it can enter into the combinations '*a* is F' and '*a* is not F' with some singular term; the capacity to form such combinations is evidently a part of the mastery of its employment. This last is not I think something we could say of a statistical quantifier, for example. '99 per cent of —— are ——' is something we can *add* to a language with the apparatus of common nouns and other predicative expressions; it does not enter into the constitution of this apparatus, though it may help to define some of its more particular terms. The terms united are themselves indifferent to this form of combination. To affirm that the situation is the same with *our* from of combination is, I think, to deny that 'when we call something an acorn we look to a wider context than can be seen in the acorn itself'.

We may say that a concept is a *species concept* if it is a possible subject of the corresponding form of judgement. A *life-form* or *'species'* (in the broad sense) is anything that is, or could be, immediately designated by a species concept or a life-form word. To this sort of *'genus'*, then, there corresponds *that* sort of generality. An *organism* or *individual living thing*, finally, is whatever falls under a species or 'has' a life-form. It is whatever might justly be designated by a phrase of the form 'this *S*' for some reading of the common noun *S* as a life-form word. Or, equivalently, an organism is the object of any possible judgement *this S is F*, to which some natural-historical judgement *the S is G* might correspond. If an intellect loses the capacity for the latter sort of 'synthesis' it must also lose the former, and with it, I think, the capacity to experience things as alive. It can no longer 'look to a wider context'.

In saying all of this I, of course, presuppose that enough has been said to isolate this alleged form of judgement and its expression in speech. Perhaps there are other types of generality which satisfy the various features registered so far. Perhaps my occasional appeal to the notion of a life-form in attempting to impart the idea of such a form of judgement has begged some question and left the essay to fall short of the standard raised by Anscombe's *Intention*. But the answer to the question, when we can say 'Enough said', will of course depend on who we are saying it to, and what else there is in our language and thought with which the intended form may be confused. For someone, I suppose, it might be 'enough' to point out a few peculiarities of the nature documentary.

Let it be thought, though, that we have at best isolated some class of what we may call 'non-Fregean generalities'. The dispiriting suggestion will be that the intended natural-historical judgements form a subclass marked off from the others by content and not by form. It may be helpful then to notice, briefly, that our enterprise can be carried further. For example, we might go on to remark that natural-historical judgements themselves possess certain further possibilities of combination—in particular, of 'teleological' combination with others of their same form. Their linguistic expressions, that is, are fit to enter into certain sorts of 'final cause'. 'They have blossoms of such-and-such type in order that such-and-such insects should be attracted and spread their pollen about.' Here the propositions joined—'They have blossoms of such-and-such form' and 'They attract certain insects which spread their pollen about'—are of the intended type. Now, any attempt to employ this fact as an instrument of 'grammatical' isolation may of course be thought to raise new difficulties: perhaps the whole idea is just a theological survival. But the insistence on an independent, 'conscious' subject who sets up the things thus teleologically expressed presupposes that the relevant 'sense of the question "Why?"' is the one about which Anscombe and Davidson disputed. It presupposes, that is, that the intended order is the order of intention.

But, of course, it is among the marks of *that* sense of the question 'Why?' that it attaches to datable descriptions of goings-on— of 'events in a man's history', as Anscombe says.[46] If someone moves behind a pillar and I ask, 'What's going on? What's the point? Why?', and am satisfied with the response, 'He's trying to avoid the Griffin Professor; he owes her a paper', then it is the movements *hic et nunc* and not elsewhere that form the object of my query. But suppose we are dissecting a living frog and— scalpel aimed at the repulsive contractions of the heart—I ask, 'What's going on? What's the point? Why?' If I am satisfied with the response, 'It's the heart, of course, and by so beating it circulates the blood', then, after all, I think, it was *not* the individual movements that interested me. I was not so much pointing into the individual, as pointing *into its form*. I do not anticipate a different reply at a different lab bench, as I would at a different pillar. The alarming truth I apprehend and query, the 'that' for which I seek the 'because', is to be formulated in a natural-historical judgement.

We are thus, I think, very far from the category of intention or psychical teleology—a fact which is also shown in this, that if the complex thought about, for example, the blossoms is true, then the judgements joined in it are also true. Here, that is, '*P* in order that *Q*' entails both *P* and *Q*. In making out this sort of connection one links a fact, not with a possibly unrealized end, but with another fact. Natural-teleological judgements may thus be said to

---

[46] Anscombe, *Intention*, 24.

organize the elements of a natural history; they articulate the relations of dependence among the various elements and aspects and phases of a given kind of life.

And so, I think, even if the Divine Mind *were* to bring a certain life-form into being 'with a view to' securing an abundance of pink fur along the shores of the Monongahela, this would have no effect on the natural-teleological description of that form of life. The description of this sort of order has nothing to do with *natural selection* either; these propositions are in no sense hypotheses about the past. The elements registered in natural-historical judgements and the interconnections registered in the natural-teleological judgements all alike belong to that peculiar 'present' which we saw contains both 'spring' and 'fall' in winter, and 'the seventh year of the cicada's life-cycle' even during the second.

This can of worms having briefly been opened, perhaps new doubts will be raised. One may wonder whether even the monstrous phrase 'teleologically articulable non-Fregean generality' can isolate our sort of judgement. Don't certain sorts of *general* proposition enter into a final-causal nexus in the description, for example, of techniques, technical processes, *technai*—and also into the description of the artefacts and bits of technology that are among their means and ends? 'The point of the lye-bath is to harden the leather.' 'The point of the carburettor is to mix the air and fuel.' It would be wrong to insist that the relevant teleology is the one Anscombe and Davidson discussed.[47] For here too we will find, I think, that 'P in order that Q' entails both P and Q.

But the distinction can be marked in other ways. For example, a kind of 'partial idealism', in Anscombe's sense, seems to hold in the technical sort of case.[48] The *truth* of a proposition of the form 'First one does this, then one does this', where it belongs to the general description of a particular technique of, say, bread-baking or aspirin-synthesis, presupposes that someone makes or has made the corresponding judgement, or at least some others belonging to the same system of judgements—though of course it presupposes more than this. An unrecognized technique is after all a merely possible one. Nothing of the sort would hold of a

[47] See Sarah Waterlow Broadie, 'Nature, Craft and *Phronesis* in Aristotle', *Philosophical Topics*, 15/2 (1987), 35–50, and Andrew Hsu, 'Artifacts', unpub. MS.

[48] G. E. M. Anscombe, 'The Question of Linguistic Idealism', repr. in *Collected Philosophical Papers*, i.

natural-historical judgement expressed in the form 'First this happens, then that happens'—which might expound the phases of the embryological development of cranes, or of the synthesis of glucose in redwoods. Natural-historical judgements are in no sense presupposed by what they are about, and unrecognized life-forms are common.

I will end with a few unguarded remarks on concepts of *good*. I have rejected any account of natural-historical judgement in normative terms, suggesting that the order of explanation must run the other way. If, though, we want to apply 'normative' categories to subrational nature, and apart from any relation to 'our interests', then the questions inevitably arise, and not so unreasonably: Where does the standard come from? What supplies the measure? The system of natural-historical propositions with a given kind as subject supplies such a standard for members of that kind. We may implicitly define a certain very abstract category of 'natural defect' with the following simple-minded principle of inference: *From* 'The *S* is *F*' *and* 'This *S* is not *F*' *to infer* 'This *S* is defective in that it is not *F*'. It is in *this* sense that natural-historical judgements are 'normative', and not by each proposition's bearing some sort of normative infrastructure. The first application of concepts of good, bad, defect, and pathology is to the individual, and it consists in a certain sort of reference of the thing to its form or kind. Once formed, though, these concepts may of course be employed in general thoughts of various types.

It is true that the judgement of natural defect, so explained, must in a sense reach beyond the 'facts' about an individual. It reaches beyond them, though, to what appear equally to be 'facts'—namely, facts about its kind or species or life-form. What merely 'ought to be' in the individual we may say really 'is' in its form. In another sense, though, the picture of a 'reach beyond' is absurd: *when we call something an acorn we look to a wider context than can be seen in the acorn itself.* A reference to the life-form is already contained in the thought of the individual and its vicissitudes. We go no farther for critique than we went for interpretation. Consider that we might attempt to explain a conception of, say, oddness, with some such rule as follows: *From* 'Most *A*s are *F*' *and* 'This *A* is not *F*' *to infer* 'This *A is* odd in that it is not *F*'. If someone then asks, 'But what does "what most of them do" have to do with what *it* does?', the answer will have to be, 'Not much, really'. But if, in the other case, someone asks, 'What bearing does "what they do" have on what *it* does?', the answer will have to be, 'Everything'. A true judgement of natural defect supplies an 'immanent critique' of its subject.

But in truth the abstract category of natural defect is an artificial one. One tends to employ more concrete concepts: sickness, need, lack, deformity—or, still more concretely: lameness, blindness, colour-blindness, etiolation, and so forth. Such concepts may be said to express *forms* of natural defect. Whether and when any of them is applicable to a given individual organism will of course depend on the character of its life-form, on the particular content of its form's 'natural history'. They are all 'species-relative', in Professor Foot's phrase.

Professor Foot has given us a striking exposition of the content and the advantages of the ancient notion that, as we may now put it, *irrationality and vice are forms of natural defect*. The sort of life in which such concepts gain a foothold is a life caught up in categories of thought and action and passion, of custom and 'culture', and of much else besides. All of these matters raise philosophical problems of their own. It is clear that the relation between *the stupidity of an individual human action*, say, and the character of its agent's life-form is something far more complex and mediated than is the relation, for example, of *the etiolation of a given geranium* to the character of *its* form. The real problem is to grasp this complexity and the distinctions that are introduced with the categories of intellect and will. But no special difficulty arises from a moralist's appeal to the life-form, named 'human', that all of us share: we make such appeal already in everything we think of ourselves and one another.

11

Categorical Requirements:
Kant and Hume on the Idea of Duty

DAVID WIGGINS

1. Would it necessarily be a good thing for everything that has to do with ethics to be demystified? Or, ought not some things to be *re*mystified—not least the frequently invoked idea of the 'point of the whole thing' (the 'whole enterprise', as people say, already gravely misrepresenting it)? But the categorical imperative—or the categorical imperative as that has so often been conceived by some sorts of moral philosophy—this *did* deserve demystification. Philippa Foot's memorable assault upon these conceptions is not her most important service to philosophy. (That is surely to have been constantly prepared to point to the quality and quantity of working moral ideas that were being arbitrarily excluded from serious consideration by positions such as prescriptivism and consequentialism.) But it is the contribution I have had here constantly in mind.

Upon me, as upon others, the long-term effect of Philippa Foot's critique was to arouse a new interest in the possibility of an intelligible conception of the categorical *ought*. I think that that is what she intended. What I doubt whether she intended is that, seeing more to admire in Hume than either she or her admirers have wanted to see there (and finding different things in him from her official opponents), one should aspire to make out the plainer conception of the moral modalities in the broad framework of

Sections 2–23 of this article represent the full text of an Inaugural Lecture spoken with omissions at Birkbeck College, London, on 21 Mar. 1990. It is reprinted here with the kind permission of the *Monist*, in which an abridged version appeared, 74/1 (1991). It also appeared as 'L'Éthique et la raison', *Studia Philosophica*, 51 (1992).

I gratefully acknowledge the stimulus and instruction I have had from reading R. C. S. Walker, 'The Rational Imperative: Kant against Hume', *Proceedings of the British Academy*, 74 (1988). For their suggestions, I thank Roger Crisp, Steven Luper-Foy, Roger Scruton, and Andrew Chitty.

Hume's moral philosophy in particular. But even if there are
exponents of our subject who would greet so unexpected a response to their work with irritation or incomprehension, my faith
is that, in the case of the particular subject for whom I here record
my affection and respect, she will see in the lecture I here dedicate
to her some of the same things—however perversely I may seem
to have misstated them—that she herself perceived about the
nature of our fallible, wavering, fitful but always somehow per-
sisting attachment to morality.

If the theory advanced below is correct, then what is the difference (I know she will ask) between the moral *must/must not* and
the *must/must not* of etiquette or the clubhouse? Looking forward
to the conclusion I shall reach, let me reply, roughly and readily,
that the difference will reside not in anything formal but in the
depth, spread, and felt authority of the attachments to which the
moral *must/must not* appeals—and categorically appeals.

2. A categorical requirement (categorical imperative) is a requirement that applies regardless of inclination. You might wonder
whether you could escape the long reach of such a thing by
simply flying the skull and cross-bones and renouncing altogether the aim of belonging to the moral community. But what
we are apt to think is that categorical requirements like moral
requirements apply to you (in some relevant sense of that slippery verb 'apply') even if you ignore them and try to renounce
every concern whatever.

Why do we think this? Are we right? And, if we are right, must
such a requirement, applying thus regardless of someone's inclination, be founded in rationality? Must it be founded in demands
that can be shown to be demands of practical rationality as such,
which can *then*, just by virtue of representing rationality, create
the demands of morality?

3. These questions arise at one of the several places in philosophy
where we witness the collision between the philosophical opinions of David Hume, whose answer to the last of these questions
(put as I have put it) would always be *no*, and those of Immanuel
Kant. In morals the opposition between Humean and Kantian
conceptions corresponds in a disturbing way to a well-recognized
division between two kinds of human personality, roughly the

warm and the austere. So it is to be feared that excessively grown-up persons who do not really believe in philosophy will take gloomy pleasure in telling us that here, as with questions like whether to marry Isabel or marry Susan or marry neither, we simply have to grow up, read our own nature and declare our allegiance to Hume (if we are warm) or to Kant (if we are cold). But I hope to convince you that the opposition we are concerned with, like those hot/cold oppositions between nationalism and internationalism or particularism and universalism that we find in politics, is not really like that. What this opposition between Hume and Kant calls for is neither eclecticism nor compromise nor some empty philosophy of pure authenticity, but mediation—the deliberate mediation of philosophical inquiry, brought to bear upon the subject-matter of morals as that is actually given to us.[1]

4. A categorical requirement applies regardless of inclination. A requirement that is not categorical is usually called hypothetical. Consider the requirement 'On the volley, you should step in the direction of the net'. The requirement is simply ergonomic. There is no more to it than this: '*If you want to hit the ball back with control, pace and direction*, then, on the volley, you should step in the direction of the net'. What the requirement is hypothetical upon is the aim supplied here in italics. The thing that is said to be required, namely stepping in the direction of the net, is required *only* by the pursuit of an aim that someone could perfectly well, without disobedience to the requirement, disown or abandon.

Let it be clear then that the labels 'hypothetical' and 'categorical' qualify only the necessity that the statement of requirement attributes to the doing of a given act. In a categorical requirement there is nothing to prevent the act itself (as distinct from the necessity to do the act) from being specified by the use of a conditional 'if' or 'when'. For instance, it is a categorical, not a hypothetical, requirement upon any of us (or so we suppose) that,

[1] In reply to a question put to me by Steven Luper-Foy about morality and self, I would add that in my opinion there is more to be learned about the self by study of the actuality and substance of morality than there is to be learned about morality by the application to morality of philosophical theories of the self. I would certainly applaud Kant's readiness to proceed in the first of these ways and would applaud equally Hume's total disregard in his theory of morals of the wretchedly thin metaphysics he gives elsewhere of the self.

if a child ask bread, then we not give him a stone, or if the child
ask a fish, then we not give him a serpent.

5. At one point Kant describes categorical requirements like this:
'The categorical imperative would be one which presented an act
as of itself objectively necessary without regard to any end' (414).[2]
Hume had neither Kant's distinction of categorical and hypothetical nor the benefit of this particular formulation, but that need not
mean that his ideas of morality and duty cannot come to terms
with this sort of requirement. We shall see whether they can. Our
real difficulty in aligning Hume and Kant with respect to the idea
of duty is not that Hume was ignorant of Kant but that Hume's
first interest in morality was that of a moral scientist or (as one
would now say) moral psychologist. His first question is not
the question of the vindication of duty (that question can arise
later), but the question of how natural beings such as ourselves
can have arrived at the point where we can even think the
refined and complex thoughts we do think about morality and its
requirements.

6. In rough outline, Hume's answer to that question ran as follows. Human beings come into the world endowed by their human constitution with the strong sentiment of self-love and the
weak sentiment of benevolence. Benevolence is variously described by Hume as fellow feeling and as the spark of friendship
for human kind. The propensity to feel this sentiment is the propensity by which we conceive disinterested desires that others
(especially, in the first instance, those close by, but then, by virtue
of the working of sympathetic processes yet to be described,
desires that others further away) should receive this or that benefit, or be relieved of this or that evil. (Hume's is still the best
exposé of the crude but apparently perennial confusions that so
often underlie the impulse to deny that such desires can be what
they seem, namely disinterested.)

From the beginning of their physical existence, Hume points
out, individual human beings, thus constituted with their benevolence and self-love, are drawn into constant converse with

---

[2] I. Kant, *Foundations of the Metaphysic of Morals*, tr. L. J. Beck (Indianapolis:
Liberal Arts Press/Bobbs Merrill, 1959). The pages cited are of the Academy edn.
of the original, as given in Beck.

other human beings. In the process of learning the sense of the public language in which there is talk of good and bad, fair and foul, beautiful and ugly, they have to learn to depart from their private and particular situation and see things not only from thence but also from the point of view that shall be common between one person and another. The only way in which someone can come to speak the public language of praise and blame or attain to any agreement with others in judgments is to learn to see his judgments and responses as answerable to that common point of view. Hume postulates no special diminution of self-love nor any cessation in the readiness to make the speaker-relative judgments that arise from it. All that he postulates are countervailing tendencies that arise from benevolence (or from the same source as benevolence)—among them the tendency to seek to cleave to the standpoint that a person can share with others to whose fate he is not entirely or utterly indifferent.

When we are drawn to try to see things from the common viewpoint and seek to grasp the sense of predicates that presuppose it, we need to learn a new set of responses and we need to see our judgments as answerable to responses beyond our own responses. Suppose that, in seeking that common viewpoint and exploring it, we are struck in one way or another by some object of attention. Then we have to ask ourselves whether others who are similarly motivated to try to take up that viewpoint are similarly struck—rather as, when we seek to establish the objective contours of a landscape, we need to interest ourselves in perspectives other than the one we ourselves happen to enjoy at a given point. We have to work backwards from a plurality of perspectives to what they are all perspectives of, allowing one perspective to supplement or explain or correct the apparent error in another.[3] Thus Hume writes in the *Enquiry*:

When [one] bestows on any man the epithets of vicious or odious or depraved he then speaks another language [than that of self-love] and expresses sentiments in which he expects all his audience are to concur

---

[3] Cp. David Hume, *A Treatise of Human Nature*, ed. L. A. Selby-Bigge (Oxford: Oxford University Press, 1978), 582, 583, 603. There is much more to say about the scope and limitations of Hume's doctrine of perspectival correction—but not here.

with him. He must here therefore depart from his private and particular situation, and must choose a point of view common to him with others; he most move some universal principle of the human frame, and touch a string to which all mankind have an accord and symphony. If he mean therefore to express that this man possesses qualities whose tendency is pernicious to society, he has chosen this common point of view, and has touched the principle of humanity in which every man in some degree concurs. (222)[4]

Marrying this claim with one Hume makes in the *Treatise*, we may paraphrase him as saying further that, if others do concur, then the judgment of odiousness is to that extent reinforced. If others do not concur the judgment is a candidate to be corrected or discarded. (Or there is one other possibility, and it is one Hume should have said something about. Sometimes we will stick to our own judgment as sound and incur the responsibility to explain the discrepancy between our own response and that of others.)

In general, one will be right in one's valuations and appraisals and others will tend to concur in these just to the extent that one succeeds in homing upon the common standard that is erected upon the interest that people have in common with one another. And now, as the passage I was quoting from the *Enquiry* continues:

While the human heart is compounded of the same elements as at present, it will never be wholly indifferent to public good nor entirely unaffected with the tendency of characters and manners. And though this affection of humanity may not generally be esteemed so strong as vanity or ambition, yet being common to all men, it can alone be the foundation of morals, or of any system of blame or praise. (*Enquiry*, 222)

The shared standard or 'abstract rule' that emerges in this way for the evaluation of characters—and (derivatively from that) of the acts that issue from characters—rests on an interest that is in each case weak. But it is the only standard that is reliably reinforced. Or, as Hume says earlier in the *Enquiry*,

General language . . . being formed for general use must be moulded on some more general views and must affix the epithets of praise or blame

---

[4] Hume, *Enquiry Concerning the Principles of Morals*, ed. L. A. Selby-Bigge (Oxford: Oxford University Press, 1978).

in conformity to sentiments which arise from the general interests of the community. (186)

7. At this point, namely the point marked by our assuming full mastery of 'general language', our imagination, our reason, our powers of analogy or of looking for similar treatment for similar cases and dissimilar treatment for dissimilar cases, the unending search for generality, have all co-operated with our benevolence, with our capacity to resonate to the feelings of others (which Hume calls sympathy) and with the other traits and tendencies benevolence fosters (such as gratitude, for instance—a virtue that Hume rightly treats as natural[5] and might usefully have stressed in its linkage with the primitive idea of reciprocity), in a way that enables us to make the shared standard our own standard of assessment. It becomes our own standard not necessarily uncritically or for every case—we are contributors to it as well as its subjects—but presumptively. And as we become better schooled in that public standard, better equipped to participate in its determination, and more and more party to the general concerns that it embodies, we shall come to feel a pleasurable sentiment of a particular kind (or an uneasy sentiment of a particular kind) in the view or spectacle of virtuous (or of vicious) characters and the actions that express them.

Genealogically or aetiologically speaking, the public standard that informs our evaluation of characters and sustains our understanding of the distinction of vice and virtue is still an elaboration of natural benevolence. But it is crucially important that that to which it has given rise reaches far beyond that original sentiment.

First, there is no clear limit upon whose happiness or misery can impinge upon the judgments that issue from the public standard. For the standard is entirely general. (This is not, of course, to say that the standard replaces the finding of particular duties with derivations of such duties from some general duty to promote utility. That is not the sort of generality at which Hume is aiming.)

Secondly, the energy that is mustered from fellow feeling and its allies (or mustered from these and self-love) can be *redirected* and put at the disposal of concerns both different from and (Hume insists) potentially *utterly at variance* with either simple or

[5] See e.g. 'Of the Original Contract', para. 33.

general benevolence, namely concerns with such things as loyalty, allegiance, justice or veracity. What is energized in this case is the adherence to the artificial or conventional observances the widespread and consistent adherence to which will further the shared or general interest. In these observances or practices we come to see what Hume calls *moral beauty*. What is more, the moral beauty of an observance is something that can outrun its basis in the original rationale for the observance (*Treatise*, 551). The demand that such observances should prevail can then begin (I think Hume thinks) to play an autonomous role in our conception of our happiness together. (In which case there must be a corresponding shift in our idea of 'the general interest'.) Finally, the perception of the moral deformity of the neglect of the observance can sustain us in the intention to do some loyal/just/etc. thing precisely because it is the loyal/just/etc. thing to do (or because not to do that thing would be disloyal or unjust).

8. Hume's full account of these matters is a wonderful work of speculative anthropology, improvable,[6] extensible, sharing striking points of similarity and of difference with current non-philosophical accounts of these matters. Among its differences are these. It avoids specious precision where the determination of detail is speculatively impossible (there is no modelling mania): and, precisely because the account arises by abduction from the phenomena of ordinary moral experience, it engages both directly and unsanctimoniously with that experience.

But what light can Hume's account cast upon the full normative force of categorical requirements? As Hume discovered (in effect) when he set out in the *Enquiry* to remedy the complaint that Hutcheson made about the *Treatise*, namely that Hume had been insufficiently warm in the cause of virtue, the main purpose of Hume's genealogy of morals was oblique to the purpose of answering that question.

---

[6] See e.g. J. L. Mackie, 'Norms and Dilemmas', in his *Persons and Values* (Oxford: Clarendon Press, 1985). Mackie supplies the point that the genealogist of morals can postulate natural tendencies less abstract than those Hume postulates, tendencies by which human beings can first combine to co-operate with others in projects undertaken for shared benefit but then identify themselves with the success of those enterprises without exact regard for the independently specifiable benefits that it will bring to them personally.

Warned by the indifferent success of the explicit answer we discover for that question in the second part of section IX of Hume's *Enquiry*, and focusing in any case on the sharper question that Kant has supplied to us, we must begin defensively, I think, by preparing to make the best use of what Hume had already supplied before he wrote section IX, part ii, and by insisting on the point that the most a Kantian deontologist can non-question-beggingly demand of a Humean philosopher working within the Humean framework is that, for every categorical requirement agreed to be counted valid, the Humean should find some sufficiently validatory explanation of the requirement. It can make all the difference to the explanation whether the requirement is to give a child bread not a stone, if it ask for bread, or the requirement to protect the innocent or the requirement to fight bravely for one's country or the requirement to repay what one has borrowed.

9. Forgetting generality then, let us focus, exempli gratia, on one case where it seems Hume ought to be on his strongest ground, namely the duty he several times mentions of kindness to children. Suppose a child asked John for bread and he gave it a stone. (Suppose for definiteness that John was the child's uncle.) At this point, Kantians will remind us of Hume's own way of criticizing such conduct (cf. *Treatise*, 518) and will say that Hume's response can only be that such conduct shows a want of natural affection or at best, deploying a phrase Kant himself arrived at during the short period when he was himself a Hutchesonian or Humean in morals, that it shows a want of affection towards the human species.[7] And then, like the mature Kant, the Kantian deontologists will say that John's behaviour as described does indeed show a lack of natural affection, but that that is not what is fundamentally wrong with it. What is fundamentally wrong has to do with John's failure to act under the general idea of duty, and his failure to act in accordance with a maxim he could will to be a general law for all rational beings.

We shall come in due course to these formulations, which are proprietary to Kant. Meanwhile, though, can we not improve here

---

[7] See Keith Ward, *The Development of Kant's Ethics* (Oxford: Blackwell, 1972), ch. 2.

on the Humean answer? Surely Hume does not need to limit
himself to saying that John is wanting in natural affection. It is not
as if Hume does not suppose that there is a duty of kindness to
children. For such a duty is enshrined in the abstract rule or
public standard for the assessment of characters and the actions
that express characters.

Marrying that obvious point with what Hume did say, I think
one should declare that the standard is indeed the way it is
because affection for children is a natural human response to
them (as well as for other reasons); but that this standard applies
to John *even if* John himself does not feel such affection.[8] Indeed
the explicit standard of morals that we came to grasp as we came
to grasp 'general language' can be silent about its own aetiology
and silent about how exactly it arose from the naturalness of
certain feelings, from utility or the rest.[9] (Such considerations can
safely coexist in consciousness with the standard. But not all of
them will figure properly in explanations that support the applications of the standard.) Finally, a third point: John simply does
not need the perfectly general idea of duty that the Kantians want
to import into this business in order to reconsider his (John's)
attitude to the demands of the child. John can apply the shared
standard and then, with its assistance, he can see his own refusal
as cruel and inhuman (which is what the standard says it is): and
then he can see it as an object of what Hume calls 'humility' and
we should call 'shame'.[10] But shame, I hasten to add, is the culmi-
nation of his commitment to the standard. It is not the basis for it.

10. Kantians will now ask how the bare fact that cruelty is condemned by the public standard that Hume describes can generate

---

[8] Putting the point for a moment in the terminology of Bernard Williams in
'Internal and External Reasons' (in *Moral Luck* (Cambridge: Cambridge University
Press, 1978)), I should claim that many reasons that might too quickly be dismissed as merely 'external reasons', and therefore practically inert, can and should
be seen by a Humean as limiting cases of internal reasons, reasons an agent can
discover and then ratify as potentially reasons *for him*. See also n. 15 below.

[9] Hume does indeed write that 'when any action or quality of the mind pleases
us after a certain manner we say it is virtuous, and when the neglect or non-
performance of [an act] displeases us after a like manner, we say that we lie under
an obligation to perform it' (*Treatise*, 517), and I suppose that this may have given
the impression that there is only an obligation where there is a feeling. But of
course the 'we' is collective and the claim is generic. It is not a part of the standard.
It is a comment on the standard.

[10] Cf. *Enquiry*, IX. i. 225, and *Treatise*, II. i. 7. Note, however, the importance here,
for this move, of taking seriously the declarative or indicative purport of moral

a duty for John and all the rest of us, whatever our feelings, to be kind to children. But the Humean may reply, why should it not? The standard is after all our standard. Does John want to escape from that standard? Is this not the standard by which John effects most of the moral distinctions he does want to effect? And that standard condemns what he has done. If he really does want to escape from its judgments, then he must follow through. Does John want to say he does not care what the standard says? If that is all that he says, why should moral philosophy regard that as a problem? He does not care. (And, as we shall see, not even the Kantian doctrine can do anything about that.) Even where he does not care, or he says he does not care, the actual features of the situation that render his actions open to criticism are features that engage with the attitudes (however fitful) that make him party to the point of view that shall be common to him with others. Or does John want to propose an alternative standard that is not so soft on children? If so, let him propose it.

If these questions are fair to John and they do not misrepresent the dialectical situation, then now is the moment to say that the Humean account of the genesis of morality, so far from explaining morality *away*, serves very well to articulate what it would take for John to make out one of the alternatives to the actual standard. For the Humean account is consistent with—and it keenly interests us in—the possibility that, once one tries to work through the alternatives to a given standard, one may find no satisfactory alternatives to it. It may be that one will find that (seriously speaking) there is really nothing else to think about how to behave to children. No other standard can (as a whole) be seriously defended. (Perhaps it would take that much to *vindicate* the standard. If so, we shall not always be able to vindicate it in these terms.) Here I would recall to you that, even about that artificial contrivance justice as it relates to property rights, Hume registered this as his own considered conclusion:

The interest on which justice is founded is the greatest imaginable and extends to all times and places. It cannot possibly be served by any other

utterance, 'my refusal was cruel' etc.—a purpose not, I think, denied by Hume and fully consistent with the link between judgment and moral approbation (see my *Needs, Values, Truth* (Oxford: Blackwell, 1987), ch. 5), however ill some may say that that coheres with Hume's own (too simply psychological or insufficiently intentional) account of sentiments such as approbation.

invention. It is obvious and discovers itself on the very first formation of society. All these causes render the rules of justice steadfast and immutable; at least, as immutable as human nature. And if they were founded on original instincts, could they have any greater stability? (*Treatise*, 620)

To understand the genealogy of morals is to understand not only *how much* but also *how relatively little* room there sometimes is for the actual standard to be varied.

11. So much for the defence of Hume against one Kantian objection. But at this point it will be helpful to hear from Kant himself *in propria voce*.

Empirical principles are not at all suited to serve as the basis of moral laws. For if the basis of the universality by which they should be valid for all rational beings without distinction . . . is derived from a particular tendency of human nature or the accidental circumstance in which it is found, then that universality is lost. (442)

There are two points here, one about the epistemological status of morality, the other about its constituency.

The first point, if directed at Hume, would amount to the claim that, on the Humean account, the standard of morals is empirical or something we learn about a posteriori from sense experience. Surely (the objection continues) the standard of morals is not something we learn from sense experience (even if sense experience can be expected to reveal the need to apply that standard more meticulously or think it through more carefully).

To this point I would reply that what the Humean standard rests upon is indeed a posteriori. If human nature had been different, then what we actually mean by morality—that is morality—might at many points be not fully intelligible to anyone. (Or so Hume might say.) There is much to say about that and I have tried to say some of it elsewhere.[11] Here, however, all that needs to be said is that aposteriority of the moral standard itself does not

---

[11] See my *Needs, Values, Truth*, 206, 347–8. This is as good a place as any for me to say that, having noted and heeded Bernard Williams's suggestion that the use of the words 'moral' and 'morality' carries suggestions that one only concerned with what he designates ethics may want to disown, I have not been able in practice to dispense with these words. As used here, they are not intended to carry those unwanted suggestions.

follow from the aposteriority of its natural foundation. We grasp the standard by participating in the practices that are informed by it (and inform it). These depend in part on sense perception, but we do not grasp (or regulate) the standard *through* sense perception any more than one under classroom instruction that is addressed to the sense of hearing and supported by examples given by sense experience grasps arithmetic simply empirically or treats his arithmetical judgments as simply empirical. What is more, the a posteriori foundation of morality does not play any large speaking part within the statement of the standard of morals itself. The standard regulating our responses to what we encounter in the world is no more answerable on Hume's account than it is on other accounts to what we learn in sense experience.

The second point Kant is making in the passage I quoted is about the definition of the moral constituency, and it is one that Kant made much of. In the preface to the work from which I have just quoted, he had written

Everyone must admit that a law, if it is to hold morally, i.e. as a ground of obligation, must imply absolute necessity; he must admit that the command "Thou shalt not lie" does not apply to men only, as if other rational beings had no need to observe it. The same is true for all other moral laws properly so called. He must concede that the ground of obligation here must not be sought in the nature of man or in the circumstances in which he is placed, but sought *a priori* solely in the concepts of pure reason. (389; cf. 408)

The point is familiar in Kant. What may be less well known is that Hume expressed himself interested in the very same point, when he wrote in his letter of 16 March 1740 to Francis Hutcheson.

I wish from my heart I could avoid concluding that, since morality according to your opinion as well as mine is determined merely by sentiment, it regards only human nature and human life . . .

If the ambiguity of Hume's words 'determined' and 'regards' did not match the ambiguity of the words 'derived' in the former quotation from Kant (442) and 'ground of obligation' in the latter (389), I should scarcely dare to intervene or say that Hume (in this letter) and Kant (in the *Foundations*) are equally in error. But surely the objection Hume fears depends for its damaging effect on the fact that these expressions suggest two different ideas simultaneously, the idea of the natural basis of the standard and the idea of justification or reasons that are made explicit in the application of the standard. Once these things are distinguished, however, Hume can return to the commonsensical point that the standard itself does not limit its constituency to human beings. The standard simply speaks against lying. It is intended to reach whoever can comprehend it regardless of whether they are actually party to the standard.

Here then we must not confuse an uncircumscribed *intended* reach with an uncircumscribed rationally *effective* reach and authority, or rush to the conclusion which Kant rushes to proclaim as the conclusion of our ordinary rational knowledge of morals, that every rational being is *ipso facto* receptive to morality as we ordinarily conceive that and *reason-bound* to submit to it. That question remains to be investigated. To reach a conclusion about this one would need a different sort of argument. (Compare Section 14 following.) How could the simple absence of anything restricting a categorical injunction to human beings prove that moral injunctions must have as their rationally effective constituency all rational beings? The circumstance that there is 'some sentiment . . . [that] render[s] the actions and conduct even of the persons the most remote an object of applause or censure according as they agree or disagree with [the] rule of right' and the circumstance that there is 'some sentiment common to all mankind which recommends the same object to general approbation' (*Enquiry*, 221)—these (as Hume says) are two circumstances. According to Hume, the connexion between them is forged by our human nature and our second nature. And so much, I would remark, not even the phenomenology of moral obligation need contradict. We feel *bound*. But why *reason-bound*? Why not say we feel bound by our moral nature, i.e. bound by those moral sentiments without which (we have concluded, if we feel bound by obligation) we should not recognize ourselves?[12] (Bound then by reason of those sentiments, one may want to say.)

[12] Peter Winch and Bernard Williams have discussed a number of ways of understanding such practical necessity. See e.g. Peter Winch, *Ethics and Action* (London: Routledge, 1972), 163, 186; and Bernard Williams, 'Practical Necessity', in *Moral Luck*. For Williams's other suggestions see the useful survey by Robert Gay in 'Bernard Williams on Practical Necessity', *Mind*, 98 (1989), 553–69. It is important to realize that such practical necessity can give *x*, who feels it, a reason, yet this can be a reason one cannot without begging the question convert into a

12. There are further Kantian objections against Hume:

> Whatever is derived from the particular natural situation of man as such, or from certain feelings and propensities, or even from a particular tendency of the human reason which might not hold necessarily for the will of every rational being . . . can give a maxim valid for us but not a law; that is, it can give a subjective principle by which we might act only if we have the propensity and inclination, but not an objective principle by which we would be directed to act even if all our propensity, inclination and natural tendency were opposed to it. (425)

The point this adds to the previous objection and presents for answer might be the following: that a scheme that is desire-driven in the way in which the Humean scheme is desire-driven—counting benevolence as a desire, or as a source of desires—cannot deliver a truly categorical requirement. At best the imperatives it delivers are hypothetical upon the aim that is sustained by the desire in question.

This is an interesting objection (and sharply to be distinguished from the vulgar post-Kantian objection, which Kant himself does not urge against Hume, that such aims are really selfish or self-centred; see 398). Clearly, the objection has been widely influential. But it is scarcely fair. What the moral standard founded in the affections that it is natural and/or promotive of the general interest for human beings to feel towards children requires of us as our duty is to give bread, not a stone, a fish, not a serpent. It does not require that of us hypothetically or only if we feel affection for children. The requirement is perfectly simple and categorical. It requires this of us 'even if all our propensity, inclination and natural tendency [are] opposed to it'. Only logical confusion, confusion about sense, confusion about scope or moralistic aversion to Humean cheerfulness could obscure the fact that Hume has just as good a right as anyone else to say this.

I do not doubt that some Kantians have fallen into this muddle. I think it can be found in the Kantian *Lectures on Ethics*, compiled from student notes.[13] But it is unlikely that Kant did himself fall into it. Perhaps Kant's own objection is not that Hume's require-

---

demonstration of someone else's *irrationality* where they are unimpressed by the considerations that create for *x* a necessity. Cf. Section 13 below, second para.

[13] See e.g. p. 13 of the Eng. tr. by L. Infield (London: Methuen, 1930), lines 13–17 from the foot of the page.

ments are only hypothetical, but that a scheme that is desire-driven, even in the special (only aetiological) way in which the Humean scheme is desire-driven, cannot put together or account for a *motive* to do what one is required to do *and* to do it regardless of propensity, inclination and natural tendency. If so, one can imagine that Kant's reflections took off from Hume's often repeated claim that 'no action can be virtuous or morally good unless there be in human nature some motive to produce it distinct from the sense of its morality'. That is speculation. What is certain is that, in his own theory of ethics, Kant believed he had found a consideration with a special power to prevail against propensity, inclination and natural tendency, namely the rational consideration of what universal law one could give to oneself as a rational being.

Here at last one catches sight of the possibility of a real objection to Hume. It is true that, as it stands, the objection mistakes the real intention of the much quoted Humean dictum. The Humean dictum is only intended to make the point that something like morality that starts out as a natural phenomenon needs a natural starting-point. The dictum was not intended to condemn morality never to rise above its starting-point.[14] But the objection can be freed of this misinterpretation: and then, where the Kantian account was already functioning as a demonstrable alternative to the Humean account, the objection might have some persuasive power. In advance of that, however, I should say that the objection was perfectly inconclusive—if only because it fails to show why a desire-driven motivation that issues in our participation in a life that is sustained by a shared public standard and can see moral beauty in certain observances (ones which are the way they are because they relate in a certain way to a shared and in part— NB here *Enquiry*, appendix III—non-egoistic interest) *could not transcend* propensity, inclination, and natural tendency. After all, it is of the essence of Hume's story that, in the light of the story, we see how morality really can 'raise in a manner a new creation' (*Enquiry*, appendix I (246)) and prompt to us concerns and perceptions that are rooted in desire but are not *themselves* desires.

---

[14] Given the main context for the dictum, which is Hume's explanation of how it is that the possessors of the artificial virtues can do what they do precisely because such a virtue demands this of them, that would be absurd. See esp. *Treatise*, III. ii. 1, paras. 9, 10.

13. Where then does this leave us? Suppose someone presses the question whether Hume can furnish a dependable motive for right action. If that is the question, Hume's answer ought to be that, for every agreed categorical requirement, he will try to furnish (i.e. remind us of) some psychologically effective, non-self-centred reason to comply with it.[15] (Not always the same reason of course.) If the question is whether this reason will always prevail, the answer seems to be *No*. Hume cannot achieve this. But then (one might say) nobody else can either.

At this point in the moral dialectic the question is usually commuted and it becomes the question whether the sort of reason that Hume furnishes for doing the required act will always prevail with the agent *if the agent is reasonable*. To that, however, I think the undogmatic Humean response ought to be to question whether any non-question-begging sense is here available for 'reasonable', in accordance with which to understand and then answer the question. (The dogmatic response will be to assert without warrant that reason is the slave of the passions.)

And now we see the most fundamental difference between Hume and Kant. Kant thinks that there is and there must be such a sense of 'reasonable'; that this sense can be given in advance (or at least independently of what comes to be at issue when we are specifically concerned with morality as such) and can be grasped by any rational being; and that a true morality must furnish a content for morality and a motivation to heed its requirements that will speak to any rational being of no matter what prior constitution or formation—again in some non-question-begging, antecedently available sense of 'rational'. In a true morality, the sort of circumstances that Hume calls 'two' circumstances will, according to Kant, *coincide*.

The time has come to put in abeyance all the doubts I have already expressed about that (see Section 11 above) and see how in the *Foundations of the Metaphysics of Morals* Kant supposes that this is to be achieved.

---

[15] As well as being non-self-centred, the reason Hume furnishes will be internal in Williams's sense—but *sometimes* (in this account of the matter) only by being a limiting case of an internal reason. See n. 8 above. The reason with which the agent is furnished will itself be founded in the much-transformed and subtly diversified standing desire that Hume calls benevolence. But being *founded* in that, it is not itself the same as that. The picture is rather that the consideration Hume will muster for an act required by some virtue—e.g. the consideration 'it would be

14. In ordinary moral thought, we interest ourselves and we think ourselves rational to interest ourselves in what can be represented to us as categorical requirements applying to anyone at all who can understand them. That is one fact. (Note that the use here of the word 'interest' comes from Kant himself. I use it henceforth in the special moral sense in which he uses it in this connexion in section 3 of the *Foundations of the Metaphysics of Morals*, not in the sense in which he uses it otherwise.) Another fact is that among requirements thus represented as categorical we sort the valid from the invalid.

These are two explananda; Kant was keen to distinguish them (for reasons closely connected with the dialectical strategy by which he aims to give morality an a priori foundation) and there is much to say about each. As regards the first, Kant repeatedly postpones until the end of his book the task of describing and vindicating as rational the moral interest that makes us open in this way to categorical requirements. (Once one attends to Kant's signposts, this is one of the salient features of Kant's plan for the book.) The problem is described by him as one of explaining how 'pure reason without any other incentives . . . can itself be practical, i.e. how the mere principle of the universal validity of the maxims' that may be willed to become universal laws for all rational beings can itself, 'without any object of the will in which we might in advance take some interest, furnish an incentive and produce an interest which would be called purely moral' (461). (Cf. 462, 448 heading, 449 *ab init.*, 450.) Let us follow Kant and bracket this question until the very end. (When we reach that point, a little more can be said about the import of Kant's decision to divide this off as a separate explanandum; see footnote 19. Meanwhile, however, it is important to see that, in his special sense of 'interest', Kant's search for such an interest is not inconsistent with his expulsion of all inclination and ordinary incentive or interest from moral motivation.)

The other explanandum is the fact that, given our readiness in principle to heed them, we sort valid from invalid claimants for

disloyal not to do *X'*—will be such as to speak to one possessed of that benevolence as thus transformed and diversified. Provided the consideration in question finds favour with him as a reason for him to do *X*, then it can become the substance of *the agent's* reason to *X*. *Consequentially upon this*, the agent acquires a context-bound desire to *X* that can be expected to be episodically sufficient to move him to act in that context.

the status of categorical requirements. How do we do this? At his best, when not trying to be 'warm in the cause of virtue' and simply following through the implications of his theory, Hume had rightly offered no single or general answer to this question. But thinking that that which sustains a valid imperative must commend it to any rational being of no matter what formation, constitution, or situation (my comment on this argument is now in abeyance), Kant does and must look for a general answer. (Compare Sections 11, 12 above; and *Foundations*, 413.) Perhaps he can persuade us. If there is such a general answer, then what is it?

15. Consider the moral injunction to protect the innocent from harm. In so far as we are prepared to see the judgment 'one must protect the innocent from harm' as possessing categorical force, we have to see it as lacking any reference to an aim one might opt out from—witness the first explanandum—and as containing positively both the idea of *universal law* (421), or of an objective principle holding for every rational being (421, note 9), and the idea of necessity. The necessity in question attaches to the act-specification 'to protect the innocent'—or to the act itself of protecting the innocent—and it itself derives from the idea of universal law. Why must it derive from that? Well, what else (Kant would ask) can such a maxim derive its necessity from than from a universal law? If there are valid categorical requirements that we can recognize as valid and as applying to anyone who can understand them, then there must be such a law.

What then—if such judgments as 'one must protect the innocent' are indeed both possible and argumentatively sustainable—must be the text of the universal law itself that sustains them? The law in question can say no more and no less than this: act only according to that maxim (or principle or act-specification, e.g. 'to protect the innocent') which you can at the same time will should hold for all rational beings: or act as though the maxim of your action were by your will (by your willing it) to become a universal law (421; cf. 402).

The formula cannot say more than this because it is to speak to all rational beings of no matter what formation and with no matter what inclinations and other aims. It must depend for its force on nothing that is not universal to rational beings.

The formula cannot say less, because nothing less would suffice to communicate unconditional necessity to maxims to which we are prepared—witness the first explanandum—to attach universal practical necessity.

16. So, *if* judgments like 'one must protect the innocent' are to have the categorical force we commonly attribute to them (Condition 1), and if that force is to have just one basis, the same basis for all correct judgments (Condition 2), and if that is to be an antecedent basis in reason (Condition 3), not just a basis that *makes* a reason,[16] then the thing that sustains these judgments can only be the a priori law for the will: act only according to that maxim (or act-specification) by (willing) which you can at the same time will that it should become a universal law.[17] Let us

---

[16] Our doubts are in abeyance but it will be necessary to keep the reckoning. Hume can accept protasis 1 as true. He will reject protasis 2, having been given no compelling reason to accept that there is *one* basis for all correct judgments of categorical requirement—and *a fortiori* no reason to believe that such a basis must comprise only the considerations Kant would be prepared to call rational considerations. Nor then can he accept that protasis 3 is satisfied. But Hume would be entitled to insist that Humean considerations can *make* a reason, and give an agent *his* reason, which can then speak to desire. (See n. 15 above.) And a *Humean* moralist need not follow Hume in his throw-away attitude to rationality. See below, Section 2.

[17] Here ends the effort to derive the formula of Universal Law from the conditions Kant states upon any moral or practically rational act. (In sum, if there has to be a moral law, and it must be shaped by these constraints, then what else can that law say?) I have been encouraged in my conviction that the matter is less straightforward than has sometimes been assumed both by Schopenhauer's discussion in *On the Basis of Morality*, tr. E. F. J. Payne (Indianapolis: Bobbs Merrill, 1965) and by Ralph Walker's doubts in his *Kant* (London: Routledge, 1987). It is Schopenhauer's discussion in particular that has encouraged me to pass over entirely Kant's first derivation of the categorical imperative (402) in favour of his second (421). The first derivation is said by Kant to speak to our ordinary rational knowledge of morals. Appealing to this, it claims that the only truly moral, intrinsically good motive is the good will, the motive to do what the moral law requires for no other reason than that is what that law requires. Kant then writes: 'What kind of a law can that be the conception of which must determine the will without reference to the expected result? Under this condition alone the will can be called absolutely good without qualification. Since I have robbed the will of all impulses which could come to it from obedience to any law, nothing remains to serve as a principle of the will except universal conformity to law as such. *That is*, I should never act in such a way that I could not also will that my maxim should be a universal law.' Surely there is a problem here. The penultimate sentence preceding the sentence with the 'that is' does not state the text or form of any law. The sentence with the 'that is' does purport to do that. But, if so, how does one get from the first sentence to the second? Here Schopenhauer's comment is still apt and must form the basis

follow custom and call this the Formula of Universal Law. All valid categorical obligations to do this or that act are for Kant impressions from this one mould. It is this single requirement that they exemplify. What our acts are morally answerable to then is always the test of universal willing. In so far as we see any force in categorical requirements, we see ourselves as answerable at this level and in this way for all our acts. On this account, I must protect the innocent because I *can* will 'Let everyone protect the innocent from harm' and I *cannot* will 'Let no one protect the innocent from harm'.

This is the answer to the question how we are to sort valid from invalid requirements. But what about the other question mentioned at the beginning of Section 14, concerning our originating rational moral 'interest' in morality? Or, to put the question as Kant reformulates it immediately after his section 2 derivation of the Formula of Universal Law, is it a *necessary law* for all rational beings that they should always judge their actions by much maxims as they can themselves will to serve as universal laws (426)? To answer that question, we must further develop in the direction of section 3 of the *Foundations* the first answer that Kant gives to the question how we sort valid from invalid requirements.

If pure practical reason proceeds on such a principle as the Formula of Universal Law, then what good is it that practical reason seeks here? What is its end? Surely this end can be nothing other than pure practical rationality itself. For there is no other end that could count as the objective ground of will's self-determination (427), or as intrinsically good or as a maxim valid for every human being (427). But for Kant pure practical rationality is effectively the alias (in so far as human beings are rational beings) of humanity. And, with this equivalence, we move beyond the

of any sincere effort to find in Kant's second derivation (420) a better argument for the formula of Universal Law. See *On the Basis of Morality*, 72–3: 'By disdaining all empirical motives of the will Kant removed as empirical everything objective and everything subjective on which a law for the will could be based. And so for the *substance* of that law he had nothing left but its own form. Now this is simply *conformity to law*; but such *conformity* consists in its being applicable to all and so in its universal validity. Accordingly this becomes the substance and consequently the purport and meaning of the law are nothing but its universal validity itself. It will therefore read "Act only in accordance with that maxim which you can at the same time wish will become a universal law for all rational beings" . . . I pay a tribute of sincere admiration to the great ingenuity with which Kant performed this trick.'

Formula of Universal Law to the Formula of Humanity: 'act so that you treat humanity whether in your own person or in that of another never as a means only, but always as an end'.

If I treat humanity as an end in itself, i.e. if I treat every other sovereign will as a sovereign will equally with my own; if every aim I conceive must be conditioned by the supreme aim of Kantian moral decency, namely the aim to treat others' wills as on a par with my own will in respect of being sovereign rational wills; if rationality-cum-humanity is, as it must now appear in the light of the Formula of Universal Law, essentially *self-legislative*; then I must treat humanity as self-legislative. And from this it then follows that I must act from maxims that can commend themselves to a will that has regard for itself as one universally legislating will among others in a systematic union under common objective laws (433) of beings that treat one another as self-legislating beings. Not only then must I so will that my will is consistent with the universal lawgiving of will (431)—consistent, that is, with the concept of each rational being as a being that must regard itself as giving universal law through all the maxims that it wills for all rational beings (433, para. 2). But also rational beings must act and will maxims as if, by our maxims, we were at all times legislative members in the universal kingdom of ends (439).

17. Now suppose a self-legislating being chooses the maxim on which it shall act not from inclination, not from incentive, not (as Kant says) heteronomously, but for the sake of the moral law or for the sake of the end of practical rationality, namely self-legislating rationality. Then his will is a law to itself and he is an *autonomous* being who sets his own end. He is the only kind of being that can rise above the level of causal determination. But now, given the equivalence between will's acting on no other maxim than that which it can will as a universal law for all rational beings, its acting on no other maxim than that which can have universal law for its object and its being a law to itself, the possibility emerges that the laws of morality—the laws that determine the conditions under which a person can count as an end in himself or as a sovereign will and which fix the terms on which one sovereign self-legislating being can properly, with due regard to the full dignity of such beings (434), treat with another self-

legislating being—are nothing other than the laws of freedom. 'A
free will and a will under moral laws are identical' (447). For, will
being the causality of living beings in so far as they are rational—
that is the stipulation Kant makes for 'will'—, the freedom of the
will is nothing more nor less than the will's property of acting
according to its own laws, setting its own end, being a law for
itself, or subjecting itself to the formula of the categorical imperative. Thus what we are prepared to expect is that our interest in
morality is not distinct from our interest in that which makes us
autonomous acting beings.

But, even given that a free will and a will under moral laws are
identical, what assures us that the will is free in this sense? Well,
practical reason has to have the idea of freedom, Kant claims, and
when we act, we have to act under this idea:

Reason must regard itself as the author of its principles [i.e. of its choice
of maxims] independently of foreign influences. Consequently, as
practical reason or the will of a rational being, it must regard itself as free.
(448)

In conceiving of ourselves as acting, we have to suppose that it is
open to us to seek to choose for ourselves the subjective principles
that we shall hold as objective principles or as universal law (449).
And now this thought becomes available: if such autonomy is a
pre-condition of rationality and constitutes our title to freedom,
how could one rationally opt out from morality? That would be to
opt out from freedom and from rational autonomy. (Cf. 452: 'with
[autonomy] is inseparably bound the universal principle of morality'.) How could one have reason freely to opt out from reason
and freedom themselves?

18. Such was Kant's interim conclusion. But he was still troubled
by two points.

First, how much light does the practical argument for freedom
cast on the question about our interest in moral requirements, the
interest inevitably brought into consideration by Kant's method
of arguing for the Formula of Universal Law, which Kant postponed to his section 3 and which we, following him, bracketed,
namely why the universal validity of our maxim as of a law has to
be the restricting condition of our action? Can we tell, simply
from what Kant has so far offered, what is the basis for the

positive worth that we ascribe to actions so restricted? In Kant's specially (here) purified sense of 'interest', what is the nature of our interest in morality? (Cf. 449–50.)

Secondly, Kant thought we ought to be troubled by the question whether that which sustains us in our belief that we can act freely and thereby sustains us in the belief that we *can* act under the idea of freedom is really the same thing as our conviction that we are answerable for our actions to the moral law (450). If so, we shall be vindicating the freedom implied by the Formula of Universal Law and its descendants by using over again the very same convictions for the sake of which freedom was invoked in the first place.

To avoid this circle and overcome his sense that in the world that Newton had explored there could be no escape from causal determination, Kant now has recourse to his well-known distinction between the world of phenomena, the Newtonian world in which we have to see our actions simply as effects and must see ourselves heteronomously as simply things in nature, and the noumenal or intelligible world of things in themselves, the world to which we each assign the basis of all our empirically given characteristics—i.e. our ego as it is in itself (451) and the pure spontaneous activity of our faculty of reason (452).

As a rational being and thus as belonging to the intelligible world, man cannot think of the causality of his own will except under the idea of freedom. For independence from the determining causes of the world of sense (an independence which reason must always ascribe to itself) is freedom. The concept of autonomy is inseparably connected with the idea of freedom and with the intelligible world there is inseparably bound the universal principle of morality, which ideally is the ground of all actions of rational beings, just as natural law is the ground of all appearances. . . . If we think of ourselves as free, we transport ourselves into the intelligible world as members of it and we know the autonomy of the will together with its consequence, morality; while, if we think of ourselves as obligated, we consider ourselves as belonging both to the world of sense and at the same time to the intelligible world. (452–3)

19. It is clear enough how this move might be addressed to the problem of freedom. Whatever the difficulties (difficulties he acknowledges (455 ff.)) of understanding better than schematically Kant's account of the dual nature that he attributes to us, the

division between phenomenal and noumenal certainly relieves the simple circularity that had troubled Kant. But how much direct help can this move give with the first point that troubled Kant (449–50; cf. Section 18 above) about our rational 'interest' in morality? How will the move make it possible for Kant to sustain the claim that morality is simply the consequence of the autonomy he introduces? (Cf. 447.) If I avail myself of my freedom to do a bad act, can I really believe that, by availing myself of it so, I renounce my own rational freedom? How does Kant's recourse to the two standpoints explain the adherence to morality of amphibian creatures like us, whose actual causality is not exhausted by their rational will (*Wille*) as Kant has defined that?

In 453 Kant writes

as a mere member of the intelligible world, all my actions would completely accord with the principle of the autonomy of the pure will: and as a part only of the world of sense [my activities] would have to be assumed to conform wholly to the natural law of desires and inclinations and thus to the heteronomy of nature. (The former actions would rest on the supreme principle of morality and the latter on that of happiness.)

This is to say that, if I were only a member of the intelligible world, rationality/humanity/autonomy would reign within me effortlessly or as a matter of course, and Kantian morality would define the mode of my spontaneous activity, the activity of my true self. And Kant's thought is that, once I recognize my participation in the noumenal, I cannot help but conceive an interest in this mode of activity, which is the same as morality. 'I must regard the laws of the intelligible world as imperatives for me' (454).

There are at least two difficulties we shall have with this idea. First, the idea of the will of a human being *in so far as it is rational* has turned into a separate entity with laws of its own, quite distinct from the normal operation of its palpable will. But this 'in so far as' and its equivalents cannot really serve to introduce some new entity. (That ought not to have been what we were accepting when we allowed the stipulation that will is the causality of living beings in so far as they are rational. See Section 17, second paragraph, above. Kant's definition of 'will' is wide open to criticism as *creative*, in logicians' parlance.) Secondly, prescinding from the scepticism about the real self and its rational will that are stirred up by the first objection, there is a difficulty in turning the activity of the noumenal ego to the philosophical advantage that Kant seeks. When we consider the question of our interest in the moral law on the level of the noumenal, moral *requirement* is not even a question. Pure rationality is simply the mode of activity of noumenal beings (noumenal beings having been denied all other springs of action) and the 'laws' of this activity are simply the general principles which characterize this activity. There is no question of what noumenal beings 'ought' to do[18]—just as there is no question of this at the simply phenomenal level, where actions can only be assimilated to things that happen.

Kant's proposal is that we should see ourselves at both levels at once, while according predominance to the noumenal as the level at which we shall find our true self:

since the intelligible world contains the ground of the world of sense and hence of its laws, the intelligible world is (and must be conceived as) directly legislative for my will, which belongs wholly to the intelligible world. Therefore I recognize myself *qua* intelligence as subject to the law of the world of understanding and to the autonomy of the will. That is, I recognize myself as subject to the law of reason which contains in the idea of freedom the law of the intelligible world, while at the same time I must acknowledge that I am a being which belongs to the world of sense. Therefore I must regard the laws of the intelligible world as imperatives for me, and actions in accord with this principle as duties. Thus categorical imperatives are possible because the idea of freedom makes me a member of an intelligible world. Consequently, if I were a member of only that world, all my actions would always be in accordance with the autonomy of the will. But since I intuit myself at the same time as a member of the world of sense, my actions ought to conform to it. (453–4)

But how, we may wonder, can the way in which a purely noumenal being *would* behave give rational reasons to one in our not purely noumenal state of being and intimate to him or her the idea of a requirement that is, *qua* normative and *qua* moral requirement, perfectly alien to a noumenal being?

20. Combing the rest of the *Foundations of the Metaphysics of Morals* for an answer to this question—an answer neither so thin that it will seem that the class of categorical requirements might be

---

[18] Cf. Walker, 'The Rational Imperative: Kant against Hume', 130.

perfectly empty (cf. 425) nor so explicit that it will seem inexplicable that Kant thought we should be content to comprehend the incomprehensibility of moral freedom and the moral imperative (463; cf. 459)—we find Kant adverting to the fact that even the most malicious villain is not immune to the claims of morality (454). The villain can abstract from the circumstances in which he has chosen villainy and from 'inclinations that are burdensome even to himself' (454) and find his true self in the intelligible world:

He imagines himself to be this better person when he transfers himself to the standpoint of a member of the intelligible world to which he is involuntarily impelled by the idea of freedom, i.e. independence from the determining causes of the world of sense. From this standpoint he is conscious of a good will, which on his own confession constitutes the law for his bad will as a member of the world of sense. He acknowledges the authority of this law even while transgressing it. The moral *ought* is therefore his own volition as a member of the intelligible world and it is conceived by him as an ought only in so far as he regards himself at the same time as a member of the world of sense. (455)

This is one of Kant's clearest statements of a thought that he puts forward several times. Even if we must not look here to explain too fully how pure reason can be practical,[19] 'which is the same

---

[19] Ralph Walker writes: 'In the *Grundlegung* [Kant] makes an attempt—a rather unsuccessful one—to show that the principles of morality are essential for all rational beings, apparently claiming that every being capable even of theoretical reasoning must actually be motivated by them. But even if arguments of this sort worked . . . [they] would only show how we, and other beings, must think . . . [For] a principle to be objectively valid it must hold whether we think it or not. But once it is clear that this sort of argument will not do, two other things become clear as well. One is that no other sort of argument will do either. The other is that no sort of argument is after all needed. It is therefore not surprising that in the *Critique of Practical Reason* the *Grundlegung* argument does not reappear. Instead of arguing, as he did in the *Grundlegung*, that a commitment to rationality is a commitment to freedom and that a commitment to freedom involves a commitment to morality, Kant just takes it as a basic fact that "the moral law is given as a fact of pure reason of which we are *a priori* conscious and which is apodictically certain" [*Critique of Practical Reason*, AkV 47 = Abbott, 136] . . . Being objective, such principles cannot be established by any kind of investigation into who holds them. Being principles, their function is to determine what inferences or actions are justified, and if inferences or actions are justified at all it is by reference to such principles as these . . . It is certainly true that the principles of deductive and inductive inference are different, and that the one cannot be reduced to the other; nor can the principles of morality be reduced to either of them . . . But the cases are parallel. In each case we find ourselves faced with an imperative, which presents itself to us

problem as that of explaining how freedom is possible' (458–9), we must surely be permitted to study the phenomenology of the process that Kant wants to describe as that of a villain's imaginatively attending for a moment to a moral demand that is a demand upon his reason. In his daydream, how does the villain connect together his empirical self and his noumenal self? And what is the temptation for the villain to look at matters, even for one moment, from the point of view of the noumenal self? Again, how can the 'intelligible world itself' furnish him with any moral incentive (462, para. 1, end).

as objective. And if we can accept this in one kind of case, we can accept it in the others' (Walker, 'The Rational Imperative: Kant against Hume', 130). One persuaded by Walker's account of the matter will then claim that what is achieved by our discussion here is at best a criticism of the division that Kant makes in the *Foundations* between what is attempted in his part III and what is attempted in his parts I and II—a division I characterized in Section 14 above (*ad init.*) as holding between our rational interest in categorical imperatives (postponed by Kant till his sect. 3) and our grasp of the distinction between valid and invalid imperatives. Such a person will say that Kant should never have conceded that there was such a division. Once Kant has established a validating procedure for categorical imperatives (it will be said), he has established the most that could be required of him. So there will be no need to take seriously either the affinity that I shall shortly try to display between the *Foundations* answer to the question of our interest in morality and the Humean answer, or any of the other affinities this one will lead on to.

No doubt, complete answer to this would have to embrace the whole plot of the *Critique of Practical Reason* and account for all the differences between it and the *Foundations*. But I believe that for anyone willing to keep objective count of the dialectical positon—see n. 16 above—an incomplete answer may suffice. In so far as the *Critique of Practical Reason* inherits the *Foundations* argument for the Formula of Universal Law, it is well placed to develop further in the way in which it does Kant's conception of the nature and sustaining conditions of our moral interest and the 'postulates' of our pure practical reason. But the *Critique of Practical Reason* is singularly ill placed to disavow the commitments into which Kant entered in the course of his derivations of Universal Law in the *Foundations* (402, 420–1).

The reason why Kant saw himself in the *Foundations* as owing us an account of reason's interest in the moral law, *as well as* an account of the general form of a categorical imperative, is surely that, while furnishing the second of these things, he needed to be able to *assume* that it is *by reason* that valid imperatives will be sorted from invalid. He needed to be able to suppose that, this being so, *all* he had to do was to find some one form in which reason can judge maxims that are putatively maxims for the rational will. (Cf. Section 15 above.)

On the condition Kant himself states, this may pass as an acceptable procedure. It brackets Humean or neo-Humean doubts about whether there need be just one such validatory procedure, and whether that procedure must arise from a concept of reason that is not already professedly moralized. What is more, it appoints a proper moment for such doubts to be heard, namely, part III of the *Foundations*. But

We might suppose that the villain could think, 'My villainy does not belong to the real me. The real me is my *Wille*.' But, in real life can anyone believe that? And ought anyone to believe it? (On the level of theory, let us not forget that the distinct *Wille* was introduced by an illicit form of definition.)

We might suppose that the villain could reflect that by renouncing morality he has renounced freedom and that in renouncing this he has renounced rational agency itself. But how could *exercising* the freedom to choose either one or another option represent the *renunciation* of freedom? It could if this were analogous to the free choice of slavery. But how similar would the villain's choice be to the choice of slavery? A Humean will complain that here Kant must rely upon the most implausible and question-begging features of his conception of a life without morality. Kant is simply repeating his view that such a life represents a servitude to desire, desire being conceived as an alien force. But what Kant has to do is to appeal to reason to convert the villain.

Should Kant then say that, in renouncing morality, the villain renounces true freedom, the freedom from tyranny of desire which would come to him from arbitrating his choice of act by the empirically untainted principle *act only on that maxim which you could will as a law for all rational beings*? Yes, Kant can say that. But here the Humean has to comment that it is a question whether that is the only freedom, or the only rationality. Could not one who acts from the principles that result from the processes of gradual refinement and intersubjective accommodation de-

---

on Walker's reading of the *Critique,* and by his defence of Kant, what happens is that in the *Critique* Kant loses his grasp of the dialectical situation and decides that the hearing of those Humean doubts can be postponed *sine die.* That is not satisfactory.

It is crucially important to remember at this point that the neo-Humean doubts about Kant's procedures are not (in the modern sense) *sceptical* doubts. They need not even be doubts about the objectivity of moral requirements. For they need not be represented as amounting to a doubt that it is rational to heed moral requirements. What matters rather is that this rationality of heeding moral requirements is conceived by the neo-Humean in a different way from the rationality that Kant seems to invoke in his derivation of the Formula of Universal Law. It can be reasonable to heed moral requirements, the neo-Humean will say, and the demand that we do so can be reasonable, without this demand's being founded in Kant's purified notion of practical reason. See below, Section 23.

scribed by Hume count as escaping from the tyranny of desire? Is
there no freedom to be had in the morality Hume describes as
arising out of the second nature of human beings—in the altogether new creation that is civilization itself?

Is the villain renouncing *rationality* then? Perhaps. But that was
what was to be shown. Surely he has not renounced anything
comparable to logic. At this point in the argument it seems evident that we need to find a new idea.

Is this the new idea? That, in persevering in villainy, the villain
turns his back on the noumenal:

> The idea of a pure intelligible world as a whole of all intelligences to
> which we ourselves belong as rational beings (though on the other side
> we are at the same time members of the world of sense) is always a useful
> and permissible idea for the purpose of a rational faith. This is so even
> though all knowledge terminates at the boundary of a pure intelligible
> world. For through the glorious ideal of a universal realm of ends-in-
> themselves (rational beings) a lively interest in the moral law can be
> awakened in us. To that realm we can belong as members only when we
> carefully (463) conduct ourselves according to maxims of freedom as if
> they were laws of nature.

If it is permissible to focus on what Kant says here, then it seems
that a view of the foundation of morality that tempted him is this:
that, at the noumenal level, a morality can be constructed that
fully satisfies the exacting requirements that Kant placed upon it;
that this morality applies to everyone who can understand it and
is rationally available to everyone who can understand it (compare Section 11 above); that the commitment to morality so conceived is founded not so much in something like the narrowly
rational requirement, given that Socrates is a man and all men are
mortal, to conclude that Socrates is mortal (surely that would be
a hopeless comparison) as in a special and glorious solidarity.
This is the solidarity of all beings that partake in the noumenal,
the solidarity of all rational beings. Even for creatures such as us,
creatures who are not completely rational, the kingdom of ends,
the systematic union of rational beings under common self-legis-
lated rational laws, is an unforgettable rational ideal. This is the
kingdom to which—in so far as we are rational—we cannot help
but aspire to belong. To belong and to be worthy to belong to this
is an aim to which we must, and must in the name of reason, be
ready to subordinate every other aim.

21. In respect of at least some of these contentions, it is hard not to take Kant's part. Is it not *rational*—is it not even a demand of practical rationality as such, perfectly independently of morality as such?—to aspire to live with rational beings on terms that are worthy of rational beings? Surely, any generous or adequate notion of practical rationality, however foreign this may be to the conceptions of rationality that dominate technical studies of that subject, will have to explain why that should be. It would be crassly disobliging to Kant to assimilate such an aspiration or interest or solidarity as this to an ordinary incentive or inclination, for instance. I myself could have no part in such a criticism. If morality and a standard of practical rationality that subsumes the solidarity of rational beings coincide, then how can there be any outright objection to allowing that rational solidarity a place within the foundation of morality?

The question that now presses is not whether a special status can be accorded to such aims and aspirations but, rather, (1) how compelling to morality the noumenal really is (here there remains our question about the definition of *Wille*, as well as the original question about the connexion of morality and rationality); and (2) whether one who rests morality on a solidarity of this kind is well placed to dismiss a theory that rests morality in *another solidarity*, a solidarity that one should equally defend from reductivist belittlement. This is not the solidarity of rational beings *qua* rational but the solidarity that Hume describes of human beings *qua* human. How well is Kant placed to criticize a theory that seeks to account for morality as the complex elaboration in the hearts and minds of the 'party of humankind'[20] of the weak but disinterested sentiment of benevolence?[21] Suddenly, when we pursue the question of rationality all the way to the last part of the *Foundations* and seek to hunt it down there, it seems that what makes all the difference between Kant and Hume—between the idea that it is reason that gives us reasons to act and the idea that it is something subtly (indeed reasonably) elaborated from benevolence that

---

[20] For the phrase, see Hume, *Enquiry*, 224.

[21] By a neo-Humean, such an account of morality could even be presented as possessing an equal right to generate rationality-claims. Or claims of reasonableness. The neo-Humean could claim that it is rational (even though not a demand of deductive rationality)—and rational or reasonable *given* our sentiments—to aspire to live with human beings on terms that are worthy of human beings. See Section 22 below.

gives us such reasons—seems to have the width of a knife-edge.

22. At this point, if we have done the best that can be done to answer the question that was put at the end of Section 19, the Humean may try to claim victory for Hume. For the whole point of the Formula of the Universal Law, delivering in due course the Formula of Humanity, the Kingdom of Ends, and all the rest was to improve on the Humean account of moral motivation. Where the foundation of that difference begins to crumble, he may say, where our interest in morality collapses into a solidarity analogous in certain respects to the solidarity Hume had postulated and where Kant has confused in ways already documented the intended and the effective constituencies of morality, no philosophical compulsion remains to accept Kant's derivation of the Formulas of Universal Law, Humanity and the rest.

I must be close to my conclusion. But this is not exactly the conclusion I can rush to. Rather than rush to it, one would have to explore the effects of a concession which I have silently assumed all along that Hume must make to Kant. I saved Hume from certain sorts of criticism by reading back into the *Treatise* an idea Hume did less with than he might have, namely the idea of an abstract rule or public standard of virtue. It is really not clear whether the Humean position can fully sustain that idea or characterize the standard as something that is at once publicly accessible and irreducible to actual received ideas—as something that both goes half-way to meet any creature of human temper and constitution and is yet essentially contestable[22]—if the Humean philosopher persists *à outrance* with Hume's stipulation that the province of reason is confined to 'matters of fact and relations of ideas', or with the rhetoric in which so many professed Humeans have delighted, that 'reason is and ought only to be the slave of the passions and can never pretend to any other office than to serve and obey them' (*Treatise*, 415; cf. 457–8). You can say that, if

---

[22] For the movement of Hume's own thought here, compare his remark at *Treatise*, 547, that 'there is just so much vice or virtue in any character, as every one places in it, and that 'tis impossible in this particular we can ever be mistaken' with his subsequent investigation of 'in what sense we can talk either of a *right* or a *wrong* taste in morals, eloquence, or beauty' (ibid. n.), namely his later essay 'Of the Standard of Taste'. See also Section 6 above, 3rd para., penultimate sentence, and n. 11 above.

you must, in introducing Hume's theory and dismissing such philosophical fictions as the eternal fitnesses and unfitnesses of things. But when the Humean theory is out there plain to view in all its explanatory glory, there is no further need to say this, and some need not to. For immanent within the practices which it seeks to delineate and leaves us free to criticize, there is something it seems unreasonable *not* to call reason.

There is unfinished business here, as there is in Kant, once we see that what Kant can mean by practical rationality is not something as tightly unassailable as deductive logic, but something substantive and contestable—the cement, as one might say, of the interpreted world of conscious beings. What needs to be explored next, before we pick our way to any final conclusion, is not so much the degree of opposition of Kant and Hume (that is obvious) but the possibility of their convergence in a reasonable notion of practical reason—a conception of practical reason correlative with something akin to the enlarged conception of reason that prompted C. S. Peirce to claim that logic itself, even the search for bare plain truth, was 'rooted in the social principle'.[23]

23. If we had elaborated such an enlarged conception, how would matters stand in the dispute between Hume and Kant? Let me simply place on record one tentative, defeasible conviction. This is that Hume would be right to dissent from the suggestion that the requirements of morality could be derived as moral requirements from pure practical reason, even as thus enlarged: unless of course they were established by a derivation that made a manifest detour through considerations that are independently recognized as moral considerations, that is through the considerations that in Hume's construction are rooted (however indirectly and non-foundationally) in humanity. If such a detour passed through the considerations that benevolence and its great progeny of other virtues ratify as authoritative, and if such a detour were itself seen as demanded *by practical reason itself*, then we should have lost the question that divides Kant and Hume. In exchange, we should have got back the problems we have been

[23] C. S. Peirce, *Collected Papers* (Cambridge, Mass.: Harvard University Press, 1932), ii. 654–5

bequeathed—if we will accept the bequest—by Aristotle's conception of practical reason. What we should then need to understand is a species of practical reason that subsumes within itself the ordinary norms of practical reasonableness, norms that both presuppose and involve (as Aristotelian *phronēsis* does, and Kantian practical reason does not) the actual human sentiments.

12

Acts and Omissions, Doing and Not Doing

BERNARD WILLIAMS

1. Preliminaries

In a famous and strongly argued essay,[1] Philippa Foot sought to explain a range of widely held moral beliefs, including some about abortion, partly in terms of a distinction between doing and allowing. Her article was not primarily directed to the analysis or explication of the distinction itself, though she was careful to distinguish it from some other distinctions that resemble it and perhaps overlap with it; she was concerned, rather, with organizing moral beliefs around it. In the enormous literature that has followed her work on these subjects, there is a rough distinction between writers who have been mainly concerned with the ethical application of such distinctions, and others who have been more interested in them as part of an attempt to understand the structure of action and action-ascriptions. Few writings fall unequivocally, of course, into one of these classes or the other, and many of them belong to what might be called 'applicable philosophy', the kind of analysis that treats distinctions in the philoso-

[1] Philippa Foot, 'The Problem of Abortion and the Doctrine of the Double Effect', *Oxford Review*, 5 (1967), 5–15; repr. in her *Virtues and Vices* (Berkeley, Calif.: University of California Press, 1978); see also 'Euthanasia', *Philosophy and Public Affairs*, 6 (1977), 85–112; repr. in the same volume; and for a more restricted account of the moral application of the doing–allowing distinction, 'Morality, Action and Outcome', in Ted Honderich (ed.), *Morality and Objectivity* (London: Routledge & Kegan Paul, 1985). The present paper offers a structure that I hope may be useful in thinking about these issues, without relating it properly to the many useful contributions to these questions that have been made in the subsequent literature, or defending it against alternative proposals. I should have preferred to do those things, but I have not been able to do so, and rather than offer a gesture towards adequacy in this respect, I have confined myself to one or two relevant references. If the paper repeats old errors or too many known truths, I apologize to any who waste their time on it.

phy of mind or action for their own interest, but keeps in mind their ethical relevance. The present paper is intended to be of that sort. Since distinctions do not exist in a vacuum, it may well be the potential moral interest of a distinction that motivates the attempt to make it out, but 'applicable' philosophy of action does stand a step further away from the exchange of moral intuitions than the other type of discussion does.

There is more than one kind of ethical relevance, and this is one reason why even the less directly ethical discussions of these notions may be ethically relevant. The first question is whether a distinction can even be coherently formulated; there is then another question, whether, even if it can be coherently formulated, it is morally relevant. Corresponding to this distinction there are, for instance, two different criticisms of the doctrine of the double effect. One claims that the distinction on which the doctrine relies, between two different causal structures relating outcome to action, is arbitrary or excessively sensitive to redescription. The other admits that the distinction can be made out, but denies that it corresponds to reasonable ethical discriminations. Coherence in a distinction does not require that there are no marginal, ambiguous, or indeterminate cases.[2] What matters is that it should be clear why a case is indeterminate, and that the explanation should be comprehensibly connected to the purpose of the distinction.

It is worth insisting, further, that it makes sense to say that a certain distinction makes a moral difference in some cases and not in others. This has been denied, in any interesting sense, by Jonathan Bennett.[3] Bennett himself makes the point that, with respect to the distinction between bringing something about and letting something happen, the fact that an example of the second may be just as bad as an example of the first does not in itself prove that the distinction has no moral force. He thinks that

---

[2] As the late Warren Quinn pointed out in 'Actions, Intentions and Consequences: The Doctrine of Doing and Allowing', *Philosophical Review*, 98 (1989), 287–312. (See also his 'Actions, Intentions and Consequences: The Doctrine of the Double Effect', *Philosophy and Public Affairs*, 18 (1989), 334–51.) In the same article, Quinn also rightly made the point which follows, about 'making a difference sometimes', and drew attention to the aesthetic analogy.

[3] Jonathan Bennett, 'Positive and Negative Relevance', *American Philosophical Quarterly*, 20 (1983), 185–94; the 'equally bad' point in 'Whatever the Consequences', *Analysis*, 26 (1965–6), 93.

someone who defends the intrinsic moral relevance of the distinction will see this phenomenon as a case of the distinction's having force in the particular case, but the force's being overcome by stronger influences. This belongs with a general additive model of moral considerations or reasons in terms of the resolution of forces: if a type of consideration (for instance, this distinction) ever in itself exerts an influence, then it always exerts an influence, and the method of agreement and difference can be used to isolate the influence it exerts. This model is equivalent to thinking that if a certain consideration provides a reason in a given context, but seemingly not in another, then the reason, properly stated, is *really* an unconditional reason which consists of that consideration conjoined with other statable considerations present in that context. I see no compulsion to accept that idea; there are surely many examples of non-moral practical reasoning, and also of aesthetic judgement, which tell against it.

2. Doing and Not Doing

'*A* is not doing anything' is, literally taken, hardly ever true, at least if *A* is conscious. Indeed, granted that *A* is conscious, it is hardly ever true even if 'doing' is confined to 'intentionally doing' (which I shall take for the purposes of this discussion to be equivalent to performing an action).[4] There is, however, a comprehensible sense of the expression, to be found for instance in a holiday postcard: there, it means that there is no *Z* such that *A* is *Z*-ing and *Z*-ing is noteworthy, what *A* would do professionally, or whatever. This gives us the basic idea of *not doing*: not doing is not doing anything of the *Z* sort, for some stated or implied *Z*.

The central point for the present discussion concerns the *causal powers of not doing*. Consider the formula

---

[4] This is to follow Donald Davidson's usage; a Davidsonian understanding of actions as events can also be assumed for the discussion, though nothing important, I think, turns on it for present purposes. I suppose (but shall not pursue the question here) that it should be possible to give an account of what it is to do something, where that does not necessarily imply intentional action, but is stronger than merely being the subject of some active verb: an account which will include breathing or blinking as something one does, but excludes being in a coma or dead. A helpful investigation is Brian O'Shaughnessy, *The Will*, 2 vols. (Cambridge: Cambridge University Press, 1980).

(I) *A* brought about *S* by doing nothing.

Though it may seem paradoxical, what is very often true when (I) is true is that some doing, and usually some action, of *A*'s was causally relevant to the happening of *S*. This follows from the conjunction of two things:

1. (I) implies that *A* exists at the relevant time, is an agent, etc. This distinguishes (I) from 'no action of *A* brought about *S*': that is true of me and the sinking of the Titanic.

2. *A* is, as already stated, (more or less) always doing something if conscious, and usually doing some action. (I) can of course be true in virtue of *A*'s being unconscious at the relevant time, but, if we leave this aside, then it will standardly be the case that if (I) is true, then there is some time-span of the life of *A*, *T*, which stands in an appropriate relation to *S*, such that *T* contains one set of actions, *X*, and if it had contained in place of *X* other actions, *Z*, which *A* might have done, then (other things being equal) *S* would not have happened. Call this form of statement about *A* (N).

(N) is not sufficient for (I), for at least two reasons:

(*a*) 'Brought about' is stronger than 'made a causal contribution to', and, in particular, stronger than 'made a negative causal contribution to', which is what (N) offers. (I) requires, in addition to (N), that there should be something that makes the fact reported in (N) salient with regard to the explanation of *S* and/or our dealings with *A*.[5] It is important that in the first instance this is a (familiar) point about cause, not a point specifically about action. But there are cases where salience arises from considerations specially connected with agency, as we shall see below, in connection with omissions.

(*b*) Even granted salience, the relation between *Z* and *X* (we may call it the 'relevant replacement relation', or 'RRR') is not enough for (I). We must add, further, that *A* did not intend *X* to prevent *S*; if he did have this intention, then it was not his doing nothing, but his poorly conceived, ineffective, or unlucky action that brought *S* about. However, we do not have to say that *A* did

---

[5] (N) seems equivalent to what Bennett, in 'Positive and Negative Relevance', calls *A*'s behaviour being 'negatively relevant' to the outcome. He indeed intends negative relevance to be a very weak notion, but I would rather say that this relation is too weak to represent, in itself, any kind of relevance.

not intend to prevent *S tout court*. He may even have acted at some other time, unsuccessfully, to prevent it, but even if he did, it will still be true, given (N), that his doing nothing *at T* brought about *S*.

(N), and so (I), contain the notion of actions that *A might* have done. What this means depends, among other things, on what use is being made of (I). If (I) is involved in blaming *A*, it is usual to say that 'might have' should imply 'could have'. If it is a matter just of historical explanation, perhaps it does not. The question is one of what range of counterfactuals is intelligible in relation to the matter in hand, and of their (usually very obscure) truth-conditions.

Two comments on the literature may be appropriate here.[6] First, even (N) can satisfy Warren Quinn's condition for harmful positive agency ('the agent's most direct contribution to the harm is an action'), if *A*'s doings at *T* constitute the nearest that *A* gets to *S*. This suggests that his condition for that notion is too weak. Second, Bennett has been much impressed by a typical feature of the RRR, namely that for given *X* and *S*, there are few values of *Z* for which (N) is true and many for which it is false. But, as Quinn and others have pointed out, this is not necessary. The important point is that the causal relevance of *X* is essentially explained by the RRR, i.e. through *X*'s not being *Z*.

3. Two Further Developments

1. It follows from the possibility of (I) that there is such a thing as acting at *T* by not doing anything at *T*. This possibility goes beyond the *causal* structure deployed in (I).[7] A particularly important example is conventional actions, where there is a specific agreement, a general explicit understanding, or a readily inferred convention that *A*'s 'doing nothing' will count as, for example, agreeing; or voting; or bidding at an auction. There are other questions, of course, about what counts as an action: e.g. whether dropping out of the bidding is one. But the present point

---

[6] Quinn, 'The Doctrine of Doing and Allowing'; Bennett, 'Whatever the Consequences', and elsewhere.

[7] It may thus go beyond what some writers have called 'negative agency', but I am not clear exactly what this expression is taken to cover.

is that there are cases in which A has certainly done an action Y at T; by doing X; where what makes X a doing of Y at T is that it is (one of many things that are) not Z, where Z is a contrary conventional action. (He bid for the Miró because he stared at his programme, or whispered to his neighbour, and did not shake his head, which is what, by prior agreement, would have counted as his not bidding for it.) Actions of this kind can in some cases be done unintentionally: whether this is possible turns on the conventions.

2. The much-discussed distinction between doing and allowing seems, at least as expressed in those terms, not to be a distinction at all. Allowing is best understood as an action, and it is usually an intentional action; whether it is allowing someone to do something or allowing things to take their course. As Philippa Foot pointed out in her original article, it is an action that may be performed by doing something. Thus it may be a conventional act of giving permission; or it may be the act of preventing someone from intervening, as when the doctor stops the nurse from giving emergency resuscitation. It may equally be done by not doing anything (in the (I) sense), as in Bennett's example of the person who by sitting still and quiet allows a blind or inadvertent man to walk off the cliff: that is indeed something this person, A, did, though of course it is not the same thing as if A had made him or encouraged him or induced him to walk off the cliff; or if A had pushed him.

No doubt there are more and less restrictive accounts of what might count as 'allowing' something to happen. What we must guard against are the two ideas that (1) there are two different relations to S's coming about, one of bringing about that this happens, and one of allowing this to happen; and (2) the first of these represents an action while the second does not. The first pair, first of all, are not exclusive of one another; moreover, allowing something to happen is, typically, itself an action, though it is one that may often be performed by not doing anything.

It may be that there are some sound moral distinctions that correspond to distinctions between certain actions and certain allowings. But if so, it is not because the first are actions and the second are not. Rather, they are (typically) different actions.

4. Omissions

I take it that the omission of an action Z may be either intentional or unintentional. In either case it is a non-doing of Z which possesses a particular kind of salience, derived from normative expectations on the agent.

I take it as given that 'normative expectation' is not pleonastic. On the day that Kant did not take his habitual walk (because he was so intent on reading Rousseau), perhaps a citizen of Königsberg, relying on Kant's walk, missed an appointment. But it would be an understatement to say that Kant was not *guilty* of an omission—there is nothing that was his omission. (This is not to deny the general point that some normative expectations can be created just by giving rise to expectations; it is a broader question when this is so, and a notoriously controversial one.)

The salience, derived from a normative expectation, can arise at two different points in the structure. It may be the salience mentioned in consideration (*a*) of Section 2, in connection with strengthening (N) to get (I). This is the relevant point when we say that by omission he brought about the (presumably bad) situation S: it selects one causal contribution from others as the cause. However, not all omissions produce bad, or any specifically interesting, results. If it is *A*'s job to Z, then his non-Z-ing (i.e. the fact that the relevant *T* contains some, different, X in place of Z) counts as an omission, even if it has no distinctive effects at all. Here the point lies just in the identification of the RRR: X-ing is identified as what was done at *T instead of Z* just because of the expectations on *A*, derived from his job.

This second point in fact presents the more basic consideration. The question with an omission always is the introduction of the RRR: the identification of X at *T*, probably otherwise uninteresting, as an omission of Z. However, the distinction between the two kinds of salience is not irrelevant. We can get directly to the RRR when we have structured expectations of a specific kind, and the *effects* of not doing will then come into the question, not in identifying an omission, but in judging its gravity and so forth. However, in other cases, the introduction of the RRR in the first place, and the identification of what the agent did at *T* as a given omission, may depend on the occurrence of the effect. This may well be so with expectations based on duties of general care; and, by the same token, expectations that are grounded in general human relations and responsibilities rather than in such things as specific job descriptions.

5. Omissions and Bringing About

The considerations about two kinds of salience, mentioned in Section 4, are relevant to a familiar kind of moral dispute (or, at any rate, dispute over moral description). I end with some rather general remarks about this.

Suppose I spend $100 on some luxury purchase; that I could have given $100 to a relief agency, and did not; and that if the relief agency had received an extra $100, then, everything else being equal, some extra person in Ethiopia would not have died of starvation. The last claim may be hard to establish, but that is not the point on which to take up the argument.

The following are among the things that might be said:

(1) I omitted to give $100 to Ethiopian relief;
(2) that omission caused someone's death in Ethiopia;
(3) I brought about the death of someone in Ethiopia;
(4) I killed someone in Ethiopia.

There is a further possible remark:

(5) I allowed someone in Ethiopia to die.

(5) perhaps implies, more strongly than (1), that I knew the relevant facts. Beyond that, I will leave (5); nothing in what has been said, so far as I can see, provides materials for denying it.

Some would deny even (1); namely those who deny any normative expectation on people to assist famine relief (though they may say that it is nice of people if they go in for it). Others would suggest that anyone living at a Western standard of life is guilty of such omissions. I suggested an indeterminately middle position when I supplied the information that it was a luxury purchase.

Many of those who accept (1) would resist (3) and (4). Various justifications for this resistance may be suggested. Some may be compatible with accepting (2); though I find it hard to see why (2) should not imply (3). It would, at any rate, be sufficient, in order to resist (3) and (4), that (2) were rejected. Whether we can reject it turns in good part on the question of the circumstances in which the salience that identifies an act as an omission also identifies it as a cause.

It clearly can sometimes do so. Inattentive life-guards certainly cause deaths from drowning. A lazy swimmer resting on the beach may do so, if he or she omits to save, but only if he or she is very saliently related to the drowning in terms of proximity, capacity to save, obviousness of what has gone wrong, and so on. The conditions for identifying the lazy person's inaction as an omission are weaker than this: weaker, that is to say, than for identifying this person's inaction as the cause of the drowning, or—as it might also and revealingly be put—for identifying his or her omission as the cause of the drowning.

In the case of the life-guard, the situation is clear. He would be guilty of an omission if inattentive, even if there were no disaster; when there is a disaster the inattention is a salient part of the explanation, because his attention is part of a system of prevention, and it is the part that failed. The general system of informal obligations to assistance, not based on specific duties, can be seen in an extended sense as such a system, but a person's inaction will have the salience needed for an explanation of a bad outcome only if quite strong conditions are satisfied. Even when those strong conditions are not satisfied, however, the inaction may still qualify as an omission, because the agent falls under a normative expectation of how we would hope he would conduct himself in such circumstances. We may hesitate to say 'in such circumstances' here or 'in the consciousness of such circumstances', because one thing that is indeterminate in these general cases is the degree to which people are required to find out about potential disasters that are not immediately obvious.

The distinction between an omission which is a cause of a disaster and one that is not (even though there was a disaster, and the disaster would not have happened without the omission) helps to focus reproach, by distinguishing from one another different things that may be wrong with the agent, and marking the point that what is wrong with the agent need not coincide with the explanation of the disaster. Utilitarians tend not to make such distinctions, and they move easily in the present case from (1) to (4). Thinking that there is only one thing needed of agents, they also think that there can be only one thing wrong with them, and hence one reproach to them. There is perhaps an uneasy join here between the idea of a system for securing desirable outcomes, on the one hand, and residual notions of personal responsibility on the other.

Select Bibliography of Works by Philippa Foot

Books

Theories of Ethics, ed. with intro. (Oxford: Oxford University Press, 1967).

Virtues and Vices, and Other Essays in Moral Philosophy, collected papers, with intro. and added footnotes, and two previously unpub. papers (Oxford: Blackwell, 1978; Berkeley, Calif.: University of California Press, 1978).

Morality and Action: Collected Papers of Warren Quinn, ed. with intro. (Cambridge: Cambridge University Press, 1993).

Papers and Replies

* Repub. in *Virtues and Vices*.

† Includes additional material.

Reprints are only noted where there are later additions, or for ease of access.

'The Philosopher's Defence of Morality', *Philosophy*, 27 (1952), 311–28.

'When Is a Principle a Moral Principle?', *Proceedings of the Aristotelian Society*, supp. vol., 28 (1954), 95–110.

'Free Will as Involving Determinism', *Philosophical Review*, 66/4 (Oct. 1957), 439–50.*

'Moral Arguments', *Mind*, 67 (1958), 502–13.*

'Moral Beliefs', *Proceedings of the Aristotelian Society*, 59 (1958–9), 83–104.*†

'Goodness and Choice', *Proceedings of the Aristotelian Society*, supp. vol., 35 (1961), 45–60.*

'Hart and Honoré: Causation in the Law', *Philosophical Review*, 72 (Oct. 1963), 505–15.

'Hume on Moral Judgement', in D. F. Pears (ed.), *David Hume: A Symposium* (London: Macmillan, 1963).*

'The Problem of Abortion and the Doctrine of Double Effect', *Oxford Review*, 5 (1967), 5–15.*

'Abortion', Discussion with T. N. A. Jeffcoate, BBC Third Programme, in A. Clow (ed.), *Morals and Medicine* (London: BBC, 1970), 29–47.

'Morality and Art', Annual Philosophical Lecture, Henriette Hertz Trust, British Academy, *Proceedings of the British Academy*, 56 (1970), 131–44

(London: Oxford University Press for the British Academy); repr. in
M. Burnyeat and T. Honderich (eds.), *Philosophy As it Is*
(Harmondsworth: Penguin, 1978).

'In Defence of the Hypothetical Imperative', *Philosophic Exchange*, 1 (Summer 1971), 137–46.

'Morality as a System of Hypothetical Imperatives', *Philosophical Review*,
81/3 (July 1972), 305–16.*†

'Reasons for Actions and Desires', *Proceedings of the Aristotelian Society*,
supp. vol., 46 (1972), 203–10.*†

'Nietzsche: The Revaluation of Values', in R. Solomon (ed.), *Nietzsche: A
Collection of Critical Essays* (New York: Doubleday, 1973).*

'Is Morality a System of Hypothetical Imperatives? A Reply to Mr
Holmes', *Analysis*, 35/2 (Dec. 1974), 53–6.

'A Reply to Professor Frankena', *Philosophy*, 50 (Oct. 1975), 455–9.

'How Good is Our Morality?' *Encyclopaedia Moderna* (Yugoslav Academy
of Sciences, Zagreb), 10 (1975), 41–3.*

'Approval and Disapproval', in P. M. S. Hacker and J. J. Raz (eds.), *Law,
Morality, and Society: Essays in Honour of H. L. A. Hart* (Oxford:
Clarendon Press, 1977), 229–46.*

'Euthanasia', *Philosophy and Public Affairs*, 6 (1977), 85–112;* repr. in R.
Stewart and B. Moore (eds.), *Western Moral Philosophy: A Comprehensive
Introduction* (Mountain View, Calif.: Mayfield, 1994).†

'Are Moral Considerations Overriding?', in *Virtues and Vices*, 181–8.

'Moral Reasoning', in W. T. Reich (ed.), *Encyclopedia of Bioethics* (New
York: Free Press, 1978).

'The Problem of Abortion and Negative and Positive Duty: A Reply
to James LeRoy Smith', *Journal of Medicine and Philosophy*, 3/3 (1978),
253–5.

'Virtues and Vices', in *Virtues and Vices*.

'Active Euthanasia with Parental Consent', *Hastings Center Report*, 9/5
(Oct. 1979), 19–21; repr. in C. Levine and R. M. Veatch (eds.), *Cases in
Bioethics: From the Hastings Center Report* (Hastings-on-Hudson, NY:
Hastings Center, 1984), 49–50.

'Moral Relativism', *Lindley Lecture* (Kansas: University of Kansas Press,
1979, 3–19; repr. in J. W. Meiland and M. Krausz (eds.), *Relativism:
Cognitive and Moral* (Notre Dame, Ind.: University of Notre Dame
Press, 1982).

'Killing, Letting Die, and Euthanasia: A Reply to Holly Smith Goldman',
Analysis, 41/3 (June 1981), 159–60.

'William Frankena's Carus Lectures', *Monist*, 64/3 (July 1981), 305–12.

'Peacocke on Wittgenstein and Experience', *Philosophical Quarterly*,
33/131 (Apr. 1983), 187–91.

'Moral Realism and Moral Dilemma', *Journal of Philosophy*, 80/7
(July 1983), 379–98; repr. in C. W. Gowans (ed.), *Moral Dilemmas*

(Oxford: Oxford University Press, 1987).

'Utilitarianism and the Virtues', Presidential Address to the American Philosophical Association, Pacific Division, *Proceedings and Addresses of the American Philosophical Association*, 57/2 (Nov. 1983), 273–83; repr., expanded, in *Mind*, 94 (1985), 196–209; repr. in S. Scheffler (ed.), *Consequentialism and its Critics* (Oxford: Oxford University Press, 1988).†

'Killing and Letting Die', in J. Garfield (ed.), *Abortion: Moral and Legal Perspectives* (Amherst, Mass.: University of Massachusetts Press, 1985), 177–85.

'Morality, Action and Outcome', in T. Honderich (ed.), *Objectivity and Value: Essays in Memory of John Mackie* (London: Routledge & Kegan Paul, 1985), 23–38.

'Von Wright on Virtue', in P. A. Schilpp (ed.), *The Philosophy of Georg Henrik von Wright*, Library of Living Philosophers, xxix (La Salle, Ill.: Open Court, 1989). This paper was submitted in 1974.

'Ethics and the Death Penalty: Participation by Forensic Psychiatrists in Capital Trials', in R. Rosner and R. Weinstock (eds.), *Ethical Practice in Psychiatry and the Law* (New York: Plenum Press, 1990), ch. 15, 207–17.

'Locke, Hume, and Modern Moral Theory: A Legacy of Seventeenth- and Eighteenth-Century Philosophies of Mind', in G. S. Rousseau (ed.), *The Languages of Psyche: Clark Library Lectures 1985–6* (Berkeley, Calif.: University of California Press, 1990), 81–104.

'Nietzsche's Immoralism', *New York Review of Books*, 38/11 (13 June 1991), 18–22.

'Justice and Charity', *The Gilbert Murray Memorial Lecture* 1992, 50th Anniversary of the Founding of Oxfam (Oxford: Oxfam, 1993), 3–14.

'Rationality and Virtue', in *Norms, Value, and Society*, Vienna Circle Institute Yearbook (Amsterdam: Kluwer, 1994).

'Moral Dilemmas Revisited', in W. Sinnott-Armstrong, D. Raffman, and N. Asher (eds.), *Modality, Morality, and Belief: Essays in Honour of Ruth Barcan Marcus* (Cambridge: Cambridge University Press, forthcoming).

'La Vertu et le bonheur', in M. Canto-Sperber (ed.), *L'Actualité de la philosophie morale: Le renouveau britannique*, Collection Philosophie Morale (Paris: Presses Universitaires de France, forthcoming).

Reviews

Review of *Godwin's Moral Philosophy* by D. H. Munro, *Mind*, 66 (Apr. 1957), 279–80.

Review of *The Varieties of Goodness* by G. H. von Wright, *Philosophical Review*, 74 (Apr. 1965), 240–4.

'Immoralist', Reviews of *Nietzsche: The Man and his Philosophy* by R. J.

344   *Select Bibliography*

Hollingdale, and *Nietzsche as Philosopher* by A. C. Danto, *New York Review of Books*, 6/2 (17 Feb. 1966), 8–10.

'Self Reliance', Review of *An Existentialist Ethics* by H. E. Barnes, *New York Review of Books*, 9/8 (9 Nov. 1967), 19–21.

'Sincerely Yours', Review of *Sincerity and Authority* by L. Trilling, *New York Review of Books*, 20/3 (8 Mar. 1973), 23–4.

'The Brave Immoralist', Reviews of *Nietzsche, Volume One: The Will to Power as Art* by M. Heidegger, *Nietzsche's Gift* by H. Alderman, and *Friedrich Nietzsche* by J. P. Stern, *New York Review of Books*, 27/7 (1 May 1980), 35–7.

'Goods and Practices', Review of *After Virtue* by A. MacIntyre, *Times Literary Supplement*, 4095 (25 Sept. 1981), 1097.

'For Lack of a Rationale', Review of *The Rejection of Consequentialism* by S. Scheffler, *Times Literary Supplement*, 4153 (5 Nov. 1982), 1230.

'Knowing What to Do', Review of *Ethics and the Limits of Philosophy* by B. Williams, *Times Literary Supplement*, 4295 (26 July 1985), 811–12.

'Life and Death', Review of J. Rachels, *The End of Life*, A. B. Downing and B. Smoker (eds.), *Voluntary Euthanasia*, and M. Lockwood (ed.), *Moral Dilemmas in Modern Medicine*, *London Review of Books*, 8/14 (7 Aug. 1986), 3–5.

Index

abortion 331
  double effect 78–81, 87
  relativism 235, 239
  virtue ethics 57–8, 69–72, 73–4
abstract rule 302–4, 306–9, 328
accidents: life processes 271
acts:
  doing and allowing 82, 85, 331, 332–3, 336
  doing and not doing 333–6
  doing well 172–4, 175–6
agency: living things 262–6
agent-relativity 83
agents, see virtuous agents
aggrandizement 209–17
agreement: social setting 41
aim-and-rule morality 86
akrasia 128–9, 135–9
algorithm for life 60–2, 68
analytical-philosophical theories 53–4, 55
animal movement 263–5
Anscombe, G. E. M. 57, 73, 202, 216 n, 249, 264 n, 275, 278, 285 n, 294
  biological acts 271–2, 276
  intention 265, 266–7, 293
  practical inference 1–34
applicable philosophy 331–2
approval 46–8
  social setting 37, 39–42, 41
  see also attitudes, non-cognitive
Aquinas, St Thomas 77, 98, 121, 257 n, 267, 281, 284
Aristotelian categoricals 153–4, 155, 267, 281, 284
Aristotle 60, 68–9, 96 n, 101, 121, 123 n, 159, 254 n, 266 n, 279 n, 284
  animals 283
  euboulia 32–4
  justice 209–17
  naturalism 149–51, 155–6, 178–9
  practical inference 5–6, 7, 8–10, 21, 30, 31, 285
  practical reason 98, 104, 329–30
  virtue 166, 171, 176–7
assailants: unjust acts 214

attitudes:
  non-cognitive 188–205
  projective theories 35–56
authority: moral considerations 223–4, 233

Baier, Karl 105 n
beauty:
  moral 304
  and pleasure 48
behaviour, animal 263–5
belief:
  ethics 38, 50–1
  practical inference 2–3, 19–20, 23, 25–8
  social setting 39, 40
benevolence 300–1, 303–4, 311–12, 327–8, 329
  universal 90–3
benign relativism 224–5, 231
Bennett, Jonathan 332–3, 334 n, 335, 336
Bentham, Jeremy 77
biological processes 261–2
Blackburn, Simon 35–56, 157 n, 170 n
Bond, E. J. 189 n
Brandt, Richard 187 n
Broadie, S. W. 294 n

cardinal virtues 90, 103–4
  see also justice; prudence
Carlson, Gregory N. 285 n
categorical requirements 297–330
causal efficacy 2–3
causality 55–6
  and omissions 333–40
ceteris paribus clause 286–7
character traits: virtue ethics 66–8
charity 72–3
Chekhov, A.: happiness 45–6
children:
  kindness to 305–7
  teaching justice to 215–17
choice 47
  and values 36–7, 38, 40